Created and Directed by Hans Höfer

INSIGHT GUIDES

NORMANDY

Edited by Roger Williams

Photography by Lyle Lawson

Editorial Director: Brian Bell

HOUGHTON MIFFLIN COMPANY

APA PUBLICATIONS

NORMANDY

First Edition
© 1994 APA PUBLICATIONS (HK) LTD
All Rights Reserved
Printed in Singapore by Höfer Press Pte Ltd

Distributed in the United States by:	Distributed in Canada by:	Distributed in the UK & Ireland by:	Worldwide distribution enquiries:
Houghton Mifflin Company	**Thomas Allen & Son**	**GeoCenter International UK Ltd**	**Höfer Communications Pte Ltd**
222 Berkeley Street	390 Steelcase Road East	The Viables Center, Harrow Way	38 Joo Koon Road
Boston, Massachusetts 02116-3764	Markham, Ontario L3R 1G2	Basingstoke, Hampshire RG22 4BJ	Singapore 2262
ISBN: 0-395-68237-1	ISBN: 0-395-68237-1	ISBN: 9-62421-202-3	ISBN: 9-62421-202-3

ABOUT THIS BOOK

normandy's well-known reputation for fine scenery, artistic leanings, sparkling resorts and good living made the task of finding expert contributors a comparatively easy one for this book's editor, **Roger Williams,** an English writer who has edited several other Insight Guides. Williams, who lives just across the English Channel in Kent, has been a constant visitor to Normandy – attracted initially, he says, because both his names are those of extraordinarily dynamic Norman kings.

The photographer for the project was **Lyle Lawson**, an American who lives in England and has photographed many Insight Guides (including those to Burgundy and the Loire Valley). Her first footfall in Europe as a wide-eyed young traveller was Honfleur's fairytale hotel, Ferme St-Siméon. "I couldn't believe it," she recalls. "I thought everywhere in Europe was going to be like this!"

Although she had been visiting Normandy's coast for many years, her assignment for this book offered the opportunity to explore the region in depth. "I was amazed at the diversity of the scenery, of the towns and châteaux, and I hope the photography in this book displays the rich variety of Norman life. There is much more to it than the half-timbered, brown-cow image for which Normandy is generally known."

The history section of this book was written by another Insight Guides regular, **Rowlinson Carter**, who has been trailing the Viking Norsemen through Denmark and Norway for the Insight Guides to those countries. "I wanted to know what happened next," he says. Also, having covered more than a dozen wars for British television, he was fascinated to visit the D-Day Landing Beaches. "The Battle of Normandy was the mother and father of modern warfare."

Like yesterday's soldiers, today's tourists march on their stomachs and, to cover the vital subject of food, Williams turned to **Marie-Pierre Moine.** A former editor of *Taste* magazine, she has written a number of books, including *Cuisine Grand-Mère, The Festive Food of France, Fast French* and *French Country Crafts.* She also volunteered to write the most sensitive of the chapters, on the Norman character. "With its quiet charm, lovely scenery and satisfying food, Normandy is my favourite route into France from across the English Channel," she says.

The region has one of the highest concentrations of literary talent in France, and the obvious choice of a writer to match them was **John Ardagh**. The author of *France Today* and *Writers' France*, he knows intimately not just the works of such writers as Flaubert, de Maupassant and Proust, but also where and how they lived and who and what gave them their inspiration.

Horse Sense

Normandy is famous for its horses, and **Jamie Reid** is a writer who has been around them for many years as a former racing correspondent of London's *Independent on Sunday* and for six years "Major Bonkers" in Britain's satirical magazine *Private Eye*. His books include *A Licence to Print Money*, about the betting industry, as well as a number of novels, the latest called *Home on the Range*. "I was first taken to Deauville by my grandmother in 1965," he says. "I fell in love with the place and I have tried to go back during the August racing season whenever

Williams

Lawson

Carter

Moine

Ardagh

possible. There is an old racing saying that 'little fish are sweet' which means that a winner is a winner wherever it is. But on the days when all our bets are losing ones, there is much to be said for being at a beautiful and sophisticated racecourse like Deauville where there are always enough compensatory attractions to make you feel that the experience has been worthwhile."

The chapters on post-war Normandy and Life Today were compiled by **Charles Lecoeur** and other contributors to *France News*, a monthly newspaper published in Caen by **Jacques Aubrée**. The paper, in English and French, is valuable to the many business people with cross-Channel links.

The Places section was assembled by a number of established Insight contributors who know the region well. **Roland Collins** has been visiting Normandy several times a year since 1950 and knows Dieppe like a native. He is our guide to the Seine Martime. "I especially like the spontaneity you get in Dieppe," he says. "It's a sort of theatre where almost anything can happen on the street – and does."

John Lloyd, author of the chapters on the inland areas of Normandy, is a freelance travel writer and photographer who has travelled widely but frequently returns to France, a country which, he says, "is dear to my heart". He has written extensively on Normandy which he has come to regard as his second home. "I just love delving into its history, much of which has strong links with my home area of Sussex."

Nigel Tisdall, author of Insight's *Pocket Guide: Brittany*, was a natural choice to cover western Normandy. A freelance travel writer who contributes to a range of British newspapers and magazines, Tisdall admits to falling in love with Normandy after being given a vintage bottle of Calvados for Christmas. While researching his chapters on Mont-St-Michel, the Cotentin and the Côte de Nacre, he made a resolution to be reincarnated as a Benedictine monk, "hoeing cabbages in the meadows beside the Abbaye de Hambye".

The invaluable and exhaustive Travel Tips section was provided by **Jill Adam**, who has a home in France and has been a regular visitor to Normandy. Her tip to visitors is: "Always call in at the local tourist office. There is usually a fair or exhibition or concert or something exciting going on."

A Helping Hand

A host of people helped bring this book into being. In particular, photographer Lyle Lawson would like to thank Gîtes de France, who helped with accommodation; Gille Clemente at the tourist office in Évreux, Armelle LeGoff in the Calvados Department of Tourism; Chantelle Olivier in Trouville; and the Houlets in Douville-en-Auge who were so helpful when her vintage MGB sports car broke down.

The book was finalised in Insight Guides' London editorial office. It was proof-read and indexed by **Carole Mansur**.

Reid

Collins

Lloyd

Tisdall

Adam

History

Features

Maps

TRAVEL TIPS

Compiled by Jill Adam

**For detailed information
see page 329**

A CIVILISED PEOPLE

The Normans have a special place in Europe. They are descended from the Viking Norsemen, one of the most ruthless and uncivilised peoples, who became, through force of arms, riches and conscience, one of the most astonishingly civilised builders in history. They had a mercurial genius. In less than two centuries, they had blossomed, spread their empires to the four corners of the Continent, from England to the Middle East, and then declined, leaving quietly like well-behaved party guests.

Suddenly this brilliant race had gone. But it had not disappeared: it was subsumed as part of the Frankish empire. Mixed with the Gaulish tribes they had conquered, these conservative, hard-working, stubborn people retained their ancient stock down the centuries, cultivating the rich land that had first brought their ancestors along its coast and up the River Seine.

Apart from 100 years spent fighting off their English cross-Channel neighbours, their life went on largely undisturbed. They could live off the land, developing their shrewd market skills while their sailors discovered Quebec and other foreign lands. Only the French themselves upset the status quo, in the 16th-century Wars of Religion and (against the wishes of the local Royalist Chouans) during the 18th-century Revolution when monasteries were again destroyed, as they had been by the Vikings.

The time for the Normans once more to take centre-stage came on 6 June 1944, when the entire Allied effort against the Third Reich was concentrated on the landing of troops on occupied Continental Europe. Normandy's beaches were the target. It was the biggest military manoeuvre of manpower in history and, though successful, its effect was devastating. Centuries of endeavour were wiped from the map. Whole towns disappeared. The landscape was ruined.

The stubborn, sturdy Normans kept their heads. Patiently the towns were rebuilt. Traditions were not allowed to die. Parisians, who had long been partial to the Normandy coast and countryside, returned for their holidays in the twinkling resorts of Deauville and Honfleur. Many bought second homes on the coast and among the tumble of old farmhouse buildings. Here they rediscovered a nostalgic France, of shrimp nets and sandy shores, and of a rural idyll of half-timbered farms where the produce of milk and cream and cheese, of apples and cider and Calvados, seemed as bounteous as it did to the early invaders. After more than 1,000 years the region's charms and promise are still hard for any visitor to resist.

Preceding pages: half-timbered house, Harfleur; on the beach; bright umbrellas on Trouville beach; Camembert cheese labels; Canadian tank memorial at Courseulles-sur-Mer; Hôtel d'Étancourt in old Rouen. Left, participant in the annual medieval Joan of Arc pageant in Rouen.

56 BC: Romans under Julius Caesar conquer resident Celtic tribes and establish regional capital at Rotomagus (Rouen).

AD 260: St Mellon is first bishop of Rouen.

486: Normandy conquered by Frankish Merovingian empire under King Clovis.

649: Abbeys of St-Ouen in Rouen and St-Wandrille at Fontenelle founded.

708: Abbey of Mont-St-Michel founded.

820: First Viking raids up the Seine valley.

911: Under the Treaty of St-Clair-sur-Epte, the Viking leader Rollo becomes the first duke of Normandy.

933: Accession of William Longsword; monastery rebuilding begins.

1066: Duke William conquers England.

1180–1223: Philippe-Auguste, king of France, reinforces castles in Normandy.

1195: Richard Lionheart, king of England, builds Château Gaillard.

1204: Château Gaillard captured by Philippe-Auguste, who goes on to conquer all Normandy except for the Isles Normandes (Channel Islands) and the duchy is united with French crown.

1315: Normandy awarded provincial status.

1337–1453: Hundred Years' War fought against England.

1415: Henry V of England arrives at Honfleur and takes all Normandy.

1431: Joan of Arc is burned at Rouen.

1437: Caen University founded.

1459: English defeated at Formigny.

1469: The French monarchy gives up the title to the duchy of Normandy.

1517: Le Havre founded by François I.

1572: St Bartholomew's Day Massacre of Protestant Huguenots; 500 killed in Rouen.

1608: Samuel de Champlain founds Quebec.

1643–1715: Louis XIV, the Sun King. During his reign his chief minister, Colbert, sets up Haras du Pin (the "Versailles of horses"), expands the port of Honfleur and initiates a lace-making industry at Alençon.

1692: Fleet sets sail from La Hougue to restore James II to English throne, and is disastrously defeated.

1756–63: Seven Years' War with England.

Preceding pages: 17th-century map of the duchy.
Left, golden leopards on the Normandy flag.

1789–92: The French Revolution leads to the First Republic. Monasteries abandoned and destroyed. Normandy ceases to exist as a province.

1793: Charlotte Corday assassinates Jean-Paul Marat.

1790s: Royalist supporters in Lower Normandy, calling themselves Chouans (screech-owls), gather support, attacking Briouze, La Ferté-Macé and Flers, and besieging Vire. They are finally defeated in 1799 and their leaders executed at Verneuil.

1804–14: First Empire is established under Napoleon Bonaparte.

1806: First horse-drawn bathing machine in use at Dieppe.

1830: Charles X goes into exile in Cherbourg.

1848: Rioting in Rouen. King Louis-Philippe leaves Honfleur for exile in Britain.

1848–52: Second Empire.

1843: Rouen–Dieppe railway built.

1856: *Madame Bovary* by Gustave Flaubert published, outraging the citizens of Rouen.

1870–71: Upper Normandy occupied during Franco-Prussian war.

1872: Claude Monet paints *Impression: Soleil Levant*, which gave Impressionism its name.

1914–18: World War I.

1923: Paris–Deauville motorway begun.

1932: The ocean liner *Normandie* breaks transatlantic records.

1939–45: World War II.

1940: France capitulates to Germany and all of France is occupied. Towns and cities in Haute Normandie ravaged by fire.

1942: Abortive Canadian raid on Dieppe.

1944 (6 June): D-Day. Allied forces land in the biggest movement of military manpower in history. Bitter fighting culminates in the Falaise Pocket, 22 August.

1957: France becomes a founder member of the European Economic Community.

1967: Nuclear reprocessing plant at La Hague starts operating.

1971: France's first nuclear submarine launched at Cherbourg.

1977: Autoroute de Normandie completed.

1994–95: The Channel Tunnel, linking England and France, opens just to the northeast; Pont de Normandie spans the Seine estuary between Le Havre and Honfleur.

Eight centuries after surrendering their sovereignty to France, the Normans retain a powerful sense of separate identity. "A turbulent race," commented the Norman chronicler Ordericus Vitalis in the days of independence, "and unless restrained by firm rule they are always ready for mischief." French chroniclers were blunter: Normandy, so-named after Viking Norsemen, was "a den of pirates".

The region has been through a number of metamorphoses, but it is the duchy of Normandy as existed between AD 911 and 1204 which underpins the Norman identity and provides the most impressive monuments. This era is most remarkable for the way four characters rose more or less simultaneously to transform a disreputable corner of France into the most powerful force in Western Europe, utterly eclipsing the nascent kingdom of France proper.

They were William the Bastard, Robert Guiscard and his brother Roger, and Bohemund, who were conquerors of England, Italy, Sicily and Syria respectively. Such power could not be achieved by wearing kid gloves. "They were all," says one authority, "in varying degrees personally repellent, cruel and coldly unscrupulous."

Roman springboard: Although Normandy has no obvious natural boundaries, Julius Caesar thought of pegging it out as a single administrative entity after defeating the resident Celts in 56 BC. He saw it as a springboard for his designs on Britain. The Romans turned a former Celtic stronghold into their regional capital and named it Rothomagus, hence Rouen. Diocletian (AD 245–313) came up with the name Lugdunensis Secunda, or Lyonnaise II, reflecting the region's second-place ranking among the 17 departments of Roman Gaul. Unfortunately, substantial Roman relics in Normandy are rare, one notable exception being the amphitheatre at Lillebonne, formerly Juliobona, in the Seine valley.

Saxon pirates, precursors of the Germanic hordes who crushed the Roman Empire in

the 5th century, had a toehold in the Bessin and Cotentin 300 years earlier. Christianity was also early on the scene. St Mellon was reputedly invested as bishop of Rouen in about AD 260, in other words some 50 years before the Emperor Constantine made Christianity official. This bishop is a flimsy figure, historically speaking, but there is definite substance to St Victrice whose St-Gervais church in Rouen, built in 386, is one of the oldest in France.

Roman Empire and Germanic tribes co-

existed long enough for some of the latter to abandon their guttural speech in favour of colloquial Latin. Throwing in some extra ingredients, they concocted the recipe for French. The Angles and Saxons who crossed the Channel did not adopt Latin quite so wholeheartedly and their hybrid became English. Back on the Continent, tribes accepting or rejecting Latin came to be distinguished as Franks and Germans respectively. The Bayeux Tapestry refers to William the Conqueror and his men not as Normans but as "Franks".

The Merovingian Clovis (AD 465–511) overthrew the Gallo-Romans at Soissons in

__Left__, arrival of the piratical Viking Norsemen.
__Right__, Roman floor mosaic from Lillebonne.

486 and rapidly took possession of the whole country between the Somme and the Loire, later extending his specifically Frankish domain as far as Bordeaux and Toulouse. The former Lugdunesis Secunda was incorporated in a western kingdom which Clovis called Neustria. Clovis married Clotilde, the pious Christian daughter of the king of Burgundy, and was infected by her enthusiasm for building abbeys. Their example was followed avidly in Normandy over the two centuries following, particularly by St Aubert, bishop of Avranches.

For the Vikings who descended like thunderbolts in the 9th century, unfortified abbeys crammed with treasure were irresistible. They

conducted their raids like routine summer outings, and prayers went up everywhere for delivery from their lusty throat-cutting. Charles I of France, otherwise known as Charles the Bald, tried bribing Viking chieftains to do their raping and pillaging elsewhere – he especially recommended England. The prospect of being paid not to lift a finger brought an increasing number of hand-rubbing Viking chieftains to their Jeufosse island base in the Seine, and among them was Rolf, son of the Norwegian Earl Rognwald of More, who particularly needed a new home because he had been banished from Norway for stealing the king's cattle. It

was in these somewhat shady circumstances that the foundations of the duchy of Normandy were laid.

Pirate settlers: Rollo, the Gallicised form of "Rolf", is the stuff of Norse legend, a man of such immense size that there was supposedly not a horse in Norway big enough to carry him without his feet dragging along the ground. Obliged to walk, he came to be known as Rollo Ganger ("the Marcher"). Very little is known about his early years in France, but sycophantic court chroniclers later made up the deficit with all sorts of fanciful nonsense, including his portrayal as some kind of Christian messiah.

Reliable chronicles make no mention of Rollo until about AD 890, or 25 years after his banishment from Norway. He evidently took part in an unsuccessful attack on Paris, consoling himself in defeat by then marching across country to the Cotentin where he sacked St-Lô and perhaps Bayeux as well. Two years later he was involved in a siege of Évreux. The resident Count Berenger was killed, and Rollo's share of the booty included the count's daughter Popa. He was now sufficiently notorious to qualify for a bribe from the king of France, by then Charles the Simple, who was prepared to recognise Rollo as the ruler of the territories around Rouen and Évreux in order to be left alone with the rest of his kingdom.

Rollo did not himself take the title Duke of Normandy but was called Patrician. The piratical Viking turned his sword into a ploughshare, donned the traditional white robe and presented himself barefoot for baptism as a Christian. On the question of marriage, however, he was an arch-conservative. The captured concubine Popa commanded his love and bore his children, while Gisella, Charles the Simple's daughter whom he married to cement their treaty, died of neglect. Her father went to the length of sending two emissaries to lodge a formal protest over her treatment. Rollo had the ambassadors removed from his presence and summarily beheaded.

The hallmark of Rollo's government was autocracy. While elsewhere in France feudalism was taking shape, Rollo and his successors kept power in their own hands and set their faces against the creation of powerful barons capable of challenging them. The most abhorrent crime was theft, a more serious matter than murder, and it is said that Rollo demonstrated his successful prosecution of theft by leaving a gold armlet dangling from a tree for three years. Anyone fearing injury to person or property had only to raise the cry of "Haro!" and it was the duty of all good men to offer assistance.

Although "Norman" was derived from "Northmen", the latter never constituted more than a modest minority among the indigenous Celtic-Roman-Frankish stock. Norwegians like Rollo were a minority among a minority as most new immigrants were Danes or Anglo-Danes. The Norwegians, however, were almost all nobles, whereas the Danes were mostly from lower social strata. In

how he was torn between the two religions. Having made a generous gift to the Church for the good of his soul, he immediately gave orders for the sacrifice of a number of Christian slaves to the gods Odin and Thor just to be on the safe side.

The house of Rollo: With a crypto-pagan Norwegian aristocrat for a father and a French Christian concubine for a mother, Rollo's son and successor William Longsword personified the confused identity of the second generation of Normans. The schism between Rouen and Bayeux deepened, and at one point the latter contingent threatened to brush the dust of Normandy from their feet and go home, which in some cases meant England.

either case, they tended to settle in towns, leaving the rural areas to Frankish peasants.

Rouen and Bayeux were very different. In the former, Norse was barely used by the second generation of Scandinavian Normans, whereas Bayeux had a large Saxon population, and as Norse and Saxon were mutually intelligible, there was less reason to abandon the old language. The Scandinavians in Rouen were rapidly Christianised; those in Bayeux clung to their pagan beliefs. The scene at Rollo's deathbed (in about AD 930) showed

Left, Vikings, from a window in St-Rémy, Dieppe.
Above, a priest blessing the abbey of Jumièges.

The French made it plain that the best possible outcome from their point of view would be to see the back of the whole lot, Rouen and Bayeux Normans alike.

Territorially speaking, however, Longsword's reign got off to a brisk start with sharp military actions followed by the annexation of the Cotenin, the Channel Islands and the Avranchin. During the course of his Avranchin campaign, which fixed the Norman-Breton frontier along the river Couesnon, Longsword espied Sprota, a Breton girl, and took her as a concubine, his reputation as an exceptionally pious Christian notwithstanding. With Sprota in tow, he took up residence at Fécamp and began rebuilding the ancient monastery destroyed by his Viking forebears. Sprota was soon pregnant and bore him a son Richard. Destined to become the first duke of Normandy proper, he was known as Richard the Fearless.

Competition between the Carolingian Louis d'Outremer and the Capetian Count Hugh of Paris for the kingdom of France was an issue which did not particularly interest Longsword, but he could not help becoming embroiled and in so doing lost his life to four assassins. His young son Richard was at once kidnapped by King Louis, an experience which caused him to turn pale and give every appearance of being at death's door.

following 70 years, Normandy became one of the most highly feudalised states in Europe. He jealously guarded his role as the supreme spiritual as well as secular power in the land and saw to it that the Norman church was generously maintained. He expanded the Fécamp monastery founded by his father and regenerated Mont-St-Michel and St-Ouen at Rouen. He was, in short, the patron of the school of Norman architecture which became so famous.

Richard II, an illegitimate son, inherited a state whose Frenchness was no longer questionable. He broke new ground for a Norman ruler by actually marrying Judith, the mother of his children, instead of settling for a "Dan-

Louis and Queen Gerberge arranged a huge banquet to celebrate the need not to murder the boy, and it was under the cover of these festivities, as noisy as they were premature, that a loyal courtier slipped through the security arrangements and carried Richard away in a truss of hay.

Richard thus survived to reign for 50 years, during which the French seemingly came to accept that the "pirates" were there to stay. Under Richard, Normandy became a powerful and wealthy state while remaining relatively small. He was responsible for introducing feudalism, which had gone against the grain of the Viking pioneers. Over the

ish marriage" neither sanctioned nor solemnised by the Church. Two of their children, the future Richard III and Robert I, were the only legitimate dukes of Normandy. On the former's succession in 1026, he was immediately in dispute with his brother Robert over possession of Falaise. Reconciliation called for a boisterous party in Rouen, after which the young king and several guests took ill and died. Poison sprang to everyone's mind, and of course Robert was the prime suspect, but even if he was responsible there were not sufficient grounds to prevent him from succeeding as Robert I.

Falaise, the cause of the fraternal quarrel,

stands high above the Ante, a tributary of the Dives river. Robert kept a castle in Falaise, and the story goes that from one of the windows he was bewitched by the sight of a girl paddling in the river below, Her name was Arletta and she was the daughter of a tanner in an age when tanning was a despised trade, if only because of the smell. To make matters worse, he ran a brewery on the side, and in the Middle Ages tanners who ran breweries were automatically suspected of depositing animal waste in their beer to make up bulk. Arletta gave Robert two children, William the Bastard (later the Conqueror) and a daughter.

After uninterrupted success both in war and internal administration, Robert's reign ran into difficulties over two refugees who took shelter in Rouen, the so-called Atheling princes of England who were the sons of Ethelred the Unready and Robert's aunt Emma. She had subsequently married Canute, Ethelred's successor as king of England (he was also king of Denmark) who had a son, Harold, by his previous marriage. At its simplest, Emma wished to get rid of Harold to further the interests of her own children by Canute, the Athelings.

Robert was cajoled into threatening Canute with war if he did not put the Athelings in line for the English throne, and he went as far as assembling a fleet at Fécamp before adverse winds made him change his mind. The impossible odds against the success of this enterprise had made some of his advisers wonder about the soundness of his mind. When he then announced that he wished to go to Jerusalem instead, their convictions in this respect strengthened.

The duke at least made arrangements in case he did not come back. Young William was nominated as his heir with the duke of Brittany the regent-designate. Between Constantinople and Jerusalem Robert met a Norman pilgrim on the way home. By then Robert could no longer ride and was being carried in a litter by black slaves. The returning Norman asked whether he could take back any messages. "Tell them," Robert replied, "you saw me being carried to Paradise by devils." He managed to reach Jerusa-

lem but died and was buried at Nicaea on the return journey. The reference to devils may explain why he is sometimes called "Robert the Devil" rather than "Robert the Magnificent", the title he preferred.

William the Conqueror: The future William the Conqueror was just eight years old when word was received of Robert's death. The general population welcomed his succession, but ruthless ambition flared and a number of barons closed in for a quick kill. As William's tutor and bodyguards, one of whom slept in the same room, were murdered one after another, his regent the duke of Brittany appealed for reason and was himself poisoned. William's mother spirited

him away to a succession of peasant communities in remote parts of the country. This peripatetic upbringing among Frankish peasants isolated William from the influence of the Scandinavian military caste, but at the same time it deprived him of the formal education which had been a feature of his immediate predecessors. When time was ripe for him to make his first public appearance as the duke, William was 14 and his character was already set in stone. He was taciturn, bitter and ambitious.

At 19 he crushed the so-called Great Revolt of the Barons at Val-ès-Dunes and not long afterwards was provoked into an out-

Left, wall relief from William the Conqueror's castle in Dives-sur-Mer. Right, William, the first Norman king of England, starts a dynasty.

rage which was to haunt him for the rest of his life. During a siege of Angevin forces occupying Alençon, the defenders beat the skins stretched along the top of the walls to deflect fire bombs and set up a chant of "Skins, skins, plenty of skins for the tanner!" William took this, no doubt correctly, as a slur on his mother. He ordered the hands and feet of 33 Angevin prisoners to be hacked off and their eyes put out. The wretches were then made to crawl back to their position as best they could.

Legend has it that William mellowed on falling in love with Matilda, daughter of Baldwin of Flanders. One version of the romance, however, has him barging into

brother. The excommunication was lifted by Leo's successor, Pope Nicholas II, after William had agreed to build in Caen the Abbaye-aux-Hommes for himself and the Abbaye-aux-Dames for Matilda.

William's *modus vivendi* with King Henry I of France was undermined by Normandy's increasing prosperity. The king wanted a feudal vassal, not a rival. Two French invasions were seen off at Mortemer and Varaville, and William's conquest of Maine in 1062 neatly rounded off Normandy's borders. In 1066, when William felt ready to turn his attention to other matters, he had been ruler of Normandy for 20 years – and he was still only 38. His plans for the

Baldwin's house and dragging her out by the hair with Matilda howling in masochistic ecstasy. Whatever form the courtship took, William urgently needed an heir: unclear succession was a recipe for intrigue and treachery. The Count of Arques was one who fancied himself as a candidate, and he was presumed to be among those who persuaded, or probably bribed, Pope Leo IX to forbid the proposed marriage on the grounds, actually spurious, of consanguinity. William and Matilda went ahead anyway with a ceremony at Eu and a writ of excommunication soon followed, issued by Mauger, Archbishop of Rouen, who was the Count of Arques's

conquest of England were galvanised by the death of Edward the Confessor on 5 January 1066, ending the line of Danish kings.

Edward left a widow, Edith, daughter of Godwin, the earl of Kent and effectively Edward's prime minister. Godwin was the rare Anglo-Saxon to hold high political office under the Danish kings, and he represented an Anglo-Saxon revival keen to reclaim the English throne, especially as Edward's policy of conjugal self-denial meant he died without issue. The Anglo-Saxons wanted Godwin's son Harold on the throne. In Normandy, Duke William believed he had a hereditary right to it through his father's aunt, the indefatigable Emma.

An enormous amount of ink has been expended on whether Edward wished Harold or William to succeed him. It hardly mattered, because the decision rested not with him but the Witan, a kind of privy council which the Anglo-Saxons dominated. There is also the thorny question of whether Harold under oath had previously forfeited his claim to the throne to William. It seems that Harold was blown ashore in France by a storm and ended up as William's prisoner. The oath was the price of his freedom. According to one of the more colourful versions of events, the oath was sworn on a table covered by a cloth and would have been a tongue-in-

hours in silent thought. The outcome was the assembly of the largest invasion force the English Channel had so far seen – between 600 and 700 ships carrying some 7,000 men, including 1,000 cavalry – and while the majority of the troops were Normans (including Anglo-Danes who were in a sense going home), they were joined by mercenaries and freebooters from all over France and the continent. A certain Rémi of Fécamp had William's promise of an English bishopric in exchange for providing one ship and 20 men-at-arms. William himself had in his pocket a Papal Bull investing him with the title of king of England.

William's victory – and Harold's death –

cheek affair had not William whipped the cloth aside to reveal that the oath had been taken on the relics of saints, a different kettle of fish altogether.

Conquest of England: In any case, Harold had a head-start by being in England when Edward died. The Witan rushed through Harold's election and he was crowned the same day by the archbishop of York. William was out hunting when the news reached Normandy, and it is said he sat for some

The Bayeux Tapestry. <u>Left</u>, William's fleet sails across the Channel to England. <u>Above</u>, a feast presided over by William and his brother Odo.

at the Battle of Hastings in 1066 gave him the English crown on Christmas Day. Thereafter William lived a double life, commuting between his roles as duke of Normandy and king of England. Much of what happened to William after 1066 belongs to the history of England rather than Normandy. September 1087, however, saw him engaged in a punitive raid against the French in Vexin. He was watching Nantes go up in flames when his horse trod on live coals and, with a crazed whinny, sent the now elderly and corpulent rider crashing to the ground. The internal injuries proved to be terminal, but the lingering weeks before death in the Abbey of St-

Gervais in Rouen enabled William to put his affairs into order as best he could.

Robert, William's oldest son, was to become duke of Burgundy and William Rufus, his second son, king of England. The third son, Henry, had to be content with a substantial sum of silver. "What shall I do with that gift," he complained, "if I have no land to live in?" William advised him to be ready to step into either brother's shoes. He indicated that, sadly, the need would not be long in arriving and that Henry would surpass his elder brothers in both riches and power.

Robert set Normandy on the road to ruin from the moment he took over. He was as courageous as his ancestors but also, unfor-

redeem the loan within five years, William Rufus would become duke of Normandy as well as king of England.

Fraternal friction: In Robert's absence, William Rufus paid frequent visits to Normandy and, fully confident that it would soon be his, expanded the duchy to include Nantes and Vexin. He was back in England contemplating further acquisitions when his customary spot of hunting after dinner went awry. A companion's cross-bow bolt may or may not have ricocheted off a deer, but in any case William Rufus was stretched out dead. His brother Henry curiously happened to be in England and at once galloped to Winchester where the royal treasure was kept. Three

tunately, "prodigal, inconsiderate, a slave to sensual passions, irresolute and vacillating". With his ready stockpile of silver, all Henry needed was a little patience. When the inevitable happened and Robert applied for an urgent loan, Henry drove a hard bargain: 3,000lb of silver (three-fifths of his inheritance) for the Cotentin, which amounted to one third of Normandy.

Robert then announced he was going off on the First Crusade. Taking the Cross was an expensive enterprise, however, and he pawned his remaining share of Normandy to William Rufus. If he failed to return from the Holy Land or for any other reason failed to

days later he was crowned king of England. "Thus," says a chronicler, "was Robert a second time deprived of the crown of England by a younger brother."

Robert returned exhausted from the Holy Land just a month later, landing at Mont-St-Michel. After attending to one or two local emergencies, he mounted the second substantial Norman invasion of England and landed safely at Portsmouth in 1101. The great Norman families had estates on both sides of the Channel and would not happily sacrifice either, so Robert and Henry were persuaded to negotiate a settlement by which Robert dropped his claim to the English throne while Henry ceded the Cotentin he had bought from him together with all other possessions in Normandy bar Domfront.

By fortifying Domfront with Tinchebrai Castle, Henry was plainly waiting for Robert to bring such despair to Normandy that he could step in and be welcomed as a saviour. He made his move in August 1106. "I have not resolved on despoiling you of your duchy," he informed his brother on landing with his army, "but, invoked by the tears of the poor, I desire to succour the church of God, which, like a vessel without a pilot, runs great danger in the midst of a stormy sea." Henry offered to settle for just half of Normandy. Robert refused, and the Battle of

in hand to have his younger son Richard acknowledged as his heir to the English throne. With his affairs in France neatly in order, Henry was feeling at "the pinnacle of human grandeur" as he prepared to sail from Barfleur for England. But the ship carrying his two sons was wrecked on tidal rocks, and Henry never smiled again.

The drowning signalled the end of the dynasty founded by Rollo because Henry had no other children and the best he could do was arrange a second marriage for his daughter Matilda, widowed young by the death of the German emperor Otto. Her new husband was Geoffrey the Fair, count of Anjou, who by wearing a sprig of broom in

Tinchebrai was joined on Michaelmas Eve 1106. Its outcome left Henry in full possession of Normandy, as his father had correctly foretold. Henry I of England thus became the 9th duke of Normandy.

Henry ruthlessly defended both kingdom and duchy. Robert was blinded and spent the remaining 27 years of his life in the castle at Cardiff. Henry got France to affirm the investment of William, his 18-year-old son, as duke of Burgundy, and arrangements were

Left, Henry II of England and Louis VII of France bid farewell to Thomas Beckett. **Above**, Richard Lionheart beating Philippe-Auguste at Gisors.

his cap earned a resounding nickname, Plantagenet (Fr. *genet* = broom). The transition was far from smooth as Stephen of Blois, William the Conqueror's nephew, seized both Norman and English crowns on Henry's death. Geoffrey concentrated on regaining Normandy while Matilda worked on England. Both achieved their objectives but Matilda quickly fell out of favour in England and was driven out to make way for the return of Stephen of Blois. Geoffrey's son Henry therefore succeeded as 10th duke of Burgundy but not to the English throne.

Eleanor of Aquitaine, divorced in disgrace from Louis VII of France because of an affair with her uncle Raymond of Antioch during the Second Crusade – she went along dressed as an Amazonian warrior – took a fancy to Henry, then 20, and brought to their marriage a dowry which made him ruler of all western France from Flanders to Spain. That gave him the strength to exact from Stephen of Blois an undertaking that he would inherit the English throne on Stephen's death. The thrones were thus reunited.

Henry's attempts to limit the power of the Church led to the exile, then the martyrdom, of his archbishop of Canterbury, Thomas Beckett. A number of Norman churches claim connection with the saint from his time in exile. Meanwhile, Henry's unbridled infidelities provoked Eleanor into a rebellious plot which was uncovered and resulted in her being locked up indefinitely. The untimely deaths of two older brothers made Richard heir-apparent. Father and son fell out when Richard learned that the woman he was supposed to marry, Alice, sister of his friend Philippe-Auguste of France, had been seduced by his father while she was a minor in his care.

Henry was still fuming on his death-bed: "Cursed be the day of my birth, cursed be the sons I leave behind."

The second surviving son whom Henry thus cursed was John Lackland, who plotted with Philippe-Auguste while Richard Coeur de Lion (Lionheart) was winning glory on the Third Crusade. News of John's activities brought Richard hurrying home, a return delayed by his capture and incarceration at the hands of the German emperor pending the payment of a colossal ransom. Richard eventually reached England in 1194 and sailed from Portsmouth the same year with a fleet of 100 ships. Landing at Barfleur, he meant to deal with both brother John and Philippe-Auguste. The former, who had been installed as governor of Évreux, capitulated almost at once, but the campaign against Philippe-Auguste continued. In 1198 Richard "fell like a lion upon its prey" at Gisors, where Philippe had to be dragged out of the river at the town's gate to add to his humiliating defeat.

The following year, Richard was besieging Chalus castle in the Limousin when he was hit by an arrow. The wound was not serious, but he neglected to treat it properly, contracted gangrene and died on 6 April

1199. His will bestowed 18,000 gallons of wine a year on Rouen cathedral and another 6,000 gallons on the archbishop alone, consignments which both continued to arrive and were presumably consumed until 1553. The rather larger matter of the duchy of Normandy and kingdom of England was settled in favour of his nephew Arthur, duke of Brittany, as Richard died childless.

Foul murder: Arthur was only 14 and John Lackland was not ready to abide by Richard's will. The windfall of wine notwithstanding, the Archbishop of Rouen also defied Richard's wishes to invest John as Duke of Normandy, and the Archbishop of Canterbury followed suit by crowning him at Westminster. The helpless Arthur's fate was sealed. John personally dragged him out of his Rouen cell where he had been kept, plunged a sword through his heart and dumped the body in the Seine. While some historians argue that Arthur was murdered at Cherbourg and dumped in the sea, there is no dispute that John's hand did it.

John's reign in Normandy was if anything more wretched than the performance in England which resulted in his being forced to sign the barons' Magna Carta in 1215. Philippe-Auguste was not slow to exploit the disaffection with all too visible preparations to seize Normandy. In England, John was curiously indifferent to the threat. "Let Philippe proceed," he remarked, "I will recover more in a day than he can gain in a year." Twelve months later, however, his possessions in France were reduced to Rouen, Verneuil and Château Gaillard, the great castle which Richard had built overlooking the River Seine.

The issue was effectively settled at Château Gaillard after a heroic defence lasting six months. That left only Rouen, and a plea for help by the deputies of Rouen was received with the same indifference. John was playing chess when they arrived and made them wait until the game was finished. He said there was nothing he could do and they ought to look after themselves. Their reaction was to hand over the keys to Rouen without further resistance, thus reversing in 1204 the independence which Charles the Simple had ceded to Rollo 282 years earlier.

Right, a pier of highly figurative columns from the abbey at St-Martin-de-Boscherville.

Incipit missa beate marie virginis

Introibo ad altare
dei Ad deum qui le
tificat iuventutem
meam Dignare
domine die isto
sine peccato nos
custodire. Confitemini domino
qm̄ bonus. qm̄ in seculū mīa eius.
Confiteor deo celi et: Confessio
beate marie virgini et oibus
sanctis dei quia ego infelix peccator
peccavi nimis contra legē dei mea co
gitatione locutione consensu visu
verbo et opere mea culpa mea culpa
mea maxima culpa. Ideo precor vir
ginem mariā et oīs scōs et scās dei
et vos orare pro me pctore. Absol
Misereatur mei omnipotens de

Normandy's relatively quiet life as a province of France ended in 1346 when Edward III of England landed his army in the Cotentin. Normandy was thus dragged into the festering Hundred Years' War between England and France. By ignoring William the Conqueror's citadel in Caen and making straight for the town's commercial centre, Edward was clearly more interested in plunder at this stage than conquest. The snubbed garrison in the citadel could only watch the women of Caen pelting the intruders with stones and furniture. To no avail: the booty included 40,000 pieces of cloth and filled 100 English ships waiting at Ouistreham.

After giving Rouen the same treatment, Edward meant to go home but found that the bridges across the Seine had been cut behind him. Pursued by a 30,000-strong French army, he looked for an alternative crossing before turning to face them just north of the forest of Crécy near Abbeville. Here the new English long-bows demonstrated their phenomenal range. At least 1,500 French knights, including many Normans, were brought down without ever reaching the English lines.

Henry of Navarre, the French king's disloyal brother, dragged Normandy deeper into the war by allowing the English to use his extensive Norman holdings as a base. After several decades of inconclusive fighting, Henry V, the last great English Plantagenet, was determined to settle the matter once and for all by conquering the whole of France. In August 1415, he set out from Southampton with 1,500 ships and nearly 10,000 men. Thanks to Shakespeare, his encouragement to the troops as they stormed Harfleur's defences has gone into the English language in the play of *Henry V*: "Once more unto the breach, dear friends, once more..."

The garrison at Rouen was a tougher nut to crack, particularly as dysentery reduced Henry to only 6,000 men in any condition to fight. Thinking the Channel port of Calais would be a softer target, Henry was well on his way when he was pulled up short by a French army five times larger than his own. The battle fought on St Crispin's Day was Agincourt, and Henry's pep-talk to the troops inspired Shakespeare to even greater heights of patriotic rhetoric.

The stunning victory at Agincourt persuaded the previously reluctant English government to give Henry as much money as he needed to complete the conquest of France. He returned in 1417 and quickly captured Caen, Bayeux, Falaise and Cherbourg. Rouen held out against a siege for six months.

Henry's ambition was within his grasp when the 1420 Treaty of Troyes promised him the French throne on the death of the lunatic incumbent Charles VI.

Ironically, Charles outlived Henry, albeit by a matter of days, and his successor, Charles VII, immediately tore up the treaty.

The martyred maid: Henry's dying words to his brother, the duke of Bedford, were to hang on to Normandy at all costs. The duke, founder of Caen University, managed to repulse a Franco-Scottish attack in 1424, but the focus of the war then moved to an Orleans peasant girl of 18 who said she could hear the voices of St Michael, St Catherine and St

Margaret. They were telling her, Joan of Arc, that her destiny was to rid France of the loathsome English. Brushing aside the barriers that would deny any other peasant a royal audience, Joan not only got to see the future Charles VII but talked him into putting 4,000 troops at her disposal to lift the English siege of Orleans. According to Bedford, the white suit of armour she affected made the English troops wonder whether they were up against some kind of divine Amazon. In any case, the English were beaten and Joan, with her banner aloft, took pride of place next to Charles as he was crowned in the cathedral at Reims, east of Paris, on 20 July 1429.

Slightly wounded in an attempt to retake

Paris, Joan recovered to take part in an action at Compiègne against the duke of Burgundy, England's ally. She was captured while leading a sortie and had a ransom of 10,000 crowns put on her head. Charles VII was not interested but the English certainly were. She was taken to Rouen and manacled in the castle to face charges of heresy and sorcery. The trial was before an ecclesiastical court of the Inquisition under Pierre Cauchon, the bishop of Beauvais, who had designs on the archbishopric of Rouen.

Cauchon planned to trick Joan into an admission of guilt, but this was to underestimate her quickwittedness. Unchastened,

Joan was taken back to the castle to examine various instruments of torture while she still had time to change her plea. This was to underestimate her courage.

Found guilty when the trial resumed, she was led to a waiting stake in the cemetery of the Abbey of St-Ouen. Joan then broke down, made a wild recantation and was escorted back to her prison cell with the sentence commuted in accordance with custom to life imprisonment. This pleased neither Cauchon nor the English.

On Trinity Sunday, 1431, guards entered Joan's cell and told her to change into male clothing. She refused to budge until, at midday, "for bodily necessities she was constrained to rise and put on the said clothes". The guards sprang into action. At her trial she had specifically renounced women who wore male clothing – like white suits of armour – and she had now gone back on this most solemn undertaking. A second trial in the archbishop's chapel in Rue St-Romain pronounced the death sentence because of her relapse into "heresy and schism".

Joan was brought under heavy guard the following day to the Rouen market place where a large crowd had gathered round a pyre. The death sentence was confirmed aloud but there was no repetition of the previous breakdown. Joan went serenely to the flames and afterwards her ashes were cast into the Seine. Curiously, she was designated Venerable only in 1904 and was not canonised until 1920.

Joan's execution coincided with the duke of Burgundy's switch of allegiance from England to France and the death of the duke of Bedford from exhaustion. England was now on the retreat, and in 1436 Paris hooted a contemptuous farewell to the last English troops. For Normandy this was not quite the end of the war because for eight more years the English fleet buzzed about the Channel and fortresses like Honfleur frequently changed hands. Nevertheless, Joan's martyrdom in the Vieux-Marché in Rouen was the symbolic turning-point.

The Norman poet Alain Chartier spoke for the French conscience during the Hundred Years' War. Born in Bayeux and educated at the University of Paris, Chartier wrote a *Quadrilogue Invective* (1422) blaming nobility and peasants equally for France's ills. "Seek," he cried sarcastically, "seek, ye

Frenchmen, the savour of delicious meats, long periods of repose from toil borrowed by the night from day, outrageous garments and trinkets, the caresses and delights of womankind. Fall into slumber, like to swine, amid dirt and the vileness of those horrible sins that have brought you so near to the end of all your days." In his quieter moments, Chartier produced widely admired romantic poems, and it is said that the Dauphine Margaret, daughter of James I of Scotland, once kissed his lips as he lay asleep, a tale which owes its poignancy to the fact that Chartier was, everyone agreed, the ugliest man in France.

Olivier Basselin, a contemporary, wrote bawdy drinking songs at his home in the things. In 1362, a party of Dieppe traders sailed down the African coast as far as what is now Sierra Leone and established a colony which they called Petit Dieppe. A century or so later, John de Béthencourt discovered the Canary Islands and triumphantly proclaimed himself king, soon to be dethroned by an unamused king of Castile. The French as a whole both hated and feared the sea, but Normans routinely fished off Newfoundland and Iceland.

In spite of the lurking hazard of the English fleet, the Ango family of Dieppe built up an impressive merchant fleet during the latter stages of the Hundred Years' War. Jean Ango, born in 1481, expanded the business

Vale of Vire. The nature of the songs and the French name for the vale – Vaux de Vire – gave rise to "vaudeville". Tradition has it that Basselin died a patriot's death at the Battle of Formigny near Bayeux in 1450. This battle was a significant postscript to the Hundred Years' War as it resulted in England losing its last stronghold in Normandy.

The great explorers: While the Normandy countryside took a battering during the Hundred Years' War, Norman seafarers ran the gauntlet down the English Channel to greater

Left, Joan of Arc. **Above**, Philippe-Auguste's castle where she was kept before being burned.

by leaps and bounds so that King Francis I, perennially short of money and therefore obliged to ingratiate himself with wealthy subjects, made him viscount of Dieppe.

Ango commissioned two Florentine brothers, Giovanni and Girolamo da Verrazano, to investigate the east coast of America. Giovanni discovered the bay of Manhattan and came across the future site of New York. Another Ango captain, Jean Fleury, captured three caravels off the Azores in 1521. It transpired that they were carrying Montezuma's treasure back from Mexico.

The Parmentier brothers, also in Ango's pay, sailed round the Cape of Good Hope to

Sumatra and Java in 1529. Paulmier de Gonneville, "gentleman of Honfleur", steered his ship *Espoir* to Brazil while Jean Denis, merely "sailor of Honfleur", explored the mouth of the St Lawrence river.

Back in Dieppe, Ango invested some of his fortune in a magnificent house built out of carved oak. It was named, like his flagship, *La Pensée*. This house perished in the Anglo-Dutch bombardment of Dieppe in 1694, but the contemporary and equally grand Manoir d'Ango at Varengeville near Dieppe, which he had built in the Renaissance style with an exotic dovecote, by Italian craftsmen, survives.

Being granted letters of marque by Francis

plary damages. Ango watched his fortune evaporate in a welter of litigation.

At his death in 1551, the family silver had gone and the Manoir d'Ango had been stripped of its celebrated art collection. Luckily, an impressive tomb in the church of St-Jacques in Dieppe, where he had been mayor, had been paid for in advance.

The French Wars of Religion, to which we shall return, wiped out most of the Norman toe-holds abroad, and it was only after them that business returned to normal.

Samuel de Champlain was born in Bordeaux but established a ship-building business in Dieppe which provided him with the means to explore the Canadian coast. On the

seemed to go to Ango's head. While he is reckoned to have seized 300 ships belonging to others, when Portugal captured two of his, he ordered his captains to bombard Portuguese coastal villages and threatened to blockade Lisbon. King John of Portugal backed down, but Ango's dealing with the French kings were less satisfactory. Having lent vast sums to Francis I, he was unable to recover the money from his successor Henry II. To compound his misery, the many commercial enemies he had made over the years found that with Henry II nodding appreciatively in the background, the courts were sympathetic to their grievances and ready to award exem-

third of these voyages, in 1608, he founded Quebec and from there set out to map large tracts of the virgin interior. Normans were a large contingent among the Frenchmen who flocked to join him. In 1612 Champlain was appointed lieutenant of Canada, and when Quebec was seized during the subsequent Anglo-French war, it was largely his artful diplomacy that returned the province to French sovereignty.

Pierre Belain of Esnambuc took possession of Martinique and Guadeloupe in the name of France in 1635, and Cavelier de La Salle of Rouen, after investigating the site of Chicago, sailed down the Mississippi to map

Louisiana. This second wave of overseas exploration needed French settlers in order to constitute a viable empire, and it was the intolerable climate in France during the Wars of Religion that provided the impetus. Thousands of Canadians today can trace their families back to Normandy.

Wars of Religion: In spite of 88 burnings at the stake, Calvinism had made considerable progress in France over a period of some 20 years before Henry II's death in 1559. Calvinists, followers of the religious reformer John Calvin who was born Jean Cauvin in neighbouring Picardy, were called Huguenots in France. They possessed powerful friends in the army, the establishment gener-

challenging Roman Catholicism's traditional hold on the French establishment. Aristocrats banded together on either side of an increasingly hostile religious divide. Francis, duke of Guise, and his brother Charles, cardinal of Reims, led the Catholics. The mere fact that the Huguenots were critical of the king endeared them to the rival Bourbons, notably Anthony of Navarre and his brother Louis, duke of Condé. A third group were Catholic by faith but could not stand the Queen Mother or the Guises. Gaspard de Coligny, admiral of France, emerged as the leader of these so-called Politiques, and as far as the Catholics were concerned, they were worse than Huguenots.

ally, and among the provincial gentry. Their strongholds in Normandy were Rouen and Caen University.

Calvinism was an intellectual revolt against sloth and corruption in the Roman Church. In the latter respect, the Church in Normandy had its own critic in Eude Rigaud, archbishop of Rouen. His *Journal of Pastoral Visits* is a sorrowful account of priests who spent their lives in brothels or taverns and went years without saying Mass.

By the mid-16th century, Huguenots were

The suspicion that Catherine de'Medici, Queen Mother and Regent to young Charles IX, was softening her attitude towards Huguenots sent the Catholics running to Spain for armed support. The Huguenots in turn looked to England and were prepared to make a gift of Le Havre as an inducement. The prospect of Protestant English pouring into Le Havre looked like the Hundred Years' War all over again: the religious bomb burst.

In Caen, Catholics held William the Conqueror's citadel and were attacked from the spire of St-Pierre opposite by Huguenot snipers. The Catholics replied with a cannon and very nearly brought the spire down. With the

Left, St Bartholomew's Day Massacre in 1572.
Above, Rouen as a sea port in the 17th century.

capture of Rouen and the defeat of the combined forces of Admiral Coligny and the duke of Condé at Dreux, the war was going well for the Catholics, but they seemed to lose steam with the assassination of the duke of Guise. An attempt was then made on Admiral Coligny's life, not so much tit-for-tat as the Queen Mother trying to abort his scheme to have Henry of Navarre, a Huguenot, marry her daughter Margaret. The dreaded wedding went ahead, and it was the sight of so many prominent Huguenots assembled in Paris for the occasion that prompted the Queen Mother to issue orders on 24 August 1572 for the notorious St Bartholomew's Day Massacre. Among the

thousands of Huguenots butchered in France that day was Admiral Coligny, whose head was chopped off and sent to the pope for approval. The massacre provoked an orgy of reprisals and counter-reprisals wherever there was a significant Huguenot presence, and in Normandy that meant Rouen especially. When the last of Catherine de'Medici's sons, Henry III, was hacked to death by an insane Jacobin, the Huguenot Henry of Navarre came on to the throne.

Arques-la-Bataille in Normandy, the 11th-century castle built by William the Conqueror's uncle Guillaume de Talou, was the test of Henry's ability to rule over the objections of the Catholic League. In the event, the defeat he inflicted on the military pride of the League at Arques put an end to taunts about "the king without a throne". Nevertheless, he had to renounce Protestantism and besiege Paris for eight months before he could properly rule as Henry IV, and by placating the Catholics he antagonised the Huguenots.

The Huguenots had a battle-hardened army of 25,000 and could not be trifled with. They demanded and were granted the Edict of Nantes, guaranteeing them freedom of worship in their castles and other specified places, equality of civil rights, judicial protection and the right to garrison more than 100 fortified towns. It created, in short, a Huguenot state-within-a-state. The Catholics insisted on a *quid pro quo*, and that was the recall of the Jesuits, who had earlier been banished from France as "corrupters of the young, disturbers of public order and enemies of both king and state".

Marvellous ruin: The Jesuits went on to wield enormous influence under Henry's successor, Louis XIV. They assured him that to revoke the Edict of Nantes would bring the Huguenots back into the bosom of the Roman Church. When in 1685 Louis bowed to the pressure, the court preacher rejoiced: "This is the worthy achievement of your reign and its true character. Through you heresy is no more. God above has made this marvel." What happened, of course, was that the Huguenots, the brains and wealth of France, packed their bags and left. For Rouen, "God's marvel" was an economic disaster.

Another miscalculation of the Sun King's reign was to get involved in attempts to restore the exiled James II to the English throne. An army was made ready in Normandy in 1692 to carry James back. The French fleet under the count of Tourville, a distinguished Norman admiral, nosed out of port to see if the coast was clear. It was not. An Anglo-Dutch fleet twice as big was lying in wait, but Tourville's valour took precedence over discretion and, after giving a good account, his flagship *Soleil Royal* was knocked out of action. From the village of Quineville James watched the destruction of his hopes of returning to England and wept.

Left, 17th-century carving of a Rouen cooper. **Right**, church window from Mortagne celebrating Pierre Boucher's colonial exploits in Canada.

The fabulous court Louis XIV maintained at Versailles tends to disguise the fact that France under him and his immediate successors was practically bankrupt. Economics and efficient taxation in particular were a blindspot, and the kings were also curiously blind to lessons littering history. An attempt to tax salt in western France in 1639 resulted in rebellion by the Avranches saltworkers. Armed bands led by Jean Quetil, "John Barefoot", went on the rampage, at one point holding the villages of Mortain and Pontorson to ransom. Draconian measures were needed to rescue the country from the so-called Barefoot Peasants' War.

The higher clergy and nobility who could afford to pay taxes constitutionally paid none at all. In 1789 the Third Estate, in other words the social ranking lower than aristocracy and clergy, proclaimed a National Assembly and converged on the tennis court at Versailles to demand a new constitution. When it became apparent that the king would side with the aristocracy against them rather than vice versa, the crowd's rage boiled over into the storming of the Bastille and the unfurling of the tricolor.

Normandy abolished: In one single night the National Assembly formally abolished everything redolent of the *ancien régime,* and that included not only names like Normandy but the provinces themselves. Normandy ceased to be a legal entity and was replaced, in the interest of "science", by the five *départements* which still exist.

Province or not, Normandy had a special role in the French Revolution as a bed of counter-revolutionary activity when, it seemed to provincial people, the Revolution had been commandeered by the Paris mob. To begin with, however, leadership of the 1791 Assembly was taken by a body of young, middle-class men drawn from the Gironde in southwest France, hence their name "Girondins". They regarded themselves as evangelists of a new international order, and it was not an order that rang

sweetly in the ears of the autocratic heads of surrounding states. The naivety which prompted the Girondins to preach war with unenlightened neighbours, however powerful they might be, was also their Achilles' heel in coping with the likes of Robespierre and the Jacobins. In their company, the Girondins were a voice of moderation and, when the Terror commenced, that was enough to condemn them, together with the royals and royalists, to the guillotine.

The chief tormentor of the Girondins was

Jean-Paul Marat, a long-time insurrectionist who had spent so much time hiding in rat-infested sewers that he contracted "a loathsome skin disease, making his naturally ugly face hideous and horrible". Marat ran a militant newspaper, *Ami du Peuple*, and by transmutation himself became "The People's Friend". A typical epithet attached to his career as a sadistic demagogue is in terms of "diabolical darkness and uncanny horror".

Caen opened its gates to Girondist refugees and they, setting up like a party in exile, fired the imagination of a young woman named Charlotte Corday, whose family history in Normandy could be traced back to the

11th century. She was descended from the dramatist Pierre Corneille and, educated at the Abbaye-aux-Dames in Caen, where her cousin was the last abbess. She became devoted to the ideals of Voltaire and Jean-Jacques Rousseau.

Having made the acquaintance of the Girondin circle in Caen, Charlotte was shocked to learn that another batch of Girondins had been sent to the scaffold in Paris. She slipped secretly out of her father's house. "I am leaving without your permission," she said in a note, "without seeing you, because I should be so sorrowful. I am going to England." It was reputed to be the only lie she ever told. Charlotte was in fact going to

grant me a moment's interview. I shall put you in a position to render a great service to the country."

Charlotte presented herself as promised but was again refused entry. She kicked up such a fuss that Marat, lying in a warm bath, asked Simone to find out what the matter was. On hearing that it was the young woman who had written the note, he asked her to be shown in. Charlotte found him in the bath with a board set up as a writing desk. He invited her to draw up a chair and tell him all about Caen.

Charlotte said Caen was sheltering 18 dangerous Girondins. "Their names?" Marat asked. Charlotte reeled them off. Marat

Paris, and her purpose was to avenge the death of the Girondins.

Marat was not at the Ministry of Interior when Charlotte called in. He was working from home, being nursed through a recurrence of his sewer complaint by his mistress Simone Évrard. Charlotte tracked down his flat at 30 Rue des Cordeliers but was twice refused admittance. She then decided to send a note by ordinary post: "Citizen, I come from Caen. Your love for your country makes me think you would like to know the miserable events in that part of the Republic. I shall present myself at your house at seven o'clock; have the goodness to receive me and

made a note of the names and passed summary judgement: "They will be guillotined." This was Charlotte's cue. She had earlier in the day purchased a cheap kitchen knife. She whipped it out from under her stays and plunged it straight into the heart of the People's Friend. He died at once.

David's famous painting and a passage in Balzac are just two descriptions of the scene in the bathroom. Other versions have Simone trying to staunch the flow of blood with her bare hand, a man called Laurent Bas breaking a stool over Charlotte's head, even a riot with all sorts of people pouring into the bathroom and, while the corpse stares vacantly from the bath, trying to tear Charlotte limb from limb.

Unrepentant murderess: At her trial, Charlotte expressed no remorse: "I have killed one man to save a hundred thousand," she said. Seeing an artist sketching the trial, she struck a proud pose. The sentence of death was assured.

"Upon the stage of her execution," a newspaper reported, "her face had still the freshness and colour of a pleased woman." As her head rolled off, a carpenter named Legros picked it up and thumped the ears, a gesture which won the approval of the crowd but earned him the pillory and a term of imprisonment on the legalistic grounds that an

spearheaded by the "Catholic and Royal Army" known by the Bas-Breton word for screech-owls, "Chouans".

Chouans used their local knowledge of heaths, marshes, close woods and hedge-bound fields to wage a classic guerrilla campaign, disappearing into the landscape or friendly houses when the enemy approached in strength, regrouping later for surprise attacks elsewhere. If the Chouans wore any identifying insignia at all it was a white cockade, the antithesis of the republican tricolor. To be caught wearing the cockade carried an automatic death sentence.

Like most guerrilla wars, the Chouan campaign resulted in atrocities by both sides,

inanimate head could not be guilty of conduct becoming such punishment.

The Girondins were not alone in using Normandy as a base for counter-revolutionary activities. A second movement owed its origins to peasants in La Vendée who opposed the Revolution because it made the clergy subject to civil authority. A proposed tax increase in February 1793 inflamed their discontent into a rebellion which royalists were quick to exploit. When the revolt reached Brittany and Normandy, it was

although these have been obscured by the romantic gloss put on the business by the writer Jules-Amédée Barbey d'Aurevilly, whose *petite noblesse* Norman family were closely involved with the Chouans. Another of the renowned aristocratic rebels was Count Louis de Frotte, whose family still owns the château of Couterne near Bagnoles. While the worst of the "Terror" ended when Robespierre went to the scaffold, Chouan resistance continued against the five-man Directory which took over. Count Louis was eventually betrayed and, with seven companions, fell before a firing squad at Verneuil. The signature on the death

Left, Charlotte Corday murders Jean-Paul Marat.
Above, *Blacksmith*, by Alexandre le Carpentier.

warrant belonged to the director who proposed, within a short space of time, to dispense with the services of his colleagues: Napoleon Bonaparte.

Napoleon came to Normandy in person to plan his invasion of England. The Bayeux Tapestry was removed from Bayeux cathedral and put on display in Paris to put Napoleon's plans into the appropriate historical perspective. He inspected Cherbourg as a possible springboard for the invasion. The port facilities did not amount to much, heavy seas having frustrated an attempt by the 17th-century engineer Vauban to build an artificial harbour. He would give Cherbourg, Napoleon promised, something to rival "the

d'Angleterre, where he lost hold of his senses. He would have the room specially furnished with chandeliers, candlesticks and flowers, and then, wearing his most splendid outfit, would ceremonially welcome his friends of old, beginning with the Prince of Wales. The room was of course empty, and the charade ended with Brummell sinking into his one armchair in tears.

He died peacefully in the Bon Saveur asylum in May 1839, leaving a disciple in Barbey d'Aurevilly, the previously noted author of tales about the Chouans, who aped Brummell's dress. While the residents of Caen quite admired the style as worn by Brummell, it was not considered suitable for

marvels of Egypt". In practice, the project was no more realised than the invasion of England. The docks and a mole were completed on a more modest scale 50 years later.

Fashion and style: The story of Normandy in the early 19th century is brightened, but hardly ennobled, by George Bryan "Beau" Brummell, the London dandy who fled to France to avoid creditors and for a while was British consul in Caen. He checked into the now defunct Hôtel de la Victoire near St-Pierre's church and, with barely a penny to his name, breezily ordered "the best rooms, the best dinner and the best Lafitte". As debts mounted he was relegated to the tattier Hôtel

a local man. "At a time when nothing any longer appeared ridiculous," Sainte-Beuve wrote, "Barbey found the means of appearing so. An intelligent man would blush to cross Paris with him, even during the Carnival." The duchess of Berry turned heads in the same period when she introduced sea-bathing at Dieppe. After undressing in a bathing hut, she was transported to the water's edge in a sedan chair carried by the wives of local fishermen.

The Normandy coast became increasingly fashionable as a summer resort when it was linked by rail to Paris. Proust revelled in being able to leave the Gare St-Lazare on the

1.22pm train and be at the Grand Hotel in Cabourg in time to dress for dinner. By 1854, when the Rev. George Musgrove dropped in, Dieppe had required an ornate casino, "where a thousand ladies in their morning or evening costume may sit at their ease, with book, crochet, or fan in hand, in a long gallery of glass, like fair flowers in a conservatory, awaiting notice and admiration."

With Trouville-Deauville coming on stream, the coast attracted many of the most famous artistic names of the day. Among celebrity visitors were Dumas, father and son, Strindberg, Henry James, George Moore, Proust, Max Beerbohm, Saint-Saens, Debussy, Grieg, Diaghilev and al-

future Edward VII, used to arrive by yacht and, unlike Wilde, passed his time vigorously, usually in the company of the delightful Duchessa Caracciolo.

The Château d'Eu, originally built by Rollo, the scene of William the Conqueror's wedding to Matilda and Joan of Arc's stop-over on her way to the stake in Rouen, became one of the favourite residences of King Louis-Philippe. Queen Victoria, landing from her yacht at Le Tréport, was twice his guest. The circumstances in which Louis-Philippe last stayed at the château, however, could hardly have been more ignominious. Driven out of Paris by the mob in 1848, the king and his family were taken

most all the painters of the period that anyone has heard of.

The homosexual playwright Oscar Wilde made a bee-line for Dieppe on being released from prison in England and was urged by friends to pay an ostentatious visit to a local brothel to rehabilitate his tarnished reputation. A crowd of well-wishers accompanied Wilde to the brothel and waited outside. Wilde let them down. He emerged shaking his head and mumbling something about "cold mutton". The Prince of Wales, the

Left, Camembert cutie; dairymaid on a donkey.
Above, most farms had their own cider press.

secretly to Dreux where he was able to borrow some money from a tenant. They paid a farewell visit to the Château d'Eu before making their way, partly on foot, to Honfleur. An English steamer was at the wharf to take them off. The king and queen left France as Mr and Mrs William Smith, to be replaced by Louis Napoleon and the Second Empire.

The Second Empire ceased with Napoleon III's surrender at the final battle of the Franco-Prussian war (at Sedan) in 1870, but that left the Empress Eugénie still at the Tuileries. She guessed that something serious had gone wrong when breakfast failed to arrive at her chamber at the customary hour.

The servants, it transpired, had heard the result of the battle and were too busy pillaging her wardrobe. Realising that she would have to flee, the empress complained that she had nothing to wear. An American dentist, a Dr Thomas Evans, smuggled Eugénie to Deauville where Sir John Burgoyne, on a yachting holiday, agreed to carry the empress to England. The Foreign Office was surprised to hear from Sir John that she was his passenger. Two English agents had been sent to Paris specifically to rescue Eugénie and they had already reported their mission accomplished. It turned out that they had in fact rescued the wrong woman, a surprised but grateful Princess Clotilde. Louis-Napo-

HAVRE-NEW-YORK
LA PROVENCE
LA LORRAINE
LA SAVOIE
LA TOURAINE

leon and Eugenie were reunited and spent the rest of their days in Chislehurst, Kent.

Normandy escaped with a minor backstage role in both the Franco-Prussian war of 1870 and World War I. The French army capitulated to the Prussians after the defeat at Metz, but Paris was still in French hands and irregular bodies of volunteers popped up everywhere. The soul of continued resistance was Léon Gambetta, a fiery orator who, when the Prussians finally encircled Paris, escaped in a balloon, a feat commemorated in the balloon museum established by the American publishing tycoon Malcolm Forbes at the Château Balleroy in Calvados.

Gambetta landed in Rouen and within six weeks raised an army of 180,000 men. This army ended up fighting not the Prussians but the Paris communists, a fanatical minority who in effect wanted to secede from France in order to found a utopia based on the abolition of property, patriotism, religion, the family, rulers, armies, upper classes and "every species of refinement". At least 14,000 died before they were silenced.

The Great War: When hostilities began in 1914, the German strategy was to put France out of action as quickly as possible in order to deal with the Russians in the east. The French high command committed every possible mistake to begin with and it looked as if the Germans would take Paris. The capital was saved by Joffré's decisive victory in the valley of the Marne. Having failed to capture Paris, the Germans were denied the Channel ports, their advance halted at Ypres. The Western Front then notoriously settled down into a war of attrition between almost static trenches. The ground fighting never reached Normandy. Instead, the Channel ports well behind the lines kept the Anglo-French campaign going with supplies from Britain and later America, a vital role whose significance made a deep impression, some years later, on Adolf Hitler.

Queen of the sea: In the 1930s the name of *Normandie* was spread across the Western world when the transatlantic liner of that name sailed into the record books. She was then the longest liner in the world and France's pride and joy. Her luxury suites included the Deauville, the Trouville, the Caen and the Rouen, the last of which had four bedrooms and four bathrooms for which more than US$9,000 a head was charged on a memorable cruise to Rio's carnival. She left Le Havre in May 1932 on her maiden voyage in which crossed the Atlantic and won the blue riband, breaking three records: for the fastest crossing, highest speed and longest day's run.

She was in New York when France fell, and was commandeered by the US navy, but a fire broke out in February 1942 and she was gutted and capsized. After her giant bulk was salvaged she became a troop transport ship, the *Lafayette*.

Left, transatlantic port: *au revoir* to the good times. **Right**, *Normandie*, the pride of France.

L'ILLUSTRATION

LE PAQUEBOT
"NORMANDIE"

PRIX 5 frs

1er JUIN 1935

One of the arresting moments in the classic film based on Cornelius Ryan's equally gripping book, *The Longest Day*, is a German officer in a cliff-top observation post above a Normandy beach making a final scan of the English Channel before going off duty. The dawn mist is lifting and, sweeping across the horizon, his binoculars suddenly freeze. "The invasion," he gasps down the line to headquarters, "ten thousand ships." Headquarters are sceptical. The Allied invasion of France was not expected yet and in any case would not be in Normandy. "Which way are these ships heading?" a voice asks sleepily. The officer lifts his binoculars for another look. "Straight at me."

The degree to which the Germans were taken by surprise is summed up by the fact that Field Marshal Erwin Rommel, the legendary "Desert Fox" to whom Hitler had given the specific task of preparing for the Allied invasion, had two days earlier – on 4 June 1944 – decided it was safe to drive to Germany for his wife's birthday. When the invasion was launched, Hitler and the high command agreed, the Allies would land further east at Pas de Calais. The Channel crossing at that point was shortest, as was the distance across the plain of northern France to the German frontier.

Ingenious defences: Nevertheless, Rommel had gone to extraordinary lengths to fortify the Normandy coastline. A string of his own inventions complemented a line of concrete fortresses and blockhouses. Devices planted in the sand between the high and low water lines were designed to destroy landing craft or at least impale them as sitting ducks for shore batteries which had plotted the range of every square inch on the beaches. The number of anti-tank and anti-personnel mines laid was no fewer than 60 million. Some beaches concealed a web of piping which, connected to paraffin tanks, would at the touch of a button spit out walls of flame. Open areas suitable for parachute landings

Preceding pages: US transports and landing craft: 7,000 ships and 200,000 men were in the first wave. **Left**, British troops disembark. **Right**, Field Marshal Rommel inspects his defences.

were flooded or laced with explosive stakes nicknamed "Rommel's asparagus".

"The first 24 hours of the invasion will be decisive," Rommel had warned. "The fate of Germany depends on the outcome... For the Allies, as well as Germany, it will be the longest day."

The war whose end Rommel could in 1944 foresee had, of course, begun in 1939 with Hitler's invasion of Poland. France was invaded in May 1940, the 250,000-strong British Expeditionary Force being evacuated

from Dunkirk as Rommel himself entered Cherbourg with his 7th Panzer Division. Hitler seemed to hold all the cards, but in reality the continued presence of a malignant Britain a few miles off his Continental conquests meant he had to defend them. Europe had to become a fortress behind an "Atlantic Wall" running from Norway to Spain.

While Hitler was preoccupied in Russia, the German garrison in Normandy had a significant proportion of second-rate units. The Germans were on the whole either too young or too old to fight on the Eastern Front, or were convalescing from wounds already received there. The balance included quite a

THE DIEPPE RAID

Compared with the small cloak-and-dagger commando operations which had preceded it and the massive scale of the D-Day landings afterwards, the Dieppe raid on 19 August 1942 looks in retrospect, says historian John Keegan in his admirable *Six Armies in Normandy*, "so recklessly hare-brained an enterprise that it is difficult to re-construct the official state of mind which gave it birth and drove it forward." The 2nd Canadian Division, as Keegan puts it, "was to sally forth in high summer from ports only 70 miles (113 km) from the German-occupied coastline and disembark on the espla-

nade of a French seaside resort." As Dieppe was excluded from the 1944 landings and consequently spared the bombardment, the port is still recognisably what it was like in 1942, and it is possible to form a picture of Operation Jubilee.

Commandos went in first, scaling the cliffs that line the Arques river to silence the German gun positions covering the port entrance. Unfortunately, this brave and successful assault did not account for other German gunners some of whom, when the Royal Regiment of Canada moved into the mouth of the gully leading into the cliffs at Puys and dropped the ramps of their landing

Above, a Canadian taken prisoner in the Raid.

craft, could aim right down the open mouths of the vessels. A handful of Canadians survived the solid sheet of fire to reach the shelter of the sea wall and, using "bangalore torpedoes", blew a hole through the barbed wire crowning it. To mount the wall and crawl through the hole, however, was to be exposed to machine-gun fire at close range. Landing craft brought in second and third waves of men to repeat the same futile exercise. Every one of the 554 men who tried was killed or captured.

Ten LCTs (Landing Craft Tanks), each carrying three Churchill tanks, undertook a direct assault on the harbour and promenade. Fifteen of the tanks managed to get as far as the promenade, only to discover that access to the town was blocked by concrete obstacles which shrugged off the sappers' explosives. Trapped in the open, the tank crews kept on firing in support of the infantry until, one by one, they were knocked out. None got away. Deprived of this small measure of covering fire, the infantry on the beaches were mown down. A German gunner later recalled: "I knew as an infantryman I wouldn't have wanted to be in the places of those Canadians, lying on those damned stones, not only having the fire come at them, but with fragments of stone flying everywhere."

Only at Pourville beach, west of the town, did the assault parties have any kind of shelter, but even so the casualties were fearsome. Five miles (8 km) above them one of the war's most costly dogfights took place between the RAF and the Luftwaffe: 106 Allied planes were lost, 48 German planes were shot down.

Of the 4,963 Canadians who set sail from England, only 2,110 returned, and of these 378 were wounded. Of those left behind in Dieppe, 1,874 were prisoners, but many of them were wounded and 72 died of their wounds. In proportional terms, the operation ranked with the first day of the Battle of the Somme in World War I as the blackest in British military history.

Arguments about the rationale behind the Raid have not yet been resolved. The majority view, perhaps, is that it was undertaken to prove to those calling for a Second Front in 1942, particularly Stalin, that the timing was wrong and that in any case frontal assaults on heavily defended Channel ports would not work. Others have said it taught important lessons about amphibious operations. As illuminating, says Keegan, as to say that the *Titanic* "taught important lessons about passenger liner design". ∎

number of Eastern Europeans – Ukrainians, Armenians, Georgians – who would serve anyone, even Hitler, rather than the tyrannical Stalin. A point which remains somewhat sensitive to this day is that the Normans got on quite well with the garrison. The cynical view is that they relished the brisk demand for their dairy products, cider and Calvados. It is said in mitigation that they patriotically robbed their customers blind.

With the United States entering the war after the Japanese attack on Pearl Harbor in December 1941, Roosevelt and Churchill were under relentless pressure from Stalin to relieve the strain on Russia by opening a "Second Front" in the West. The Americans

bases in southern England, not more than 200 miles (320 km). Moreover, the beaches would have to be sufficiently long and sheltered for the unloading of troops and stores until a nearby port could be captured.

Chosen beaches: The Normandy beaches in the western half of the Bay of the Seine – with Cherbourg and Le Havre close at hand – were just the ticket in all but one respect, the weather. Meteorological records revealed that even in June, the most likely date for an invasion, fair weather could not be relied on for more than three consecutive days, not nearly enough time to be sure of taking a port. That was a problem for the boffins.

The answer to questions about the weather

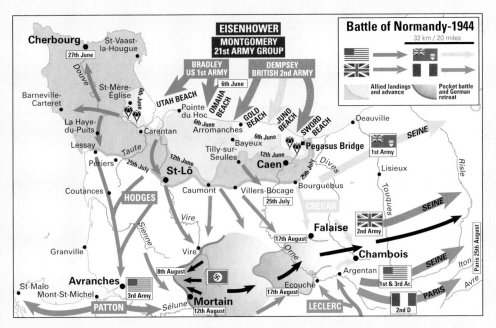

were sympathetic to the idea of a cross-Channel invasion while Churchill argued that a premature assault would be repulsed with demoralising effect by the German forces already stationed in France.

It is said that the ill-fated Canadian raid on Dieppe (*see facing page*) went ahead to underline, especially for Stalin's benefit, that an effective Second Front in France would require an immense amount of planning and preparation. Landings in France would have to be within the operational radius of fighter

Above, in just a few weeks the Battle of Normandy devastated hundreds of towns and villages.

was that the landing forces would have to take artificial harbours ("Mulberries") with them. The general idea was that old ships ("Gooseberries") would be sunk in line to form an outer breakwater. Within them was a semi-circle of of hollow concrete boxes, "Phoenixes", the largest displacing 6,000 tons, and they were connected to shore by floating roadways, "Whales". The components for two Mulberries were constructed in great secrecy. Starting on the afternoon of D-Day, they were to be towed across the channel at 1½ knots and assembled on site, one for the Americans and one for the British.

In the event, the American Mulberry at

Omaha Beach was destroyed in the Great Storm of D-Day + 13, but its British counterpart at a more sheltered position off Arromanches survived (as pieces still do) to provide 39,000 vehicles and 220,000 men with dry landings.

The code-name "Mulberry" contributed, as we shall see later, to a minor but intriguing aspect of war-time Intelligence. It was actually chosen from a list of deliberately meaningless possibilities, and it was only after the war that one of the principal architects, Colonel V.C. Steer-Webster of the Royal Engineers, come across a biblical quotation from Luke xvii, 6: "And the Lord said, If ye have the faith of a grain of mustard-seed, ye might

identified and immediately reported, but to no avail. The Allies, it was said, were hardly likely to announce their arrival in France over the radio.

The first wave of the invasion was already in motion for a 5 June landing when deteriorating weather caused General Eisenhower, Chief of the Allied Expeditionary Force, to agonise over whether he ought to call a postponement. In the event, the main body was turned back but there was no way of communicating with two midget submarines whose job was to surface less than a mile offshore and transmit directional signals to the approaching fleet. The five-man crews of the two submarines, each squeezed into a

say unto this Mulberry tree, Be thou plucked up by the root, and be thou planted in the sea; it will obey you."

Coded messages broadcast by the BBC warned the French Resistance that the invasion was imminent. The first went out on 1 June 1944 as the opening line of Paul Verlaine's *Song of Autumn*: "The long sobs of the violins of autumn…" It was followed up on 5 June with the second line: "Wound my heart with a monotonous langour." Admiral Wilhelm Canaris, chief of German Intelligence, had been tipped off about the significance of these messages and told monitors to keep an ear open for them. They were

single 8ft by 5ft (2.5 by 1.5 metres) cabin, spent a tough night and day on the seabed off Ouistreham and Le Hamel, 20 miles (32 km) apart, not knowing what was going on.

Day One: Operation Overlord began in earnest as the clock struck midnight to herald 6 June. At its simplest, the plan called for a vanguard of airborne troops and commandos to secure the flanks of the beach-head and neutralise the gun batteries trained on it. The US 82nd and 101st Airborne Divisions were to seal off the northwestern perimeter against counter-attacks by German forces concentrated around Cherbourg. The British 6th Airborne was to hold the eastern approaches.

The five beaches within the corridor thus created were Utah and Omaha, for the 1st American Army, and Gold, Juno and Sword, for the 2nd (predominantly) British Army. The intention was to break out as quickly as possible with the Americans curling round to take Cherbourg and the British going straight for Caen, the German strongpoint.

Poor visibility and high winds played havoc with the initial airborne landings so that paratroopers were scattered all over the place, some as far as 25 miles (40 km) off-target. The unluckiest fell into flooded areas. The typical American paratrooper had a jump-suit over his battledress and wore or carried a helmet, boots, gloves, main and reserve

towed across the Channel by bombers and then unhitched for powerless descent, carried about 30 men each. Their night's work began with a crash landing – there was no other way – sometimes right on top of the positions they planned to take. There were many acts of valour in the early hours of D-Day. A British glider unit is credited with the first victory: a blinding 10-minute fight which captured the vital Pegasus Bridge near Bénouville. Thanks to *The Longest Day*, one of the most unfortunate of the early American air drops became one of the most celebrated: Private John Steele, dangling helplessly from the Ste-Mère-Église church, his parachute wrapped around the steeple.

parachute, Mae West, rifle and pistol with anything up to 700 rounds of ammunition, a selection of knives and a machete, an anti-tank mine and up to a dozen grenades, slabs of TNT, a spade, blanket and raincoat, one change of socks and underwear, five days' rations and two cartons of cigarettes. They could barely stand up under the weight. Landing in water, they drowned.

British paratroopers used hunting horns to find one another in the darkness, the Americans clicked toy crickets. Wooden gliders,

Left, US naval guns ceaselessly pound the coast.
Above, Allied troops on 6 June in Hermanville.

Secrecy about the place and timing of the invasion had been maintained to a miraculous degree. Rommel, as we have seen, was driving obliviously to Germany. All but two of the 124 aircraft of the Luftwaffe's 26th Fighter Wing had the previous afternoon been moved from their base near Lille. The crack 21st Panzer Division, veterans of Rommel's Afrika Korps, were alerted to what was happening and, 25 miles (40 km) southeast of Caen, had their engines running. They received no orders to move, perhaps because intense bombing had neutralised much of the German communication network. Three serviceable boats of 5th E-boat

Flotilla at Le Havre represented the sum strength of the German navy. They went into immediate action, pounding towards – they knew not – the biggest fleet ever assembled.

The vanguard of the invasion fleet consisted of 7,000 ships, of which 713 were warships including a number of battleships with guns capable of pounding Caen 15 miles (24 km) inland from their off-shore stations. Some 11,500 aircraft and 200,000 sailors and soldiers made up the order of battle in the first wave alone, the landing forces being mustered in 59 separate convoys, each preceded by minesweepers and organised so that they landed in the correct sequence. In the 87 days after the landing,

the Allies put ashore 2,052,299 men, 3,098,259 tons of stores, and 438,471 vehicles. The stores alone would have filled a goods train 900 miles (1,450 km) long.

As the fleet approached the beaches, mother ships disgorged square-faced landing craft under an umbrella of shells from battleships and cruisers and salvoes of rockets from specially converted barges. Landing craft, said to have "a capacity for rolling all ways at once which fortunately is unrivalled by any other sea-going vessel", quickly filled with water to the acute discomfort of the troops who, almost to a man, were wretchedly seasick. Not a few sank, and worse was

in store as the water grew shallower and the craft triggered Rommel's devices. The force of one explosion blew an amphibious tank 100 feet (30 metres) in the air, sending it tumbling end over end.

The opposition was stiffest at Omaha Beach in the American sector. Fewer than a third of the men survived the wade from their landing craft to dry land under withering fire from the cliffs above. Only half the tanks made it ashore. Ironically, the landings at Utah Beach were relatively easy because the troops were put ashore in the wrong place. Brigadier-General Theodore Roosevelt, at 57 the only general to land with the first wave, was not too bothered. "We'll start the war from here," he announced.

At Sword Beach, Lord Lovat's 1st Special Service Brigade was piped ashore (*Highland Laddie* followed by *The Road to the Isles*) by a kilted William Millin waist-deep in water. At Gold Beach, the 47th Royal Marine Commandos lost all but one of their landing-craft and had to swim ashore under machine-gun fire. "Perhaps we're intruding," one remarked. "This seems to be a private beach." At Juno, the Canadian 3rd Division fought through a maze of pillboxes and trenches.

Even at between 10,000 and 12,000 Allied casualties (killed and wounded), the cost was much lighter than feared. The Germans are thought to have lost between 4,000 and 9,000 men, but that would not have concerned Hitler. "If only they would land half a million men," he had once mused, "and then foul weather and storms cut them off in the rear. Then everything would be all right."

Day Two: Many of the men at D-Day later said they were so keyed up that they could not think beyond the actual landing. The troops awoke on the blustering morning of 7 June cold, stiff and dirty after a fitful sleep in a shallow hole in French soil, in most cases their first on *terra firma* for three days. Their first thoughts were astonishment at still being alive, followed by a psychological adjustment to the realisation that there was still a long way to go. To pick themselves up for another day of fighting – and how many more after that? – was not easy, but of course that is what they did.

General Montgomery, in command of the Anglo-American troops, arrived off the Normandy beaches before dawn, having crossed from Plymouth in the destroyer *HMS*

Faulkner. His intention was to consolidate the five landing beaches into a continuous secure beach-head and then strike hard while the Germans were still off-balance and wondering whether the Normandy landings were a red herring for the real invasion in the Pas de Calais. The British 50th Division at Gold Beach stormed on to liberate Bayeux which, being taken so early, was the only town in Normandy to escape heavy damage. The Canadian Division at Juno managed to seize part of the Caen-Bayeux road and railway line but plans for the swift capture of Carpiquet airport proved to be extremely naive, as was the hope that the British 3rd Division at Sword could snap up Caen.

mand was still inclined to view the Normandy landings as a diversion, and within these constraints Rommel saw his duty as confining the Allies to the smallest possible area as he brought up a panzer force strong enough to drive them back into the sea. With one hand tied behind his back by the Allied air forces and pinpoint naval bombardment, Rommel had the other shackled by Hitler. In response to desperate appeals for the release of panzer units still being kept in reserve for the "real" invasion around Calais, Hitler's unhelpful order was that "every man shall fight and die where he stands".

Hitler had another compelling reason for protecting the Pas de Calais at the expense of

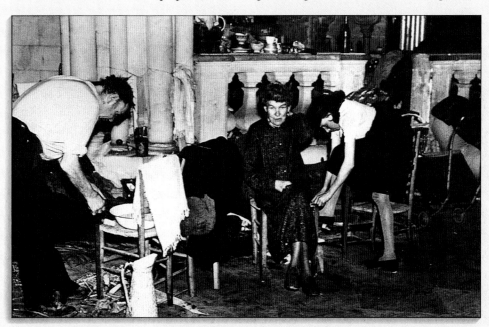

At Utah Beach, where the landing had been relatively comfortable, the main task was to consolidate the two Airborne Divisions whose scattered landings were epitomised by Pte Steele's lonely vigil beneath the church steeple of Ste-Mère-Église. At Omaha Beach, where the reception had been hottest, the Americans had to fight inland from their shallow beach-head against a crack German infantry division.

Rommel returned from his ill-timed trip to Germany on D+2. The German High Com-

his forces in Normandy. It was the launching pad for the secret weapon which he believed would turn the tide of the war regardless of D-Day, the V1 "doodle-bug" rocket. To witness the start of the V1 bombardment of England and perhaps to emulate Churchill's visit to Normandy on 10 June, Hitler went to France. Conferring with Rommel in a bunker near Soissons, Hitler wanted only to talk about the miraculous properties of the war-winning rocket. The next day, one of the rockets went beserk and crashed by the bunker. Hitler returned to East Prussia at once and never again set foot in France.

At the time of Hitler's brief visit, the

Left, a gift from the US 8th AAF. **Above**, citizens of Caen seek shelter in the Abbaye-aux-Hommes.

Americans had taken Carentan and thus both joined up Utah and Omaha Beaches and cut the Cotentin peninsula in half, isolating the German forces in Cherbourg. In the British sector, however, things were not going at all well. Montgomery's plans to take Caen with an elaborate pincer movement failed, giving the newly arrived 51st Highland Division, veterans of the Western Desert, a bitter taste of the very different conditions in Normandy.

Memoirs of the Normandy fighting are haunted by the word *bocage*, used to describe small fields enclosed by hedgerows, "ridges on a monstrous waffle". Hedgerows grown since Celtic times had so stiffened the banks with their roots that the Americans

war of attrition. This was to the Allies' advantage as long as their replacements and supplies came across the English Channel faster than the Germans could receive theirs, but on 19 June the worst summer storm in living memory struck the coast. The American Mulberry at Omaha was damaged beyond repair and no fewer than 800 supply ships were driven ashore. The loss of the Mulberry made the capture of Cherbourg all the more imperative. This was accomplished on 27 June, but only after the Germans had done such a thorough demolition job that the port was not serviceable for several weeks.

The Caen front showed no improvement, and the Allied air forces needed Carpiquet

eventually had to improvise a special kind of bulldozer to cut through them. In the meantime, troops working their way through *bocage* confronted at intervals of 100 to 150 yards (90 to 135 metres) an interminable succession of perfect defensive positions for snipers, machine-gunners or worse. The roadways between the hedgerows had been worn so deep beneath the level of the surrounding fields that they could conceal a defensive tank. For advancing tanks, the hedgerows made such narrow roadways that they could not traverse their turrets.

Summer storms: In the middle of June, the Normandy campaign threatened to become a

airport as badly as the navies needed Cherbourg. On 26 June Montgomery launched Operation Epsom with a view to encircling Caen from the west and at the same time attracting German armour to the British sector, thereby improving the chances of an American break-out from their position. The offensive focused on capturing and holding "Hill 112" overlooking the airport. This much was done, but the hill was almost immediately lost to a ferocious counter-attack. Thereafter so much firepower was trained on the hill that neither side dared occupy it. Although Epsom did not win Caen, it did succeed in drawing a total of 725 panzers, which left the Americans with only 140 to worry about. Now, it seems, Hitler also had things to worry about.

Sacking Field Marshal von Rundstedt, his Commander-in-Chief West, Hitler decided that operations in Normandy required his personal attention. While his field staff strongly recommended drawing back the German line so that it was at least out of range of naval bombardment, Hitler hated the idea of giving up any territory. "The present positions are to be held," he ordered, and that applied also to the 15th Army chained to the Pas de Calais in anticipation of "Patton's Army". The Germans always assumed that General George Patton, whom they knew

as did Carpiquet airport. Omar Bradley and Montgomery arrived at the same conclusion: St-Lô and Caen would have to be pulverised.

Caen bombed: On the evening of 7 July, 267 bombers dropped more than 2,500 tons of bombs on Caen. The infantry were not sent in until the following morning, by which time the Germans had recovered. If anything, the destruction hampered the attackers. Craters blocked the path of vehicles, whole streets had been reduced to rubble, and maps had no meaning. Only after two days of street fighting was the town north of the Orne river captured, and at the same time the airport. Ominously, the Germans managed to hang on to high ground south of Caen and so

only too well from Italy, would be given a decisive role in the invasion of France. "Patton's Army" was apparently still poised in Kent for a Channel crossing; in reality, it was a decoy army of cardboard cut-outs.

The American and British armies had a more or less common problem in their sectors. The market town of St-Lô controlled the main road out of the Cotentin in the same way as Caen controlled the road network in the east, and both remained in German hands,

On the beaches. <u>Left</u>, Eisenhower with Ernest J. King, C-i-C US Fleet. **<u>Above</u>**, Montgomery with Winston Churchill on his fleeting 10 June visit.

commanded the gateway to the coveted Caen-Falaise plain.

After a similar aerial bombardment, St-Lô fell to the Americans on 18 July, the day Montgomery launched the Goodwood offensive to get the Germans away from Caen and open the way for the push on to the Caen-Falaise plain. The simultaneous American offensive was to be Cobra, a punch through the German defences in the west to enable them to move into Brittany.

Goodwood began with the biggest air operation in support of ground troops in the entire war – 1,600 heavy bombers, 400 light bombers, and 2,500 fighters and Typhoon rocket aircraft. Nearly 750 guns lent their support. On the ground, the assault was led by three armoured divisions (750 tanks) and infantry divisions accompanied by a further 350 tanks. Rommel was waiting for them with several hundred tanks, 200 guns, about 100 of the wickedly efficient 88mm anti-tank guns, some 270 multi-barrelled *nebel-werfers* ("Moaning Minnies") and a strong body of infantry in well-prepared defensive lines 10 miles (16 km) deep.

Rommel wounded: On the eve of what was clearly going to be the major offensive of the campaign, Rommel had been out as usual to inspect the defences. On his way back to headquarters near the Seine, Rommel's spot-

mitted suicide in October rather than face charges of complicity in the von Stauffenberg plot to blow up Hitler three days after his encounter with the Spitfire.

With or without Rommel, the German defences managed to hold out against Goodwood. The British lost 400 tanks in the process, but these could be repaired or replaced. The Germans lost far fewer, but they could not be. In case there was any doubt left in Hitler's mind about the authenticity of the Normandy campaign, it would have been banished by the knowledge that Cobra, the American counterpart to Goodwood, was to employ the services of Patton and a real-life 3rd Army. After an initial error that killed

ter warned that two Spitfires were flying along the road in his direction. "The driver was told to put on speed and turn off on to a little side road," an officer in the car recalled. "Before we could reach it the enemy aircraft, flying at great speed only a few feet above the road, came up to within 500 yards of us and the first one opened fire." Both Rommel and his driver were hit and the car overturned. He was dragged out of the wreckage unconscious and seriously wounded. The nearby village to which he was carried for first aid was called, ironically, Ste-Foy-de-Montgomery. Rommel eventually recovered but took no further part in the war. He com-

558 American troops, the bombs went in on target and obliterated the Panzer Lehr, a significant proportion of the reduced tank force on the American front. Coutances was captured on 28 July and Avranches two days later. It was now time for Patton to show his long-awaited hand. In three days he manoeuvred 100,000 men and 15,000 vehicles down the single road out of Avranches and by 4 August had reached Rennes, the capital of Brittany. The 3rd Army then wheeled towards an emotive destination: Paris.

Montgomery switched his push drive east of Caen to the western flank, enabling the British 2nd Army and the American 1st to drive south almost side by side. The newly established 1st Canadian Army, of which about half the troops were either British or belonged to the 1st Polish Armoured Division, were left with the unresolved problem of fighting through the German defences in order to drive down the Caen-Falaise road. The distance to William the Conqueror's birthplace was only 20 miles (32 km), but every inch would be contested.

Canadian vendetta: For the Canadians, the long slog down the Falaise road was something of a personal vendetta. On D-Day they had come up against the 12th SS Panzer Division formed largely of fanatical Hitler Youth near the Abbey of Ardenne near Caen.

rection and begin a pincer movement aimed at snapping the trap in what became known as the Falaise Pocket. On 15 August the Allies landed in the South of France, and on 16 August Hitler's Commander-in-Chief advised him that the only hope for the German army in the north was to retreat across the Seine. Hitler sacked him on the spot.

Hitler notwithstanding, the German retreat was in full swing. "The floor of the valley was seen to be alive with stuff," a British gunner noted. "Men marching, cycling and running, columns of horse-drawn transport, motor transport, and as the sun got up, so more and more targets came to light. Soon the whole Regiment was banging away with

Twenty-three Canadians were captured, led into the abbey and shot. In their second encounter, still near the abbey, another 45 prisoners were taken and again shot. Barring their way to Falaise was the 12th SS again, but this time they met on more equal terms.

The battle for Normandy was moving towards a climax. Patton had surged as far as Chartres and Orleans when it appeared that, largely owing to Hitler's bungling intervention, the German forces in Normandy could be encircled. Patton was told to change di-

Left, a helping hand from an American MP.
Above, family life somehow manages to go on.

all it had, and the cry for more ammunition went up on all sides. It was a gunner's paradise and everybody took advantage of it."

The Canadian Army still had the 12th SS Panzer Division between it and Falaise but not for much longer. They entered Falaise on 17 August and closed in on the last of the Hitler Youth. In the end, only four of them were alive to be captured, and they were all wounded. That did not quite end the Normandy campaign for the Canadians, and in fact a Canadian major went on to win the Victoria Cross in three days of hand-to-hand fighting at St-Lambert.

Among the heroes of the final phase of the

battle for Normandy was the smallest contingent among the Allied forces, the 1st Polish Armoured Division. While waiting to go into action in Normandy, they listened to news of the Warsaw Uprising which began on 1 August and bit their nails. When on 17 August they at last received their battle orders, some could not wait for the 2am start-time and went off at once without their re-supply of fuel and ammunition.

The Poles took up positions on a "long whale-like ridge" with a commanding view of the valleys and roads around Chambois. The position, which they called "The Mace", was excellent, but it was isolated and happened to be within territory still German. In

fact, Germans were pouring by on all sides and their only hope was to stay put with their 1,500 infantry and 80 tanks despite serious shortages of food, water, fuel and ammunition. The Germans saw the Poles on the Mace as an obstacle between them and escape from the Falaise Pocket, so the position was engulfed in fire from all directions.

On 20 August, coincidentally a critical day in the course of the Warsaw Uprising, the Germans directed their heaviest attack yet on the Mace. The assault was supported by armour, the fresh 2nd SS Panzer Division just arrived to spearhead a desperate German counter-offensive. They penetrated the Mace

perimeter that evening. "Gentlemen," the Polish commander told his troops, "all is lost. I do not think the Canadians can come to our rescue. We have no food and very little ammunition... Fight all the same. There is no question of surrender. Tonight we shall die."

Polish stand: The night actually passed quietly, but in the morning the Germans meant to finish off the Poles. A supply drop by American Dakotas, the Poles' last hope, landed 5 miles (8 km) away. The garrison commander had signalled that he could "no longer stand up from physical exhaustion when the distinctive sound of Sherman tanks was heard – the Canadian Grenadier Guards. "The scene," one Grenadier recorded, "was the most savage the regiment had ever encountered... There were corpses everywhere, unburied and dismembered."

The sense of relief was ruined by the news that the Warsaw Uprising was doomed. It was left to Royal Canadian Engineers to mark the spot where the Polish exiles had done their bit. It simply read, in English, "A Polish Battlefield".

Hitler's keen prospect of destroying 500,000 Allied troops on the beaches of Normandy was heading rapidly towards disaster. The battle of the Falaise Pocket had annihilated Army Group B, the largest in his Army. The 2nd SS Panzer Division, which had only just arrived when it went into action against the Poles on the Mace, was down to 450 men and 15 tanks.

All in all, the battle for Normandy cost Germany 300,000 casualties. The figure for the Allies who, being on the offensive, would have expected more, was 209,672, including 36,976 killed. The German formations in Normandy remained a fighting force until 27 August, but it was really all over at Falaise on the 22nd.

General Eisenhower said that only Dante could have adequately described the scene. "It was literally possible to walk for hundreds of yards at a time stepping on nothing but dead and decaying flesh." A reconnaissance pilot flying over the battleground said that at 1,500 ft (450 metres) the stench penetrated the cockpit and assailed his nose.

Left, back in unharmed Bayeux, 14 June, the first time that General de Gaulle has been in France since the occupation. Right, the devastation of Caen after two months of fighting for the town.

AFTER THE WAR WAS OVER

On 1 September 1944, the Battle of Normandy, which had started in the morning of 6 June on the beaches of Calvados and the Manche, finally ended. Normandy was liberated, but at a price. The cost of the fierce battles, which for nearly three months had been contested on Norman soil between the troops of the Third Reich and those of the American, Canadian and British armies, was appalling.

Added to the damage caused by the German invasion in 1940 was the damage by the seaborne landing missions, and by the airforce and artillery that assisted the Allies' breakthrough. It left towns and cities, industrial sites and communication systems totally or partially destroyed. Worst affected were St-Lô, Caen, Lisieux, Vire, Falaise, Rouen and Le Havre where it would be two years before ships could use the port again. In many places Normandy was deprived forever of priceless riches, of works of art and, particularly, architecture. Whole half-timbered towns had disappeared.

The Norman countryside had also been a stage for fierce fighting and it left a trail of destruction. In August 1944 in the Argentan-Chambois area in the *département* of Orne, the fighting was so violent that Germans who had taken part in the invasion of the Soviet Union unhesitatingly compared the Battle of the Poche de Falaise to that of Stalingrad.

After four years of occupation, many Normans became the hostages of the retreating German army, and the innocent victims of both sides in a necessary war. Thousands of men, women and children either became refugees, or were killed or wounded by the aerial bombardments and artillery. In the *départements* of Calvados and the Manche alone, civilian casualties amounted to about 10,000 dead and 35,000 wounded.

Dark days: Once the pangs of the war were over the Normans slipped into a dark period lasting many years while reconstructiuon took place. Before 1939, Normandy was the most prosperous region in all France. World War II put paid to that and it seriously jeopardised the region's future. This once-hospitable place and fashionable tourist centre was reduced to an enormous field of ruins, littered with masses of debris.

As soon as the fighting ended the Normans set to work clearing away the ruins to build a new country that would combine 20th-century living with the values they cherished from the past. No one was in any doubt about the enormity of the task. Over nearly the whole of Normandy reconstruction was needed. The economy of town and country, public services and the environment, were all victims of the war. What was worse, the communications systems, without which the economy could not begin to take off, were virtually unusable in most areas.

These enormous undertakings could not be financed without big loans. But central government had requests for money from many quarters, compounding frequent political crises, and it turned a deaf ear. What money it did give was for bare necessities and was only a drop in the ocean. The Normans had to wait 20 years before their country was back to anything like normal.

Most of the other French regions developed, modernised their industry, their agriculture, their communications systems and exchanges, and set off to win new markets. In the meantime, Normandy was growing poorer, losing its trump cards one by one. Powerlessly it watched its skilled workers set off for Paris or other cities which offered immediate employment. With them went the hopes for its textile industry, boat building, ironworks and transport sectors.

If the competition against the other French regions became particularly strong, the difficulties encountered in trading with other countries was formidable. The only consolation the Normans had was the creation of a large number of temporary, unskilled jobs in the construction industry or in maintenance work for the public sector. This enabled a large number of labourers to get back to work and it also attracted many agricultural workers who were either unable to find employment or had decided to leave their trade for something that was better paid.

The numbers of unemployed in Normandy

Left, the people of Falaise return to what is left of their homes: 586 towns had to be re-planned.

increased every year until the end of the 1960s. The progressive decline in the number of vacancies in agriculture and building forced workers to leave for other places, just as those with qualifications had done a few years earlier. A large part of Normandy was thus further depopulated.

As agriculture went into recession, the rural communtiy felt it was being dragged down an inexorable decline. Until 1960, the shortage of raw materials, the stopping and then the control of trade and the decrease in buying power brought hard times for Normandy's "home-made" products: its meats, ciders, Calvados and cheeses which had made it a fortune under the Second Empire.

for two types of agriculture in Normandy: arable farming; and livestock farming of both beef and dairy cattle which has gone hand-in-hand with apple orchards and cider. Until 1939, livestock farms were the most profitable but, after the war, mechanisation and the expansion of the cereal market favoured arable farmers. The livestock regions, located in the most beautiful countryside and picturesque places, would have to await the increases in tourism for a new rise in fortune.

In spite of the difficulties, agriculture remained the driving force of Normandy until quite recently. Today, in terms of turnover, it comes second to tourism. From the beginning of the 1980s, the pace of decrease in

The rural exodus also took away the large number of labourers essential just to carry out the various jobs on the small-holdings. A farm of an average 75–100 acres (30–40 hectares) once had up to 15 workers. Now that number was reduced to two or three: the owner, his wife and a part-time helper.

Production methods were mechanised and livestock farmers stopped making their own products, selling instead the raw materials directly to the increasing number of dairies and industrial cider plants. Among them were Uln, Besnier and Elle et Vire.

Since the 19th century the mixture of flat, open country and wooded hills has provided

holdings has slowed, mainly as a result of farmers who began to specialise.

Industrial revival: While agriculture was suffering a loss of jobs in the 1950s, industrial, business and communication systems began to revive around Caen, Rouen and Le Havre. To complement their traditional businesses, and to make up for the disappearance or reduction of others (iron works at Caen, passenger transport to the US from Le Havre) these three towns took on new industrial developments such as petrochemicals, and mechanical and electronic engineering. The Le Havre-Rouen basin began to expand with refineries built at Ganfreville, Notre-Dame-de-Gravenchon, Petite Couronne and Port-Jérôme, where the first synthetic rubber factory outside the US was built.

The construction of the Paris-Rouen motorway, later extended to Caen, the linking of the two banks of the River Seine by the Tancarville bridge in 1965, and more recently, the Brotonne bridge, all contributed to the rise of these centres.

To avoid creating a "two-speed" Normandy, elected representatives and economic advisers tried and succeeded, from the 1960s, in establishing new industries across the whole region. Their aims were helped when central government called for the industrial decentralisation of the Paris region. This led to the creation here and there of new, usually small, factories.

Animal feed and agricultural machinery were the two main industries in Normandy, but local help was given to relaunch small traditional industries. Aiguiules, an iron-smelting business at L'Aigle in the Orne, precision engineering and metallurgy in the Eure, and Moulinex, manufacturers of electronics and electrical goods, all revitalised areas of industrial depletion. Normandy's proximity to Paris and improved communication systems enabled it to establish numerous businesses throughout the 1980s, though many of these were for unskilled labour.

Added to the industrial growth was the decision in the 1960s by central government to site three nuclear power stations in Normandy, which have been important to the region's economy. Two are in Seine Maritime and one in the Manche, and in 1967 a reprocessing centre for nuclear waste was set up at La Hague, near Cherbourg. In 1971 France's first nuclear submarine slipped out of the harbour at Cherbourg, now known as "Plutonium City".

Tourists return: The last factor in Normandy's "renaissance" was tourism. Nearly the whole coast, as well as a large number of tourist sites inland had suffered terrible damage, and several hundred leisure centres, hotels and guest houses had been destroyed or seriously affected. Roads, railways, and ports were mostly unusable. With the exception of the top tourist attractions, such as Mont-Saint-Michel, Bayeux, Lisieux and

Deauville, this industry was not able to relaunch itself until the 1960s, and it had to wait until the end of the 1970s for tourism to really take off. The Jeanne d'Arc church covering the damaged Vieux-Marché in Rouen was not opened until 1979 it was not until the 1980s that the Abbaye-aux-Hommes in Caen was fully restored.

To develop the tourist market in inland Normandy as well as along its borders, it was essential to begin by trying to sell its natural riches: its countryside, gastronomy and heritage. Regional committees and the Department of Tourism, the "Syndicats d'Initiative" (information centres), consular organisations, local groups and associations tried to make

people appreciate what Normandy has to offer, and through their efforts even the rural population has realised the economic and other benefits of tourism. The development of sea travel for cross-Channel passengers at Cherbourg, Le Havre, Dieppe and more recently at Caen-Ouistreham, was the cause of an influx of new clients.

Today Mont-St-Michel brings 850,000 visitors a year, but even more numerous are the 2.5 million who come to see the Landing Beaches and the Battle of Normandy sites. The event which ravaged the country and from which it took so long to recover, is now, ironically, contributing to its prosperity.

Left, agriculture went into inexorable decline.
Right, Cherbourg sky-rises from the rubble.

Europe today has a two-speed economy: one speed in the south, where agriculture is the main occupation, the population is widely dispersed and production centres far from the markets they serve; another in the north, with a Europe where people live in big cities well-placed for industry and agriculture, and where there are the vital communication systems needed to service a modern economy.

In the centre sits Normandy, though it occupies a marginal position: an agricultural area in a well-populated region close to the French capital. In many ways the region shares the fate of the rest of Europe, having entered the 1990s in the recession common everywhere. It has one of the highest unemployment levels in France: Lower Normandy's largest employer, for example, is Société Metallurgique de Normandie, a steel works due to close in 1994. Nearly three times as many people work on the land compared with the rest of France, but agriculture holds little interest for young people and service industries, in particular tourism, will be the mainstay for the foreseeable future.

Beyond that, the region sees its future in moving in three directions. It wants to build preferential economic relations with its inland neighbour, the Île de France, as a natural extension of the lower Seine's industrial basin. It wants to see its ports of Cherbourg, Dieppe and Le Havre opened up to Europe and indeed to the world. And it wants better trade with northern Europe.

But post-war history of impoverishment and neglect has left the region a reputation of "mal normand", and it needs to convince the rest of France – and Europe – of its excellence in services and commmunications if it is going to achieve its aims.

It is this basic belief, that once the infrastructure is right, the rest will follow, that keeps the public works programme pushing ahead on the road, rail, sea and air fronts. Among projects in hand are the A29 and A28 autoroutes, the Pont de Normandie spanning the Seine estuary to link Le Havre with

Honfleur, the electrification of the Paris-Cherbourg railway line and the creation of a new Transmanche link to the new Channel tunnel across to England just up the coast.

Rural roots: With a working population of more than 130,000 in Normandy, agriculture remains the main activity. It covers 90 per cent of the countryside and employs a workforce of more than 60,000. Traditional agricultural production (meat, dairy products and *cidricoles*), helped by the development of tourism and the consumers' return to

natural foods, should see a rapid expansion in the years to come. Normans are very fond of the traditional landscape responsible for this food, and though some old orchards, particularly in Upper Normandy, have been grubbed up and modern, smaller fruit-tree stocks introduced, many traditional farms continue to hang on to their huge, boughed trees, and practise mixed farming with their spotted Normandy cattle which still give good milk yields on the rich grass.

Lower Normandy produces 10 percent of all France's milk products. Over the past decade this western region, made up of Calvados, the Orne and the Manche *départe-*

Preceding pages: farmer in the Perche region; modern Cherbourg. Left, Le Havre's port, second busiest in France. Right, Le Havre's skyline.

ments, has had the lowest decline in the numbers of farmers.

In their endeavours to keep to small and mixed farming and the old ways of life, farmers have had some help from the EC and central government, a great deal of local sympathy, and the opportunity to share their pleasure by turning old barns and out-houses into *gîtes.* But methods and crops have had to change. Cereal farming, for example, now occupies nearly 40 percent of Lower Normandy's farmlands.

There has also been a need to research new market openings and today studies are going on for opportunities outside the food industry, such as in bio-carburants. This is hap-

cially in the manufacturing sector, Normandy has lost numerous businesses and a corresponding number of employees.

After agriculture, the fishing industry is the oldest and most traditional activity in Normandy. There are more than 1,000 boats and 3,500 fishermen, and though the fishing industry remains an extremely active part of the economy, it has had to fight its corner, and its fishermen have had to contend with territorial disputes in the waters around the nearby Channel Islands.

As elsewhere these days, traditional fishing yields little profit and the future of the industry lies in a new type of long-range trawler, like those being used out of Dieppe

pening because agro-food production in Normandy since the war has progressed more slowly than in any other agricultural region of France – even in neighbouring Brittany it has undergone considerable expansion. Situated principally in Lower Normandy, agro-food production employs around 20,000 workers. Their produce is easier to sell as it has a good reputation with most French consumers, and Normandy is conveniently close to Paris.

With 865,000 acres (350,000 hectares) of forest, including beech and oak, the timber trade and its allied industries represent a major activity in the region. Here too, espe-

and Fécamp, which have facilities to freeze fish on board.

Industrial base: Among the oldest industries in Normandy are those of mechanical and metallurgic construction which today employ more than 20,000 salaried workers within a large number of small businesses. The car industry has followed in this tradition, and it plays a dominant role in the region's economic life.

The largest companies are Renault and Citroën in eastern Normandy who employ 19,000 and 2,000 respectively. These car giants create work for a multitude of small fitting businesses and sub-contractors who swell the total employment figures in the car industry to close on 35,000.

Shipbuilding is no longer the great employer it was, and today it is mainly based in Lower Normandy, while an aeronautical industry is set up in Upper Normandy. The electronics industry, scattered throughout the region, has had a hard time keeping up with the needs of modernisation.

Le Havre is still the second-largest port in France. Exports of cars, agricultural machinery and chemical products are principally destined for Spain and Germany, followed by Italy, Great Britain and Benelux and, finally, for the eastern countries. A rather soulless, rebuilt town, Le Havre neverthe-

the base chemical and fertiliser sectors. Occupying second place in regional industry for value per employee, chemicals are now the leading export in Normandy with excellent forecasts for the end of the century.

Nuclear power: The refineries are just a part of Normandy's huge energy resources, which include three nuclear centres producing more than 60 billion kW/h per year. These have been seen as welcome investment in the region. The La Hague nuclear reprocessing plant at Cherbourg is, along with Sellafield in Britain, the largest of its kind in the world. Waste plutonium is sent here from Germany and Japan, provoking protests from international campaigners – but, perhaps because

less thrives on being the entry point to the "River of Petrol". From the Côte de Grace above Honfleur you can see a skyline of green storage tanks which mark the first of the four most important refineries on the right bank of the lower Seine. Here 34 percent of France's petrol is treated and it is a leading area of petroleum research.

The chemical industry, located in the same geographical region, employs more than 23,000 people of whom more than half are in

Left, Greenpeace, keeping an eye on one of Europe's main plutonium reprocessing plants. **Above**, tourism is an important money-earner.

people fear possible job losses, local opposition has been muted.

Funds for research and development have been released so that a 21st-century Normandy can pursue its atomic evolution. Some of the most important research establishments and laboratories are located near Caen.

Rouen is home to aerothermochemicals and toxicology and, in the Seine valley, near Le Havre, private research centres in the fields of petroleum, chemicals, pharmaceuticals and electronics have been opened. Alençon, in the Orne, is the centre for the promotion of work in the plastics industry.

Of the ports, Le Havre has been noted for

its promotion of business outside the region since the beginning of the 1980s with its slow but sure increase in assisting exports. Consumables and equipment are the principal imports, mostly for the petroleum and chemical industries and arriving from other European countries (mainly Britain and Germany), North America and the Middle East.

New markets need to be conquered to end the reliance on the petroleum industry. Much is being done, through balanced economic development by elected and appointed experts who have been trying to ensure that the rural and stricken industrial zones may benefit from the best equipment and from industrial or artisanal materials adapted to their

needs. This essentially political action has borne fruit: around 5,000 businesses are started up in Normandy every year. Among the most interesting of the promotional organisations involved in this programme are the Agropole at St-Lô, which was started up to encourage the local food production, and Techno-Rice, the Anglo-French innovation centre in Caen.

Of continuing major concern is the lack of qualifications held in the Norman workforce. There is an imbalance between those demanded by companies offering employment and those seeking work. This has largely contributed to the deterioration of the employment situation in Normandy, which today is one of France's most affected regions. Training programmes are being funded on both a national and a local level.

Tourism tomorrow: The future for the region undoubtedly lies to a large extent in tourism. Normandy annually welcomes more than 10 million visitors. It is one of the leading touristic regions of France and employs around 80,000 people. The British represent 70 percent of foreign visitors, either in transit or staying in Normandy.

Professional tourism is considered an industry in itself, and it offers new products and opportunities. Coastal tourism has been the touristic activity essential to the summer season in Normandy for many years and now "green" tourism has, in the last few seasons, developed strongly: cattle from Scotland and the Camargue have been introduced to the Brotonne regional park; forest land has increased, and the beech forests of Upper Normandy and the oak forests of Lower Normandy are on the tourist maps.

The River Seine, meanwhile, has seen its traditional barges, which link Normandy to Paris and the whole waterways system of Europe, in decline. In their wake have come pleasure boats which are hoping to make the trip from Rouen to the sea, or even Paris to Honfleur or Le Havre, one of the great river trips of Europe.

But a full third of the people who spend their holidays in Normandy are French, mostly from Paris, for the capital's citizens have long used the coast and the countryside as a place of easy escape. The fact that so many of them have second homes here accounts for a shortage of property for holidaymakers to rent.

The rich and famous have been coming to the region for years – the writer Françoise Sagan has a Normandy home which was once owned by the celebrated actress Sarah Bernhardt (1844–1923) – and the new meritocracy have helped to preserve some of the old buildings from decay. These sophisticated Parisians know a good thing when they see one, and they are as keen as the Normans themselves to preserve the buildings and traditions of the region, enjoy its incomparable food and help maintain its way of life.

Left, apples are still a major part of the rural economy. **Right**, the dry dock at Granville.

THE NORMANS

If you ask someone from Normandy what most readily sums up the Norman character, he or she may reply: "*Pt'être ben q'si, pt'être ben q'non.*" This phonetic rendering is approximate, but "Maybe yes, maybe no" is an accurate enough translation of an old country saying of Normandy.

The Norman is a canny type who is happy to hesitate and to linger over a decision while he weighs up the pros and cons of the situation. He hates to make up his mind in a hurry. As he is also very stubborn – *têtu comme un Norman*, the rest of France calls it – this can be infuriating for the other person, but it is an extremely good bargaining technique. And the people of Normandy are nothing if not good negotiators. Like Monsieur Rouault, the shrewd but lazy father and a Norman *paysan* of the old school in Gustave Flaubert's *Madame Bovary*, they are "formidable bargainers on market-days, loving the tricks and haggling of the trade".

Best sellers: Normans enjoy the whole business of buying and selling. There is a story that if a Breton has four cows to sell, he will take them all to town on the first market day and do his best to get a good price for them. The idea is to get the unavoidable transaction over and done with as quickly and as painlessly as possible. Not so our Norman friend. On the first market day, he will take one cow into town and have a good time selling her. He will ponder, plan and plot until the next market day, when he will bring out the second of the four cows and have another successful outing.

This native talent for commerce, combined with the rich resources of the region, made Normandy prosper and change earlier than other French provinces in the 19th century. The proximity of Paris via adequate roads and the waterway of the Seine was an important factor in the region's development. Fresh fish and seafood packed in seaweed, fruit, vegetables, butter and cream were soon transported daily to the capital.

Preceding pages: cheerful Dieppe fisherman; time to chat, St-Lô; Michel Touzé, maker of Pays d'Auge cheese. Left, two farmers, enjoying the business of buying and selling on market day.

The money earned was spent wisely, invested in building suitable houses and furnishing them in an appropriate manner.

Because of this early and enduring prosperity, the regional furniture of Normandy has a strikingly confident and solid quality. Cupboards, dressers and clocks tend to be handsome, in the spirit of Louis XV furniture and on the large side. The most typical piece of Norman furniture is the *armoire*, the cupboard that was traditionally presented as a wedding gift to a young couple by the bride's parents – the custom of giving a cupboard rather than money survived until recently.

The wedding cupboard is decorated with carved doves, flowers and fruit motifs – all

niture shining with the patina that can only come from years of conscientious elbow grease. The Normans are a clean and tidy lot – practically Swiss. This is reflected in their neat small towns and villages.

Traditional cupboards and case-clocks (the latter straight or sometimes with the pinched waist of the *horloge demoiselle*) are still very popular. Qualified cabinet-makers able to recreate to a high standard of skill the old pieces of the region's furniture can earn an honest living in Normandy today. Fellow Normans come to them to order *meubles* just like the ones they were brought up with, the reassuring dressers, cupboards and clocks they saw as children in their grandparents'

suitable symbols of happiness, love and prosperity. It had pride of place in the living-room and was used to store a family's most precious possessions – linen, best clothes, souvenirs and relics. The woods used vary, often oak, pine near Caen, mahogany in the Manche. As the family fortunes prospered over the years, other pieces of furniture appeared, perhaps a dresser, *un buffet*, a chest of drawers, *une commode*, or a clock, *une horloge*, always substantial-looking, with straight or triangular cornices and ornately decorated with carved floral or rural motifs.

The Norman sitting-room is without fail impeccable and dominated by gleaming fur-

kitchens and dining-rooms. Once a Norman always a Norman: even Normans in exile and their descendants still feel part of the old province. Furniture is one way of keeping up the link and they are excellent customers for the traditional artisans.

Enthusiastic hosts: For the visitor to Normandy, the local character manifests itself in a number of positively enjoyable ways. Tourism is all-important commercially in the region and treated with the utmost seriousness. More interestingly, the Normans who are so proud of their province and its history are prepared to work hard and enthusiastically at communicating this passion to visitors. They want people to care and understand. Of course it makes commercial sense but there is more to it than that. The needs and interests of *les visiteurs* are more intelligently and sensitively catered for in Normandy than in many other parts of France. Caen's Peace Memorial is an unforgettable experience that will leave no one unmoved, whatever their degree of knowledge about, or experience of, World War II.

A small town like Bayeux, dominated as it is by its famous tapestry, has managed to set the scene for it in a way that makes a visit a fresh, exciting experience for children and blasé adults alike. A set-piece the tapestry may be, but it is not allowed to become

prepared and able to answer questions. And the compact town is crammed with delightful visual surprises.

The Normans have become masters at interactive tourism. Much of it comes under the category of what tends to be referred to in France as *le tourisme artisanal*. Artisans, shop-keepers and hoteliers have grouped together to open up specialist circuits which take you on *la route du verre* if glass-blowing is your hobby, *la route des métiers* if you prefer an all-round approach, *un circuit gourmand* for those who have an appetite for *dégustations*.

They have produced leaflets and opened up their workshops to visitors, a sound com-

fossilised. We are a long way from the sheepish guided visits where people shuffle their feet round some château or other and listen to a dull commentary.

In Bayeux off-season, say late autumn or early spring when there are few visitors around, as well as absorbing the joys of the tapestry at leisure, it is possible to have a satisfying two or three days. From the lacemakers at the Conservatoire de la Dentelle and at the Atelier de l'Horloge to the people who run the half-closed hotels, everyone is

Left, foodstalls are popular in Rouen's streets.
Above, bikers get together in St-Aubin-sur-Mer.

mercial ploy that almost invariably loosens the tightest purse-strings. You have to be very strong-willed indeed to resist buying a copper pan in Villedieu-les-Poêles after seeing the unusually enjoyable informative film and watching copper being hand-crafted to a glittering smooth finish in the Atelier du Cuivre. And if you don't buy your pot in the Atelier, you are unlikely not to buy something in one of the dozens of copper shops which line the streets. Beware of cheap imitations, though: some of the stuff on sale in the shops is imported. But since you are in Normandy, you might as well emulate the natives and practise your bargaining skills.

The very rich, believed F. Scott Fitzgerald, are mystically different to the rest of us. "That's right," retorted Ernest Hemingway, who was less deferential about these things, "they've got more money." Fitzgerald never set a novel in Deauville but the creator of Gatsby and Daisy Buchanan and of the Riviera settings of *Tender is the Night* would surely have appreciated the place.

It's overcrowded. It's overpriced. Some of its attractions are frankly vulgar rather than smart, kitsch rather than chic. But in spite of these objections, Deauville's combination of beach life and high life, of grand old seaside hotels and ultra-modern fashion, of racetrack and casino, retains a glamour and a romance that is impossible to deny. On high summer weekends in July and August the approach roads from other parts of the Côte Fleurie are jammed with the cars of the seriously rich and the merely profligate. With bouffant women in Chanel and shades. With bare-chested men in shorts. All searching frantically for a space on the beach. For a seat at a café table. Or just for a place to park.

Best address: Deauville's position as the premier social address on the Normandy coast was once held by the cheerful old fishing port of Dieppe further north. Dieppe may have the nearest beach to Paris but it has always had a special attraction for visitors from the other side of the Channel who could get there easily once the Newhaven packet boat opened up its daily service in the 1850s. Oscar Wilde went to Dieppe to die. Sickert went there to paint. A little colony of expatriate English aristocrats almost took over Dieppe society around 1900. At their head were Lord and Lady Cecil who lived in a villa at Puys. They imported English kippers and sausages for breakfast. They also imported snobbish ideas about how to treat the locals.

The incomers' favourite vice was the casino, once a splendid old *fin-de-siècle* gaming hall that was sadly flattened during the ill-fated British and Canadian raid on Dieppe in 1942. One of the casino's best patrons was

Preceding pages: the polo crowd. **Left**, Deauville Jazz festival. **Right**, nightclub queen Régine with singer Gérard Lenorman at the casino.

the beautiful Lady Blanche Hozier, mother of the future Clementine Churchill, who used to queue up patiently with a picnic basket waiting for the tables to open.

Queen Victoria, who twice passed through Dieppe on her way to visit King Louis-Philippe at the nearby château at Eu, probably didn't approve of the casino. Her son Bertie, Prince of Wales, almost certainly did approve although he was not exactly welcomed by the stuffier expatriates when he came over to see one of his mistresses, the

Duchess of Caracciola. The duchess didn't allow their rebuff to slow her down, later marrying a baron and becoming a fashion photographer for *Vogue*.

The turn of the century was also the high point of popularity for Trouville. It had grand hotels, a casino and a boardwalk when its neighbour Deauville, just across the River Touques, was still little more than a gleam in a developer's eye. Then the Trouville authorities made the fatal mistake of putting up the rent of their casino and the casino owners decided to move next door. Deauville's expansion began and didn't stop while for many years Trouville drifted out of fashion and was allowed to slide rather charmingly downhill, enjoying the status of a looked-down-upon, middle-class relative of the fast-money joint up the road.

Today Trouville is popular once again and deservedly so. Its atmospheric waterfront brasserie Les Vapeurs is renowned as a sort of Normandy equivalent of the Brasserie Lipp on the Boulevard St-Germain in Paris. On warm summer nights half the buskers in Deauville seem to turn up outside, hoping no doubt that some of the smart but casually dressed diners are really members of the jet-set going ever so slightly down-market. Trouville's fishing boats and narrow back streets and small family-owned shops give it

length of the beach. Les Planches may have been the backdrop for a hundred different fashion spreads over the years but it is still the "in" place for a spot of constructive posing. The unchanging spectacle of sand and sea and sky and of the red-and-blue umbrellas billowing in the wind is a hard act to beat – especially if savoured over a coffee and *calva* or a large glass of pastis while among the beautiful people at an outside table at the Soleil Bar or the Bar de La Mer.

Les Planches is also the setting for Ciro's, the most fashionable and expensive restaurant in Deauville. The former pools tycoon and leading racehorse owner Robert Sangster keeps a permanent booking at Ciro's through-

an alive and year-round feel that persists even in mid-winter when Deauville can sometimes feel like a theme park in hibernation.

Trouville's serene old Edwardian villas still look down on the town from the Corniche above the sea. Deauville has its own Edwardian villas and streets full of large and comfortable-looking half-timbered houses built in 1930s mock-Tudor style. It also has a flash modern yacht marina and no shortage of the sort of luxury apartment blocks that have nearly overwhelmed Monte-Carlo and Cannes. But the central and most charming focal point of the town remains Les Planches, the old wooden boardwalk that runs the full

out the season and if you feel in the same financial league then you too can enjoy lobster and asparagus tips at 290 francs a time while the paparazzi queue up at the entrance waiting for a "face".

Film favourite: The old-fashioned bathing cabins further down the Planches have the names of famous film stars emblazoned on their sides. This conjures up a kind of *Hollywood Boulevard* aura, encouraging you to believe that if you pay to slip on your swimming costume in cabin number 13 or 23, for example, you may be changing in an atmosphere once sanctified by the hallowed presence of Rita Hayworth or Gregory Peck. The

French film-maker Claude Lelouch bestowed cinematic immortality on Deauville with his celebrated 1966 love story *Un Homme et une Femme*. Lelouch owns a house at Villers-sur-Mer and continues to use Deauville as a backdrop to his films, as do many other film-makers. Gérard Depardieu and Jeanne Moreau are other French film stars with places in the area.

The town continues to salute the movies with its annual Festival of American Film in early September. The festival may not quite be able to rival the shenanigans that go on down in Cannes earlier in the summer but it has proved charismatic enough to lure stars of the lustre of Jack Nicholson, Michael

horse-racing seems to move down to Normandy for the *vacances*. Each morning the horses are exercised on the beach and allowed to paddle by the water's edge. The ambience may be a relaxing one but the action on the track at Deauville is competitive and highly prestigious. The principal races, such as the one-mile Prix Jacques le Marois and the six-furlong Prix Morny for two-year-olds, are among the foremost events of their kind in Europe and the big English stables regularly challenge the top French trainers for the money.

Deauville's elderly red-brick grandstand, its graceful old Norman-style weighing room and the profusion of horse chestnut trees that

Douglas and Sharon Stone to pose on the boardwalk in recent years. The Film Festival pretty much brings Deauville's short but frenetic social season to a close, a season which begins unofficially at the end of July with the staging of the first two race meetings at the elegant flat-racing track at Deauville and at the smaller but even prettier Clairefontaine one mile away.

Just as no self-respecting Parisian sophisticate would be seen dead on the streets of the capital in August, so the entire cast of French

<u>Left</u>, café society in Dieppe, 1930s. <u>Above</u>, Robert Mitchum with Lucien and Martha Barrière.

shade the paddock create a perfect setting and one in which enthusiastic tourists mingle freely with the *soigné* racing professionals. No bookmakers are permitted on French racetracks. Punters have to queue up, sometimes interminably, to place their bets with the French Tote (PMU). The good news is that it is remarkably cheap to get in, little more than 200 francs even for the biggest Sunday programmes and less than that on weekdays. But the French make no effort to segregate their customers at the turnstiles: that comes in the clubhouse restaurant. A good lunch for two in Le Brantôme at Deauville, whose glass walls are erected each season under a fabulous white canopied roof, will leave you with little change from 1,000 francs. The big eaters may not always be the big punters too, but even when they are they don't allow the tedious events on the track to interfere with their enjoyment of their *sole normande* and *filet béarnaise*.

When the racing is over you can glance at the Grand Prix polo tournament in the centre of the course or wander down the road to the sales pavilion and catch a preview of the yearlings that will be on offer that evening. Or you can stroll back into town and enjoy a drink in the Normandy Hotel, Deauville's largest and most sumptuous hostelry. This resplendent half-timbered fake was actually

built in 1911 and inside it feels as if it had been created by a combination of Scott Fitzgerald and Noël Coward. You keep expecting to see blazered lounge lizards lurking behind the display cases for Lanvin and Cacherel and looking out for suitably rich widows whose fortunes they can tease away.

The Normandy's Bar Americain is a most luxurious pub and, as well as a long list of cocktails, the head barman André Pallares can offer a choice of up to 80 Scotch whiskies. M. Pallares's drinks, all tall and refreshing, come with a sufficient kick to strangle your screams as you look down at the bill.

Bathing, posing, drinking, dining, racing:

Deauville offers a fully integrated menu of delights. There is even a Thalassotherapy Centre in Trouville to clean you out, tone you up and calm you down when you feel you have been overdoing it. But the climax to any visit to the resort has to be an evening at the casino. This magnificent old white wedding cake of a building, fully floodlit at night, occupies a prime position looking out towards Les Planches and the sea. It was put up in 1911 like the Normandy and, like the hotel, and like just about everything else in the town that makes money, it is owned by the Barrière hotel group.

Casino Royale: Deauville was the model for Royale-les-Eaux in Ian Fleming's first and best James Bond novel, *Casino Royale*, with the unforgettable opening line about the nauseating "scent, smoke and sweat of a casino at three in the morning". These days Bond might find himself diverted by Régine's nightclub and the casino's camp Las Vegas-style floor show with its mixture of tigers and former Folies Bergères dancers in what are still coyly referred to as "revealing costumes". And Fleming himself would no doubt be distressed to discover that the outside hall of the casino is lined with slot machines and that the only night of the year when you still need a dinner jacket is in August on the occasion of the annual jockeys' black-tie ball. The late M. Lucien Barrière, who presided over much of Deauville's prosperity, hotly defended these changes on the grounds that they were financially unavoidable.

The chandeliers and the pile carpets are still there in the main salon along with the sleek aura of soft and velvety expense. And there is still something undeniably erotic about the spinning wheel, the cries of "*Suivi*" and "*Banco*" and the feel of the crisp, clean playing cards and the gleamingly cold chips. If you play and win, you can celebrate with a bottle of Roederer Cristal champagne up at the casino bar. If you lose, untie your imaginary black tie and stroll back nonchalantly through the night towards one of those 80 or so stiff whiskies in the Normandy. As you go, lift your head and sniff the sea air. And smell the flowers and the ozone and the faint but discernible whiff of money drifting back towards you on the breeze.

Left, the Aga Khan, a leading society figure of Deauville in the 1920s. **Right**, the casino today.

THE BIRTHPLACE OF IMPRESSIONISM

Normandy was the great outdoor *atelier* of late 19th-century French artists. Dieppe, Étretat, Le Havre, Trouville, Deauville… each of its resorts could be represented in a weighty anthology of works by the greatest modern French painters. Here they set down their easels and tried to give a true impression of the bucolic farms, the cloud-soaked skies and the surf-spattered, grey-green sea. This is where Impressionism was born.

Some of the artists came from Paris, others were attracted from further afield: J.M.W. Turner, John Sell Cotman and Richard Parkes Bonington began a cross-Channel exchange of ideas from England; Johann Barthold Jongkind arrived from Holland; and James Whistler and John Singer Sargent were in the vanguard of American artists who later came in waves to find Claude Monet painting at his home in Giverny.

One of France's greatest painters, Nicolas Poussin, was born in Les Andelys in 1594, but it was the 19th century that brought a second Norman Achievement. Théodore Géricault was born in Rouen in 1791, and he knew the young Eugène Delacroix who went to school in Rouen. Jean-François Millet was born near Cherbourg in 1814, Eugène Boudin in Honfleur in 1824, Raoul Dufy in Le Havre in 1877 and Fernand Léger in Argentan in 1881. Georges Braque and Camille Pissarro ended their days here.

The most faithful was Boudin, who was born at 27 Rue Bourdet in Honfleur, the pretty little port opposite Le Havre on the estuary of the Seine which still has the air of a painter's paradise. He has left us with enduring images of the bracing beaches of nearby Deauville and Trouville, of bonnets and ballooning dresses, petticoats and parasols, of blustery seas and great billowing skies. He also left us Claude Monet, supreme Impressionist, for it was Boudin who persuaded the local young cartoonist from Le Havre to get out and paint.

Boudin's father was captain of a ferry boat that plied across the Seine estuary between Honfleur and Le Havre where the family

Preceding pages: Monet's lily pond at Giverny. **Right**, the grand old master in Giverny's studio.

moved when Eugène was 10. He left school at 12, and at 20, after being apprenticed to a paper-maker, he started up a stationer's and frame-makers in Rue de la Communauté.

Among those he served and began to admire was Millet, the son of a peasant who was one of the first French painters to depict rural poverty. Ten years his senior, Millet had been trained by a local painter in Cherbourg, then in Paris where he continued to paint landscapes and peasant life. In 1849 he moved to Barbizon in the forest of Fontainebleau just south of Paris where he spent much of his life in poverty quite equal to most of his subjects'.

Surrounded by painters' paraphernalia,

reputation as a caricaturist and he sold his drawings through various outlets, which is how, aged 18, he came knocking on Boudin's door. Monet did not, apparently, like Boudin's style of painting, but Boudin clearly thought Monet had potential. He took him under his wing and persuaded him to work out of doors, and to follow his example by studying the effects of daylight and the changing aspects of the shifting skies.

"First Impressionist": Boudin remained Monet's mentor, but both were also touched by the wild card of Johann Barthold Jongkind, one of several painters now referred to as "the first Impressionist". Born near Rotterdam, Jongkind had met and befriended the

Boudin began to sketch. He was encouraged by Millet and other artists who came to his shop, including Constant Troyon, to whose paintings Boudin would later add the skies, and the landscape and marine painter Eugène-Gabriel Isabey. In 1844 Boudin visited Holland where he met Gustav Courbet and became impressed by Dutch 17th- and 18th-century landscape paintings. In 1851 he went to Paris to study informally, mostly by copying the works of the great masters.

Monet, born in Paris the son of a grocer, had meantime been growing up in Le Havre since the family moved there when he was five. In his teens he gained a minor local

sociable Isabey in Paris in 1846 and they had travelled through Normandy painting together. But even to Isabey, who made cider drinking fashionable as a result of his visits, the bouts of drunkenness and erratic behaviour of his protégé were excessive. They parted company and Jongkind returned, a lost cause, to Holland.

Monet had not met Jongkind but his reputation as an artist and an alcoholic was sufficient for him to write to Boudin: "Do you know that the only good marine painter we possess is dead as far as art is concerned? He is quite mad."

But by 1862 Jongkind had been taken in

hand by various concerned parties and reha-bilitated. As a result he revisited Le Havre where he made a lasting impression on both Boudin and Monet, who had just returned from military service in Algiers. He stayed on the coast for four consecutive summers, at Honfleur, Le Havre and Ste-Adresse, where Monet's parents had a summer home. The three painted together, and Jongkind exerted his influence through his sensitivity and light-ness of touch, especially in his water-col-ours. Monet has referred to Jongkind as his "true master" who "completed the teaching I had already received from Boudin".

In 1864 Monet moved to Honfleur, which was becoming more of a hotbed than a haven.

artist Louis-Alexandre Dubourg suggested that there was when in 1868 he presented the town hall with works by himself, Boudin and Jongkind. These pictures became the basis for the art museum of Honfleur of which Dubourg was the first curator. But the artists did form themselves into a group, calling themselves the Société Anonyme des Artistes-Peintres.

One misty spring morning in 1872, Monet set up his easel in Le Havre and swiftly covered a 20 inches by 25 inches (50 x 65 cm) canvas with a mix of blue and red paints. Before him the sun was rising, flicking its light across the water toward him. The mauve of the brightening sea and sky was rubbed

Isabey had taken to staying at the 17th-century Ferme St-Siméon in Rue Adolphe-Marais just outside the town overlooking the Seine estuary. Over farm cider and Mme Toutain's excellent meals, art would be dis-cussed with Corot, Courbet, Diaz and Daubigny whom he brought along. Sisley, Pissarro and Cézanne also found their way here, and the poet Baudelaire would add to the discussions.

There was never a real School of Honfleur, as there was at Barbizon, though the local

Left, wild Channel waters at Étretat by Monet.
Above, Trouville beach figures by Boudin, 1865.

with the darker marks of jetties and cranes and sailing ships, while a small rowing boat just in front of him darkened in the quiet water as it became silhouetted by the sun's warming rays.

Salon sensation: Monet called the picture *Impression: Soleil Levant* and exhibited it together with the works of other members of the Société Anonyme des Artistes-Peintres in the former premises of the photographer Nadar at 35 Boulevard des Capucines in Paris, two weeks before the 1874 main Salon exhibition. One critic, Louis Leroy, writing in the magazine *Charivari*, contemptuously dismissed the work of what he called

Impressionnistes. The rest is history: eight Impressionist exhibitions were held between 1874 and 1886 after which the members of the group continued to develop as artists in their own separate ways, returning again and again to the Normandy countryside.

The painters did not live off the fat as a result of their fame – or infamy. For years Boudin and Monet, like the rest of them, often begged and borrowed and starved. Monet was thrown out of a hotel in Falaise and Renoir, with whom he painted La Grenouillère, a favourite resort on the left bank of the Seine, stole bread for him.

It helped, of course, if the places the artists painted were fashionable. Boudin, who moods, the west front of the cathedral at Rouen, which no reproduction can fully convey. In 1890, two years before he began the series, he settled in the beautiful house and gardens in Giverny in the Seine valley between Rouen and Argenteuil, the nearby Paris suburb where Monet, Renoir, Sisley and Manet had worked together for a number of years. At Giverny he established his magnificent water garden which he went on painting up until his death, at the age of 86, in 1926.

The house and gardens are now immaculately restored and however many visitors are crowded into them it is still possible to feel the presence of the simple, single-minded,

shared much of his outlook with the likes of Millet, nevertheless had as his subjects the Empress Eugenie and the bourgeoisie on the beach at Trouville rather than peasants stooped in their daily grind. He made enough in the end with his "gold mine" pictures, the familiar seafront scenes peopled with what he called his "little dolls", often oil sketches on canvases no bigger than large envelopes, called *pouchades*.

Monet, between bouts of extreme depression, remained true to Impressionism and produced paintings of extraordinary vivacity, in particular his series of pictures of haystacks, of poplars and, in 20 different grand old man of Impressionism, a stocky figure, breathing heavily as he quickly worked over his huge canvases, cigarette smoke curling up over his nicotine-stained whiskers.

Dieppe connection: By the time the Impressionist group broke up, the resorts were in full swing, stretching up the coast eastwards to Dieppe. Monet and Renoir were both familiar with this port. Camille Pissarro, who had lived in Normandy since 1894, painted the town and harbour in 1901, just before his final project in Le Havre, producing in his painting of St-Jacques one of his finest works.

Walter Sickert, a pupil of Whistler and the

leading light of the "London Impressionists", regarded Dieppe as his second home. He lived here from 1899 to 1905 and was indebted to the town's most charismatic figure, Jacques-Émile Blanche, a painter and collector with the best of connections. In summer the drawing room of "Blanchie's" mother's house, the Chalet du Bas Fort Blanc, echoed to the opinions of Aubrey Beardsley, André Gide, George Moore and Edgar Degas, Sickert's mentor.

Le Havre revival: As the century turned, the scene was given a fresh impetus by two painters from Le Havre: Raoul Dufy and Georges Braque, whose family had moved to the port in 1890 when he was eight. Braque

fashionable Impressionist style for a while, until he discovered Matisse and the Fauves. It was impossible for him to have avoided the influence of Monet and Boudin, and there is a hint of them both in his 1904 painting *Beach At Sainte-Adresse*, but it is hard to imagine a painter more different from Monet and his circle.

Dufy was a hedonist who eschewed politics (he worked in Paris throughout the Nazi occupation, for example) and sought trouble-free subject matter. He was fresh-faced and a smart dresser who went to the opera rather than the music hall.

His images of Normandy are as enduring as Boudin's, and his fascination for boats

started out as a decorator, and was taught at the local art school by Charles Lhullier, before going to Paris. First Fauve, then Cubist, along with Léger, whom he met in 1910, Braque spent his last years at Varengeville-sur-Mer and has a lasting memorial in the Tree of Jesse window at the church of St-Valéry where he and his wife are buried.

Charles Lhullier had a few years earlier taught Dufy, the son of an accountant and one of nine children who became a friend of Braque. In Paris Dufy followed the by-now

Left, festive yacht at Le Havre by Dufy, 1904. **Above**, Monet's milestone impression of sunrise.

and racehorses stayed with him all his life. There is a fine collection of his work in the André Malraux Musée des Beaux-Arts in Le Havre, given to the town by his widow. The port's sailing boats have never looked breezier, the resorts never more festive, Deauville's thoroughbreds never more lively than under his cheerful brushstrokes.

In the Musée de Beaux-Arts in Rouen, beside Géricault's stallions and stormy seas, is a large Dufy triptych of the Seine, a homage to the river from Paris to Rouen, from Rouen to Le Havre, which serves as a celebration of this river and coast that has inspired such remarkable talent.

Normandy has produced more great writers, or inspired more great literature, than almost any other region of France. Some of the writers were non-Normans who came from outside, such as Jean-Paul Sartre who lived for a while in Le Havre and made it the setting for his first novel, *La Nausée*; or Marcel Proust, who spent many seaside holidays in the Grand Hotel at Cabourg, which he transmuted into the "Balbec" of *À la recherche du temps perdu*. Others were Normans born and bred, such as Guy de

Maupassant who acutely portrayed the stubborn peasantry of the Pays de Caux; or Gustave Flaubert (in fact Norman only on his mother's side) who dissected with a sharper scepticism the middle-class snobberies of his native Rouen. The wild Cotentin country to the west has been luridly evoked by that strange Gothic-romantic novelist, Barbey d'Aurevilly, truly Norman.

The heartland of Norman writing is the neat little triangle between Le Havre, Rouen and Dieppe. Both Le Havre and Rouen have stronger literary associations than many much larger French towns such as Toulouse or Marseille. Maupassant, Sartre, Queneau and

Salacrou all wrote vividly about the great seaport of Le Havre. The dramatist Pierre Corneille was born in Rouen, where his house now holds a small museum of his work. He attended a Jesuit college (now the big state-owned Lycée Corneille) whose glittering list of alumni includes Flaubert, Maupassant, the painter Eugène Delacroix, and André Maurois who was born at nearby Elbeuf and lived there for 30 years.

Above all, Rouen belongs to Flaubert (1821–80), that walrus-moustached scourge of the local bourgeoisie. His father was head surgeon of the Hôtel-Dieu, still one of the city's main hospitals: here the family's former home, in one wing, is today a museum. You can visit Gustave's bedroom, from whose window he watched carts bearing corpses during a cholera epidemic. That famous green stuffed parrot here stands in its glass case. An attendant may assure you that this was *the* actual parrot that Flaubert borrowed to stick on his desk while writing *Un coeur simple*.

Three miles away beside the Seine is the village of Croisset where Flaubert lived for years until his death. His elegant mansion is no more, but the squat garden pavilion remains, where he would come to read or talk with friends. Here are more Flaubert souvenirs, including *another* green parrot, also claimed to be the authentic one. A painting on the wall shows how pretty Croisset's pastoral landscape must have been in Flaubert's day. Today it is cluttered with the mess of industrial Rouen.

In central Rouen, rebuilt after wartime bombing, little remains of the garish bohemian quarter where Flaubert's Emma Bovary "walked amid a smell of absinthe, cigars and oysters". But the cathedral itself has been well restored; and with the novel in hand as guidebook, you can retrace the famous comic scene where Emma uses the alibi of a guided visit to stave off the advances of her beloved Léon, "her tottering virtue clinging for support to the Virgin." This scene was found shockingly blasphemous, and helped lead to the book's prosecution.

Tragic saga: Just east of Rouen, the pretty village of Ry is probably the original *bourg* of Yonville where Emma lived with her dreary, doting husband. And the true and tragic saga of the Delamare family of Ry lends a curious detective-story mystery to the question of what inspired Flaubert to write *Madame Bovary*. A Dr Eugène Delamare, former pupil of Flaubert's father, settled in Ry in the 1840s and married a local farmer's daughter. There are records to prove that she died in 1848, aged only 27, and he a year later. According to some accounts, he hanged himself, though his tomb today stands clearly in the village churchyard, where no

he had met his first love, Elisa Schlesinger.

Guy de Maupassant (1850–93), Flaubert's disciple and close friend, also loved the Normandy coast which features in much of his work. He was born in the fishing-port of Fécamp, and spent most of his childhood and parts of his later life in Étretat, a staid bathing-resort where he set the sad story of *Miss Harriet,* an English spinster who dies of thwarted love. Even sadder is *Une vie*, about a married woman's wasted life, set in the gentle country just inland from Yport: the

suicide would have been buried. Ry now cashes in with an active Flaubert industry, including a museum of Bovary automata.

Flaubert chose Pont-l'Évêque, his mother's home town, as the setting for *Un coeur simple*, his sad tale about the noble Félicité, comforted in her old age by her *live* green parrot. The nearby coast also features evocatively in this story – the daily return of the fishing-boats to Trouville, the walks on the hills above. Flaubert was deeply attached to Normandy beaches, and to Trouville where

landscapes, altering with the seasons, reflect her varying moods.

Of Maupassant's two famous tales about prostitutes, *Boule de Suif* is set partly in Rouen during the Prussian occupation, partly in nearby Tôtes at the Hôtel du Commerce (based on the Hôtel du Cygne, still there today). The joyful brothel in *La maison Tellier* was in Fécamp – "a homely looking house, quite small, with yellow walls". There actually was a *maison de passe* on that spot at that time: but the area has since been totally rebuilt. And the Fécamp that Maupassant describes, a great prosperous deep-sea fishing-port, has declined into a somewhat

Left, Gustave Flaubert. **Above**, one of his parrots and the book that shocked the people of Rouen.

gloomy little town where today's unemployment might be too high for Tellier-type commerce to flourish so busily.

The harbours, chines and chalky cliffs along this coast, so often painted by Claude Monet, were equally known to Maupassant who gives a vivid picture of one coomb in *Pierre et Jean*: "The fallen rocks looked like the ruins of a great vanished city which formerly overlooked the ocean." This novel, about a middle-class family in Le Havre, also has a remarkable portrait of the busy prosperity of that mighty port in its heyday.

"Liners were expected from Brazil, the River Plate, Chile and Japan, also two Danish brigs, a Norwegian schooner and Turkish

scene. Le Havre has changed utterly. First, world shipping is not the same. Secondly, the port area was blasted to bits in the war, then rebuilt in a dull concrete style. Even the vivid portraits of Le Havre written by Sartre, Queneau and Salacrou in the 1930s are totally outdated.

Sartre's port: Jean-Paul Sartre spent five years there, teaching at the Lycée François-Premier, which still exists. He chose to live in a seedily sinister hotel near the port. On his free days he would go to Rouen to be with Simone de Beauvoir, who was teaching in a lycée there. But many free evenings he spent in the low-life bars and bistros of the port area, notably the red-light St-François quar-

steamer... Above Sainte-Adresse, the two electric beacons on Cap de la Hève, like two gigantic twin Cyclops, threw their long powerful beams across the sea." And the commercial harbour (near the present P&O ferry terminal) was "full of shipping which overflowed into other basins, in which the huge hulls, belly to belly, were touching each other four or five feet deep. All the numberless masts along several kilometres of quays, with their yards, mastheads and cordage, made this open space in the middle of the town look like a great dead forest."

Dead-looking indeed it has become today, and a ferry-goer would not recognise that

ter now so tidy and dull. One biographer, Annie Cohen-Solal, has written: "In this city Sartre acquired daily habits he would never relinquish... he turned his patronage of cafés and hotels into a moral necessity."

His first novel, *La Nausée* (1938), is set in Le Havre, though he changes its name to "Bouville": here are its clanking trams (now no more), garish cafés, lecherous sailors, workers' marches and sea promenades. The book merges Sartre's fascination for low life with his hatred of industrial ugliness and human misery, along with the central philosophical theme of the main character's disgust at all tangible matter.

Something of the same desolate quality permeates *Un rude hiver*, a novel by Raymond Queneau (author of *Zazie dans le Métro*) who was born and brought up in Le Havre. Set in the 1914–18 war, it traces its bourgeois hero's mournful revulsion against "a world of work and horror" in a city of slums "bedecked with linen and crawling with urchins... the closest earthly image of hell." In different ways, Sartre and Queneau exemplified writers' reactions to Le Havre's sharp social contrasts of those days.

Queneau's hero visits the graves of his family in a hilltop cemetery, noting also the tombs of English soldiers who were wounded at the front in 1916–18, then died in hospitals

ville, northeast of Le Havre. Gide on his father's side was of Protestant stock from the south, but his mother came from a wealthy family in Rouen, where he spent part of his childhood. He married his first cousin Madeleine, whose parents owned a hilltop manor house at Cuverville. This became the Gides' by inheritance, and he made it the setting for his sublime novel *La Porte Étroite*.

For all his bisexual free-roaming nature, Gide's marriage was fairly happy and should not be seen as the original for the loving but tragic relationship in the novel. However, the physical setting at least is precisely true to life: a big white building with a score of large windows, "then, at the bottom of the

here. These were not the first Englishmen to have perished here on active service. Just east of the city is the old seaport of Harfleur, now a tangle of factories and refineries. Here in 1415, as related by William Shakespeare (who probably never visited France), the young Henry V summoned his dear friends once more unto the breach – "or close the wall up with our English dead!"

Still on the subject of graves: André Gide (1869–1951) and his wife Madeleine lie buried in the little village churchyard at Cuver-

Far left, Guy de Maupassant. **Left**, Pierre Corneille. **Above**, Victor Hugo's house at Villequier.

kitchen garden, a little gate with a secret fastening." The lovers in the novel, like Gide and his cousin in real life, would go out by this highly symbolic *porte étroite* to sit on a bench in the beech-copse. The house and garden are still as he described them, though rather run-down. The famous little gate carries a picture of a dog with a Keep Out notice, "*Je garde ces lieux: vous y entrez à votre péril*" – a suitably Gidean spiritual warning.

Whereas Gide was half-Norman, Sartre came to the region from outside; as did an earlier writer, Victor Hugo, whose link became one of personal tragedy. He was friends with a wealthy family of Le Havre shipowners, the Vacquerie, who owned a handsome manor by the Seine near Caudebec, at Villequier; and in 1843 his daughter Léopoldine married Charles Vacquerie. Six months later the young couple drowned in a sailing accident in the river. Hugo had idolised the girl, and for years he was shattered. Later he wrote about his feelings in one of his best-known poems.

Today the scene of the disaster is marked by a statue of Hugo on the river bank, with a line from the poem. The couple lie buried in the churchyard behind the manor, together with Hugo's wife and his younger daughter Adèle who died insane. The manor is now an elegant museum with interesting souvenirs.

A contemporary of Hugo's, Jules-Amédée Barbey d'Aurevilly, is the leading writer of western Normandy (the Cotentin) and one of the most startling figures in French 19th-century literature – romantic Royalist, arrogant dandy, devotee of the macabre. It is odd that he is not better known outside France. He was born into the local gentry in the village of St-Sauveur-le-Vicomte, where his bust by Rodin stands by the castle and a tiny museum is devoted to him. In Paris he became a flamboyant Byronic figure, a leader of fashion and brilliant critic. Yet he remained deeply attached to the Cotentin peasantry and their traditions; and his best work

deals with that rugged region, which in his day was still rife with witchcraft, superstition and bizarre legends. He saw himself as its Walter Scott, giving a voice to the local people and their Royalist ("Chouan") aspirations which had been crushed in the turbulent years after the Revolution.

Many of his stories and novels contain a Gothic element of mystery and terror, telling of morbid passions leading to strange crimes; but they also have a poetic resonance, and his feeling for the Cotentin's lonely landscapes is real and moving. The little port of Carteret is the setting for *Une vieille maîtresse*, about a young man ruined by his Spanish ex-mistress who writes him letters in her own blood. By the lighthouse on the headland, you can visit the ruined Roman lookout-post where they trysted, and the caves in the cliff where they made love.

Witches' tales: A more strange and powerful novel than this is *L'Ensorcelée*, ghoulishly steeped in blasphemy and witchcraft. Barbey sets it on the Lande de Lessay, a moorland today neatly cultivated but in those days more sinister, "the terrain of mysteries, the property of spirits, ever trodden by prowling shepherds and sorcerers." To this blasted heath there comes the awesome Abbé de la Croix-Jurgan, tall and proud, his face horribly scarred by tortures during the Chouan wars: "Never perhaps, since Niobe, had the sun lit up so poignant an image of despair."

As the tale unfolds, a squire's wife falls in love with this charismatic monster, but is then found drowned, bewitched by the *abbé* himself or by nomadic shepherds possessed of magic powers. Croix-Jurgan inhabits the sinister half-ruined Abbey of Blanchelande (northeast of La Haye-du-Puits), where as he prepares to serve Easter Mass he is shot dead at the altar by the vengeful squire. Ever after, travellers crossing the heath at night can hear a mournful bell tolling from the abbey whose windows are weirdly lit; inside, the *abbé*'s ghost is saying a Mass he can never finish. This beautiful abbey, nicely rebuilt, is set idyllically by a lake and has been taken over by a youthful group of religious hippies, who say they have heard no midnight bells, seen no phantom priest.

Last but far from least, we come to the still quite stylish bathing-resort of Cabourg, where a great white wedding-cake of a *belle époque* hotel, the Grand, stands on the Promenade

Marcel Proust: he stayed here many times between 1881 and 1914, and Cabourg in his novel he called "Balbec", at once a terrain of precise sociology and a metaphoric dream-destination like the walks at "Combray". Proust came to the hotel first as a child, to seek relief from his asthma, then alone as an adult. So the "Balbec" parts of the book are a fusion of poetic childhood memories and mature social satire on the rich upper classes.

With his phobias against noise, draught and hot sun, Proust as an adult led an odd life in the hotel, often wearing a winter coat even in August; he might book three rooms and keep the two side ones empty, to ensure quiet. He both loved and hated the Grand, "this cruel and sumptuous hotel with its deafening and melancholy tumult", yet an ideal forum for his social curiosity: it was then very fashionable with Parisian society.

He also loved the shifting moods of the view from his bedroom, where the sun "pointed out to me far off, with a jovial finger, those blue peaks of the sea which bear no name on any map". He loved the hotel's dining-room, which in a famous phrase he compared to "an immense and wonderful aquarium" where the poorer people of Balbec would press their faces against the huge window from outside, to gaze in wonder at "the luxurious life of the occupants", as strange to the poor "as the life of strange fishes or molluscs."

Proust's legacy: Cabourg today is not as smart as it was but it happily flaunts its Proustian connections. It serves all guests an obligatory *madeleine* for breakfast, its luxury restaurant is Le Balbec and its beach-club L'Aquarium, while its bar will serve a sea-green "cocktail Proust" (the bar of the adjacent casino is even called "Du Côté de Chez Swann"). The hotel has been well restored in *belle époque* style: the "Marcel Proust" bedroom has the right period fittings – but a very modern telephone. Proust's "Balbec so long desired" remains today much the same Cabourg of traditional villas. Some are the holiday homes of well-to-do Parisians, who today arrive by the *autoroute* and no longer on Proust's "beautiful, generous" 13.22h train from the Gare St-Lazare.

Cabourg for him was also an erotic terrain.

While staying at the Grand in 1907 he began his romance with a Monégasque cab-driver, Alfred Agostinelli (when in the 1980s the newly-named Promenade Marcel Proust was formally inaugurated, the mayor tactlessly proclaimed, "What a shining example Proust sets to the young men of today!", which set the journalists tittering and the Prefect choking with embarrassment).

Proust's love for the cab-driver was his inspiration in part for the unique and unforgettable Albertine of the novel – a homosexual writer's sublime tribute to heterosexual love. She is first glimpsed on the promenade, "a girl with brilliant, laughing eyes and plump matt cheeks, a black polo-

cap crammed on her head", as she and her "little band" of lively young friends "progress… like a luminous comet". Later, as the narrator's love for Albertine intensifies, he comes to equate her in his mind with Balbec. As he watches her asleep, in the Paris flat where he is virtually holding her prisoner, "Her sleep… was to me a whole landscape. Her sleep brought within my reach something as serene, as sensually delicious as those nights of full moon on the bay of Balbec, calm as a lake over which the branches barely stir." Few sentences are more profoundly erotic than this, a high point of this most poetic of the world's great novels.

THE GREAT ABBEYS

"The place had an aura of immense antiquity. Grey stone walls soared to a Gothic timber roof, and, above the Abbot's table, a giant crucifix was suspended. As the monks tucked their napkins into their collars with a simultaneous and uniform gesture, an unearthly voice began to speak in Latin from the shadows overhead."

This description by the English writer Patrick Leigh Fermor of his first meal at St-Wandrille de Fontenelle, published in *A Time to Keep Silence* in 1957, could have applied at any time during its occupation over the past 500 years. The Benedictine abbey, in the Valley of the Saints in the lower reaches of the Seine, lives in perfect peace with itself, its guests and its congregation.

A simple canteloup tithe barn from Eure serves as its church, brought here by the monks in 1969 and added to the beautiful and battered ancient buildings. Each morning devotees at Mass seated in its cool, clear silence, wait for the first murmurs of the distant Gregorian chant. It rises from the secret cells of history, calling clear across the stone colonnades of the 15th-century cloister, and as the brown-robed monks enter, the barn-church becomes spellbound by the simple plainsong. What better place could a writer choose to help to concentrate his mind on finishing a book?

Sunday choice: Although the land is soaked with the names of its saints, the Normans are not steeped in pilgrimages and tradition as, for example, their Breton neighbours are. The region's singular cult is of the young 19th-century nun, St Thérèse of Lisieux (*see page 266*), who attracted a nationwide following. In general, Normans are conservative, church-going Catholics, but for daily Mass or Sunday worship they have a choice of churches from an astonishing collection of former abbeys.

The church was always the keystone to administrative power and ecclesiastic impetus came in three waves. First under the Franks, who by the 9th century had founded

episcopal sees in Bayeux, Coutances, Avranches, Sées, Lisieux, Évreux and Rouen plus 35 monasteries, one-third of them along the valley of the Seine. The second wave was the greatest, the splended and most enduring aspect of the Norman Achievement. Finally, in the 17th century, between the Wars of Religion which saw off the Reformation, and the Revolution which saw off monks and monasteries, there was a spirtual regeneration under the followers of St Maur.

Europe's monastery networks, established

in 7th-century Italy by Ireland's St Columban in Bobbio and St Benedict at Monte Cassino, soon reached Normandy, though missionaries coming across the Channel had already begun forging links that have continued, in spite of the Reformation, until this day. St Mellon, from Wales, is credited as founding the first bishopric in Rouen on AD 260, but it was not until the arrival in 640 of St Ouen, a high-ranking official at the Frankish court, that missionary zeal was backed by sufficient funds for large-scale building to begin. His first ecclesiastical task had been to oversee the building of a monastery at Rebais, east of Paris, after which, at the age of 41, he

Preceding pages: figures from St-Martin-de-Boscherville. **Left**, the abbey ruins of Jumièges. **Right**, Rancé, founder of the Trappist order.

took holy orders and became the bishop of Rouen, from where he set about trying to convert all he could, starting at the local monastery of Sts Peter and Paul which he enlarged into what was to become the Benedictine Abbey of St Ouen. Its much rebuilt central church beside the Hôtel de Ville contains his remains.

Under the encouragement and influence of the saintly and politically ambitious Ouen, the monasteries of St-Wandrille and Jumièges were established 25 miles (40 km) downriver from Rouen on the right bank of the Seine. The monastery of Count Wandrille, a man of such grace and beauty he was called "God's athlete" and a man so unspeakably

saintly he forsook the pleasures of his wedding night to join the order, was originally called Fontaenelle. The first history of a western monastery, *Epic of the Abbots of Fontenelle,* was compiled here in AD 831, and so many saints followed in Wandrille's wake that the abbey celebrates, uniquely, its own All Saints' Day.

Jumièges, founded six years after St-Wandrille in 654, was put under St Ouen's protégé, St Philibert, a Gascon. His inexperience had lost him the first post St Ouen had given him, as Rebais's founding abbot. Philibert continued to be in favour at court and King Clovis II gave over the forests at Jumièges for his

monastery, which was built around three sanctuaries. It became a centre of learning and one of the largest monasteries in France.

These two monasteries only 10 miles (16 km) apart, were symbols of Frankish power and civilisation until the whirlwind violence of the Norsemen interrupted their progress – and before successive generations of the same Norsemen, with a vigour unprecedented in history, resurrected them and other abbeys and left Western Europe a far, far better place, architecturally, than they had found it.

Norman style: It was a 19th-century Norman historian, Arcisse de Caumont, who first put a name to the style that evolved out of the Carolingian period and was exemplified in France's first major abbey, at Cluny. He called it Romanesque. It was the style William the Conqueror brought to Britain in 1066 where it is simply called Norman. It is characterised by rounded arches, stout round pillars, decorated capitals, sculpted tympanums and ornaments with zig-zags, chevrons, billets, nail-heads, cables and frets.

In Normandy it took on a special style. It favoured patterns rather than figurative decoration common to Romanesque elsewhere, and sometimes whole walls were ornamented, as in the nave at Bayeux. Without buttresses nave walls were so thick that the upper storey, the clerestory, could conceal a wall passage. Stone vaulting appeared in side aisles, though nave roofs remained timbered.

There was plenty of material to choose from. Wood was abundant in the forests, though carving did not really take off until the Renaissance. (Normandy's exemplary wooden church is Ste-Catherine's, Honfleur, hurriedly hewn by local axe-masters after the Hundred Years' War.) There was flint in the chalk hills around the Seine valley and the Pays de Caux. In the west there was granite from which monumental buildings such as Mont-St-Michel grew; and the southern Perche region had iron-red sandstone known as *grison.* But, most importantly of all, there was the easily-shaped light Caen stone, from which the great abbeys were built, as were many churches throughout southern England.

Normandy's first great Romanesque abbey was at its then capital, Fécamp, where there had been a monastery since the 7th century. Richard I, who had begun the building at Mont-St-Michel which he populated with 50 monks from St-Wandrille, built Fécamp's Holy Trinity church and made his son, Richard the Good, promise to build a Benedictine abbey. Richard, impressed with what he had seen of Cluny, brought Guglielmo da Volpiano, an abbot from Dijon, to Fécamp in 1003, though it was in Bernay under Volpiano that the clerestory wall passage was first introduced.

Today Fécamp's huge and imposing abbey church, one of the largest in France, seems cold and lifeless, but in its heyday it was lively and rather exotic. Gilded and ornamented with silver and silk, it was the focus of pilgrimages, some from England who would make it their first Continental

Avranches, the episcopal see of Mont-St-Michel. Two years later he became a monk at the newly established monastery at Bec-Hellouin, on the south side of the Seine beside the River Risle, where he was shortly made prior.

William the Conqueror came into contact with Lanfranc during his three-year siege of nearby Brionne and Lanfranc later negotiated with Pope Nicholas II the lifting of the excommunication of William and Matilda, distant cousins whose blood relationship should, according to Rome, have prohibited their marriage. The price extracted by the Pope was that they should build their two abbeys in Caen, the Abbaye-aux-Hommes

stop on their way to Santiago de Compostela in Spain. It became known as the "Heavenly Gate" and its fame was broadcast by troubadours who were always made welcome.

The Fécamp style was continued at Bayeux, built by William the Conqueror's half-brother Odo, and William and Matilda's churches in Caen. The Caen churches can be attributed to one of the most powerful ecclesiastic figures of the time, Lanfranc, who was born in Pavia in Italy in 1005 and educated as a lawyer. In 1039 he went to teach at

dedicated to St Étienne (St Stephen) where William was eventually and unceremoniously buried, and, a mile distant, the beautiful, honey-stoned Abbaye-aux-Dames (La Trinité).

The abbey at Bec-Hellouin had not long been founded when Lanfranc arrived. It was begun in 1034 by a knight named Herluin who had hung up his sword and, the story goes, swapped his charger for a donkey and built a small cloister. Bec is Norse for small stream, and the setting of the abbey, in a broad valley where wood pigeons call, is still remarkably peaceful. There were 32 monks there when Lanfranc arrived, and it soon

<u>Left</u>, St John, from an old manuscript, Alençon.
<u>Above</u>, monks distilling Bénédictine at Fécamp.

became one of the major monasteries in Europe with an impressive library. Lanfranc continued to advise William and after the conquest of England he became the first archbishop of Canterbury, and *de facto* regent when William was away.

He was succeded both at Bec and Canterbury by the Italian theologian and philosopher Anselm, and a plaque on the 15th-century St Nicholas Tower at Bec-Hellouin records the number of archbishops and bishops in England provided by the abbey over the years. (Canterbury's saintly Thomas Beckett was abbot of the nearby monastery of Val Richer.) The connection between Canterbury and Bec has remained, in spite of

Canterbury's break from Rome, and recent archbishops have continued to use Bec's abbey as a retreat.

In the Middle Ages Norman society was divided into the nobility, the clergy and the peasantry. The nobility defended the clergy who were not allowed to hold a sword: though William's half-brother, Odo, the bellicose bishop of Bayeux, is seen enthusiastically waving a club in the Bayeux Tapestry. When a knight grew tired of war and the hunt and when celibacy no longer meant sacrifice, he would retire to the abbey he had spent his life defending, bringing with him a gift of his best steed.

Monks had rights of tithe over the villages, and they created their own clearings in the woodlands for farming. Vines were first planted at St-Wandrille and by the 11th and 12th centuries there were some famous and prosperous vineyards, but these did not last, and today water is more likely to be served at the monks' tables than wine.

The famous Benedictine liqueur was made by a Venetian monk, Vincelli, who arrived at the monastery at Fécamp in 1510. He used 27 herbs and spices for the concoction, which he hoped would keep away the adverse affects of the Normandy weather, and today it is factory-made.

Mont-St-Michel: Fécamp was eventually surpassed as a centre of pilgrimage by Mont-St-Michel (*see pages 323–26*) whose clergy in time became some of the richest in France. Like all great vassals of the crown they had the rights of justice, of *cheminage* and of *fornagium*, of measuring and gauging, of sea fishing of seaweed and treasure trove, and harbour dues. They owned the whole coast, had a lordship that stretched over hundreds of acres and nominated all local legal and administrative appointments.

The nobility had been the initial patrons of the abbeys: the Hautevilles, Tancarvilles, the counts of Bellême, Hambaye, Brécy and Perche. But changes of fortune meant changes of patronage and when, at the beginning of the 16th century, laws were passed to allow the unordained to be granted abbacies it was only a sign of how far things had slipped. Among new absentee landlords was Henri de Lorraine, who was appointed abbot of Mont-St-Michel at the age of five.

What Abbot de Rancé found when he arrived at the Cistercian monastery of La Trappe in 1664 was probably typical: just seven monks, who had long since abandoned their robes and their religion. It is ironic that the most severe order ever to have been established in the monastic system was introduced by someone whose pendulum had spent the previous part of his life pointing priapically the other way.

Armand Jean le Bouthillier de Rancé was a godson of Richelieu and a womanising spendthrift who had a blinding conversion after the death of his lover, Marie de Bretagne, duchesse de Montbazon. "I resolved to be God's as utterly as I had been the world's," he declared as he sacked the incumbent monks and got down to devising the formidable Trappist regime of anonymity, abstinence, manual labour and perpetual silence.

The abbey of Le Grande Trappe remains reclusive in its forest, but visitors can visit its shop and buy souvenirs. Only men are allowed to visit Normandy's other Trappist monastery, Notre-Dame-de-Grâce just outside Briquebec, though women may attend services in the abbey church.

Rancé was a man of vision and influence but he was also a man of his time. He lived during the Counter-Reformation when Catholicism was re-asserting itself. Its leading lights were the Maurists, followers of St Maur, a 6th-century monk brought up by St

which at its height had sustained 500 monks and dependents, was down to 15 monks in 1790 when it was turned into a stone quarry. Lord Stuart de Rothesy, the British ambassador to Paris, took advantage of this outcome: he bought the decorated arches over the main and cloister doorways to embellish his English home in Highcliffe, Hampshire. Mont-St-Michel became a prison fortress and was initially used to hold 300 priests.

One by one, however, the monks began to return. But their lives would never be quite the same. Never again would there be the great riches of a powerful kingdom to lavish on their treasures, and today's communities often inhabit more convenient modern homes.

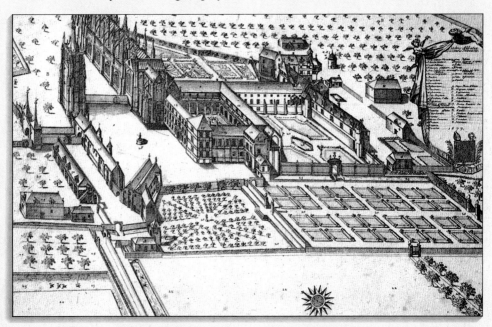

Benedict. They re-established the communities at Bec-Hellouin where Guillaume de la Trambaye, a brother architect and sculptor, designed the refectory which has become the new abbey church. He was also the architect of the conventual buildings at William and Mary's abbeys at Caen. Other buildings of the time include Mondaye's fine neoclassical church, built under Prior Eustache Restout.

But the reform ended dramatically in 1789 with the French Revolution which devastated all the monasteries of France. Jumièges,

Although the Revolution forced abbey buildings – dormitories, refectories, libraries and cloisters – to be put to other uses or closed down, many of their churches remained.

Today these outsized prayer houses tower over small communities, such as Beaumont-en-Auge or Lonlay, or are majestically cast adrift in the countryside, such as the beautiful church at Cérisy-la-Forêt. Even in towns such as Fécamp or St-Pierre-sur-Dives the abbey churches are too vast for their congregations, but they stand as monuments to a time when material and spritual greatness converged and the church was the symbol of the power in the land.

Left, a monk at Bec-Hellouin. **Above**, the abbey before it was pulled apart during the Revolution.

FOOD

For the visitor to France intent on enjoying not simply the dishes that are placed in front of him or her but also on appreciating the culinary culture behind the *spécialités,* it always pays to consider the fat of the land – the butter, cream, olive oil, goose fat or pork dripping that flavour the food.

What could be more different than *marmite dieppoise* and *grand aioli* (poached fish and seafood prepared with a delicately rich cream and butter sauce or served with a gutsy garlic, and olive oil mayonnaise)? Or than *poulet Vallée d'Auge* and *cassoulet* (chicken with velvety cream, apples and Calvados, and a hearty casserole of pork, sausage, poultry and beans redolent of goose fat)? Or than those kings among French cheeses, Brillat-Savarin and Roquefort (sumptuously reduced cow's milk, and ewe's milk at its salty savoury best)?

France stretches from the dairy lands of northwest Europe to the sunny olive-oil shores of the Mediterranean and the cooking of its regions intensely reflects the country's climatic differences. Normandy is the great northern dairy base for a whole spectrum of French cooking. *Poulet Vallée d'Auge, marmite dieppoise*, Brillat-Savarin... many of the best examples of the food of the dairy land come from Normandy, the natural home and finest illustration of the cuisine of cream and butter.

Land of bounty: A region of orchards and plenty, the province is also bordered by several hundred miles of coastline. The bounteous products of pastures and farms are complemented by gifts from the sea. Also endowed by the sea is the grass of the salt meadows. Rich in iodine and minerals, it delicately flavours the flesh of lambs and the milk of cows. It is as if a gastronomical deity or gourmet fairy godmother had favoured Normandy among all the regions of France.

Faced with such an abundance of riches, the Normans have always had the good sense to keep their cooking techniques simple. The traditional dishes of the region are unpretentious. Top-quality ingredients need no embellishments, no disguises. Spices are used sparingly and the more pungent herbs are used in moderation – a little shallot, chives, chervil, sorrel in season.

The contribution of cream and butter – however luxurious – remains discreet. White wine is used rather than red in cooking, but less frequently than cider or Calvados, which add a distinct but subtle flavour all of their own. Apples are a savoury garnish as well as the basis of innumerable tarts and desserts.

Normandy is an ideal place to acquire a taste for seafood. Even the most reluctant shellfish eater will find it hard to resist a bowl of tiny shrimps, served hot with the sweetest of creamy butters, and perhaps with close-textured *pain brié*, the traditional ridged bread of the region. Take a small handful of minuscule cooked shrimps, snap off their heads, peel if you wish (only if you are a perfectionist – it takes a good 30 minutes to shell an average helping), place on a slice of buttered bread, season with a touch of pepper from the mill and eat. You should experience love at first bite.

Crevettes grises are best eaten hot and by

the seaside. Try them in the splendid brasserie Les Vapeurs on the main street near the market in Trouville-sur-Mer.

From shrimps onwards and upwards, the true shellfish lover's progress will inevitably confront him or her with a *plateau de fruits de mer*. Seafood has to be absolutely fresh: when you order it in a restaurant, it is always reassuring to see plenty of other guests tucking into still lives of crustaceans and molluscs served on beds of ice and seaweed (not a terribly pretty sight; this is messy eating however good your table manners).

A platter of Normandy seafood is a copious affair, involving a serious communal *dégustation* of oysters, mussels, clams,

affordable are mussels. While in Normandy, make the most of *moules marinières* or *moules à la crème*. They are ubiquitous on menus and seldom disappointing, even in very simple restaurants. A steaming bowl of mussels and a side-plate of crisp golden *frites* to toy with only requires a glass of sharp Muscadet-sur-Lie to make a perfect light meal.

Mussels are used to flavour *sole normande*, the quintessential fish dish of Normandy. *Sole dieppoise* is probably the most celebrated version. Fillets of sole are poached in stock with mushrooms and the liquid is reduced to a fragrant concentrate. In typical Norman cooking style, *crème fraîche* is added and the whole thing left to simmer before

whelks, shrimps, prawns, crab, baby lobster (sometimes), limpets and winkles. If you are the only shellfish-lover in your party, there is no need to deny yourself. Many restaurants put on the set menu a more modest *assiette de fruits de mer* which turns a first course into a private treat.

Plump and meaty, smooth, ridgy, long or oval, all manners of oysters are grown along the Cotentin peninsula, a fifth of France's total production, with the main parks in Isigny-sur-Mer, St-Vaast-la-Hougue and Blainville-sur-Mer. If you prefer your seafood cooked, firm sweet scallops are an expensive must in and around Dieppe. More

chilled *beurre doux* is briskly whisked in. Prawns are an optional extra. Sole is the favourite fish of the region. The larger the better; but Normandy cooking also excels at preparing small lemon soles, *limandes,* and delicate plaice, *carrelet*.

Crème de la crème: Probably ever since the original Normans brought with them their sturdy cattle from Scandinavia over a thousand years ago, milk, cream and butter, *le lait, la crème et le beurre* have been the foundation of the cooking of the region. The modern pedigree Normandy breed of cattle (white, cream and cream-and-brown animals), produces more than a quarter of

France's dairy needs and each gives up to 6½ gallons (30 litres) of cream-rich milk a day.

The French are good at protecting their own and the Normans better than most: *crème fraîche d'Isigny*, pale, golden, with a *soupçon* of tartness under the sweetness, is the only *appellation contrôlée* cream in the country. An accolade *crème fraîche d'Isigny* certainly deserves but this rankles with other cream producers.

In the old days cream was allowed to rise to the surface of the milk and *crème fraîche* was left to ripen naturally. There were always bowls of *crème* on the Norman table – the writer Gustave Flaubert included great quivering dishes of yellow cream in his

butters have *grand cru* status: Isigny, Ste-Mère-Église, Neufchâtel-en-Bray, Gournay and Valognes. Totally unsalted, these butters have a delicate, pure taste and fine texture. Sold in great slabs in the markets, they are worth sampling on their own – or on a piece of fresh bread if the idea of unadulterated butter brings out the puritan in you.

A full cheeseboard: The other famous *plateau* of Normandy is, of course, the cheeseboard, *le plateau de fromages*. Local cheeses tend to be soft and made with rich cow's milk. Farm cheeses are produced all over the province, signs advertising *fromages fermiers* or *fromages artisanaux* beckoning enticingly at regular intervals, but the centre of tradi-

memorable description of Emma and Charles Bovary's wedding feast. The couple's initials adorned with a flourish the smooth surface of the cream.

Self-respecting Normans have always found life unendurably hard without a fair daily ration of butter, a fact witnessed by the Tour de Beurre in Rouen Cathedral. The story goes that this tower was built with money paid by the good people of the city for the dispensation to eat butter during Lent. Nowadays no fewer than five Normandy

Left, the traditional method of making Pont-l'Évêque cheese. **Above**, *andouilles* from Vire.

tional cheese production is really the Calvados region: five *appellation d'origine contrôlée* cheeses in a single *département* is very good going indeed and significantly above the French average.

A good Normandy cheeseboard will include at the very least three local cheeses. Many of these cheeses have a "bark" that is considerably worse than their "bite" – their smell tends to be much stronger than their taste. An honest selection will include a square Pont-l'Évêque, 50 percent fat, with an orangey-yellow rind and a ripe, earthy aroma that is stronger than its tender flavour and texture on the palate. There will be a

CALVADOS

In France a good meal always calls for a bottle of good wine, preferably local, *une bonne petite bouteille*. For a region with so strong a tradition of culinary excellence, Normandy is unique in not having its own vineyards. The local drinks are apple-based.

Cider sweet and dry, *cidre doux* as well as *cidre sec*, is made from carefully mixed different varieties of cider apples. With their rosy hues, their sharp greens or their russet tones, these apples look pretty enough to eat but they often taste much sourer than eating apples.

Although ordinary cider has lost ground to

beer as an everyday drink, the better quality bottled ciders, *cidres bouchés*, often slightly sparkling, are well-presented, well-marketed and gaining a new audience. An apéritif worth asking for is *kir normand*, cider (or sometimes *poire*, perry) with a spoonful or two of *crème de cassis*, blackcurrant liqueur.

Ordinary rough apple brandy is called *eau de vie de cidre*. It is much coarser than the celebrated spirit of Normandy, Calvados. High in alcohol, golden to amber in colour, fiery Calvados is made from distilled cider and slowly aged in oak casks.

Above, Calvados from the Pays d'Auge, the only region to have its own *appellation contrôlée*.

In times past, every self-respecting Normandy farmer distilled his own Calvados, often on the quiet, and to lethally potent alcoholic strengths. Travelling stills were a common sight. Since the mid-1960s the French authorities have tightened up regulations in their fight against alcoholism. The Calvados industry is today strictly controlled and distilling permits are no longer automatically passed on from father to son.

There are two different grades of Calvados. *Calvados appellation réglementée* is made in 10 areas of Normandy using the single distillation method. Each *appellation* has its own distinctive flavour and characteristics. These 10 Calvados areas are Pays de la Risle, Vallée de l'Orne, Perche, Pays du Merlerault, Pays de Bray, Mortainais, Domfrontain, Cotentin, Avranchais and Calvados.

The finest of all Calvados, the only one to enjoy an *appellation d'origine contrôlée*, comes from the Pays d'Auge in the *département* of Calvados. Here it is made from local cider and twice distilled. Every spring there is a public tasting and grading in the town of Cambremer. This is at the heart of the "*route du cidre*", and cider farms hope to be awarded the annual *cru de Cambremer* at the same tasting event. The winning farms can then display signs and may be visited.

All Calvados is then aged in oak barrels, moving from young casks where it acquires its warm toffee colourings to older casks where it matures in peace. Different years are blended to achieve a given Calvados's house style, with the most recent year determining the age under which the bottle will be labelled. Three-star Calvados has spent two years in the barrel, *vieux* or *reservé* three years. VSOP Calvados is five years old, including four years in cask. Calvados *hors d'âge* must be at least six years old, five of which are spent in the barrel.

A distinguished after-dinner drink, Calvados is also the secret taste behind traditional Normandy cooking, an ideal partner for *crème fraîche* and at home with fish, poultry, pork and desserts. It is also traditionally served chilled in the middle of a meal to revive flagging appetites – these days often in delectable sorbet form. This is rather bluntly known as *le trou normand*, the Norman hole. Calvados is added to coffee to make *café calva* (coffee in the old days was a luxury kept warm for several days on a corner of the stove and much in need of a little *je ne sais quoi* to improve it) and mixed with apple juice to make *pommeau*, a pleasant, born-again apéritif. ∎

round Livarot with a shiny, reddish, washed rind, pungent aroma, elastic texture and sweet flavour. There might be a Brillat-Savarin, created in the 1930s by the great Monsieur Androuët, doyen of modern French cheesemakers. A dietary hazard, this round cheese with a pale, velvety crust is made with triple cream and has a 75 percent fat content. Not suprisingly, its taste is mild and buttery and its texture very smooth. There might be a square Pavé d'Auge with its spicy tang, a delicate Neufchâtel on its bed of straw.

One of the oldest cheeses in Normandy, Neufchâtel was probably already around before William and his men set sail for England. It has a soft, velvety texture and a solid, chalk-like or runny. A good Camembert has a distinctive, rich, smooth taste that is slightly salty, and the taste lingers satisfyingly on the palate.

Should you want to buy one in a shop, do as the natives do. Take the cheese out of its little round wooden box, and press the centre with your thumbs to check that it gives a little, rather like well-inflated children's armbands. If the texture feels right, sniff discreetly – there should be a cheesey whiff but nothing too pronounced. You might see people testing half a dozen cheeses until they are satisfied they have the perfect Camembert. Like the rest of their compatriots, the Normans take their cheeses very seriously. And like

somewhat salty taste. And, of course, there will be a genuine *Camembert de Normandie*. Ordinary supermarket *camembert pasteurisé* is produced practically everywhere in France but authentic Camembert has to come from one of the five *départements* which make up Normandy.

The connoisseur's Camembert has a 45 percent fat content and is made of raw milk cured for at least three weeks in small dairies. It has a crust tinged with orange and its texture should be bouncy firm rather than

Above, Calvados, apple brandy, ageing in oak casks at Pierre Boulard's distillery, Pays d'Auge.

the rest of their compatriots, they believe passionately that the cheeses of their *pays* are the best in France.

Meat for a feast: On the table at Emma Bovary's wedding feast were "four sirloins, six chicken *fricassées*, pot-roasted veal, three lamb gigots and, in the middle, a pretty roasted suckling pig surrounded by four *andouilles* [sausages] flavoured with sorrel". The meat-safe of prosperous Normandy has changed little since Flaubert described it in the middle of the 19th century. Among the fresh meats, veal is more popular than beef, but even more typical of Normandy is the lamb bred on the salt marshes of the Manche

near Mont-St-Michel, *l'agneau de pré-salé*. Young salt-meadow lamb is tender, flavoursome and lean and requires very little in the way of accompaniment.

Succulent chickens, squabs and guinea fowl are bred in farmyards all over Normandy and still *fricasséed* with velvety cream sauces. Among the notable absentees from Flaubert's roll-call are a few braces of *canetons*, the long-breasted ducklings which come from Yvetot and Duclair with a deep, gamey flavour, stuffed with liver, lightly roasted, and served in a wine sauce. This is *canard rouennais,* one of the classic dishes of Normandy.

Tripe and sausages: The pigs of the region (most survive beyond their suckling days) thrive on a diet of windfall orchard fruit. Normandy black pudding ranks among the most celebrated in France. Every year in March the town of Mortagne-au-Perche hosts an international black-pudding festival and competition, *la foire du boudin* and the *concours du meilleur boudin.*

Perhaps the most notable *charcuterie* of Normandy is beef tripe, *les tripes*. Best known of all are the slowly simmered *tripes à la mode de Caen.* These are cooked with plenty of vegetables and the flavourings include a little Calvados, and they are good and filling, as all workers' food should be. Also well worth trying are the aromatic skewered *tripes en brochette,* a speciality of La Ferté-Macé in the Orne.

Andouilles and *andouillettes*, large and small blood sausages, are also popular with connoisseurs – if not to everyone's liking. *Andouilles* and *andouillettes de Vire* are famous throughout France. An acquired taste they may be, but they deserve an experiment. Like many another *spécialité de charcuterie*, they taste infinitely finer on the spot, very freshly made and in the place where they were made.

The traditional desserts of Normandy are dominated by apples and pears, which make superlative *tartes* with subtle fillings and excellent *confitures*, jams and jellies. Other sweet specialities worth a little detour are *brioches de Gournay,* freshly made caramels d'Isigny and in Fécamp *truffes* and *chocolats à la Bénédictine.*

Left, the daily covered market on Trouville quay, for fresh fish, shellfish and fish soup.

HORSES

Horses are as quintessential a part of Norman life and the Normandy landscape as apple trees, Calvados and half-timbered barns. The vivid pictures in the Bayeux Tapestry provide a telling reminder of the use to which William the Conqueror put mounted horse-power in his battle against the Saxon foot soldiers at Hastings in 1066. These days the contests that the pride of Normandy horse-flesh can expect to be subjected to take place not on the battlefields but on the premier racetracks of western Europe.

The two French national studs, one at St-Lô in the Manche and one at Le Pin in the Orne, each stand a complement of more than 200 stallions. But the progeny of these sires will be predominantly trotting horses, cross-breeds and show-jumpers. The two studs are also the breeding base of the Percherons, that distinctive strain of dappled grey or black dray horses. Both studs are open to the public and the *haras* (stud) at Le Pin, which was planned around a château in a forest by Louis XIV's guileful minister Jean-Baptiste Colbert, is especially worth a visit.

But it is with the production of top-class thoroughbred racehorses, rather than cobs and hacks, that the Normandy region is most famously associated. The elite private stud farms like the Aga Khan's Haras de Bonneval near Mesnil Mauger, where rich Charolais cattle share the pastures with the mares and their foals, are never open to the public. Unless you are a racing insider you will have to be content with tantalising glimpses of these fairytale settings, seen down the end of long gravel drives or over white paddock fencing as you journey through the lush green country.

Money and class: There can be few other multinational industries in the world that are still conducted in such evocative surroundings as thoroughbred breeding. Elegantly cut lawns, immaculately maintained stallion boxes, old trees and even older houses, blue blood, money and class – Normandy has all of these things. What it also has, and what has made its fortune as a thoroughbred cen-

tre, is good-quality grass. The great Kentucky horsemen have traditionally attributed their phenomenal success in horse-breeding to the excellent grazing provided by the celebrated Kentucky Blue Grass which, so it is claimed, is more productive and less green than the Virginia Blue Grass further north.

In truth, the smooth stalked meadow grass to be found in Kentucky is little different from the extensive pasturelands of the great European breeding regions around Newmarket in England, in Tipperary and on the plain

of Kildare in Ireland – and in Normandy.

The big difference between the two sides of the Atlantic is that Normandy pasture is more watery than Kentucky Blue Grass and grows on a much thicker layer of soil. American breeds, with such an abundance of fine grazing, often tend to be bulkier and more forward-looking juveniles than French- and European-bred horses but they sometimes revert to a coarser and more purely sprinting type of animal later on. Which is why American owners and breeders have continually returned to the top European bloodlines to replenish their stock with those qualities of stamina, soundness and speed over middle

Preceding pages: neck and neck at Deauville. **Left**, paddock bound. **Right**, Touques stud farm.

distances that the best French, Irish and English-bred horses are felt to display.

The most dominant and influential owner-breeder in European racing during the 20th century was the third (or "old") Aga Khan, who bought his first yearlings at Deauville in 1921 and summered there regularly in his own private villa. According to the colourful racing writer and *boulevardier* Quentin Gilbey, the Ismaili Prince was particularly fond of giving large quantities of rough Normandy cider to his guests at lunch and then sitting back to watch the effects on them throughout the afternoon.

The old Aga was very much a trader and not averse to selling some of his best stal-

the highlight of Deauville's month-long August racing season.

Countess Margit Bathyanny's Haras du Bois Roussel at Bursard has been a stud farm since 1802 when the Emperor Napoleon gave it as a present to his imperial minister, Count Roederer. The octogenarian countess, whose home-bred filly San San won the Prix de l'Arc de Triomphe in 1972, is a long-time friend and rival of the Rothschild family, owners of the Haras de Meautry at Touques. In 1977 Baron Guy de Rothschild, the then president of the French Thoroughbred Breeders' Association, controversially persuaded the French government to ban all non-EC bred horses from competing in the lesser

lions to the Americans when the price was right, but for the most part the plutocratic owners of the old school could afford simply to breed to race and to race predominantly among themselves. The old Aga's leading rival in the pre- and post-war era was the French textile millionaire, Marcel Boussac, who for 59 years owned the Haras de Fresnay-le-Buffard at Neuvy-au-Houlme in the Orne. This fabulous 650-acre (262-hectare) stud farm is now the property of Stavros Niarchos, the Greek shipping tycoon and veteran racehorse owner. Fresnay-le-Buffard sponsors the £100,000 Prix Jacques le Marois, one of the championship mile races of Europe and

French races. The baron may have believed that he was protecting his colleagues' interests but lack of competition was unhealthy.

Strictly business: Since then thoroughbred breeding in France, as in every other first-division racing country, has been strictly a business. And it is the players with the least insular outlook who have thrived. Of all the great Normandy stud farms none displays a more romantic exterior nor conceals a more business-like purpose than the Haras du Quesnay at Vauville, some 6 miles (10 km) south of Deauville. The château at Quesnay was built by the Count de Glanville in the 16th century; the stud farm was established in 1910 by the American millionaire William Vanderbilt who had won the 1908 French Derby with a horse called Sea Sick. Vanderbilt sold on his racing and breeding interests to his compatriot A. K. Macomber for 12 million francs in 1920. Macomber gradually lost interest in horses in later life and by the time the champion French trainer Alec Head took the stud over in 1958 there had been nothing much doing there for over 20 years.

Alec Head, who gave up training on his own account in the 1980s but whose family remains one of the most distinguished racing dynasties in Europe, is an exceptionally shrewd as well as a charming and charismatic man. During the 1950s his foremost

the great stallion stations and stud farms of the world. Among the horses that have been bred there have been two Prix de l'Arc de Triomphe winners and two winners of the French Derby or Prix du Jockey Club. And the Le Quesnay stallions, some of them later exported to the US, have included Riverman, sire of two more Arc winners in consecutive years, and Lyphard, sire of the immortal Dancing Brave, and grand-sire of the 1993 Epsom Derby winner, Commander-in-Chief.

Alec Head's racetrack and sales ring successes have been intimately bound up with his relationship with the late Count Roland de Chambure, the silver-haired banker-cum-horse breeder who died suddenly of a heart

patron was the equally dashing Prince Aly Khan, son of the old Aga Khan and father of the present Aga. On Prince Aly's death in a Paris car accident in 1960 his heir informed Head that if he was going to continue to go into the breeding business on his own behalf he could no longer train for the Aga. Head declined to back down and although he lost the patronage of the Aga his skill at moving out of the tack-room and into the boardroom can be measured from the fact that he has since transformed Le Quesnay into one of

Preparing the season's winners: <u>Left</u>, pre-race exercise. <u>Above</u>, grooming and mucking out.

attack in 1988. Head and Chambure were once one half of a quartet of French owner-breeders referred to enviously by their competitors as "Le Mafia". The count was only 19 years old when he inherited the 100-acre (49-hectare) Haras d'Étreham near Bayeux on the death of his father Count Hubert de Chambure in 1953. The old count was every inch the sporting aristocrat of yesteryear, a reckless gambler who was in the habit of giving away nominations to his best stallions whenever he had a particularly irksome gaming debt to settle. His son recognised that if he wanted to hang on to his inheritance in the changed social and financial climate of the post-war era he would have to expand the stud on commercial lines. He was helped out at the beginning by a loan from his family's own merchant bank. But it was a sound investment. Today the stud farm that has passed on to his children runs to 600 acres (240 hectares), employs a permanent staff of 50 and has boxes for around 150 horses.

The Haras d'Étreham and the Haras du Quesnay each keep some 60 mares permanently on the farms, half of them owned by the stud and the rest belonging to patrons of the stud such as the international art dealer Daniel Wildenstein. The patrons pay to have their mares board at the farm and to have them covered by one of the resident stallions.

Head and Chambure skilfully used the money and the contacts that they amassed from their domestic breeding interests to buy nominations for their own mares, including some of the world's leading stallions in Kentucky.

Yearling sales: The count sold his first yearlings at Deauville in 1954 and each year the majority of the Étreham and Quesnay yearlings are sent to the sales with perhaps five or six out of 50 being kept back to race in the breeders' own colours. Men like Marcel Boussac would never breed a mare to a stallion that they didn't own themselves, or sell a homebred foal at a public auction unless it was a cast-off that they had no use

for. But to France's commercial breeders the Deauville sales, which take place in the second half of August and which are the biggest European yearling sale outside Britain and Ireland, offer a premium opportunity to sell their wares to a large and captive audience at the height of the Deauville season.

The Deauville sales complex is a short stroll away from the racecourse and the main sessions are timed to begin in the early evenings just as the horse racing is finishing. You don't need a ticket or an invitation to attend. All you need to do is pick up a sales catalogue and then amble around the picturesque barns and paddocks with the requisite degree of self-confidence. Watching the serious buyers scrutinising the lots that they may be considering making an offer for that night. You can then wander through into the ultra-modern bidding theatre where bids are flashed up on an electronic screen in francs, pounds, dollars and yen. Providing you don't scratch your nose at the wrong moment the spectacle of well-heeled wallets and powerful egos duelling for the choicest lots can provide engrossing free entertainment.

The Deauville record of winners produced is one of which any sales company would be proud but the pedigrees of these star graduates have not always been fashionable enough to attract the game's biggest high rollers like the Maktoum brothers from Dubai. One effect of this trend has been to make Deauville excellent value for money for the purchaser.

The top lots recently have rarely gone for more than 2 million francs (£250,000/ $375,000) whereas the top lots in Kentucky in July can still reach $1 million or $2 million a head. This may not be such good news for the smaller French breeders but, having been less dependent on Arab money during the bloodstock boom of the 1980s, the Deauville sale has caught less of a cold than its rivals now that the Arabs are breeding rather than buying a majority of their own stock.

Canny professionals like Alec Head remain quietly confident that the age-old allure of horse racing, coupled with the other attractions of Normandy and the glamour of Deauville in particular, will always be enough to entice wealthy punters to want to own, rather than simply to bet on, racehorses.

Left, inside the top stables at Le Haras du Pin.
Right, exercising on the beach at Deauville.

Normandy's name evokes a pastoral picture: mottled cattle munching in knee-high buttercup meadows beneath laden apple boughs; vast barns and farmhouses, their half-timbered walls infilled with earth-red brick or honey-coloured clay, creaking and weary with use and age; a seriously rich green land which yields a bounty of cider, Calvados, butter, cream and cheese.

The ideal picture is also the real one, and it is exactly what a visitor can expect to see. But Normandy is by no means a uniform place. There are forests and flatlands, sandy shores and granite coasts, hidden valleys, old villages and the scars of war grown over with memorials and modern towns.

Most noticeable is the difference between the eastern and western halves of the region. Haute or Upper Normandy lies along the banks of the River Seine and stretches north and eastwards to neighbouring Picardy. To the west, bordering Brittany, is Basse (Lower) Normandy, where timber gives way to stone and the countryside is ensnared in the *bocage* and lanes sink between fields enclosed in ancient hedgerows.

Motorways make light of the whole region, which can easily be driven through, but off the beaten tracks, where some of the greatest rewards are, it is impossible to hurry. Layered over these rural havens is a modern society and an industrial heartland, centred on the River Seine which arrives, through a system of locks, from Paris, passes through Rouen, France's fifth largest port, and meanders down to Le Havre, the second largest. Rouen is Normandy's ancient capital and today it is a handsome provincial French town. It remains the capital of Haute Normandie and the Seine Maritime. Caen, home of the great abbeys of William and Matilda, is the capital of Basse Normandie.

Preceding pages: rapeseed field; rainbow over Trouville; canoeing on the Orne; Bayeux bogeymen. **Right,** Pays d'Auge farmer.

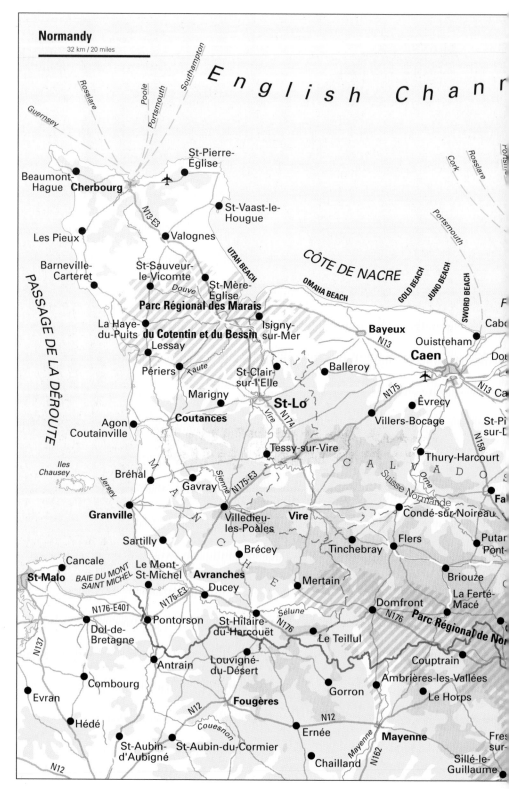

Normandy

32 km / 20 miles

English Channel

Rosslare
Poole
Portsmouth
Southampton

Guernsey

Cork
Rosslare
Portsm

Portsmouth

Beaumont-Hague **Cherbourg**

St-Pierre-Église

Les Pieux

Valognes

St-Vaast-le-Hougue

N13-E3

UTAH BEACH

CÔTE DE NACRE

OMAHA BEACH

GOLD BEACH

JUNO BEACH

SWORD BEACH

Barneville-Carteret

St-Sauveur-le-Vicomte

St-Mère-Église

Douve

Parc Régional des Marais

F

Cabo

La Haye-du-Puits

du Cotentin et du Bessin

Isigny-sur-Mer

Lessay

Périers

Taute

St-Clair-sur-l'Elle

Marigny

Coutances

St-Lo

Agon Coutainville

Vire

Tessy-sur-Vire

Iles Chausey

Bréhal

Jersey

Gavray

Sienne

N175-E3

MANCHE

Granville

Sartilly

Villedieu-les-Poêles

Brécey

Vire

Isigny-
sur-Mer

Bayeux

N13

Ouistreham

Caen

Ballery

N175

Dou

Êvrecy

Villers-Bocage

St-Pi
sur-L

N158

Thury-Harcourt

CALVADOS

Suisse Normande

Orne

Fa

Condé-sur-Noireau

Flers

Putar
Pont

Tinchebray

Cancale

St-Malo

Le Mont-St-Michel

BAIE DU MONT
SAINT MICHEL

Avranches

Ducey

Mertain

N176-E401

N175-E3

Pontorson

St-Hilaire-du-Harcouët

Sélune

N176

Le Teillul

Domfront

N176

Parc Régional de No

Briouze

La Ferté-Macé

N137

Dol-de-Bretagne

Antrain

Louvigné-du-Désert

Couptrain

Ambrières-les-Vallées

Evran

Combourg

Gorron

Le Horps

Hédé

N12

Couesnon

Fougères

N12

Ernée

N12

Mayenne

N162

Fres
sur-

St-Aubin-d'Aubigné

St-Aubin-du-Cormier

Chailland

Sillé-le-Guillaume

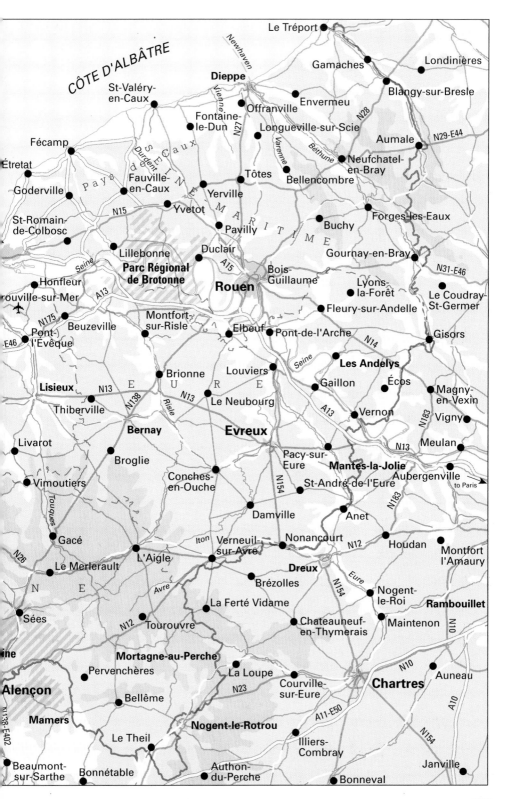

ROUEN

The capital of Haute Normandie and the region's largest city with a population of 380,000, Rouen lies on the River Seine between Paris and the sea. Forget the Romans. There is nothing of Rotomagus, their old trading place, to be seen above ground except in the Museum of Antiquities. Look ahead to where Normandy was baptised, with Rouen as capital, on a handshake between Rollo, head of the plundering Norsemen, and Charles the Simple, king of France. The year: 911. With the boundaries of the new duchy of Normandy agreed, Rollo changed his name to Robert and married the king's daughter, initiating three centuries of rule by Norman dukes with Rouen as their power base, and provoking the bitter struggle with England which Joan of Arc helped to resolve in the early 1400s.

Story in stone: Much of the place's history is in the open book of the **Cathedral**, whose St Romanus and Butter towers of its Gothic facade look down over the heart of the old town. Stand where Claude Monet put up his easel before these great towers of the west front for his series of paintings in 1894, and start reading bottom left. The story begins here at the foot of the **Tour St-Romain** with 12th-century stones set on the foundations of a cathedral built by William the Conqueror, seventh in the line of Norman dukes, just three years before his forces invaded England. From the brutalism of the lower stages of the tower, Gothic arches soar to the extravagances of the Flamboyant style that sets the character of the remainder of the west front.

By 1250 the cathedral we know today was complete, but in the succeeding centuries a fretwork of embellishments and the demands of restorers must have put it permanently under wraps. As the 19th-century English critic John Ruskin complained: "The beasts of workmen have scaffolding everywhere." Porches, St Jean-Baptiste on the left and St Étienne (St Stephen) on the right, formed part of

the old cathedral and survived the heat of a fire in 1200. Above them, in the storeyed galleries, sculptured figures act out the life and martyrdom of St Jean's and St Étienne's cruel treatment at the hands of the mob – touching reminders of intolerance long ago.

In the central porch, not completed until the 16th century by Jacques Roux and his nephew Roland, the Flamboyant style gives way to the Renaissance. The Roux had just put the finishing touches to the right-hand tower, the **Tour de Beurre**, which owes its name to a popular belief that it had been paid for in exchange for a dispensation to eat butter and drink milk during Lent. Jacques Roux would be relieved to know that the tower is still standing, because the tower, they said, was built not on butter, but a subterranean lake. Soon after construction began it started to lean, but the cracks were filled and building went on to its exquisite conclusion in the octagonal lantern in 1517.

The central tower completes and unites the composition, rising through

the 13th to the 16th centuries to the lantern which so dramatically lights the space below and supports the tapering spire. Love it or hate it, but admire the innovative skill of the architect who substituted the wood and lead of its predecessor with, of all things, cast-iron. In 1834, when Alavoine, the architect, died, he had been working on it for 11 years, but it was another 40 years before it was completed. Monsieur Eiffel's tower was still to be dreamt of.

Sculpted entranceways: Opening from the Rue St-Romain on the north side of the cathedral is the **Cour des Librairies**, once filled with booksellers' stalls, and beyond it the entrance to the north transept through the **Portail des Librairies**. Angels and monsters crowd the pages of this "encyclopaedia of the Middle Ages". In a corresponding position on the south side is the **Portail de la Calende**, a 14th-century masterpiece, covered from top to bottom with sculptures inspired by French ivories.

After the rich display of the exterior of the cathedral, first steps inside bring something of anticlimax, of chill even. The soaring heights, the sheer magnitude of the enclosed space and absence of decoration reveal its many creators' solemn intention.

Its beauties must be searched for in such details as the slim, clustered columns that support the central tower, their strength disguised in elegance; in the mighty organ above head-height, whose voice can make the whole edifice tremble; in the Booksellers' Staircase (1480) by the Portrait des Librairies; in the 13th-century windows in the ambulatory, and Chartres-blue glass in the rose windows; in misericords in the choir stalls, mirror of life in the 15th century in which they were carved; in the chapel adjoining the south transept in the tomb of Rollo, Normandy's first duke, who died in 933, "Founder and father of Normandy of which he was at first the terror and scourge, but afterwards the restorer".

Amongst other tombs of the great and the formidable are those of William I, duke of Normandy, died 942; Richard

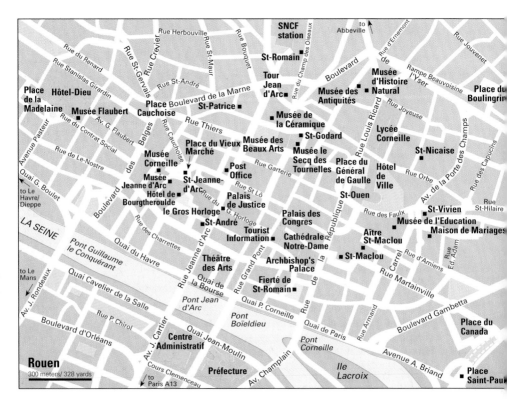

Rouen
300 meters/ 328 yards

Lionheart's brother Henry; the effigy of Richard himself, his heart in a casket in the stone beneath; Roland le Roux's Renaissance masterpiece of Cardinal Georges d'Amboise, Louis XII's minister and virtual ruler of France who gave Rouen fresh water supply and sanitation; his nephew, the second cardinal, is the other figure; Louis de Brézé, seneschal of Normandy, died 1544, a knight above, a naked corpse below, mourned by a kneeling Diane de Poitiers.

Before leaving, look at the St-Julien windows in the north choir aisle. Flaubert did, and found inspiration for one of his novels in this story of a man destined to kill his parents.

On the river side of the cathderal, across the Place Notre Dame, the **Rue du Gros-Horloge** offers a natural (and traffic-free) introduction to the core of the old city. Once it was a main artery leading to the Vieux-Marché, and now, though bisected by a modern boulevard, still rich in buildings of the Renaissance. The tall, timber-framed mansions nod overhead to their opposite neighbours, oblivious of the 20th century reflected in the shop windows below. In a side street, the Rue de la Vicomte, the carving of craftsmen centuries ago faces the surprisingly picturesque graffiti by years of visitors.

Spanning the street ahead is the **Gros-Horloge**, a delightful Renaissance pavilion set on an arch with the most splendidly embellished clock. It began life in 1389 in the belfry tower at its side, until Rouen, flushed with civic pride, gave it its present richly-gilded setting. One-handed, it tells the hour and week and moon's phases through a bull's eye above. Two great bells, La Rouvel and Cache-Ribant, share the **Tour du Beffroi**, and from here the curfew is rung at 9 o'clock each evening, postponed an hour as a special privilege granted his capital city by Duke William. These bells rang for the people, calling them when decisions had to be made, when their rights were threatened, or when revolt was the only way to resist oppressive rule.

At the foot of the belfry tower is the

Below, the **Booksellers' Staircase**. **Right**, tomb of Rollo, first duke of Normandy

keeper's lodge, a perfect house in miniature, and beside it is a charming 18th-century **fountain** that tells how the nymph Arethusa was changed into a fountain by Artemis to save her from the attentions of the river-god Alpheus, who is the Seine. A fate worse than death?

The old market: The Rue de Gros-Horloge leads to the **Place du Vieux-Marché**. This was a market-place nearly 1,000 years ago, an open space outside the city walls. The tall, timber-framed houses that surround it now were yet to be built. There was no hint it was to be the theatre of judicial murder and the catalyst of France's heroic and ultimately successful struggle to throw the English out of Normandy. It was here that Joan of Arc was burned alive on 30 May 1431, and her ashes thrown into the Seine. Despite the gaiety that restaurants, cafés, shops, market stalls and visitors contribute to the market-place today, it remains a haunted corner.

Near the spot where the flames were lit, traced out in stones and marked by a 65-ft (20-metre) cross, is the **church of St-Sauveur**, mute witness to the scene, and nearby in tribute to the Maid's faith is the 1979 **Church of Ste-Jeanne d'Arc**. Like a beached ship, this modern building sits uneasily under a ski-slope slate roof and pyramid gables, but glows warmly inside with the brilliant lustre of old stained glass.

In a strange echo of the beginnings of Joan of Arc's crusade, you too can hear voices in the **Jeanne d'Arc Musée** on the south side of the square. A taped commentary in four languages complements the waxwork figures that bring nearly to life the characters in her story, from childhood in Domrémy to her death at the stake.

Within shouting distance of the stallholders in the Vieux-Marché is **Musée Corneille**, in the Rue de la Pie. France's great playwright was born here in 1606, and as a dramatist Pierre Corneille might have been lost to the Law Courts had he been more successful in setting up as a barrister. Fortunately the reception given his comedy *Mélite* tempted him to Paris, where his

Left, the old Hôtel de Bourg-theroulde. **Below**, shop in the Vieux-Marché.

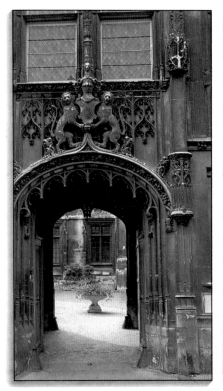

genius won him the sponsorship of Cardinal Richelieu, until the popularity of *Le Cid* led the cardinal to try to have it panned by the critics.

At 40, the acclaimed master of both French comedy and tragedy, Corneille, married and returned here to the Rue de la Pie, seldom leaving except to stay in his country house at Petite Couronne. In 1662 he returned to Paris to live, giving way in public esteem to an up-and-coming young verse-maker, Racine. Drama, off-stage, links Corneille with the Revolution through his descendant, Charlotte Corday. Her hatred of the Jacobins led her to seek out Jean-Paul Marat in his bath and plunge a knife into his heart.

Turn right from the market into the Place de la Pucelle (The Maid, again) and discover the **Hôtel de Bourgtheroulde** (call it *Boortrood*), the town mansion Guillaume de Roux built for himself in the early 16th century. He was counsellor to the Exchequer at the time. Thanks to a bank (in whose hands could it be safer?) we can enter the

One of the richest Gothic buildings in the world, the Palais de Justice.

courtyard and admire the octagonal staircase tower, the surviving Flamboyant Gothic end building and the fine Renaissance gallery along the south side. In its six arches is the sculptured frieze of the *Triumphs of Petrarch*, his triumphs somewhat dimmed by the passage of time, and on the stone below the celebrations of the Field of the Cloth of Gold, again somewhat tarnished by weathering. Guillaume de Roux's son, the abbot, was there at the meeting between England's Henry VIII and the king of France in 1520 near Calais. At this Field of the Cloth of Gold, each tried to excel the other in lavish entertainment to cement an alliance which ended three years later in the English invasion of France.

Near the Gros-Horloge, and glimpsed up a side-street in the Rue des Juifs, is the **Palais de Justice**, the Law Courts. Built near the end of the 15th century by Roland le Roux, architect of the cathedral, it is one of the world's richest examples of Gothic architecture. And it has survived not only restorers, war and

desecration, but also restorers restoring the work of restorers. Here was the seat of Normandy's parliament, a private place, hidden behind towering walls, its beauty not for the public eye. Now, only railings interrupt the view, and we can marvel at the artistry with which the facade ascends through the comparatively plain lower storeys to the glorious profusion of flying buttresses, lantern windows, turrets, tracery and crockets rising like champagne bubbles against the steeply sloping roof.

The wing on the left, the **Salle des Pas Perdus**, has a theatrical connection. When the old court, the Vicomté de l'Eau, was shifted here from its temporary home in the cathedral, a table of white marble came with it. The great Corneille, Rouen's dramatist son, must often have thumped it when addressing the court as advocate.

In the central block are the handsomely decorated staircase, the great hall, and the judges' retiring room which so tastefully interrupts the main front. It was once the king's private room. Res-

toration of the courtyard cobbles in 1976 produced surprising and hitherto unknown evidence of Rouen's history: a 12th-century Jewish building in the Romanesque style.

Rue St-Romain to the left of the cathedral skirts the **Archbishop's Palace**. In the forbidding wall only the ruined windows survive from the **Chapelle d'Ordres** where the final act in the trial of Joan of Arc took place. The next day she would be burned at the stake. In some of the houses opposite lodged the canons who condemned her to death. Can it be true that the iron cage in which she was chained is still there behind one of those lovingly restored facades? So a workman said. Not, surely, behind the decorative ironwork of Monsieur Roussel the printer? In this street, as elsewhere in the city, the old wooden houses attract sympathetic businesses, and the displays of dealers in antique furniture, books and prints put a welcome brake on "progress".

What a delight it is to come on **St-Maclou**, oppposite the Archbishop's

166

Palace on the far side of the main Rue de la République. This pyramid of pure Gothic is possibly the finest in the Flamboyant style in France; the burning zeal with which it was begun in 1437 persisting to its completion only 33 years later. The west front is an astonishing *tour de force*, its bow window of five great arches and gables carried up against flying buttresses "crowned by fretted niche and fair pediment – meshed like gossamer with inextricable tracery". The English critic John Ruskin said it all.

Oiled palms: Somewhere in that forest of pinnacles are two oil jars in stone. The 6th-century saint to whom the church was dedicated was a Scotsman who seems to have been canny enough to win the concession for supplying holy oil to the diocese. The carving on the entrance doors is attributed to the celebrated sculptor Jean Goujon. So, too, are the black marble columns which support the organ in its loft, reached by a spiral staircase of great delicacy – in carved stone.

The Rue Martainville on the left of St-Maclou is an attractive, half-timbered street of old print and bookshops which hides a ghost train funfair ride of indescribable horror: the **Aître St-Maclou**. Enter its passage and push open the door. You are in a quadrangle surrounded by two-storeyed buildings. Young people stand chatting in groups or pass from one side to the other. These are the studios of the **École Régionale des Beaux-Arts**. Look now at the carved wooden frieze above the ground floor on the timberwork gallery. Skulls, crossbones, coffins, hourglasses, shovels, buckets, beds – all the gruesome paraphernalia of death are here, for this quiet retreat was a plague pit with bones heaped in the centre, under the once open cloister and in the space above as well. Rouen's victims of the Black Death, who are believed to have numbered 100,000 in the 14th century alone, were led into Paradise by St Michael, whose altar once stood here.

Two hundred years later the surrounding galleries were built. The bodies of the well-off were accommodated under

Gruesome carvings in St-Maclou cloister, once used as a plague pit.

the cloister, and the poor in the open centre space. Eventually the first floors received the overflow, yet more and more were invited to this *dance macabre*. Before the Huguenots defaced them, you could have joined the dance in the sculptures on the stone columns.

The view framed between the timbered house-fronts of the Rue Damiette, north of St-Maclou, catches the breath with the beauty of the lantern tower of the **abbey church of St-Ouen**. Unlike the cathedral, closely confined in a protective huddle of streets and houses, Rouen's second great church rises from lawns, trees and the wide open spaces of the Place du Général de Gaulle. These roughly cover the grounds and buildings of the Benedictine abbey founded in 1318, but still not complete 200 years later. Though the proposed lantern towers to the west front of the church could have been finished, they were demolished in the 19th century and insensitively replaced with the spires in sham Gothic we see today. We should be led blindfold through the doors.

The interior, often described as having great unity, impresses rather by its great size, over 400 feet (20 metres) from end to end beneath an unbroken roof, and its great height, 108 feet (33 metres) to the nave ceiling. Light floods in from windows so vast it does not seem possible their slender stone frames can support the enormous weight of the roof. In fact, the walls are propped by the flying buttresses outside, their strength concealed in beauty. Windows plain and stained apart, there is little in the interior of interest beyond the organ in its gallery and the wrought-iron grilles which bar approach to the high altar.

History's black marks: The church has always needed friends. There is too much evidence of the damage done by the Huguenots in the 16th century, and revolutionaries in 1793, when shortage of weapons led them to set up a munitions factory inside. The smoke from the forges still blackens the stone.

After the Revolution the old town hall next to the arch of the Gros-Horloge was abandoned in favour of the new

Left, diners beside St-Maclou. **Below**, Rue Damiette and St-Ouen.

Hôtel de Ville built here in the abbey lands on the north side of St-Ouen in the central Place Général de Gaulle. Where monks once walked the cloister, civil servants tread the corridors of power.

Just beyond the Place is a former Jesuit College named the **Lycée Corneille** after its star pupil, though later students did not do so badly either – Flaubert, Maupassant, Delacroix and, later, the writer and critic André Maurois also attended.

No doubt they would have been fascinated by the collections of the **Musée d'Antiquités** and the **Musée d'Histoire Naturelle** just above the lycée on the left. The antiquities were housed in the glazed cloister and buildings of a former convent, and if the eroded reliefs in the courtyard of the Hôtel de Bourgtheroulde conveyed little, here are the plaster casts to show just what the Field of the Cloth of Gold was like originally. Plenty of evidence, too, of the Romans in Rouen. A mosaic Orpheus charms the animals and Apollo pursues a reluctant Daphne, rescued from the Roman baths in Lillebonne. Locks, chimney-pieces, tapestries, ivories and carved woodwork fill the gaps in Rouen's history made by time and man's relentless hand.

There seems to have been precious little sentiment and precious little sense of history about the subsequent treatment of the castle Philippe-Auguste, king of France, built in Rouen in the early years of the 13th century. Of its seven towers only one remains, and that owes its survival to its association with the Maid. Behind the museums the **Tour Jeanne d'Arc**'s conical roof thrusts like a rocket's nose cone above the surrounding modern buildings, a bow-shot from the ring road and close to the city's railway station. Stones hurled from the wooden hoarding at the top of the tower today would make holes in roofs.

Before long, the castle suffered the indignity of being used as a quarry for building elsewhere. Then, after a spell as a convent, it became a cotton mill. Its failure brought back the nuns, this time running a girls' school, and there were more demolitions to make a garden. The

tower itself was threatened. At this point the conscience of France was roused, the tower saved, and the scene of Joan of Arc's humiliation, the only remaining place which knew her presence, was preserved.

Here she was brought from her prison cell in the Tour de la Pucelle (the Maid's Tower) and, in a scene reminiscent of early cinema melodrama, she was confronted with the instruments of torture. Had she not given the right answers under interrogation, they would undoubtedly have been used. The English soldiers looked on, not understanding a word of the proceedings.

From iron to glass: Henri Le Secq des Tournelles worked as a clerk in a lawyer's office handling house sales and marriage contracts. Flights of fancy were strictly reserved for his leisure hours. Then the iron really entered his soul. Henri conceived a passion for the blacksmith's art and began collecting wrought-iron. When he died in 1920 he bequeathed the collection to Rouen, and in an inspired decision it was found a home in the redundant church of St-Laurent in the Rue Jacques Villon, now the **Musée Le Secq des Tournelles**. Henri's catholic taste embraced an astonishing variety of objects from keys to corkscrews, flat-irons to jewellery, household tools, decorative ironwork from forgotten buildings, even a chastity belt – all commonplace articles (except for the latter, perhaps) which have been elevated by the metalworker's art.

The ironwork museum has for near-neighbour the church of **St-Godard**. If ever a light was hidden under a bushel this is it, the light being the glory of its 16th-century stained glass, so famous that, if you wanted to compare the strength of colour you would describe it as being "as red as the windows of St-Godard". In spite of heavy restoration, you may still confront that dreaded monster, the *gargouille,* in the east window, and struggle with the imagery of the roots of the Tree of Jesse growing from Abraham's head.

Opposite the two churches is the **Musée des Beaux Arts**. One of the

Balcony scene from a timbered town house.

finest art galleries in France, it thinks of itself as "*fraîche*" and invites a new, fresh look at the work of the great and famous artists from the Spanish, Italian, French and Flemish schools. Velásquez, Veronese, Caravaggio, Rubens, La Tour, Ruysdael, Ingres, Géricault, Delacroix – all are represented here by important canvases. Closer to our time, you can renew acquaintance with Sisley's sensitive Impressionism, with Monet's superb west front of Rouen cathedral, and with Dufy's *joie de vivre*.

In the sculpture garden, classic figures pose in frozen immobility under the glass roof. Can it be true that there was a model of the church of St-Maclou made of breadcrumbs once displayed here? And if you're interested in knowing what Pierre Corneille looked like, there he is in terracotta, and, looking rather fierce, in oils.

Rouen faïence: France's reputation for the manufacture and decoration of china and earthenware nowhere stands higher than in Rouen. Within a few steps of the art gallery the gracious rooms of the Hôtel d'Hocqueville overflow with its finest examples of faïence, such as the horn of plenty that is so conspicuous a motif of its decoration. This 17th-century mansion in the Rue Faucon is the **Musée de la Céramique**, tracing the history of the potter's art from the world's earliest civilisation to its flowering in the 17th and 18th centuries.

Faïence is most typical of the local ceramics, and modern copies are on sale throughout the city. Rouen plates – made of a mixture of local clays covered with a white tin-based enamel and finished off with colourful designs, decorated with maxims, plays on words, and expressions of love – speak volumes, revealing an intimate glimpse from their sideboards of the warm humanity of their owners.

Aside from the Sèvres porcelain, the museum's collection has such oddities as the terrestrial globe painted by Pierre Chapel in 1775 and a violin made by some Delft Stradivarius.

From the Vieux-Marché the Rue de Crosse and the continuing Avenue

Celebrants in the annual Joan of Arc festival.

Gustave Flaubert lead to the vast complex of the Hôtel-Dieu, Rouen's old hospital. Behind high walls in the brick pavilion on the Rue de Lecat lived Achille-Cléophas Flaubert, surgeon to the hospital, and here Gustave was born in 1821. What effect his early life within the surroundings of the hospital had on his upbringing may perhaps be measured in the morbidity and pessimism of his works and his hatred of bourgeois values. However, his undenied achievement is celebrated here in the family home, now the **Musée Flaubert et d'Histoire de la Médecine**.

The poster outside says it all through the images of a brace and bit in a case of surgeon's tools. Inside there is some original family furniture and paintings and the famous parrot under a glass dome. But the surgeon's manuals may make your hair curl.

Beyond the centre: The centre of Rouen has much more to offer that only patient exploration on foot can reveal, but cross the traffic-ridden encircling boulevards that mark the line of the ancient walls, or the streaming traffic on the motorway that separates city from river, and the reminders are there that this is not only an industrial centre but also one of France's four largest ports.

Cross the bridges at your peril. In the vast conurbation beyond the Seine there is little to invite interest except the view back to the roofs and spires of old Rouen, though the **Jardin des Plantes**, in the middle of a built-up area, offers a breathing space and a retreat from the rain in the tropical hothouses.

Farewells to Rouen are best taken at sunset from the heights of Saint Catherine's Hill, and the most spectacular views of river and city are to be had from the hairpins of the **Rouen Corniche** on the road to Paris. (Leave the city on the N31 signposted to Beauvais, and take the turning just before Darnétal.)

A souvenir? What better than the little paper tube with a beautifully printed label and inside, apple-sugar, the fruit of Eden – and Normandy.

Right, traditional beam and plaster town dwellings built above street-level shops.

THE SEINE VALLEY

Born in Burgundy, brought up in Champagne and reaching maturity in the cider orchards of Normandy, the 479-mile (771-km) Seine shows a marked reluctance to reach the sea. The Celts christened it the Seine from their word for "bend", a name well-earned by its firecracker contortions as it struggles below cliffs and through forest, carrying in its slow progress the silt that is an ever-present threat to its navigable life.

For France the Seine has been a mixed blessing. A highway for trade in tin with England's Cornwall, for the expanding culture of Rome and the founders of the great abbeys, it was also the open door for invaders from Scandinavia, the Vikings. The Normans, predators and pillagers of abbeys, churches and wealth, struck a deal with the French that gave them control over the occupied territory north of the river. Poachers turned gamekeepers, they restored the abbeys, rebuilt the churches, and brought the region prosperity and stability.

The rest is commercial history: embanking in order to improve the passage of large vessels to Rouen and Paris; the reclamation of the flood plain to extend docking facilities at Le Havre and Rouen; and the construction of the Tancarville Canal so that barges could reach Le Havre from the river without braving the estuary.

River traffic: The barges that ply the river can go on to connect up with the immense network of waterways which stretch throughout Europe, though the number of traditional barge operators has been in sharp decline. Now the waterway is looking for tourists to climb aboard sparkling luxury passenger boats that ply from Paris to Honfleur. Depending on the tide, the journey takes up to four hours on the navigable waters from Rouen to the sea.

Leaving **Le Havre** by the Tancarville road does little to reassure you that you are about to embark on the most fascinating, picturesque and richly varied excursion this side of the Rhine. The first port of call is one no longer. **Harfleur**, swallowed in the city suburbs, has a surprisingly attractive heart, and there is a lot of local effort going on to return to it some of its former pride.

This was once the chief port of Normandy until it was literally choked to death by sand. Where once navies anchored, there are now roads, wharves, waste and pipelines separating it from the sea. The 15th-century church with its stone spire alone holds up its head against the indignity of it all, reserving for itself its best view from the bridge over the sluggish stream of the Lézarde.

In 1415 England's Henry V with 30,000 men besieged the old port, and, taking it, threw out the inhabitants and installed his soldiers. But a local hero, Jean de Crouchy, rallied the remaining residents and ousted the attackers. A month later came Henry's triumph at Agincourt, and soon Normandy was back under the English crown.

With white chalk cliffs dominating the river road east it is an almost surreal experience to drive below, like being in

receding ages: the iver Seine at es Andelys. eft, mist on iver barges. ight, the old wn at arfleur.

an amphibious vehicle. In the distance is the thin, spider's web outline of the Tancarville bridge, and at the cliff foot the wooden chalet rural retreats cling like washed-up debris on a shore. On the heights above, and best reached from Harfleur through Gonfreville, is the **Château d'Orcher** and the cliff-top **Orcher Terrace**, the view from which the *seigneur* is gracious enough to share. From this eyrie, 295 ft (90 metres) above the river, framed by oil installations on reclaimed land below and Le Havre's enormous presence on the estuary, is the misted vision of Honfleur under the Côte de Grâce on the far bank.

Modern French engineers have a light touch. For a bridge the size of **Tancarville**, nearly a mile (1.6 km) with its approaches, the lightness of the concrete and the slightness of the filaments supporting the latticed steel highway are a nice contrast to the work of their medieval predecessors in the massive remains of the castle that overlooks it. The impact the bridge has made on the economic life of the region has been tremendous. Before 1959 the Seine effectively isolated Upper from Lower Normandy, forcing long detours through the first bridging point at Rouen, or acceptance of the uncertainties of the numerous ferries. Now the even more ambitious **Pont de Normandie**, linking Le Havre with Honfleur, will alter the pattern of life in the estuary once again.

It would be a pity if our quest for improved communications interfered with a legend. Where the Tancarville bridge joins the other side of the gorge is the cliff called Pierre du Géant. The giant Gargantua used to sit on the rock while he washed his feet in the Seine below. Legends galore mingle with fact in the history of **Tancarville Castle**. Its spectacular situation on the cliff, once even more formidable when the Seine flowed at its foot, was chosen by Tancred, a 10th-century Norman *seigneur*, for his stronghold. Not till the early 1300s, when the last Tancarville fell in battle, did it leave the family, one member of which was William the Conqueror's tutor. Subsequent owners ex-

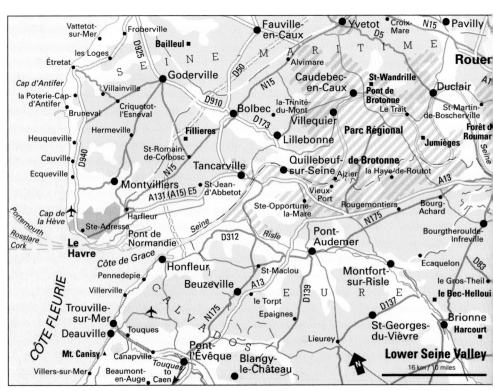

tended the castle, but later wars and the Revolution reduced it to today's still impressive ruins. Round, restored, and oddly triangular inside, the Tour de l'Aigle once stored the archives. It introduces the cliff terrace and the broken walls and towers cradling the modern château begun in 1710.

The Tour Carrée has the longest history, surviving intact till the Revolution, but it is overshadowed by the great Tour Conquesart, some 300 years its junior. Between them are the remains of the chapel and banqueting hall. The Tour du Griffon was reserved for important offenders against authority, though making the walls nearly 10 ft (3 metres) thick seems like overkill. The devil appears to have reserved the Tour de Lion for himself, since it is always referred to as the **Tour du Diable**. However, the awful hole he inhabited is empty. The local priest, alerted by the people, evicted him with a dash of holy water and a few well-spoken words. Exit the devil, grimacing horribly.

What of the occasion when three kings referred a duel between Robert de Tancarville and the Sire de Harcourt over possession of a mill at Lillebonne? Thinking, for reasons unknown, that they could not afford to lose either man, the kings of France, England and Navarre stopped the fight. Less testing times prevail in Tancred's castle. Customers of the terrace restaurant named after the giant's rock can leave their swords at home.

Roman roots: As the road from Tancarville turns inland across the flat plain of the Marais (marshlands) that separates **Lillebonne** from the Seine, it is difficult to believe it was once a port. Yet, covered by the river silt are the traces of dock installations to prove it. The Gauls knew a good site when they saw one. Here, at the junction of the Bolbec river with the Seine, the Calètes tribe from Belgium established their capital. Julius Caesar must have had the same idea. Following his conquest of Gaul in 51 BC he selected Lillebonne as an administrative centre, guarding the Seine valley and the highway to the

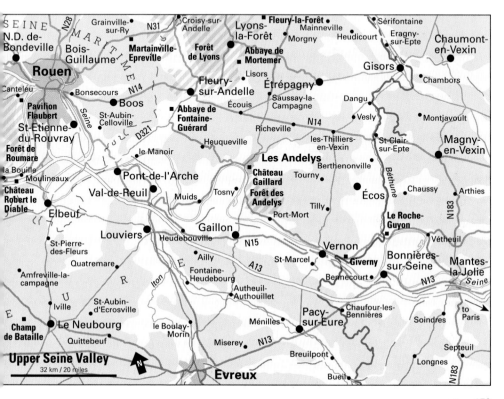

Upper Seine Valley
32 km / 20 miles

coast. So Juliobona was born and named in honour of Caesar's daughter, Julia. Lillebonne is its modern survival. Evidence that this new town became a settled community and not just a military staging post is dramatically there, plumb in the middle of the main street: the **Roman theatre**.

A small natural amphitheatre of the 1st century was transformed in the next into a stone-built theatre appropriate for a population of something like 25,000 people. The 10,000 spectators, Gauls and Romans, conquered and conquerors, sat on the stone terraces, now mostly grass-covered, reaching their seats and leaving after the performance through seven exits to the vaulted passages at the top. The Romans had an expressive word for them – *vomitorii*. The site of the proscenium lies under the feet and the wheels of people in the Place Félix Fauré, but what precisely was performed on that stage nobody knows.

The Roman city under Lillebonne's modern shopping streets sleeps on, waiting for foundations to be dug or sewers laid to be brought unexpectedly back to life. Imagine the delight of the café proprietor who uncovered a mosaic of hunting scenes in his back garden, the site of a temple to Diana and Apollo. To Lillebonne's loss it is now in the Musée d'Antiquitées in Rouen. Only one wall remains of the great hall in the hilltop fortress opposite. This is where Duke William called a meeting of his supporters to discuss invading England.

The circular tower built by the Harcourts in the 13th century seems to have had a charmed life. Henry V captured it, but left it unscathed, and it was spared, too, by the *nouveau riche* cotton-spinner who acquired the castle in the 19th century. Giving not a fig for history, he built himself a château among the ruins. At that time the valley between Lillebonne and Bolbec was humming with the mills of spinners and weavers, and it was known as the **Vallée d'Or**, the Golden Valley. After World War II they had completely disappeared.

If Lillebonne lost a port to the silted river, it gained one in **Port-Jérôme**,

The Roman amphitheatre Lillebonne.

though Napoleon III would have been surprised to learn that his uncle Jérôme had given his name to petro-chemical installations. Certainly he would have been proud of the obvious prosperity they have brought to Lillebonne.

Car ferries regularly cross to the Viking port of **Quillebeuf**, which seems abandoned to its long quays on the opposite shore. Modern bustle passed by this wide stretch of river on the other side. It was rescued from the ravages of war by Henry IV in gratitude for being the first Norman town to recognise his sovereignty, though renaming it Henricopolis can't have been too acceptable. The fortifications have gone, but the fine Romanesque church and old houses with carved timbers, including Henry's, recall former glories.

Drowning tragedy: Eastward from Lillebonne the roads divide and part company with the river, the more inviting D81 hugging the high ground for 10 miles (15 km) till the forest sweeps down to take the little town of **Villequier** in its green embrace. Where the Seine curves gently into a bay the beauty of the place is almost an invitation to tragedy, and that is what it is indelibly associated with. The well-to-do local family of Vacquerie with a flourishing boat-building business were overjoyed when their son Charles married Victor Hugo's daughter Léopoldine in 1843. Six months later they were both dead, drowned while boating on the river.

In *À Villequier* from Victor Hugo's collection of poems, *Les Contemplations*, considered his greatest poetic achievement, he expressed his grief. In the church, his beloved "Didine" and her husband lie together along with the writer's wife Adèle, and the whole tragic affair is laid out in the **Musée Victor Hugo**, in the Vacquerie house. The family might almost still be there so sensitively is the atmosphere of the period evoked by the original furniture, paintings, books, letters and photographs that fill the rooms. Outside, flower gardens slope down to the river, and ships change pilots for the journey upstream.

Caudebec, just over a mile further

on, is a shadow of its former self, but enough of its old buildings remain for the imagination to flesh out the bones of the skeleton and see it again as a town of wood, the tall jettied houses huddled together like nowhere else in France.

Caudebec's fate had always been tied to the nearby abbey of St-Wandrille, and the transfer of the market from there in 1130 began its slow growth to become the chief port and market town of the Caux region. When the town's plea for independence from the abbey was refused several monks were murdered. Justice seems to have been satisfied, however, with the hanging of two of the ringleaders.

For 30 years the English occupied Caudebec. Two years after their departure the kings of France and Sicily dropped in with assorted nobles and an army of thousands, which must have stretched the town's hospitality a little. Henry IV came in 1592 and charmed everybody by calling the church the "most beautiful chapel in the kingdom", and then dashed their pride by adding "but the jewel is badly mounted". The town's fortunes began to slide when the Edict of Nantes in 1685 sent half the population into exile, taking their weaving skills with them, but the final straw came with the Revolution; Yvetot was made capital of Caux in its place.

With nothing left to do but die, the town fell back on its natural virtues – a wonderful situation in the green hills against the ever-changing backdrop of the river, the Saturday market, the enduring attraction of the **church of Notre-Dame**, and the surviving cluster of old Norman houses.

The church of Notre-Dame, emerging unscathed from the fires of the last war, faces its most serious threat from water as the corrosive elements blur the intricate detail of the carved limestone. Nothing, however, can obscure the beauty of that tower, the triple-crowned spire, the triple porch (reminiscent of St-Maclou in Rouen), and the rose window above. Guillaume Letellier, the 15th-century master mason who conceived it all, lies buried in the Lady **La Haye de Routot yew.**

Chapel. Pointing down from the arched ceiling a stone of immense weight provides ample evidence of his skill.

Happily, much of the flavour of Caudebec's past is proudly displayed in its oldest house, the stone-built, 13th-century **Maison des Templiers**. The Biochet-Bréchot collection it contains links the primitive artefacts of pre-history with the achievements in art and culture in more recent times. The little River Gertrude, on whose banks the old house was built, has its own memories of being almost arched over by the upper storeys of wooden houses.

Wildlife haven: The **Parc de Brotonne** was once a ferry away from Caudebec, but the new toll-bridge has brought the hidden pleasures of this great beech forest within easy reach. The French take their forests seriously, with the aim of protecting and enhancing them as wildlife habitats, at the same time allowing complete freedom of access and encouraging appreciation of the many associated crafts and activities that sustain rural life. Aberdeen Angus and Camargue cattle have been introduced and bird hides set up for the public.

The flat valley has a distinctive character, which can be seen in the architecture on the **Route de Chaumières**, the Cottage Route, which skirts the park to the north. Scattered round the fringes of the wooded area are a clog-maker's workshop, a bakehouse, a flax and linen centre and a gaily decorated windmill, all near **Routot**. At **La Haye de Routot** 2,000-year-old yew trees in the churchyard are so large that shrines have been carved out of their trunks. There is an apple centre and also a blacksmith's forge at **Sainte-Opportune-la-Mare**.

A short walk upstream of Caudebec, the **Abbey of St-Wandrille** is situated in the village of that name in a lovely valley running down to the Seine – a valley of horror. Theft and pillage, fire and massacre dogged this place from the moment when Wandrille, deserting his bride on their wedding night to devote himself to the service of God, set his monastery here in AD 648. He reckoned without the Norsemen. They

arges on he Seine.

burned down the abbey in the 8th century, and returned to do the same two years after it was rebuilt. The monks fled, not to come back until AD 960. A new abbey, consecrated in 1033, was burned down and again rebuilt only to have the spire collapse and demolish most of the building. The Benedictines conceded defeat, and at the Revolution the ruins were sold by the State, and a spinning mill established.

Monks' return: An English nobleman, the Marquis of Stackpole, rescued the abbey, and on his death in 1894 the monks bought it back, only to be evicted seven years later. Maurice Maeterlinck, the Belgian dramatist, was the next owner, till in 1931 the Benedictines returned to stay, converting a 15th-century barn they brought from the Eure as the monastery church. The only voices raised today at St-Wandrille are in the Gregorian chant. On the wooded hill behind the abbey is the little chapel of **St-Saturnin**, mute witness for 1,000 years of its neighbour's vicissitudes.

Jumièges lies 10 miles (16 km) above the shipyards of Le Trait, where the river doubles back on itself. Above the forest trees rise the ruined towers of what was once one of France's most important and influential monastic institutions – the **Abbey of Notre-Dame**, served by 900 monks and 1,500 lay brethren. St Philibert seems to have left the royal court at the same time as St Wandrille to found his abbey here in 654. Like St-Wandrille's abbey it was destroyed by the Norsemen two centuries later and the monks massacred. The consecration of the new abbey church of Notre-Dame in 1067 was witnessed by William the Conqueror on his return, triumphant, from England.

The 14th century saw extensive additions in the choir and chapels, and successive abbots added new building and increased the abbey's material wealth. The dispersal of the monks at the Revolution heralded change and decay, unfortunately connived at by the parishioners of Jumièges who refused to swop church for abbey. Soon it was being looted for building material, even dyna-

The abbey at St-Martin-de-Boscherville.

184

mited by an impatient timber merchant, until rescue came in the shape of the Lepel-Cointet family.

Sympathetic reconstruction and stabilisation of threatened structures ensure that the pleasure of ruins at Jumièges will be with us for a long time to come. Below the great ivory towers the remaining walls trace out the vast dimensions of the original building, and exercise the imagination to re-create its former glory. A doorway in the south wall leads through a passage to the **church of St-Pierre**, the abbey's modest predecessor.

The former abbot's lodge is now the **Museum**, filled, not surprisingly, with fragments salvaged from the abbey, tombs, gargoyles and statues, but nothing more moving than the black marble slab that covered the heart of Agnès Sorel. On the death in 1449 of Charles VII's mistress it was presented to the abbey. **St-Valentine's**, the parish church which roused such local pride, has an unfinished air, though it was started in the 11th century, and suffered over-sized additions in the 16th century in anticipation of replacing the abbey.

Sailing scenes: Back to river business, and **Duclair** on the D982 towards Rouen. From the stalls of the quay or the gallery of the **Promenade du Catel** on the cliffs above, the Seine offers an ever-changing moving-picture show. From the stars of the big cargo vessels Rouen-bound to the sail-on parts played by the weekender, it is a continuous performance framed prettily in the lime trees of Liberation Quay. "Liberation" recalls the wartime devastation Duclair suffered – so invisibly mended since.

Serenely untroubled, the belfry of the **church of St-Denis** still springs from 12th-century arches and offers some 16th-century stained glass. From the clifftop cemetery, where tombstones flourish amid the wild flowers of the chalk, the Promenade du Catel looks over the sweeping curve of the river downstream and the riverside drive below the cliff to the abbey that became, not a ruin, but the parish church of **St-Georges** at **St-Martin-de-Boscherville**.

It is undoubtedly one of the most perfect examples of Norman Romanesque architecture in France. Unaltered and undamaged, only its west turrets added since it was completed in 1125, it replaced a church founded in 1050 by Robert de Tancarville, William the Conqueror's chamberlain.

The abbey of St-Georges, to which it belonged, escaped the fate usually reserved for abbeys at the Revolution by being adopted as the rather over-endowed parish church. It has an impressive nave of eight arcades, a beautiful apse, delicately carved capitals, and in the Chapter House a unique room, the Salle Capitulaire, the architecture of which is a reminder that the Normans once had a kingdom in Sicily.

Painters and picnics: The river takes another plunge southward here round the Roumare forest. The only escape is via the ferry to the left bank at **La Bouille**, where the inhabitants of Rouen love to picnic and Monet loved to paint. On a hill overlooking the river is the **Château Robert-le-Diable**, more intriguing for its name than the remnant of a fortress that looks real only at a distance. Robert the Devil enjoys in legend a sort of Jekyll-and-Hyde personality, since he is more probably Robert the Magnificent. duke of Normandy and father of the Conqueror, he was a highly estimable character who would never have poisoned his way to dukedom, let alone haunt the place as a wolf.

Views of the Seine apart, and those from the **Qui Vive Monument** and the **Roches d'Orival** must satisfy the most avid fancier, the less elevated road between the Forêt de Rouvray and the river leads 5 miles (8 km) through paper mills and oil refineries to "the house in the fields", the country retreat at **Petite Couronne** that Corneille inherited from his father in 1639.

In the timber-framed 16th-century cottage the atmosphere and character of the family's occupation for nearly a century have been wonderfully recreated. Standing by his original writing desk it seems more than possible that the author of *Le Cid* could come

Château Gaillard, built by Richard Lionheart.

through the door from his garden bakehouse, hands white with flour.

Canteleu, on the opposite, right bank upstream, is poised above Rouen's port area, its chimneys echoing the spires of the city. At its feet is **Croisset** and **Flaubert's House**, or rather the surviving wing, now a museum. *Madame Bovary* first scandalised society here in 1857. Above Croisset Rouen's great port takes the Seine to its heart.

Above Rouen: The thread is picked up again on the other side of the city at **Port-St-Ouen** 6 miles (10 km) upstream, where the D18E's short-cut leaves the river to make the long loop to **Elbeuf**. There are memories of a lost woollen industry and abundant evidence of its replacement by car manufacturing and chemical plants. Birds and butterflies in the Hôtel de Ville and stained glass in the churches do little to soften the harsh reality that in Elbeuf industry is king.

Pont-de-l'Arche, 7 miles (11 km) east, just below the junction of the river Eure with the Seine, was given its first bridge by Charles the Bold to deter Vikings sailing upstream. Its effectiveness can be judged in the stained-glass window in **Notre-Dame des Arts**, which shows a boat being hauled with difficulty through an arch of the bridge.

On the north side of the river the D321 follows the Andelle valley past the haunting ruins of the 12th-century **Fontaine-Guérard Abbey** to **Lyons-la-Forêt** (*see page 208*).

The Seine as a tidal river stops at **Amfreville Lock** just above the Andelle valley and, with the Poses Dam, it shares control over the canalised reaches above. The lock is overlooked by a hill named after a legend, **Côte des Deux Amants**.

Louviers, the main town on the left bank, is engaged in light industry which in no way detracts from its fine church and celebrated Porche Royal. The nearby Municipal Museum has a good ceramic collection and an account of the town as a textile centre.

Opposite Louviers, the road from **Muids** to the attractive half-timbered twin towns of **Les Andelys** hugs the river under chalk cliffs that look like

Monet's much-painted garden pond at Giverny.

broken teeth and are strangely echoed in the ravaged, ivory castle of **Château Gaillard**. It was a trade-off; Richard Lionheart got the site in exchange for releasing Dieppe, amongst other places, to Philippe-Auguste, but it was a deal that went wrong. Legend says Richard promptly built his massive fortress in a year. It really took three. Philippe besieged and eventually took the castle, but the state it is in now is down to Henry IV, who allowed two religious houses to take away stone for building. In the haggling that followed the château came off third best.

Beautifully sited, it remained good material for painters such as J.M.W. Turner, who came in the 19th century, though he was not the first. In 1593 the court painter Nicolas Poussin was born near Great Andelys and the **Nicolas Poussin Museum** is in Rue St-Clotilde.

Gaillon, Normandy's first Renaissance château perched on a rocky outcrop, offers a choice of roads to **Vernon**, where the Seine enters Normandy. Of its wilder days as a frontier stronghold,

only a few walls and the **Tour des Archives** remain of Henry I's castle. A number of old, timber-framed houses, some of which house the **Poulain Municipal Museum**, and the **Collegiate Church of Notre-Dame** invite pleasant exploration of the town,

Just west of the town is classical **Bizy Château**, still in the hands of a family connected to Napoleon Bonaparte as well as his marshals Suchet and Massena. It has some fine tapestries and pieces of furniture. The garden, which has a car collection in its stables, was laied out by King Louis-Philippe.

Monet's home: On the east side of Vernon a a handsome stone bridge links the town with Vernonnet on the right bank. A right-turn here leads shortly to a village with the world's most famous lily-pond, the model for some of the best-known impressionist painting. **Giverny** was home to Claude Monet from 1883 to his death in 1926.

In spite of the crowds, it is a wholly delightful place, beautifully renovated, from the bright and colourful interior of the house, set off by Monet's collection of Japanese prints and ceramics, to the gardens, reached through a tunnel under the road. You can become part of the picture, crossing the Japanese bridge and looking down on the cluster of lily-pads in the pond. Monet's large studio, hung with huge copies of his works, is now a souvenir shop.

The modern **Musée Américain** nearby demonstrates the influence that Monet and French Impressionism had on American painting. It was paid for by Daniel J. Tarra, a former US Ambassador at Large for Cultural Affairs, and was opened in 1992. Among its interesting paintings are works by Mary Cassell, the only American to exhibit with the Impressionists.

Giverny lies on the Normandy border. Welcoming the Seine on its journey from Paris into Normandy one is reminded of Napoleon's pronouncement that Paris, Rouen and Le Havre make the river "a difficult street to cross".

Left, Monet's restored house at Giverny.
Right, Vernon, an idle backwater.

DIEPPE

Dieppe is "deep". The Vikings had a word for it, and as Dieppe it has stayed. Carved from the estuary of the Arques river, the safe harbour that gave protection to the longships has been enlarged and extended to today's great port system to satisfy the demands of the fishing fleet, worldwide seaborne trade and the cross-Channel ferries.

The town's importance grew following the Norman conquest of England, which effectively made both sides of the Channel one country, but exposed it to the depredations of both sides. Captured by Richard Lionheart in 1188, sacked by Philippe-Auguste in 1195, its prosperity ruined during English occupation from 1420 to 1435 and recovered in the next century, Dieppe's fortunes rose on the performance of its navigators, who "discovered" Guinea, Cape Verde, Brazil and the Bay of New York.

Trade with the new-found land brought lucrative cargoes of saffron, pepper, ginger, cinnamon and, significantly, ivory through the port. One of the merchant princes, Jean Ango, became a key figure in Dieppe's history and powerful enough to conduct wars on his own account. It was left to the combined fleets of England and Holland to destroy virtually all the town's timber-framed buildings in bombardment from the sea in 1694, but the rebuilding gave the town its distinctive and elegant arcaded brick terraces.

Tourism starts here: At the beginning of the 19th century, the popularity of sea-bathing under the patronage of the duchesse de Berry, and the birth of tourism through passenger traffic from England, gradually introduced the resort as we know it. History does not stop there. Dieppe was to play a crucial part in World War II, and has still to adjust to the changes which a Channel tunnel will inevitably bring. Meanwhile, new harbour arms extend from the port entrance ready to embrace the future with foresight and optimism.

In the streets of the old town or on the *plage* it is impossible not to feel overlooked, though from its eminence on the height of the western cliff there can be no more benevolent surveillance than that of Dieppe's own **château**. Now the **Musée**, it is a reformed character. Four pepperpot towers (now three) and flanking walls were raised against the English in the 15th century. A prison during the Revolution, a barracks until 1906, it narrowly escaped demolition to become the town's museum in 1923.

The roofless tower of **St-Rémy**, one of three churches to bear that name, props the flank wall of the fortress. Pillaged for material to build a new Renaissance church, it suffered the further indignity of being blown up by the Germans during World War II because of the munitions it sheltered.

The château is a movable feast of the arts, mounting the most delectable exhibitions in a new gallery exchanged for the living quarters of the soldiery against the background of the permanent collection. Its strength is in ivory. Raw ivory came into the port from the 17th

eceding
ges: ferry
riving at
eppe. **Left,**
e old town
ound St-
cques.
ght, the
urch's eagle
ctern.

century onwards, and was fashioned or scratched by sailors into keepsakes. In the hands of artists it was made into objects of great delicacy. Your very presence in the same room as the model of the ship *La Ville de Dieppe* makes the ivory shrouds tremble and ivory sails strain against ivory spars.

Breath-holding, too, are the paintings by Pissarro, Sisley, Renoir, Courbet and Sickert interpreting, with love surely, the magnetic attraction of the town. The mystery is why Pierre Graillon's fame for his carvings in wood and modelling in terracotta is only local. He is to Dieppe in sculpture what the writings of Dickens are to London. Georges Braque – another local resident, since he came to live and die in neighbouring Varengeville – is represented by a remarkable series of prints.

As you leave the château by the bridge over the moat, you can share the view with Delacroix, though he was hardly bowled over by it. He wrote in his *Journal* on 30 August 1854: "A heavenly morning; I went out alone and climbed the hill behind the castle. I sat down in a field where corn had just been reaped, and made a sketch of the castle and the view – not that it was particularly interesting, but so as to retain the memory of this exquisite moment."

Most prominent in that view is the tower of the **church of St-Jacques**, Dieppe's only high-rise building, dominating the market-place and filling every street in the surrounding quarter with the riotous detail of its Gothic tracery. An earlier church on the site was burned down (a good old Normandy custom it seems), and St-Jacques today survives as the rebuilding of 1282. However, the work was to be painfully extended in the 15th and 16th centuries and by serious restorations in the 19th century.

King of the sea: Overhead, gargoyles grimace, buttresses fly, rose windows bloom and statues shelter in niches. Inside, 20 chapels march the length of the 13th-century nave, each one with its own dedication, altar, rights and privileges. Treasures abound: the carved relief on the oratory of Jean Ango with his

Ivory ship from the town museum.

194

coat of arms; Adam and Eve and a cat-headed snake; the sacristy built at his own expense by the "king of the sea", Jean Ango, its frieze peopled with natives of Brazil, and visual proof of the discovery of America by Dieppois; the superbly carved oak staircase inside; near the floor, graffiti of a 15th-century galleon cut with great accuracy by a Dieppe sailor on his knees. Presiding over all from below the rose window is the Louis XIV organ with the voice of 2,800 tubes and the mute support of two carved figures with trumpets.

The second great church, **St-Rémy**, is the third of that name, and a refugee from the confines of the château, where the surviving tower threatens players on the tennis courts below with falling stones. Work on St-Rémy in the town was begun in 1522, the choir and side chapels being completed by 1545, then, the Wars of Religion intervening, work was not resumed until 50 years later. Progress in the 17th century was slow. The Anglo-Dutch bombardment of 1694 and the vandalism of the revolutionaries

in 1789 were further setbacks. Not until the 19th century was this Gothic building completed, because Gothic it had started and Gothic it had to finish. Only the facade to the little square and the side doors acknowledge the change in style to the Renaissance. The second of the two towers was never built.

Inside, the panelling in the choir, the beautiful Renaissance decoration of the sacristy and the Rococo organ defy the passage of years, but outside is another story. Wind and weather have smudged the detail, and masons strive to make crockets curl just as they did 400 years ago. Incidentally, there is a delightful 19th-century painting of St-Rémy in the museum. Seen from the Rue Richard-Simon, it shows a farm cart being unloaded of its precious cargo of redcurrants cradled in big leaves.

Keeping close company with the Casino, the **Tourelles** look like an offspring of the château, and are the only survivors of the walls and gates that once surrounded the town. The **Porte du Port Ouest**, to give the twins their

n the shade
*n the
shingle.

proper name, has outlived five casinos and two generations of hotels as neighbours, served as a prison during the Revolution, and suffered the indifference of a State so ungrateful as to sell it to a private buyer in 1850.

The old gate gives on to the quiet backwater of the Place Camille-St-Saëns, where parked cars are a reminder that it was once filled with carriages of the rich and favoured on their way to the theatre. It is still there, buried in the grey, anonymous building behind the Tourelles. Beneath a painted ceiling, bare-breasted nymphs stretch arms invitingly from the boxes in gilded abandon, trailing the fruits and flowers of a forgotten Elysium.

Salty cures: Scene: the **Plage**, June 1578. Henry III steps gingerly over the pebbles, a rope round his waist in case he should need to be rescued from the waves. He was suffering from a skin complaint, and under doctor's orders to bathe in sea-water. Twenty-five years later the governor of the château, who frequented the court, was indiscreet enough to declare his love for Henry IV's mistress. Banished to Dieppe, the king sent him his dog Fanor, thought to have rabies. The governor personally bathed the dog in the sea and gained a pardon from Henry, who cried: "Who loves me, loves my dog."

These are the touching beginnings of a reputation for curative powers that led to the tents and cabins on the beach and finally a permanent building, "Les Bains Caroline". This was the first **casino**, named after the duchesse de Berry, who came here from 1824 to 1830. Not only was sea-bathing good for you, but it was patronised by royalty. Hot-water baths followed, gardens were laid out, concerts were given. The *plage* had arrived.

Attention turned to the rest of the seafront; the Empress Eugénie even sketched a plan for the lawns. By 1857 the elegant Regency building had given place to a new glass-and-iron casino that had obvious affinities with London's Crystal Palace.

Thirty years later, the dilapidated building was replaced with yet another **Fishing boat.**

casino in the then popular Moorish style, its domes and minarets complementing the twin chimneys of the tobacco factory further along the *plage*. In the gardens and on the terrace, Dieppe's English colony met to exchange views on art, music and literature with the French, or listened to the 60-strong casino orchestra, unaware that the ballrooms would later become bedrooms for wounded soldiers.

After World War I the fourth casino was built in a less flamboyant style. The era of night-clubs, jazz bands and cocktails had arrived. "Operation Jubilee" of World War II put an end to all that (*see page 62*). The *plage* was the focal point of the 1942 reconnaissance, and the prime objective on "White Beach" was the casino. After the attack had been repulsed the ruined building was levelled by the Germans. A Thalassotherapy centre, swimming bath, tennis courts and car-park now cover the site.

Between the port end of the *plage* and the ferry terminal is a quarter called **Petit Veules**. It takes its name from Veules-les-Roses along the coast, which had its churches pillaged during the Reformation. When this was followed by a succession of storms when the sea swept into Veules, the fishermen and their families conceded defeat. Putting their salvaged belongings into their boats they sailed eastwards until they came to a spit of land at the entrance to Dieppe harbour that had been uncovered by the shifting channel. Here they built their huts, brought their catches ashore, smoked their fish, made new boats, and were accepted into the community as the folk of Petit Veules.

Their troubles, and those of Dieppe, were not over. The Anglo-Dutch fleet, set on destroying the Channel ports, suddenly appeared off the coast. By 6 o'clock next morning 3,000 bombs had set the town in flames from end to end. Then, at 11am, came the ultimate horror, an "infernal machine", an unmanned ship full of bombs and incendiaries was directed ashore. Happily it exploded before reaching the target. A handful of houses survived, a few in

Fishmonger.

Petit Veules amongst them. That was the bombardment of 1694.

The **Tour aux Crabes** is something of a tower of mystery. Once an important defensive position in the wall encircling the old town, it is rather odd to discover it has a garden on top. At its foot, where crabs drew themselves out of the water at the river mouth, are the prosaic landing stages of the marine station. At the top of a steep diagonal stone stair is a tiny square garden with dwarf espaliered apple treees and rose bushes, surrounded on three sides by cottages. The Ruelle Beauregarde will return you beside the tower to the **Place du Moulin à Vent**, a little open space which was a coal market in 1759. There was still a coal merchant in business here a few years ago.

The **Quai Henri IV** alongside the marine station holds surprises if the eye can be diverted from the menus of the restaurants that march solidly down its length. **No. 33** for one. Where there is now a school building, Jean Ango built himself a palace in the 16th century called "La Pensée". "Pansy" was appropriately enough set in a fabulous garden. From his windows, nothing escaped him – his fleet at sea, his cargoes being unloaded in the port and the wagons on the road to Arques. He magnificently entertained François I here, and Henry IV used it as a hotel. In 1694 it went up in flames.

No. 49 was the Hôtel d'Anvers, and on the reverse of the entrance archway is a relief sculpture of the city of Antwerp. When Delacroix first came to Dieppe he stayed at the Hôtel de Londres at **Nos. 5 and 7**, wrestling with boredom most of the time. His friends bored him, people he disliked bored him, and he was bored with walking on the pier. There was a deeper cause of his unhappiness – the failed search for his lost youth. Twenty years after his celebrated *Liberty Guiding the People* he was within a year or two of his last showing at the Salon. On the facade of the old Hôtel Mr Michelin joins Mercury and another Greek gentleman in what looks like some sort of ball game.

Restaurants on the historic Quai Henri IV.

Across the road, Dieppe's fishwives sprinkle water on the heaped mussels in the **Poissonnerie**, the covered fish market at the harbour head, and in the **Café Suisse**, under the **Arcades de la Bourse** opposite, steaming bowls of moules marinière are served – with memories. The 4.30am boat has just arrived from Newhaven and Oscar Wilde is breakfasting on sandwiches, a bottle of red and a bottle of white wine with his friends Reggie Turner and Robert Ross. Diners under the Arcades and the Poissonnerie get double protection, from the elements and for the buildings. Built after the bombardment in 1696, they are listed ancient monuments.

The **Grande-Rue** is a street of contrasts. Couture shops happily neighbour *charcutiers*; bookshops, boutiques; greengrocers, antique shops. Chocolate sardines in a tin or a set of *boules*, they are all there in a street that would not be out of place in one of the smarter quarters of Paris. On Saturday, market day, it becomes part of a country market town overflowing with all the produce of the Norman countryside. From elderly farm wives with a basket's contents of beans or spring onions to enormous vans with more varieties of cheese than you ever knew existed, the tide of this most animated, most colourful, most mouth-watering display flows on into the Rue de la Barre, the Rue St-Jacques and the **Place Nationale**.

Late Admiral: Presiding over all is the spirited statue of Duquesne, Dieppe's honoured admiral, and a specialist in bombardments. The "admiral" is posthumous. Louis XIV could not confer the title on him in his lifetime because he belonged to the reformed church. Even his ashes had to wait until 1894 to be returned from Switzerland.

The Grande-Rue begins in the **Place du Puits Salé**, a reminder that until the 16th century salt water at high tides often mixed with fresh water in the well. Here at the heart of Dieppe is the **Café des Tribunaux**, an impressive old inn of uncertain age always the social centre of the town. The clock gave it its former name in 1736 of the Cabaret de

Fresh farm cheeses and charcuterie.

l'Horloge. The café has often posed for artists, Sickert and Blanche amongst them, and at a table on the terrace the content of *The Savoy*, the influential English magazine of the 1890s was thrashed out between Aubrey Beardsley and his editor.

Besides the Tribunaux, the vista is closed by the tower of St-Jacques in an area developed as a whole after 1694, the **Quartier St-Jacques**. From the window of his room at the Hôtel du Commerce in the Place Nationale, Camille Pissarro had an Impressionist's eye view of the church. He painted no fewer than eight variations on St-Jacques, including St-Jacques in the rain, with the market in full swing below, and the swings and roundabouts of a visiting fair. He wrote to his son Lucien: "The fair is here just now. Wooden horses, music by Gounod and other classics on the steam organ. I can't sleep!"

New flats replacing run-down tenements edge into the Place Louis Vitet, once a meat market. Framed by the arches of the old school is Dieppe's

finest timber-framed building; built in 1621 as a residence, it survived the fires of 1694 to become a warehouse for the tobacco factory on the *plage*.

Italian link: There is another Dieppe. Cross the bridges to **Le Pollet** to discover a different world. As "foreign" in speech and appearance as in manners, the Polletais are the lingering evidence of an Italian connection that began when ships called in here from Venice on the way to Flanders. Above the houses the cliff rises honeycombed with caves that provided homes for fishermen's families and hovels for yesterday's dropouts, and was once the platform for heroic endeavour.

From here, the fortified hill of La Bastille, the English in 1442 threatened the town. Nothing the French could do would dislodge them until the young Dauphin, the future Louis XI, flung himself on the walls in an attack his officers felt obliged to follow. The successful though costly exercise was to be echoed in the Normandy landings on the beaches below 500 years later.

From the Rue du Petit-Fort with its well-preserved brick and flint fishermen's cottages, steps climb to the Semaphore and the church of **Notre-Dame de Bon Secours**, with magnificent views from the cliff. Down on the quay **Notre-Dame des Grèves** suffers a facade nibbled to Swiss cheese by the greedy elements, but the Abbé Cochet's description of it as a *bâtard et hermaphrodite* seems a little strong. It overlooks a whales' graveyard where the hulks of old ships are beached to die.

Dieppe's attractions stretch a long arm beyond the town's streets. Watch that downward swing on the breezy heights above the château. The **Golf** is a short drive up the hill and round the hairpin bends of the road to Pourville, a clifftop course to put air in your tyres. The obstacles are different at **L'Hippodrome**, where the road to Arques tangles with the railways and by-passes of Dieppe's suburbs. Between jumps, sheep nibble and shepherds watch on this most pastoral of racecourses. "The People's Sport" has been king here for over 140 years.

Left, crane operator in Dieppe harbour. **Right**, the 15th-century château.

INLAND FROM DIEPPE

Get on your bicycle in Dieppe and join Oscar Wilde for breakfast at the Clos Normand. "Do you remember," he wrote, "the pretty girl at the little café by the river at **Martin-Église** where we drove together with Robbie and More on bicycles behind us?" Dieppe's favoured rural excursion is a short pedal up the road beside the River Arques, and the mellow red-brick building, once a farm, has tables set out in an apple orchard through which a trout stream runs. Water music is the perpetual accompaniment to a meal. Nearby a statue of the Virgin keeps sentry duty from her box on a bridge, and there is a strong local tradition that Joan of Arc crossed it on her way to death in Rouen.

Arques, or as it came to be known after the event, **Arques-la-Bataille**, lies beside the D1 a few bungalows and a forest further on, with an obelisk on the hillside to remind us that here in 1589 the Protestant Henry IV with a handful of men fought and won a resounding victory over the overwhelming forces of the Catholic League. A bas-relief over an archway in the château itself pays a belated tribute, since it was put there only in 1845, and shows Henry, now worn nearly bodiless, on a galloping horse and approached by a figure offering the crown of France.

The château is reached up a steep road through a gap in the outer wall. Built by William the Conqueror's uncle, it became a pawn in the aspirations of assorted kings till the invention of gunpowder made its possession a liability rather than a military asset. Even in its romantic decay, broken walls crumbling into grassy earthworks, and a fallen stair rendering the great keep unassailable, it remains a most impressive ruin and a vaguely threatening place.

Kissing fields: Mermaids, creatures with pointed ears and the recumbent figure of a "chevalier" upright with his feet above ground invite a visit to the church at **Envermeu**. From here to the River Bresle and the Picardy border are the kissing fields, old apple orchards heavy with mistletoe, and only the shock horror of **Foucarmont** between. Three bells in a hooped frame, sub-Corbusier columns, and a bunker pierced with holes (for guns?) signal the church – a 1959 firework display of coloured glass and concrete cancer inside.

South of Dieppe the Scie valley's apple orchards promise, and deliver from the presses at the **Cidrerie Duche de Longueville**, Normandy's answer to the produce of the grape. Longueville lies 10 miles (16 km) south of Dieppe, and between the two, on the N27, cornfields and beech avenues lead to the **Château de Miromesnil**, a building of delightful and inventive design begun in 1589, but completed only in 1630. Top left is the window of the room from which the infant Guy de Maupassant first announced his existence, though something of a mystery surrounds his birth. Did the confinement take place here or at a more modest address nearby? It seems his parents, determined to give their child the best of starts in life, chose

the silver spoon of a good address by taking a short lease of the château. Certainly Gustave Flaubert was present as godfather when he was baptised in the private chapel of St-Antoine in the park in 1850. Among the souvenirs exhibited in the château of the writer who was to achieve fame not only in France but all over the world is a cup lettered with the word "*Amitié*", the natural friendliness that inspired his interest in all classes and conditions of men.

Social hub: Fields away, **Offranville** bears the imprint of a painter and writer who had a profound and benevolent influence on art and letters in the early part of the century – Jacques-Émile Blanche. To the 16th-century **Manoir du Tôt** during Blanche's 40 years as a tenant came Jean Cocteau, André Gide, Walter Sickert and James Whistler.

Today many more come to the manoir. Its farm and buildings have been happily brought back to community life as the **Centre de Loisirs du Colombier**, accommodating leisure activities as diverse as riding (there is a large covered school), camping, tennis, miniature golf, and exhibitions in the converted dovecote. Blanche's work is courteously shown on request at the Mairie, and as a war memorial in the church of St-Ouen in the village.

On the River Dun 8 miles (13 km) west is **Bourg-Dun** which has a magnificent 16th-century house, gable-ended to the road, in flint, brick, stone and wood, and in **Notre-Dame** a village church of extravagant proportions, part 11th and 12th centuries.

The little River Dun is accompanied on the east by la Sâane and joined at Gueures by la Vienne before reaching the sea at Quiberville. Fortunately, the rivers are closely followed by roads inland, and it is a most rewarding experience to pursue a leisurely exploration of this little known countryside.

Flainville is a case in point, just up the road towards the coastal resort of St-Aubin, but centuries further away in time. The road that serves it stops abruptly at a 16th-century calvary and becomes a cart track across fields of

Grey slates and poppies.

flax. The farmyard of the old manor with its still surviving barns and sheds hides the most remarkable and, unfortunately, most neglected monument of Normandy's Middle Ages: the **Chapelle de Flainville**. Built in 1324 by the seigneur Estout de Gruchet, its walls and ceilings once exquisitely decorated, the chapel retains a beauty from which not even damp and decay can detract.

Much further west, on the inland side of the D925 just before it reaches Fécamp is the town of **Valmont**, made sturdy and prestigious by the Estouteville family who built the gaunt 15th-century château where François I used to stay, and the 12th-century Benedictine abbey, its church now a haunting ruin.

Caux capital: It is easy to be dismissive of **Yvetot**, southeast of Valmont on the N15 halfway between Rouen and Le Havre. It is capital of the Caux region and largely a postwar re-creation. The **church of St-Pierre**, whose stained glass is measured in square metres, they say, believably, you cannot ignore. **Allouville-Bellefosse**, just south of where roads divide for Fécamp and Le Havre, had no history to lose, but it does have a very elderly inhabitant – an oak tree 1,200 years old, 52 feet (16 metres) in circumference at the base, and in its hollow heart two chapels. These were the inspiration of the parish priest in 1696, and the tree has recently had to undergo heart surgery. Hidden down lanes nearby is the **Musée de la Nature** whose objectives are difficult to resist. Local fauna and flora get supportive treatment here, and injured wild animals and oiled seabirds are rehabilitated in their own natural environment.

To the east, 10 miles (16 km) due north of Rouen, is **Clères**, which has its feet in the waters of the Clérette. It runs the length of the main street under little bridges, past the market hall and the Auberge du Cheval Noir, tables beneath a canopy, looking for all the world as if captured on canvas by an Impressionist. Across the road the **Musée d'Automobiles et Militaire** solicits interest outside with a 1942 vintage torpedo and, inside, with motorbikes, bicycles

Forêt de Lyons.

and cars from Red Flag days. Everything looks harmless enough. Next door the **Parc Zoologique** offers sanctuary and freedom to 2,000 birds of more than 250 species and beasts like antelopes, deer, kangaroos and monkeys, all in the garden of a Renaissance château.

East of Rouen on the N31 is **Martainville** where an early 16th-century château contains one of the best **folk museums** in Upper Normandy. Just beyond it is the **Château de Vascoeuil** where a delightful waterfall, literally a water staircase, courses through the grounds. You can almost tell from the proud bearing of the restored 12th-century building that it won a "Masterpieces in Peril" award. Although one end is modestly half-timbered, it progresses storey on storey in golden coloured stone to the soaring heights of the rocket-like lookout tower.

In the garden below, the baronial dovecote has found a new purpose in life as a gallery, but its chief attraction is permanent: a massive wooden ladder that revolves on a central pivot to give easy access to the nesting places. The château itself, as a lively regional arts and history centre, hosts exhibitions of painting and sculpture, some of which spills over into the garden. There is a room in the tower devoted to Michelet, the French historian who wrote many of his books in his study there. When you consider that his *Histoire de France* alone ran to 24 volumes, you can understand how the place could have become a little neglected.

Musician's retreat: The château is on the northern edge of the **Forêt de Lyons**, a former hunting ground of the dukes of Normandy, and a regular place for dropping supplies for resistance workers in World War II.

At the heart of the 26,430-acre (10,700-hectare) forest is the popular, tranquil town of **Lyons-la-Forêt**. Off the main roads amid massive beech trees, it was chosen as a retreat by the composer Maurice Ravel, and in his half-timbered house in Rue de la République he wrote *Le Tombeau de Couperin* in 1917. Five miles (8 km) away in a glade in the woods are the remains of the splendid **Abbaye de Mortemer**, the first Cistercian monastery in Normandy. It was destroyed in the French Revolution, though its 17th-century convent building remains, and there is a museum of monastic life. The 15th-century dovecote in the grounds was rebuilt in the 17th century and used as a prison.

Fortified border towns: On the southern side of the forest, lies **Gisors**, one of a number of fortified towns along the border and following the valley of the Epte. It was designed by the early Norman dukes to keep out the French.

Dominating the town is its **château**, begun in 1097 by William Rufus and expanded by Philippe-Auguste who occupied it in 1193 when its owner, Richard Lionheart, was held captive in Germany. Prisoners here elaborately decorated the walls of the Tour de Prisonnier during the 15th and 16th centuries. The **church of Saints Gervais-et-Protais** dates from the time of Rufus, but is mainly 13th–16th century.

The D915 border road continues to the north, past **St-Germer-de-Fly**,

Lyons-la-Forêt, home for Ravel.

which is in fact just the wrong side of the border in the *département* of Oise, but the abbey church which dominates the small town is the grandest in what can still be called the Bray region. Entrance to the church is through the town hall in the 14th-century fortified gate.

Gournay-en-Bray is the next border town. Here lived one of those inventive Norman farmers' wives who mixed fresh cream with curds to produce Petit-Suisse. The capitals of the **church of St-Hildevert** have some wonderfully primitive figurative carvings.

There is a grey sadness about **Forges-les-Eaux** 12 miles (20 km) to the north. It was an iron-working centre in the Middle Ages, but the discovery of the spring waters' beneficial qualities in 1573 brought new prosperity and royal patronage. Anne of Austria took the waters, hoping that she could provide her husband with an heir, but not till six years later was the future Louis XIV born. Cardinal Richelieu joined their majesties here in the beautiful, wooded park below the spa building, now a casino. Had they come today, they could have spent from 3pm to 3am on the fruit machines. A grotto and the facades only of 17th and 18th-century buildings contribute to the wistful appeal of this haunted place, which the **French Resistance Museum** in the grounds of the Hôtel de Ville serves only to reinforce.

The road north ends this circuitous tour of the Bray region, arriving at its heart at **Neufchatel-en-Bray**, renowned for its production of the heart-shaped Coeur de Neufchatel, the oldest cheese in Normandy. In 1940 the town's heart was almost completely destroyed, but one building, a Norman manor house, survived to become the **Musée d'Art Régional**. The tools of rural arts and crafts, such as cheese and clog-making, pottery and earthenware, cooperage and saddlery, share elegant rooms, and in the garden there is a Norman market hall with apple presses and a well. In another garden, this time in the rebuilt Civic Centre, a massive female head with nostrils flaring flashes cartwheel eyes outside the Palais de Justice.

View from the castle ruins, Gisors.

THE ALABASTER COAST

In choosing a popular name for this fine stretch of the Normandy seaboard – 75 miles (120 km) from Le Tréport to Le Havre – the French, as usual, erred on the side of elegant sophistication. Streaked with sand and crusted with soil these jagged, switchback, white chalk cliffs suddenly drop sheer from the platform of the Pays de Caux to the sea below, making the drive along the winding and picturesque roads a dramatic and exhilarating experience.

Le Tréport, 20 miles (32 km) east of Dieppe, is poised above its harbour at the mouth of the Bresle. It has a personality happily split between commerical shipping and fishing and the seaside resort sheltered snugly below the last and highest cliff this side of Picardy. The two worlds meet on the quays, which are always crowded, lively and colourful, but a few steps up the hill, reached through a gate by the old Hôtel de Ville, are the quiet streets of the old town. The 16th-century **church of St-Jacques**, still smarting at never having had the spire it was promised, dominates the harbour from the site of successive churches burned down in raids by the English. There are good views from the garden behind the church, and even better from Les Terrasses at the top of a punishing flight of steps up the west cliff. Secure in the old prison is the **Musée des Enfants du Vieux Tréport**, the "children" in question being objects associated with Le Tréport's historical and cultural heritage.

Royal retreat: Two places link closely with the town: the little bathing resort of **Mers**, across the Bresle in Picardy, its hotels and villas the late 19th-century Parisian's fantasy of rural retreats by the sea, and the other, **Eu**, 2½ miles (4 km) upstream. Always connected with the royal families of Normandy and France, Eu possesses a faded glory. The **château**, now shared between the Hôtel de Ville and the **Musée Louis-Philippe**, was begun in 1578, but the unfortunate red-brick building we see today is of indeterminate age, like the service lift between the floors. It was intended for Napoleon, but Louis-Philippe fell in love with it, and during his occupancy twice entertained Queen Victoria here. The **Chapelle du Collège** was built by Catherine of Cleves in 1620, widow of Henri Guise (was he really surnamed *Scarface*?), murdered on the orders of Henry III. In their marble mausoleums they lie each side of the altar.

The church of **Notre-Dame et St-Laurent** is dedicated to an Irish archbishop here on a mercy mission in 1181. Lawrence O'Toole came to make peace between the king of Ireland and Henry II, and died in Eu. It contains some fine 13th-century tombs.

By-roads hug the cliff westwards through **Mesnil-Val** to **Criel-Plage** at the mouth of the Yères and **Criel-sur-Mer** in the green valley inland, where the 17th-century **Château Chantereine** on the banks of the trout stream grandly satisfies the demands for leisure. If leisure includes climbing the 340 ft (104 metres) of Mount Jolibois on the cliff,

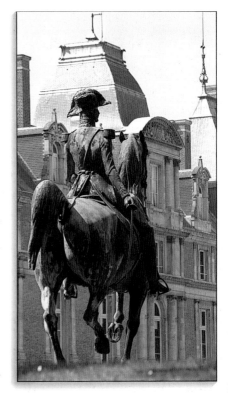

then the views from the belvedere of the Yères valley and up the coast to the River Somme are glorious. There's no other word.

South and west the coast road sends out lanes to farms and villages scattered among the patterned fields. The difference with Penly is that its output is measured not in bushels or tonnes, but in MWes, 2,600 of them in fact. **Penly Nuclear Power Station** makes a dramatic interruption in the cliffscape, carving a deep scar of roads behind, and thrusting a platform of space-age buildings and industrial development into the sea in front. Visitors are welcome to this "major attraction".

Wilde's hideaway: The breach in the cliff at **Berneval** is a natural one and the beach itself perfect for bathing. The resort, at the top of the steps cut in the rocks known as the **Giant's Staircase**, is the sort of place in which a stranger could lose himself, specially if he had just left prison. Oscar Wilde (last address, Reading Jail) booked into the Hôtel de la Plage under the assumed name of Sebastian Melmoth to do just that. The next year, 1897, he was celebrating Queen Victoria's Diamond Jubilee with a fête for the local children, presenting them with toy trumpets and accordions. The charm of the rustic idyll soon faded, and Wilde left for Naples and Alfred Douglas.

That personal tragedy is eclipsed by Berneval's part in the horror of 19 August 1942. The success of the Allied raid on Dieppe depended on silencing the huge coastal batteries (*see page 62*). That of Berneval was assigned to Canada's No.3 Commando, whose men were landed, scaled the cliff and engaged the battery. None got away.

Earlier struggles are recalled in **Caesar's Camp** in the fields by the sea, the hill-fortress of a tribe of Gauls captured by the Romans. There is a sharp descent into **Puys** on the outskirts of Dieppe, the scene of another disastrous assault in 1942, ending in the massacre of the Royal Regiment of Canada. Alexander Dumas *fils* built a house here in 1870 in which his father died, and in Villa Cecil Lord Salisbury spent his holidays, until a zealous customs officer demanded duty on whisky he had sent from England. In a huff he sold his house and never returned.

West of **Dieppe** the coast road, hostilely commanded by pillboxes, drops down hairpin bends to Pourville, crosses the Scie by a bridge bitterly fought over in the Raid, and wanders through the delightful hamlets of **Varengeville.** The Cubist painter Georges Braque made his home here, and created a rustic Chartres in the tiny barn-like **Chapel of St-Dominique**, his big oriel window glowing golden with the *galets*, the stones

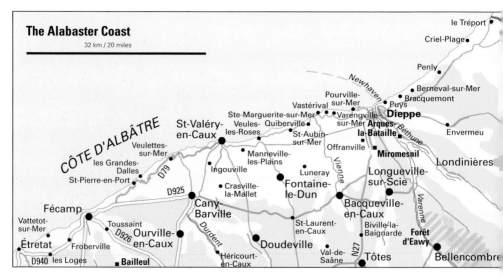

from the beach. Nearly opposite an avenue of trees leads to the **Manoir d'Ango**, the Renaissance palace Jean Ango, Dieppe's merchant prince, built on the spoils his ships brought from India, Brazil and the New World. In the courtyard is the finest *colombier* in the region, providing Ango with fresh meat in the winter from 600 pairs of pigeons. The sailors' church on the cliffs, recorded in innumerable canvases by Monet, has Braque's Tree of Jesse window, and in the cemetery a white bird spreads its mosaic wings over his grave.

Of Varengeville's **Parc des Moustiers**, the architect Sir Edwin Lutyens wrote: "It is so lovely here, so quiet and delicious." The house he built for banker Guillaume Mallet in 1898 has the most beautiful situation at the head of a wooded valley with gardens running down to the sea. Irresistible. After pine forests that hide the elusive lighthouse of **Phare d'Ailly**, discover the twisted columns and high altar in the church of **Ste-Marguerite**, dating from 1160.

The road then dips to watering places, climbs again and skirts the watercress beds at **Veules-les-Roses**. Here rises France's smallest river, reaching the *plage* just 1,300 yards (1,194 metres) away, providing a delightful footpath walk along its banks, over bridges, past thatched cottages, flower gardens and old watermills. Not surprisingly the path

begins as the Chemin des Champs Élysées. Paris should be so proud!

The **church of St-Martin** is a gallery of sculpture in wood and stone. Figures with plumed hats, ships, mermaids, beasts and angels climb the columns to the wooden-vaulted roof. A beggar on a crutch asks for alms of a man on a horse flourishing a sword. The colouring and the carving is crude, but the effect is immediate. Saints proliferate, given shelter here from churches elsewhere. Victor Hugo loved Veules, often visiting the house of his friend Paul Meurice where the elaborate memorial is by the *plage*. The ruins of another church, **St-Nicolas**, on the hill behind, were in Meurice's garden. Outside his house by the river a man sits roasting coffee beans over a fire, turning the handle of his simple machine and poking them with a stick. Time does not stand still at Veules; it has been put into reverse.

"How many sailors, how many captains, have blithely left for far-off journeys?" Victor Hugo wrote in appreciation of the brave men of **St-Valéry-en-Caux**. The little port, hemmed in by the steep cliffs of the Caux, now owes more to *boules* and baccarat, sailing and sunbathing than fishing. As a resort it mounts a programme of events every year in which almost everything from Henry IV to herrings has its festival. Henry stayed there, so they say, in the rather

Watermill, Veules-les-Roses.

grand, timber-framed house on the west quay. The **Maison Henry IV** was built in 1540 and, preserved and restored, doubles as Tourist Information and exhibition centre. Up a steep street behind the old house is the **Penitents' Cloister**, now a hospital, but founded in 1623 as a monastery. Before the Revolution the garden was lovingly tended by Friar Antoine. When the monastery was seized the brothers were turned out, and the convent became the headquarters of a Jacobin club, later a barracks and military prison. Friar Antoine, however, refused to leave his garden, and finished his days there in 1816, aged 66. The last of the penitents is recorded simply as "Antoine Dubourg, gardener, formerly Friar Antoine".

On the western cliff is a memorial to the French Cavalry Division, which together with the Scottish Highlanders fought a desperate rearguard action in the port after France's collapse in 1940. The Scottish monument on the east cliff overlooks a town risen from the rubble.

"Pleasant little watering places" is guidebookese for the seaside villages that fill gaps in the cliffs between St-Valéry and Fécamp, though **Paluel** does not quite answer to this description. "Electrifying" would be more appropriate, since its nuclear power station supplies 10 percent of France's needs. In **Veulettes-sur-Mer** it is difficult to resist an excursion through the lush water-meadows of the Durdent to **Cany-Barville**, where the château built by the uncle of the architect of Versailles managed to keep its furniture from the revolutionaries. The artefacts of a rural past are looked after here by the **Moulin St-Martin Ecomuseum**.

Monks' tipple: In **Fécamp** they worship cod and the amber liquid we call Benedictine, produced in a building you might be forgiven for confusing with the abbey, if the remnant of that great monastery, the church of **La-Trinité**, did not dominate the big fishing port. Legend determined its siting at the spot where the trunk of a fig tree was washed ashore with a vessel containing blood from the wounds of Christ concealed

Seafood sale at St-Valéry-en-Caux.

inside it. Earlier churches perished, but by 1220 a most impressive church of cathedral-like proportions with a central lantern-tower was erected here. It is a treasure-house of early stained glass, altar pieces, tombs, carved screens and a tabernacle containing relics of the Precious Blood. The adjoining 18th-century town hall is all that remains of the Benedictine abbey buildings.

In the Rue Alexandre-Legros, a busy city street, the **Musée Centre des Arts** lives in some splendour in a former private mansion with, hidden behind it, a fascinating woodland garden. Apart from the Rouen ware and ivory on display, a typical interior of the Caux region has been reconstructed in the attics. The **Benedictine Palace** was a late starter, built in 1892 in a regrettably florid style at variance with its religious associations, but it does exhibit priceless collections from the old abbey and throw in a taste of Benedictine. A monk, Dom Vincelli, first produced his liqueur here in 1510 to a recipe of herbs and spices that is still a secret.

The cliffs put on a spectacular performance at **Étretat**, embracing the curved beach and tiny esplanade in the arms of the **Porte d'Amont** on the right, and on the left the **Porte d'Aval**. Both are pierced by doorways worn through the chalk by the sea, and near the latter is the famous needle-pointed **Aiguille d'Étretat**. Though Marie-Antoinette had her own private oyster bed here it was artists like Corot and composers like Offenbach who brought popularity to the resort. Sadly, the thatched boats used as stores by the fishermen have become restaurants. On the Amont cliff is a memorial and museum devoted to two aviators, Nungesser and Coli, who set off from here in 1927 to make a first crossing of the Atlantic and died trying.

Was the lighthouse at **Cap d'Antifer** flashing on the night of 27 February 1942? Close by at **Bruneval** British paratroops destroyed a German radar post near the beach and re-embarked. Beyond, the cliffs march on to be broken finally by the Seine's abrasive flood and the villas of Ste-Adresse.

Rod fishing on the beach at Fécamp.

LE HAVRE

In the league table of French ports, **Le Havre** ranks second only to Marseilles, yet it didn't exist before the 16th century, and both port and town were almost destroyed in World War II. That it rose, phoenix-like, from the ashes to develop into today's thriving port and industrial centre (population: 200,000) shows remarkable resilience in its people and formidable courage in their commercial and strategic decisions.

It was a particularly shrewd strategy which prompted François I to begin the harbour in the silted-up mouth of the Seine in 1517. It would make an ideal base, he thought, for an assault on the English. François-Ville as he called it, with a nice show of modesty, was not an immediate success. The royal ships ran aground on sandbanks until the church tower was pressed into service and beacons lit to guide them in.

All at sea: Tides played havoc with the town, carrying the fishing fleet into the flooded streets. Worse followed: the English under the Earl of Warwick sailed in and took possession for 10 months. There was nothing for it but to change the name, and François-Ville was hopefully abandoned for Havre de Grâce. Richelieu, Minister of State to Louis XIII, took it in hand, deepening the harbour and later joining it to the neighbouring town of Harfleur by canal.

The English were back again in 1694 after bombarding Dieppe, and, though a shift in the wind made them retreat, it was not before they had destroyed much of the port and hundreds of houses. The Havrais responded by building themselves a new harbour of stone. In 1759 the persistent English were back with similar effect, but peace and an alliance with the American colonies brought stability and prosperity.

Louis XVI, taking up a suggestion by the Emperor of Austria, built new docks and put walls round the town, happily resisting the temptation to call it Louisville. Under Napoleon's threats to invade England the town grew in status and importance. Following Le Havre's support for the "rebels", ties with the United States grew stronger and in 1864 their first steamship, the *Washington*, arrived, initiating a lucrative exchange of trade.

Calamity had to wait for the 20th century. Le Havre was to suffer from friends and enemies alike in the devastation of World War II, from German bombs in 1940 and as the target of Allied bombing in 1944. Though Paris had been liberated, Le Havre was still occupied. Given the extent of the devastation, the Havrais could have been excused for abandoning the almost insuperable task of wholesale renewal.

That they succeeded in doing just that is due largely to the breadth of vision of one man, the Parisian architect Auguste Perret, and his pioneering use of one material: reinforced concrete. Borrowing from Belarmato, the Italian architect who laid out Le Havre in the 16th century, Perret retained the chessboard pattern of streets, but gave his new town space and wide boulevards opening on

Preceding pages: the yacht marina. **Left,** triathlon competitors in the town centre. **Right,** the second busiest port in France.

the port. There are cynics who would call them ways of escape from the concrete jungle.

Central to the design is the **Hôtel de Ville**, superbly sited on one of Europe's largest squares, liberally planted with flowers, trees and fountains. From here the Avenue Foch points west to the boundless sea and the Rue de Paris south to the ferry quays. Here in these apartment- and office-lined boulevards is the "grand, large, original" look so admired by its champions. Perret brought rainbow hues to his concrete, varying the colour according to the situation, the light and the character of his buildings. Would they inspire Claude Monet today to paint his Havre masterpiece, *Impression: Sunrise*?

Of the original Rue de Paris, nothing remains except for one building, the church of **Notre-Dame**, and of that only the facade. The descendant of a sailors' chapel, it has a tower dating from the 16th century, on which the English, invited in by French Protestants in 1562, mounted their guns and fired on the French camp. Cardinal Richelieu made the church a present of the carved oak organ case in 1657.

There is a nice contrast between Notre-Dame and Perret's church of **St-Joseph**. The concrete tower, which has affinity of outline with the Empire State Building, rises 348 feet (106 metres) to its belfry above the Boulevard François. On entering from the street, the feeling is of visiting a super cinema. You expect to be shown to the tip-up seats by a girl with a torch. Clustered pillars support the tower above the central altar, and the whole interior is speckled with constellations of coloured light from what used to be called stained glass set in the walls and ablaze with sunshine.

Brazilian conrtribution: St-Joseph's closes the vista west from the **Bassin du Commerce**, now filled with leisure craft, but the view is interrupted by the "elephant's foot". Leisure nowadays takes on strange forms, and the Brazilian architect Oscar Niemeyer must have recognised this in designing the **Espace Niemeyer**, his arts and recreation cen-

Old Le Havre Museum in a 17th-century family lodge.

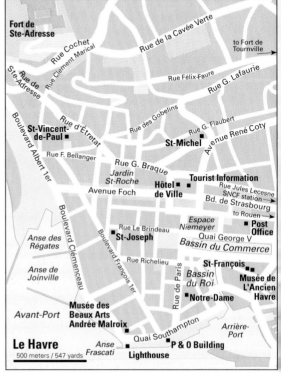

tre completed in 1982. Inevitably it earned itself the descriptive nickname, though it is officially "Volcan" and curiously described as "bubbling" in promotion literature. On Sundays there is a large market between here and the port.

By contrast, the **Musée de l'Ancien Havre** in the heart of the city, south of the Bassin du Commerce, is appropriately housed in a restored 17th-century lodge belonging originally to an old Havre family. The city's history from 1517 to its great days as a transatlantic port to modern times is brought vividly to life through maps and engravings, photographs, models and paintings. They all leave you with enormous admiration for its formidable powers of renewal and achievement.

The port is too important not to have a museum devoted to itself, though the **Maritime and Port Museum** turns out to be more of a celebration. Worldwide links in the days of the multi-funelled transatlantic liners are recalled, merchant ships and the cargoes they carried – cotton, wool, coffee and oil – the men who sailed in them, the perils of the sea and the threat of fire. Hoses at the ready, the fireship *Le Havre III* is moored at the quay outside.

Curiously, the pleasure boat that tours the docks from the Quai de la Marine is named after a lizard supposed to live in fire. From the cabin of the *Salamandre* something of the immensity of port operations and the size of the docks, some as big as lakes, can be seen in comfort.

The width of a street is all that separates the ferries from England and Ireland and Le Havre's most distinguished building, the **André Malraux Fine Arts Museum**. Opened in 1961, it is as modern as tomorrow, perfectly adapted to its function of displaying pictures and sculpture, regardless of period, in the best possible conditions. The glass-and-steel gallery is strikingly simple in construction and layout, with a moated entrance that has a medieval feel about it. Inside, no walls. Screens can be shuffled into place like playing cards to give the interior new spaces, new volumes, new shapes. Aluminium blinds in the

laminated glass roof filter the natural light as required.

The paintings more than deserve their setting, progressing through the European schools to outstanding works by Eugène Boudin, Raoul Dufy and his contemporaries. There are revelations, too, in the black cavern where Dufy's drawings glow like jewels and there is furniture designed by Bugatti's father, Carlo, when driving meant behind a horse and not at a wheel.

Fashionable resort: Across the road the ferries slide into their berths with almost less noise than the ducks on the moat, and the Boulevard Clemenceau lures us away to Havre's other persona as a seaside resort: the yacht harbour and the *plage*.

On the rising hill beyond is the suburb of **Ste-Adresse**, giving a passable impersonation of Nice, villas crowding the slopes above the Seine estuary, nudging each other for a share of the magnificent view. The proprietor of *Le Figaro* newspaper fell in love with it and bought himself a house in 1841 surrounded by open farmland. Writers, painters and musicians followed, and by World War I the last farm had disappeared. Sarah Bernhardt, Alexandre Dumas *fils*, Gabriel Fauré, Raoul Dufy and Claude Monet all had villas here. Monet said: "I have everything here that pleases me – light and water."

Ste-Adresse once belonged to Belgium. At the French government's invitation, the large Dufayel Palace became the seat of that country's government in exile during World War I. In 1914 it was used as the general headquarters for the American army.

From the terrace of the **fort** there is a wonderful panorama over the port across the Seine estuary to the Côte de Grâce. Visitors like to linger over meals in the Nice-Havrais restaurant, one of the best fish restaurants in town with a grand view. A favourite Havre excursion skirts the hill past the "Pain du Sucre", the sugar loaf-shaped mariners' monument, takes in the nearby Bernhardt villa with its mosaics, and continues to the lighthouse on **La Hève** headland. The views are unforgettable.

Another worthwhile excursion takes you in the opposite, inland direction to a hilltop above the Rouen road on the urban fringe of Le Havre – the **Graville Priory**. Relics had a rough ride in the 6th century, and St Honorine's were no exception. The shrine built to protect them had no guarantee of respect from the marauding Normans, so her remains were spirited away to Conflans, near Pontoise, for safe keeping. Happily, her tomb is now back in the priory. From the wooded setting of the old cloister there is a spellbinding prospect of the Seine on its way to the sea.

The **Museum**, in surviving monastic buildings, has a remarkable collection of church sculpture in stone and wood – processional crosses, gravestones, alabaster statues, documents revealing the chequered hisory of the priory, and intriguing relics of the Black Madonna. The Madonna is there as you leave by the Rue de l'Abbaye entrance and its colour signifies the mystery of Jesus, and mourning for the child born to die on the cross.

Left, annual chores. **Right**, the leisure yacht marina.

CAEN

Visitors penetrating the mesh of ring-roads, industrial estates and post-war housing that surround modern-day Caen may find it instructive, even therapeutic, to while away the traffic lights with sustained fantasies about the city's earliest incarnations. Try Catumagos, the fledging Celtic settlement that grew up here on an island at the confluence of the Orne and Odon rivers. Or the Gallo-Roman port of Cadomus, with its neighbouring villages scattered across fields and marshland now graced with concrete and tarmac.

Twin abbeys: Better still, return to the mid-11th century, when this walled town became William and Matilda's favoured residence and their major power base in western Normandy. These monarchs put Caen on the map, and bequeathed the city its two great abbeys, the Abbaye-aux-Hommes and Abbaye-aux-Dames, both founded on the north bank of the Orne in penitential response to the lifting, in 1059, of the papal excommunication imposed following their cousinly marriage nine years earlier.

Today these His 'n' Hers abbeys act as towering book-ends between which everything of historic interest in Caen can be found. Midway between them stands the hilltop **Château de Caen**, a castle founded by William and much enlarged by his son, Henry I. It is still the city's hub, though no longer its heart – World War II stopped that, when the "Battle for Caen" reduced three-quarters of the city to rubble. Pause on the castle's western ramparts, though, and you can still contemplate a skyline punctuated with spires and belfries, a poignant hint of what Caen must have been like before the bombs rained down.

From the ensuing decades of hasty reconstruction and utilitarian town-planning, Caen has emerged as a functional and busy city, its industries benefiting from the 1855 Caen canal that links it to the Channel 7½ miles (12 km) to the north. As the capital of Basse Normandie and Préfecture of Calvados, this city of 120,000 has worked hard to regain its cultural stature. A lengthy process of restoration (still very much in evidence) has preserved many monuments, and a good spread of lawns, parks and gardens, planted courtesy of Allied bombers, have been incorporated into the city centre. This can be easily toured on foot, along streets well-stocked with affordable shops and restaurants, and kept lively by a 24,000-student university to the north of the castle.

For many visitors Caen begins with the **Place Courtonne**, and the best way to arrive is surely by water, sailing up to join the serried yachts and pleasure boats that moor in the adjacent **Bassin St-Pierre**. During the week the square functions as a car park and bus junction, but on Sunday mornings is given over to an antiques-and-anything market. At its northern end stands the **Tour Guill-aume-le-Roy**, a stubborn remnant of the town's ramparts that once looked out over the Odon, but which is now a chess-piece castle stranded in traffic.

A short walk north, along Rue Buquet,

is the **Vieux Quartier de Vaugeux**. This is a pleasantly pedestrianised fraction of old Caen centred on the Rue du Vaugeux. Its timbered buildings are home to a useful variety of restaurants offering everything from fast junk and couscous to Madagascan cuisine and the gourmet dishes of one of Caen's best-known restaurants, La Bourride.

At the southern end of Rue du Vaugeux, Rue des Chanoines leads eastwards up to the **Abbaye-aux-Dames**, the first of William and Matilda's twin abbeys to be built. Nine centuries ago it would have stood amid meadows sloping down to the Orne, with its own attendant village, known simply as Le Bourg-l'Abbesse. A few remnants of St-Gilles, its parish church, can be seen standing in a garden opposite the west front of the abbey's church, **La Trinité**.

Begun in 1060 and consecrated six years later, only a few months before William invaded England, Matilda's church is a monument to both the grace of the Norman Romanesque style and the creamy sensuality of Caen stone.

Despite the loss of its spires in the Hundred Years' War, a zealous revamping of the west front in the 1850s and the well-scrubbed homogeneity that has resulted from the recent restoration of the interior, there is much to enjoy. The nine bays of the nave, roofed with pointed vaulting in the 12th century, are textbook Romanesque, while the crypt, forested with columns, has hardly changed since the day it was built. Directly above this, in the choir, a black marble slab marks the tomb of Queen Matilda, who died in 1083.

The crypt is often locked, but can be viewed if you join one of the daily guided tours (2.30pm and 4pm only) around the adjacent **conventual buildings**. These were laid out in 1704 by Guillaume de la Tremblaye, who designed a similar ensemble for the Abbaye-aux-Hommes. The Revolution prevented the completion of the fourth wall of the cloisters, but the abbey's classical buildings and formal gardens have since been restored to make an harmonious residence for the Conseil

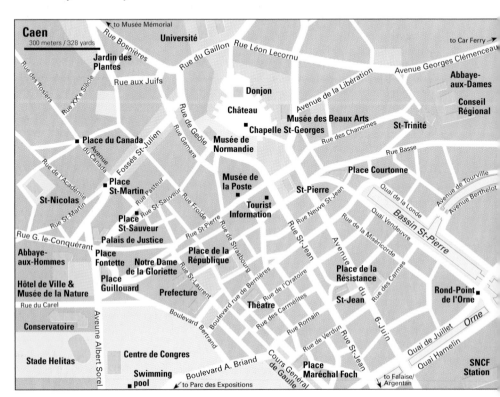

Régional de Basse Normandie. Among its grand halls and fluid staircases is a portrait of the last abbess, Madame de Pontecoulant, whose cousin Charlotte Corday assassinated the Jacobin leader Jean-Paul Marat.

Spiritual heart: William and Matilda's abbeys may be the most venerable religious buildings in Caen, but the church closest to the hearts of its citizens is the **church of St-Pierre**. Just west of the Tour Guillaume-le-Roy, it remains lovingly unrestored and grimy – although archaeologists are now excavating the adjoining cemetery. Begun in the late 13th century, St-Pierre's orderly Gothic nave contrasts with the richness of its Renaissance eastern end, the dripping decorations paid for by wealthy Caennais. The spire and roof were destroyed in the war, and their impressive reconstruction is easily appreciated when you climb the steps that lead up to the château further north.

Caen's **castle** is today a grassy ghost town, with the few buildings that survived the war now used as museums.

The ruins at its northern end are the most tangibly feudal, where thick, massive walls emerge from the surrounding lawns like the teeth of a badly-buried giant. Here you can see the outline of the castle's **Donjon**, a moated keep raised in 1123 by Henry I but felled by the Convention in 1793. To its west is a lonely survivor from the 12th century, the **Salle de l'Échiquier** (Exchequer's Hall), the great hall of Henry's palace.

In the south of the castle precincts two museums lie either side of the small **Chapelle St-Georges**, dating from the 12th to 15th centuries and now an exhibition space. To the east, the renovated **Musée des Beaux Arts** boasts a wide-ranging collection of fine paintings and prints, with some of its choicest works acquired by Napoleonic pillage. It is particularly strong on 17th-century French and Italian painting, though the artists represented stretch from Van der Weyden and Dürer to Courbet and Dufy.

To the west of St-Georges, the **Musée de Normandie** occupies the former residence of the city's governor, with a medieval **Jardin des Simples** (medicinal garden) laid out alongside. Its rooms are a résumé of life in Normandy down the centuries, with informative exhibits describing the region's diverse styles of agriculture and architecture, displays of crafts such as the making of cider, cheese, lace and copper, and an esoteric collection of liturgical candle-making equipment from a factory in Cherbourg.

From the northern end of the château a path leads out across the Esplanade de la Paix to the Orwellian landscape of **Caen University**. Although it was founded in 1432 by the Duke of Bedford, regent of England's Henry VI, the present campus is a serene pool of 1950s tower blocks and parkland sprawling across 82 acres (33 hectares) of northern Caen. On the western edge of its grounds, hardly noticed by either students or drivers hurtling along the Rue du Magasin à Poudre, is Caen's small and overgrown **Protestant cemetery**.

The English have always been attracted to Caen, from the booty-hunting troops of Edward III who sacked it in 1346 to the cross-Channel coach parties

St-Pierre, lovingly unrestored.

that now raid its hypermarkets for cheap wine and beer. For 33 years after the Battle of Agincourt, Caen was under English rule, and in the mid-19th century the city hosted an expatriate community of more than 1,000. Among their number was England's best known dandy, George "Beau" Brummel, who was consul here from 1830 to 1832. At the age of 20 he inherited a fortune that enabled him to live with impeccable flamboyance for the next 18 years, until gambling debts forced him to flee to France. A tragic decline into penury, prison and paralysis culminated in his death in 1840, and the inelegant headstone that now marks his grave.

Shopping centre: The western side of Caen, from the château to the Abbaye-aux-Hommes, is the city's most active and energetic. Its main artery is Rue St-Pierre, while Boulevard du Maréchal Leclerc, which follows the Odon's old course, winds south past large department stores such as C&A, Nouvelles Galeries and Monoprix. Within this compact grid of shop-lined streets – which include a good supply of bars, *salons de thé* and heartlifting *patisseries* – are a scattering of historic buildings worth discovering rather than seeking out.

On the west side of Église St-Pierre, Caen's Tourist Office is located in the restored **Hôtel d'Escoville**, an Italianate mansion built in the 1530s. A short walk north at 31 Rue de Geôle, and easily seen from the château, is the 15th-century timber-latticed **Maison des Quatrans**. In the opposite direction, down Rue St-Jean, you can see the gnawed towers of the **church of St-Jean**. Begun in the 14th century, it was never completed as it was built on unsteady marshland. Despite the noticeable slant of its west front and internal pillars, it is still in use.

West along Rue St-Pierre, two 16th-century half-timbered buildings stand stoically at nos. 52 and 54. Inside the first the **Musée de la Poste** (Postal Museum) boldly romanticises the delivery of mail, from the galloping messengers of the Bayeux Tapestry to the brightly-anoraked heroes of today. **Crêpe-maker.**

A short walk further west is the curiously attractive **church of St-Sauveur**, known as Notre-Dame de Froide-Rue, which consists of two naves built side by side, one 14th century and the other 15th. From here Rue St-Pierre continues west into the Rue Écuyère and an area known for its antique shops, beyond which is the Place Fontette, dominated by the octagonal hulk of Caen's **Palais de Justice**. This is the most direct route to the Abbaye-aux-Hommes, but a preferable detour is to take one of the narrow streets, such as Rue Froide (next to that church) or the Rue aux Fromages (off Rue Écuyère) that lead north to the spacious Place St-Sauveur.

Lined with 18th-century houses, the square is the scene of Caen's principal **market**, held every Friday. In its centre is a statue of Louis XIV masquerading as a Roman emperor. Continuing north, Rue Pémagnie leads into the Place St-Martin, where an equestrian statue of Bertrand du Guesclin takes on the city traffic. From here there are views west to the spires of the **Abbaye-aux-Hommes**, which can be reached by walking down Rue St-Manvieu.

As with Matilda's Abbaye-aux-Dames, William's abbey consists of an abbey church, **St-Étienne**, abutted to a grandiose ensemble of 18th-century conventual buildings. The imposing west front of the church is reached via Rue Guillaume-le-Conquérant, where a small square and cul-de-sac to the left gives visitors the chance to gaze up at its 269-ft (82-metre) towers.

The harmony of this facade belies St-Étienne's battered history. Work on the church began in 1067 and was virtually complete by the time of William's death 20 years later. The Conqueror's funeral turned out to be a farcical affair, with the route of the cortège disrupted by a fire in the town and the burial service interrupted by a townsman claiming his father had owned the land where the grave was dug. This canny Caennais left only after the bishop paid him 60 sous in compensation. When the coffin was eventually lowered into its vault William's decomposed corpse burst,

Dog's dinner.

creating such a stench that the congregation fled. His tomb was desecrated by the Huguenots in 1562, and again in the Revolution, and it is said that only a solitary femur now rests beneath the inscribed slab set in front of the altar.

Roofing first: Despite such indignities, St-Étienne has remained William's triumphal mausoleum. The west front and nave are remarkable for their restrained decor and exquisite sense of proportion, while the sexpartite vaulting that roofs the latter, from the first half of the 12th century, is one of the earliest examples in Europe. In the next century Gothic spires were added to the towers and the choir and east end built.

The abbey buildings to the south of St-Étienne now house Caen's **Hôtel de Ville**. Their entrance and most prestigious facade are in the Esplanade Louvel, which can be reached by turning left along Rue Duc Rollon after leaving the church. Skirting round the abbey, you meet the small but diverting **Musée d'Initiation à la Nature**, housed in its old bakery. This offers a concise guide

to the Normandy countryside, with aromatic gardens, a *chemin géologique* and displays of stuffed birds and animals.

Guided tours of the **Hôtel de Ville** (daily at 9.30 and 11am, 2.30 and 4pm only) allow a limited inspection of its monastic chambers and cloister. Designed in 1704 and completed 60 years later, the abbey buildings were turned into a school by Napoleon in 1802. Most of the rooms, which have splendid wood-panelling and furnishings, serve civic purposes: the chapter house is a registry office, the refectory a reception hall. In the former sacristy is a small display of the enormous lace head-dresses (*coiffes*) which ladies wore in the last century.

A separate building, the 14th-century **Salle des Gardes**, was where the abbot received his guests. After its restoration in 1974, the results of the excavations were set under glass. Here, as if you were looking through the window-panes of history, you can gaze on the walls of the Gallo-Roman port of Cadomus, and at the 3,000-year-old skeleton of a young woman, one of Caen's earliest citizens.

William the Conqueror and his Abbaye-aux-Hommes.

THE CAEN MEMORIAL

On the northwestern outskirts of Caen stands a smooth, monolithic building, split in two by a rough-hewn fissure marking its entrance. Surrounded by well-trimmed lawns and fluttering flags, it might be the flashy HQ of a multinational software company – until you read the uncompromising text carved in its facade. *La Douleur m'a brisée, la Fraternité m'a relevée, de ma blessure a jailli un fleuve de Liberté.* (Pain broke me, Brotherhood lifted me up, from my wounds sprang a river of Liberty.)

Composed by a citizen of Caen in tribute to the Allied forces that liberated the city, these words herald the forceful world of Mémorial, a war museum dedicated to the pursuit of peace. Opened by François Mitterrand on 6 June 1988, it differs spectacularly from the D-Day museums found elsewhere in Normandy.

Built on three levels, Mémorial uses a barrage of audio-visual techniques to set the Battle of Normandy into the context of World War II, with thematic links to previous and subsequent international conflicts. Shot through with symbolism, its centrepiece is a walk-down spiral gallery chronicling our century's descent into war, from the failure of the peace that followed World War II to small screens proffering multiple Nuremberg rallies. Darkened rooms evoke the dark years of Occupation, wide spaces mirror the world-widening of the conflict in 1942.

Three "spectacles" supplement this historical expedition (if you are pushed for time, see these first). First a film montage, using both real and fictional footage, vividly recounts the events of D-Day as simultaneously experienced by both the Allied and German forces. A series of illuminated maps then outlines the subsequent progress of the war. A second film, *Hope*, concludes with images of continuing conflict and idealistic calls for world peace. This enduring aspiration is picked up in a separate gallery, housed in a former German bunker, that honours Nobel Peace Prize winners.

Mémorial has its critics: some see it as bumptious and narcissistically hi-tech, a slickly-marketed piece of civic aggrandisement engineered by Caen's mayor, Jean-Marie Girault. How can a museum promote peace without sensationalising the achievements of war? Is it "Un Musée pour la Paix", or just a hypermarket selling history to clipboard-wielding schoolchildren who come only to test its efficacy as an echo chamber?

Whatever its failings, Mémorial's chosen subject is too serious to be ignored, and its displays undoubtedly prick the emotions. You may not be moved to start a pacifist petition, but something will linger – a photograph of Russian Jews being hung, a child's boot from Auschwitz, film from Stalingrad. After Mémorial, D-Day is never quite the same – particularly if your visit coincides with one of the groups of veterans that frequently tour the museum. Sporting berets and regimental ties, and inevitably grown frail or grey or fat, their presence twists the experience. Some are moved to tears, others to jingoism. "We come every year," they patiently explain to a generation fortunate enough to have never known war. "Those that can. It's a pilgrimage." ■

Mémorial is on the Caen ring-road (N13), to the west of its junction with the D7. By bus take a no. 17 from the Place Courtonne.

Nations united in peace.

THE D-DAY BEACHES AND BAYEUX

To the men in marketing, the coast of Calvados between the mouths of the rivers Orne and Vire is known as the **Côte de Nacre**, the Mother-of-Pearl Coast. For most visitors it is, and always will be, simply the **D-Day Beaches**. The events of 5–6 June 1944, when 135,000 troops landed on this embattled shore as part of **Operation Overlord**, have irrepressibly dented what would otherwise be an undemanding string of seaside resorts and quiet ports devoted to harvesting its excellent shellfish.

Half a century on, the Côte de Nacre bristles with an absorbing legacy of fortifications, memorials, museums and military cemeteries that stand at ease amid the beach hotels, aquaria and mini-golf courses of what has become a popular summer holiday destination – more subdued than the queenly resorts of Cabourg and Deauville to the east, but still graced by fine stretches of sand, breezy cliffs and postcard-picturesque fishing harbours.

With the development of **Ouistreham** as a cross-Channel ferry port in 1986, new roads, hotels and hypermarkets have sprung up around the Orne estuary. The Caen canal, constructed in the mid-19th century to link the city to the sea, runs parallel to this river. Now deepened to take ships of up to 30,000 tonnes, it is spanned near the town of **Bénouville** by the **Pegasus Bridge**.

Tour of the beaches: The D-Day landing beaches stretch the length of Calvados's great sandy shoreline as far, in the east, as Cabourg and the Côte Fleurie coast. To the west they spill into the Cotentin where the American forces landed on Utah Beach (*see page 305*). Inland at St-Mère-Église is **Milestone 0**, the start of the **Liberty Highway**, which runs, via the 0-km marker on Utah Beach, 711 miles (1,145 km) to Bartogne in Belgium, with markers every kilometre.

Finding your way around the beaches is made easy because of the enormous continued interest in the events of D-Day, helped by popular museums and well-kept monuments.

The Pegasus Bridge, at the eastern end of the beaches, was an early objective in the campaign to establish an eastern foothold on French soil, and is a natural starting point for a tour of the D-Day beaches. Just after midnight on 6 June 1944, gliders and paratroopers of the British 6th Airborne Division (whose insignia is a flying horse) landed in the nearby fields and quickly secured the bridge. The Café Gondrée, at its western end, was the first French house to be liberated, and is today an affectionate port-of-call for returning veterans. Next door the **Musée des Troupes Aéro-portées** (Airborne Troops Museum) recalls the events of that night.

On the east bank of the Orne two associated sights are worth a detour (D514) and are typical of how, in this not forgotten corner of Normandy, the glory and the price of the Allied landings often lie side by side. In the village of **Ranville** the British and Commonwealth war cemetery contains 2,536

eceding ges: sand chts ply ah Beach. ft, Gold each near romanches. ght, the 0-n marker on e Liberty ghway that etches to lgium.

dead, including that of Lt. Den Brotheridge, the first Allied soldier killed in the invasion. Neat lawns, rows of white headstones and a parish church built in the Norman style from soft-toned Caen stone paint a very English scene.

If one of the contemplative pleasures of touring the D-Day beaches is to compare the different styles with which nations choose to honour their dead, another is to try to imagine the ferocious dramas that took place around what are now dull and twisted lumps of concrete.

Just beyond **Sallenelles** (a village which is apparently still living in the 1940s) are the remnants of the **Merville battery**, a heavily armed brick in the Atlantic Wall. Capturing it proved a costly affair – 70 men were lost, and its guns turned out to be not as powerful as believed. Today the battery resembles a mid-20th century tumulus: cows and horses graze nonchalantly beside its casements, while a small **museum** struggles to be an *aide-mémoire*.

West of Pegasus Bridge, the D514 follows the shore for the length of the Côte de Nacre, with a well-signposted **Circuit de Débarquement** indicating the beaches, memorials and museums associated with, as the French know it, J-Jour. The first three landing beaches, lying between Ouistreham and Port-en-Bessin, were given the code-names **Sword**, **Juno** and **Gold** and are where the British and Canadian troops disembarked.

Many of the resorts along the coast here were re-built after the war, paying homage to their liberators with street names such as Rue de Southampton and Avenue de Amiral Mountbatten, while the village of Colleville re-named itself **Colleville-Montgomery**.

Even today memorials are being added to town centres, and new museums opened to honour a particular troop division or action. At the same time seaside life goes on: some visitors come to **Courseulles-sur-Mer** to see the Sherman tank dragged out of the sea in 1971 to decorate its seafront, others to enjoy the best oysters in Normandy.

Washed-up port: West of this resort the mock-Austrian villas and casinos give way to campsites and wheatfields as the land rises to a coastline indented with cliffs and bays. Near the village of **St-Côme** a windy viewpoint overlooks the port of **Arromanches-les-Bains** – the best place to survey the startling remains of the ingenious artificial port towed across the Channel as part of the invasion force.

One of the pioneering achievements of D-Day, the **Mulberry harbour** was built by sinking 146 caissons (hollow rectangular concrete boxes) to form a semi-circular harbour wall, with further protection from a breakwater of scuttled

Washed-up Mulberry caisson at Arromanches

ships behind. Floating piers and pontoons, which could rise and fall with the tide, were used to create 10 miles (16 km) of waterborne roads over which vehicles and equipment could be driven ashore. The **Musée du Débarquement** in Arromanches has photographs and Admiralty film of "Port Winston" in action, complete with barrage balloons, battleships and tanks rolling ashore.

American beaches: A short drive westwards, at **Longues-sur-Mer**, the D104 leads seaward to the stubborn remains of the Longues battery. Here, four well-preserved casemates, some still armed with guns, crown the cliffs. West of the fishing port of **Port-en-Bessin** lies **Omaha Beach**, which, along with **Utah Beach** on the eastern Cotentin Peninsula, was where the US troops made their landings. Another Mulberry harbour was established here but destroyed on 19 June 1944 by storms.

The heaviest casualties of D-Day were incurred at Omaha, and the **American cemetery** at **Colleville-sur-Mer** overlooks the cliffs and beach where much of the fighting took place. The Americans repatriated many of their dead, but the cemetery, which is spread over a 172-acre (70-hectare) site, nevertheless contains 9,386 burials. At the entrance a Time Capsule dedicated to General Eisenhower has been buried, which contains reports of D-Day landings. It will be opened on 6 June 2044. Within the cemetery, a semi-circular memorial is decorated with maps detailing the developments of the war and a soaring bronze statue representing the Spirit of American Youth.

Behind this memorial a Garden of the Missing records the names of those whose bodies were unidentified or lost at sea: David Mahan, a pharmacist's mate from Texas, Robert E. Bonnesen, a radioman from Iowa, Ed Hopkins, water tender 3rd Class, from New York... Towards the sea a viewpoint looks down on the sands where the fighting occurred, while to the west grids of white crosses and Stars of David are laid out with tight-lipped precision on an immaculate carpet of grass, a visual correlative of infinity.

A short way inland (D517) the village of **Formigny** was the scene of another famous battle for Normandy: the final conflict of the Hundred Years' War. Here, on 18 April 1450, the French finally ousted the English from their country. While the early triumphs of the English troops were won by devastatingly acurate use of the long-bow, it was the French cannon that finally expelled the occupiers.

The most telling memorial to the fighting that took place along the Côte de Nacre on D-Day can be found at **Pointe du Hoc**, a headland 7½ miles (12 km)

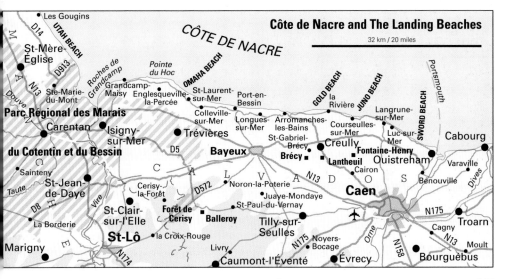

Côte de Nacre and The Landing Beaches

32 km / 20 miles

further west. The ground remains emphatically pockmarked with bomb craters, and the ruined bunkers have been left much as they were after US 2nd Rangers stormed the cliffs to destroy a six-gun battery positioned here. The **Musée des Rangers** in the nearby fishing port of **Grandcamp-Maisy** commemorates their achievement.

A short drive south at **La Cambe** (D113), you can see the quite different way with which the Germans, with restrictions imposed by the French, buried their dead. Here 21,160 soldiers lie beneath rows of horizontal headstones, grouped around a central funereal mound. The graves are shadowed by oak trees and sets of symbolic black stone crosses.

The Teutonic melancholy of La Cambe is a marked contrast to the stiff-lipped formality of the American cemetery at Colleville-sur-Mer, or the chin-up epitaphs that distinguish the graves of the British. Anyone whose interest in war cemeteries is aroused by the D-Day beaches should also seek out one more:

the German mausoleum at **Mont d'Huisnes**, just south of Mont-St-Michel. Here 11,887 dead are buried in a concrete circle of graves, stacked like mailboxes six bodies high. It is the grimmest statement of the price of war you could find.

The inland Bessin: Inland from the Côte de Nacre lies an undulating plateau of land known as the **Bessin**. Its clay soil gives rise to a lush pastureland famous for its dairy products, and the brand name of **Isigny-sur-Mer**, an otherwise insignificant market town at its western end, is now a familiar sight within Europe's fridges. This is also, according to the EuroDisney publicity machine, where the family of its founder comes from: the Disneys were "d'Isigny".

The Bessin countryside is peaceful, with enough woodland, châteaux and idiosyncratic museums to provide a useful refuge from the hullabaloo of the war. The **Forêt de Cérisy**, straddling the border with the Manche *département*, is a remnant of the medieval beech forest that once surrounded the village of

The German cemetery at La Cambe.

Cérisy-la-Forêt. A Benedictine abbey dedicated to St-Vigor was founded here in the 11th century by William the Conqueror's father, Robert the Magnificent. Though the abbey is no longer there, its huge restored church is one of the finest in Normandy, standing out like a beacon in the quiet countryside.

To the northeast three traditional Bessin industries are celebrated in the villages of **Le Molay-Littry** and **Noron-la-Poterie**. In the first, the **Musée de la Mine** is devoted to a coal mine that operated here for two centuries following the discovery of the fuel in 1741.

Nearby the **Moulin de Marcy** is a restored 19th-century flour mill and farm. Further east, Noron-la-Poterie has been producing *grès au sel* (salt glaze pottery) since the 13th century. Modern examples, including cider pitchers, are sold in the village's shops and studios.

At the eastern end of the Forêt de Cérisy, the **Château de Balleroy** is the first recorded extravagance to be designed, in 1626, by François Mansart. Then 28 years old, the architect was later guilty of working on the Château de Blois. Balleroy and its attendant village is best approached along the road from Castillon (D73). Behind the château's stately exterior lie richly decorated salons that have survived since the late 17th century. In the 1970s the château was bought by the late Malcolm Forbes, a multi-millionaire publishing magnate and thrill-seeker who created a **Musée des Ballons** (Hot Air Balloon Museum) in its outbuildings.

Mansart is also thought to be responsible for the enjoyable 17th-century formal gardens that adjoin the **Château de Brécy**, to the east of Bayeux. The nearby **St-Gabriel-Brécy priory** is a cultural centre and has attractive gardens. The château lies just off the D82 that runs southwest from **Creully**, an attractive town built above the Seulles valley. In June 1944 a makeshift BBC studio was rigged up in one of the towers of Creully's Mairie, from where news of the Battle of Normandy was broadcast.

In the nearby **Château de Creullet**, which is closed to the public, Field-

THE BAYEUX TAPESTRY

In 1476 an inventory of Bayeux cathedral noted that amongst its possessions was "a very long and very narrow strip of linen, embroidered with figures and inscriptions representing the Conquest of England, which is hung round the nave of the church on the Feast of Relics and throughout the Octave".

Often referred to in France as the "Tapisserie de la Reine Mathilde" (Queen Matilda's Tapestry), this 230-ft (70-metre) church hanging should, strictly speaking, be called "Bishop Odo's Woollen Embroidery". If the historians have got it right – and every now again someone pops up to claim the whole thing is a fake – then it was Odo, bishop of Bayeux and half-brother of William, who, perhaps as early as 1067, commissioned English women from Kent to embroider a length of linen with scenes recounting the story of 1066 and all that.

Odo is a prominent character in this narrative, and it may be that the Bayeux Tapestry was specifically created for the consecration of his cathedral in 1077. The

pivotal act in the story (Scene 23), where England's King Harold swears allegiance to William's cause upon holy relics, is set in Bayeux. Guillaume de Poitiers' chronicle says it took place in Bonneville-sur-Touques.

Later we see Episcopus Odo supervising the building of the invasion fleet, and blessing the troops' food and wine. Forbidden by the scriptures to draw blood with a sword, he charges through the Battle of Hastings wielding a club. The bellicose bishop was well rewarded for his participation – created duke of Kent, with the port of Dover as booty. By 1086, as the Domesday Book records, he was the largest landowner in England after William.

But was Odo merely the tapestry's patron, or is he the creative genius behind its story, so subtly woven with economies of truth, so coolly didactic? Of the many pleasures this 11th-century comic strip offers modern eyes, one of the most engaging is the spectacle of seeing history in the making – literally being fabricated.

Its creators omit to tell us, for example, how William's fleet was forced east by storms from the mouth of the Dives to the Somme estuary; or of Harold's victory in Scotland, and how his battle-weary troops marched 250 miles (402 km) south in 12 days. Instead everything is directed towards the big moral lesson that justifies the Conquest – Harold broke his oath, and suffered the consequences.

The value of this cartoon as propaganda was not lost on Napoleon, who in 1803 had it put on display in Paris in an attempt to drum up support for a repeat invasion of England. Most likely its viewers were, as we are today, captivated more by its minutiae than its message. We marvel at a *petit* Mont-St-Michel and Halley's Comet, note the stubble on the chin of Edward's doctor, watch the jackalish corpse-robbers, and wonder how they knew about shish-kebabs.

Though generally seen as an historical document, the Bayeux Tapestry is equally a great work of art and has an inherent universality. Scene 47, where a woman and child stand by as William's troops torch their home, provides an emblematic portrait of the refugee. And somehow, even though he is not on their Bayeux Trail questionnaires, schoolkids always find the man in the margin with the sword-sized penis. ■

Harold of England is knighted by Duke William.

Marshal Montgomery parked his straw-camouflaged caravan, where he entertained dignatories such as Winston Churchill, Field-Marshal Smuts and King Edward VI.

Châteauholics should also pay a visit to **Fontaine-Henry** 3 miles (5 km) to the east. Here the remains of a 13th-century castle have been capped with splendid Renaissance buildings that are notorious for their steep roofs, which in the northern wing rise taller than the walls that support them.

Popular centre: The capital of the Bessin is **Bayeux** (population: 15,250), a city that attracts hordes of visitors but which somehow maintains its sanity. Perhaps it has grown used to occupation, having been variously overrun by Romans, Bretons and Saxons before becoming one of the first towns to be colonised by the Vikings – Norse was spoken here as late as the 11th century.

In this century Bayeux was occupied by German forces, but was fortunate to be the first French city liberated by the Allies. As a consequence it was spared the destruction wrought elsewhere, and has an agreeable nucleus of historic buildings located to the south of its central thoroughfare, Rue St-Martin. This runs into the pedestrianised Rue St-Jean further east, from where waterside paths follow the course of the Aure.

Since 1983 the famous **Tapestry** (*see facing page*) has been displayed in the **Centre Guillaume-le-Conquérant**, which occupies a former seminary, built in 1693, in the Rue Nesmond. Today *la tapisserie* resides, like a Garboesque recluse, in a dimly-lit, bullet-proof glassed gallery. A guided commentary is available on headphones, though this rather races along and it is advisable to spend a preliminary hour or so in the Centre's upper floors, where a cinema and exhibitions set out the background to the tapestry.

To the northwest of the seminary rises Bayeux's **Cathédrale Notre-Dame**. Of the original church begun in the 1040s and completed by Bishop Odo in 1077, only the crypt and parts of its west towers survive. The bulk of the stone-

work is Gothic, though the central tower was added in the 15th century and capped with a 19th-century dome that has attracted phenomenal disapproval from critics. Look out, too, for the small house that a hermit had built on the roof. The work of successive centuries is clearly visible in the interior too, where the decorated arches of the Romanesque nave are surmounted by a 13th-century clerestory and vaulting – though the eye is inevitably caught first by the pulpit, installed in 1787 and inspired by an *île flottante*. The crypt is decorated with delightful Gothic frescoes of angels playing musical instruments.

On the north side of the cathedral, its entrance shaded by a magnificent 200-year-old plane tree in the Place de la Liberté, is the **Musée Baron-Gérard**. Cool, dark and soothingly crowd-free, this former Bishop's Palace now houses a collection of fine art, lace, porcelain and furniture gathered in the 19th century by Baron Henri-Alexandre Gérard, whose undiscriminating tastes led him to acquire anything from local porcelain and lace, to a portrait of romping nymphs and a still-life of fried eggs.

Between the 17th and 19th centuries Bayeux became a centre of lacemaking – by 1860 there were 10,000 workers in the area. The Musée Baron-Gérard has a room devoted to examples of the sooty cobwebs worn by women of that time, while on the south side of the cathedral an **Atelier de Dentelle** (Lacemaking School) currently teaches the craft to 25 students. The school is part of the 18th-century Hôtel du Doyen, which also houses the **Musée d'Art Religieux**, containing religious treasures from the cathedral. One room re-creates the scene in which the 15-year-old St Thérèse asks the bishop of Bayeux for permission to enter a convent.

Celebrated leader: A short walk southwest, along Rue des Chanoines, is **Le Mémorial du Général de Gaulle**. This museum celebrates the life of the French political leader, who was rapturously welcomed into the city on 14 June 1944. To the west is a tree-lined park, the Place Charles de Gaulle, where a column celebrates the victorious speech he made that day.

Further south Rue St-Loup leads into Boulevard Fabian Ware, part of the city's ring-road, with the **Musée Mémorial de la Bataille de Normandie** to the right. This provides a thorough account of the war in Normandy with the aid of maps, black-and-white photos, newspaper front pages and enough weapons, vehicles and military equipment to mount a *coup d'état*. Its introductory film compilation, using newsreels of the day, is one of the best of its kind to be found anywhere.

A little further along Boulevard Fabian Ware is the largest World War II **British and Commonwealth War Cemetery** in France. It contains 4,648 graves, including soldiers from Canada, South Africa and Australia. Across the road a **Memorial to the Missing** bears 1,805 names, and a Latin epitaph uniting the two great historic events that collide at Bayeux: *Nos a Guilielmo Victi Victoris Patriam Liberavimus* (We, once conquered by William, have set free the Conqueror's land).

Left, Bayeux cathedral. Right, stilted medieval pageant in the town.

DEAUVILLE AND THE CÔTE FLEURIE

The Côte Fleurie is the high spot of Normandy's seaside. Here are the Sahara-size beaches, the vast villas and apartments and the dazzling lights of casino and grand-hotel chandeliers – even though some may have seen more glorious days.

As well as the poodles and poseurs, the gourmands and the smart yachts, there are camp-sites and sand yachts and shops selling large shrimp nets to trawl the shallow shore. Between sunshine and showers is a brief glittering social season in Deauville, while little Honfleur, pretty as a jigsaw picture, cannot help attracting weekend visitors all the year round.

The coast proper, in the *département* of Calvados, lies between Cabourg and Honfleur, a 25-mile (40-km) stretch of the D513. At two points it rises up from the shore into unexpectedly rustic corniches, above the Falaise des Vaches Noires rocks between Houlgate and Villers-sur-Mer, and along the Côte de Grâce above Honfleur, once a thriving port, which still has the makings of an old maritime town.

On the other hand Dives-sur-Mer and Touques, the other two medieval ports on the coast named after the rivers on which they stand, have silted up and been left high and dry behind the 19th and 20th-century resorts which have grown up on their extended estuaries.

Rivers also provide the coast's western and eastern boundaries: to the west, the Orne arrives from Caen and the Suisse Normande through the marshland beside the Route du Marais; to the east the Seine's last meanders are contained inside the reclaimed Parc Régional de Brotonne, and soon a new bridge will span it, connecting the coast to Le Havre and the Alabaster Coast beyond. Inland are the rolling green hills of the Pays d'Auge.

Crossing from Caen: Easily approached, the coast is shadowed by the A13 Rouen–Caen motorway. From the east, the new Pont de Normandie will bring visitors from Le Havre. Coming from Caen's ferry port of Ouistreham the D514 slips across the Orne and passes through **Sallenelles,** a centre for wildlife with a small **Natural History museum.** Inland the lanes wander through the marshes and the Route du Marais, a pleasant backwater not quite as flat as it sounds, with *gîtes* and manor farms selling their products. Centre for this district is **Troarn,** on the high ground behind where a small, boarded-up Gothic **priory of St Martin's** sits on the edge of a modern estate.

On the coast **Merville-Franceville** heralds the Côte Fleurie. Its modern buildings and camp-sites are strung out along a great desert of a beach and its singular attractions are a couple of military sites. On the west end of its seafront is an 18th-century redoubt built in the style of the great French military architect Vauban. Just inland, among the fields, is the 40-acre (16-hectare) German Merville battery (*see page 240*).

Past modern-day bunkers in the sand dunes of the local golf course, the road

Preceding pages: going into the marina at Deauville. Left, the Vieux Bassin in Honfleur. Right, Sunday market, Dives-sur-Mer.

continues to **L'Home** where a promenade leads towards the Promenade Marcel Proust at **Cabourg**. From 1907 the writer spent his summer holidays at the resort's house of hedonism, the Grand Hotel, a great cream mansion which dominates the main square. Its marbled, pillared hall and chandelier-dripping lounges should be visited even if only for a cup of coffee, while serious gastronomers may head for the hotel's Balbec restaurant looking over the sea, which Proust called "the aquarium".

Proust's association with the place, which is now run by Pullman International Hotels, is further milked in the Marcel Proust suite, room 414, charging 1,200 francs a night. During the season the resort awards a Marcel Proust literary prize.

Cabourg, a one-shopping-street town, has fine examples of late 19th- and early 20th-century châteaux-on-sea architecture, incorporating steep gables, slate roofs, tall chimneys and the fanciest finials you can find. But the glamour has begun to fade, and next door to the Grand Hotel the casino, dulled by sea salt and flaking in the wind, has been undergoing restoration.

Conqueror's port: Behind Cabourg, on the far side of the River Dives, is **Dives-sur-Mer,** which is now s*ur terre* with no sign that it ever was a port, let alone the spot where William the Conqueror with his barons and prelates and soldiers from all over Gaul set sail, via St-Valéry-sur-Somme, on 12 September 1066. For a month the fleet of open boats were fitted out in the port, among them *Mora*, Matilda's gift to William. In 1861 Arcisse de Caumont, the well-known archaeologist from Caen, had the names of William's heroic fellow knights inscribed on a plaque and placed inside the **church of Notre-Dame**, which was built as a thanksgiving by William in 1067.

The history of Dives's large church is familiar on this coast where religious relics were washed ashore with miraculous regularity in the 10th and 11th centuries. Sixty-six years before William arrived a crucifix appeared on the beach

William the Conqueror's tourist village in Dives.

and a shrine was made in a chapel under the eye of the abbey at Troarn. It became a centre of pilgrimage until the crucifix was destroyed in 1562 during the Wars of Religion. Today, with flying gargoyles characteristic of the 14th–15th-century local Gothic churches, it has a tumbledown air, and sparrows call out from its fan-vaulted aisles.

Opposite the church is the Michel Dupont *chocolatier* with a *salon de thé* and the road to the right leads to the old market square and a fine wooden market hall, **Les Halles**. It dates from the foundation of the town market in 1554, and was entirely rebuilt after the war. The square's other old building is the **Lieutenance**, residency of the duke of Falaise, which was restored in 1920 when the rest of the buildings in the square were torn down.

A further collection of ancient buildings in this small town is the **Village d'Art de Guillaume le Conquérant**, a tourist trap which for three centuries served as the Auberge de l'Epée Royale, the *relais de poste* on the coast road

from Rouen to Caen. This coaching inn was renamed in the 19th century, statuary was imported for its courtyards and it is now a pleasant spot to stroll through.

Dives's port today lies around a collection of small fishing boats on the quay beside the river, left roped to the wall when the tide goes out. On sale are live pink crabs and grey shrimps and mussels by the litre, freshly caught the previous night.

Within a mile (2 km) the River Dives reaches the sea at **Houlgate**, and on the beach here M. de Caumont erected a pillar to commemorate William's departure. Behind it the Chemin de la Cascade leads through a pretty little valley of thatched houses topped by irises, pigeon lofts and a watermill. But otherwise Houlgate is another resort of classic Norman château architecture, of timber balconies, rafters and balustrades, concave roofs, dormers, domes and witches'-hat towers.

Houlgate's Grand Hotel, a mammoth Second-Empire building in the railway-station style (complete with clock) has

now been converted into apartments, though the casino on the beach in front of it still operates a bar, cinema and the Manhattan disco.

The resort is attractively sited against a hillside, which tumbles into the sea over a pile of rocks called **Les Vaches Noires** because they looked to somebody like a herd of black cows. It is possible to walk over these rocks to the town of **Villers-sur-Mer**, but only, be warned, at low tide. Otherwise the road climbs back over the hills, reaching a panorama point with a *table d'orientation* which signposts the landfalls visible westwards (Arromanches) and north-northeast (Cap de l'Havre and, invisibly, Canterbury beyond).

There have been good fossil finds on this part of the beach, and a small collection of them is housed on the second floor **Museum of Palaeontology** in the Maison des Jeunes behind the market in Villers-sur-Mer. This is another family resort, with more of a feeling of a real town. Activity is centred around the popular seafront seafood café and restaurant, Mermoz. The casino here is modern, ugly, fully functional, and open until the small hours every weekend. Beyond Villers are a couple of resorts tucked into the hills, **Blonville-sur-Mer** and **Bénerville-sur-Mer**.

Up behind Bénerville is **Tourgeville,** in the middle of a short but very scenic route. The small town has a cluster of thatched, half-timbered houses and there is a wonderful view down across the bright lights of Deauville. British and German fallen lie side by side in the cemetery here.

Although he set sail from Dives, William and Conqueror had his principal residence on this coast near **Touques** on the parallel river of the same name. Above the port, at **Bonneville**, he had a better command of the coast. There is not much left of the chalk-white walls and towers: just part of the outer wall, the *donjon* and the stumps of five towers. An underground passage leads from the old gate to the river. There is an adjoining estate and it is all privately owned, with limited opening hours,

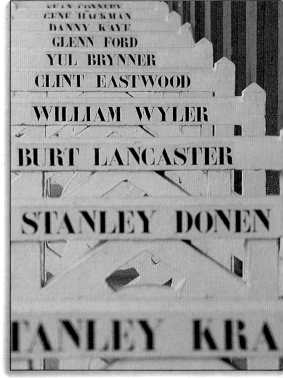

Deauville beach brollies and huts named after the stars.

which if missed can be compensated for by a fine view over the Touques valley.

Touques itself is a plain little town, and many young people move here from the coast because property is cheaper. It has two good churches: **St-Pierre**, from the 11th century and now deconsecrated, and 12th-century **St-Thomas**, named after its founder, the Archbishop of Canterbury. There is a statue of him in his mitre and crosier, but the interior is rather empty and dull. On the short road between here and Trouville is a large pottery making traditional Normandy glazed earthenware.

The high life: The Côte Fleurie's two best-known resorts of **Trouville** and **Deauville** lie each side of the Touque estuary, and each has a quite different flavour, which is easy to detect after only a few hours' visit. Deauville is the showcase: its casino the most glittering, its hotels most grand, its restaurants and cafés most expensive. When people are in Deauville, they are on parade, along the famous boardwalk, the *planches,* or cruising the streets in their spotless

motors. In Trouville real life enters in. This is where everyone runs to, to eat and to drink and be themselves, to have a bowl of *moules frites* at Les Vapeurs or the Central after the casinos are closed: as long as there is a light on, the restaurants boast, you will be served.

Trouville started it all. The small oyster-fishing village on the estuary of the silted-up Touques attracted artists in the 1830s, and the fashionable soon followed, as did the habit of bathing and the railway from Paris. On the west bank, under a consortium headed by the duc de Mornay and advised by Dr Oliffe, the British Ambassador to Paris, the marshes were drained and an entirely new town, Deauville, was put in place. As in contemporary England where the Prince of Wales took his court and camp followers down to Brighton, so in France Emperor Napoleon III and the Empress Eugénie favoured these ritzy Channel resorts.

Deauville, with two marinas, is still a much smarter place, but Trouville's geography gives it a trump card. Its

liveliest street, Boulevard Fernand Mourneaux which runs beside the river, faces south: when the sun is shining, it shines on it all day. Life can be lived *en plein air* all the year round and some restaurants have gas-lamp heaters beside their pavement tables so that even in January people can sit outside. Regulars from Deauville will usually cross the Pont des Belges to Trouville when they want to go out to eat.

Activity centres on the daily **fish market,** built in 1935 on the site of former markets, and on Wednesdays and Sundays a regular market stretches the length of the quay. Two landmarks are unmissable: the 1912 **town hall** and the **casino**, which begins the boardwalk along the shore to the north, towards the aquarium, one of the largest in the country, and the yacht club. The older streets and shopping lanes are down around this end of the town.

Among many mansions beyond it, on the way out to Honfleur, is **Villa Montebello** (1865), which houses the town **museum**. Paintings by Isabey, Huet and Charles Mozin, who was the first French painter, show what they saw, revealing to us how it has changed. Among them is a vast canvas by Mozin of Louis XVI in a gold state carriage, with a company of 200, riding across the sands of what was then Dives-sur-Mer during his royal passage to Cherbourg.

Though not as grand as its neighbour's, Trouville's 1912 **casino** is unimaginably large. It contains a water therapy centre, a gala room and conference halls, cinema, restaurant and of course the gaming rooms, done out in the style of a Louisiana paddle steamer. And still no more than 10 percent of the building is occupied.

The one-armed bandits at Trouville casino pay out less and more often than at Deauville, and both pleasure palaces have to be visited. The **casino** at Deauville is just back from the beach where dinner is expensively served in the pink, knicker-rouched boudoir of Ciro's by immaculate, silent waiters. At night the casino's sumptuous halls and star-spangled chandeliers are a beacon

Trouville's châteaux by the sea.

to the hedonist moths. A government tax is levied for anyone entering the gaming rooms, but there is action to be seen among the one-armed bandits, and in the bar where a roulette wheel spins. Check out, too, the exquisite little theatre, venue for weekend and summer shows, where champagne can be served at the tables in the gods.

The Côte de Grâce: The bright lights are followed by a dramatic dawn on the rural corniche that heads for Honfleur. Here there is typical Pays d'Auge country, of cows in buttercup fields beneath old orchard boughs, with the addition of the Channel waters beneath.

En route is **Villerville**, a small town that tips down precipitous streets to the sea. At **Pennedepie** there is an attractive 12th-century church with a busy interior which includes two alabasters from England.

Shortly beyond it are two high spots worth visiting from Honfleur even if you are only there for half a day. The first is the 17th-century chapel of **Notre-Dame-de-Grâce**, three-quarters of a mile (1 km) from the centre of Honfleur, which gave its name to this coast. This is a delightfully idiosyncractic little building of great vitality, which still attracts pilgrims and votive offerings. The little shop at its side is busy all day.

People also come for the view. From this rural setting, in a glade on the high ground, there is a grand panorama of Le Havre and the Seine estuary which the new **Pont de Normandie** impressively spans. There is also a good view from the terrace of the **Ferme St-Siméon**. In the days when it was a farmhouse all the artists and poets would come to eat and drink and have their say. Today it is ridiculously expensive and it has altered much. Nevertheless, should the temptation arise to have a look around the pretty flower-draped buildings and to take a coffee on the terrace, it should not be resisted.

Honfleur is, without doubt, the jewel of Normandy's coast. Its maritime credentials are impressive, too: it came to prominince in the Hundred Years' War when Charles V fortified it and installed

the Admiral of the Fleet, Jeanne de Vienne, as the town governor. From 1419 to 1450, when **St-Étienne church**, now housing the **Musée de la Marine**, was built it was occupied by the English whose ultimate departure was celebrated with the building of the wonderful wooden **church and belfry of Ste-Catherine**, roofed with chestnut shingles, at the heart of the old town.

Among many discoverers and South-Sea island traders who set sail from Honfleur, was Samuel de Champlain who founded Quebec, and Rabelais' fictitious giant who went in search of Utopia. Shipbuilding flourished and the surrounding salt marshes gave the town a commodity to trade in. Two salt stores with impressive oak roof timbers can be seen in Rue de la Ville. These were put up under Louis XIV's able chief minister, Jean-Baptiste Colbert, who greatly improved the port, adding the **Vieux Bassin** around which the old town is centred today. The **Lieutenance** on the river side of the dock is the former Caen gate and is the only surviving part of the old town wall.

From the old dock and the attractive St Catherine's quay, where the tall, slate-fronted buildings date from the 16th century, nothing is hard to find. A visit to the **Musée Eugène Boudin** is essential. It is housed in the chapel of a former convent where Lady General Aupick, Charles Baudelaire's mother, used to attend Mass. Expanded by various gifts over the years, it now contains a good collection of local paintings apart from a number by Boudin. The pictures by Jongkind, who so inspired Boudin and Monet, are interesting, and a plaque in the Rue de Puits shows where he stayed.

The town is thick with plaques of the famous, among them one for the composer Erik Satie, born in Rue Haute in 1866. André Hambourg, whose work figures prominently in the art museum, is one of a number of contemporary painters still irresistibly drawn to this artists' haven and who may one day be rewarded with a plaque of his own.

Right, the annual Blessing of the Boats at Honfleur, held on Ascension Sunday.

CAMEMBERT AND CALVADOS COUNTRY

Between the Caen Plain and the lower Seine is a rather secretive land, hidden among hills and valleys and forests. It is a rich countryside, full of old orchards and dappled cows, chequerboard manor houses and châteaux and half-timbered farms. It is also the heart of the production area of Normandy's three particular delights – cider, Calvados and cheese – and to help you find your way around the country lanes to the farmyards where regional produce can be sampled and bought, the tourism-conscious local authorities have mapped out a *Route du Cidre*, a *Route du Poire*, a *Route du Fromage* and a *Route du Camembert*.

Two rather separate regions, based on the main stretches of two parallel rivers, are included in this chapter. To the east is the **River Risle** which flows through the *département* of the Eure in a broad valley of meadowlands where the great abbey of Bec-Hellouin flourished. Its two largest towns are Pont-Audemer and, on a tributary further inland, Bernay. Both have a diversity of hotels and make good bases for touring.

To the west, entirely in the *département* of Calvados, is the **Pays d'Auge**, a distinctive region centred on the town of Lisieux and riven by the Touques which flows into the sea between Deauville and Trouville. Rural *gîtes* and *chambres d'hôtes* are seldom far away.

Calvados country: Between Lisieux and the sea, where the A13 autoroute whistles from Rouen to Caen, is the town of **Pont-l'Évêque** which gives its name to one of three Pays d'Auge cheeses. This is a square, soft cheese with a full flavour and it comes in a box. The town has a grand church, **St-Martin**, which has been well restored since the war and has dramatic and effective modern stained-glass windows.

On the N177 just north of the town is the **Père Margloire Calvados distillery and museum**, where you can discover all there is to know about apple brandy and its associated crafts during regular 45-minute tours which include a film show. There is also a model of the *El Calvador*, the Spanish galleon washed ashore in 1588 which gave its name to the *département* and the drink.

Just beyond the museum at **Canapville** is the **Manoir des Évêques**, which until recently was thought to have been one of the original homes of the bishops (*évêques*) of Lisieux. It is certainly grand enough. There are guided afternoon visits in summer around its two 15th-century half-timbered buildings and 13th-century core. To the south of Pont-l'Évêque on the same road, opposite a leisure lake, is the imposing **Château de Betteville** and in a large ancient barn beside it is the **Musée de la Belle Époque de l'Automobile**. Among a collection of 100 cars is a stuninmg blue-and-black Bugatti Petite Royale from 1932 which must have wowed everyone on the seafront at Deauville.

The next turning south on the right, the D580, leads up into the hills of the Pays d'Auge at **Pierrefitte-en-Auge**. *Auge* means a "trough" in both the geographical and farmyard sense, and it

describes the undulating landscape. This little village is approached through a charming motley collection of old farm buildings leading up to a little bistro, Les Deux Tourneux. Its church has excellent 17th-century paintings.

The next community on the D580 is **Saint-Hymer**, made up of only a handful of buildings including a pleasant restaurant and a huge abbey church. Among the large easel paintings strung up on its walls and not improved by the outdoor atmosphere are pictures of St Hymer and St Martin by the 18th-century Rouen artist Jean Restout. There is still a retreat in the grounds of the abbey which dates back to 1067 when it was a dependent of Bec-Hellouin. In the early 18th century the Benedictine monks adopted Jansenism, a severe discipline which became centred here after being outlawed in Paris by Louis XIV.

Rather than submit to Jansenism, the abbey at **Beaumont-en-Auge** just to the north-west, closed its doors and gave itself over to a military academy. Among its pupils was Pierre Simon, a poor local farmer's son, who became one of France's most distinguished astronomers and scientists, president of the French Academy and Marquis de Laplace (1749–1827). A plaque marks his birthplace in Place du Verdun where a statue of the man was erected in 1932 with the help of the Carnegie Peace Foundation. From the end of the square a view over the surrounding fields gives an idea of the height the land has reached. Martins fill the air, and green woodpeckers flash their bright red heads as they flit between trees. Sometimes a buzzard appears overhead.

Seven miles (10 km) west on the main N175 is the roadside town of **Dozule** and just beyond it the D49 picks up the Route du Marais, marshlands that slip down to the sea. Turn left to **Putot-en-Auge,** which has a small church with a fine Romanesque portal and a graveyard of young Allied soldiers who did not live long after D-Day. A couple of miles (2 km) to the south is **Beuvron-en-Auge**, a conservation village with a fine manor, farm products and several

Print-maker in Beaumont-en-Auge.

restaurants. Above it, at **Clermont-en-Auge**, park the car and walk down to the delightful little chapel founded in the 11th century and containing a fine 15th-century wood crucifix. From here, 325 feet (100 metres) up, there is a view over the Touques valley, which in the 19th century supplied Paris with 70 percent of its red meat requirements, and across the Caen Plain to the Normandy Hills.

Famous connections: From Beuvron-en-Auge follow the **Cider Route**, a 25-mile (40-km) trail which wanders happily among these hills, past a number of manors and châteaux, most of which are private and remain closed: **Val de Richer**, home of the great 19th-century statesman François Guizot, built on the Val de Richer abbey where Thomas Beckett was first abbot; **la Roque Beynard** where André Gide was mayor; **Manoir du Champ Versant** at Bonnebosq, now a *gîte*, though occasionally open to the public.

A score of farms in this area have a signpost outside advertising Cru de Cambremer, where cider and often Calvados can be sampled and bought, and a tour of the business offered. **Cambremer** is a town on the south side of these hills and each May producers bring their cider, Calvados, and *pommeau* (a sherry-strength apéritif made of Calvados and apple juice) to an old barn here for tasting. Those that make the grade are accorded a sign outside their establishments. Pays d'Auge *appellation contrôlée* Calvados differs from other Normandy Calvados in that it is made by a double distillation process, rather than by single, continuous distillation. This, the locals believe, marks it out as the real McCoy. A good place to see the huge copper stills in action and for a tour is **Calvados Boulard** at **Coquainville** on the D48 on the eastern side of the Cider Route.

South of Cambremer the road falls away to **Crèvecoeur** where **Le Château de Crèvecoeur** is a collection of old buildings, including a fine pigeon loft, assembled by the Schlumberger brothers, Conrad and Marcel, from Alsace. They were successful mining engineers

Manor at Beuvron-en-Auge.

ST THÉRÈSE OF LISIEUX

Around 100,000 pilgrims a year climb a hill in Lisieux to the basilica of St Thérèse of the Child Jesus or, as she is generally known in the English-speaking world, the Little Flower of Jesus. As a place of pilgrimage, it ranks second in France only to Lourdes, with which it shares not only a reputation for working miracles but also a degree of commercialisation.

The centre of attraction was born in Alençon on 2 January 1873 as Marie-Françoise-Thérèse Martin, the daughter of Louis Martin, a successful watchmaker, and Zelie Guerin, who married after being separately turned down for conventual life. M. Martin informed his bride on their wedding night that he did not intend then or ever to consummate the union, but resolve weakened and the couple in due course had nine children, of whom Thérèse was the youngest. "Nine flowers bloomed in this garden," wrote one of her biographers in the kind of prose characteristic of practically everything written about Thérèse, "of which

four were transplanted to Paradise before their buds had quite unfolded."

The survival of the frail infant Thérèse is the first of the many official or unofficial miracles associated with her. Her mother died when she was four, however, and with that the family moved to Lisieux and a house called Les Buissonnets (The Shrubbery). It was an exceptionally pious household. Thérèse had her own altar, where she prayed daily, and the first word she recognised in print was "heaven", probably because when the family circle read together, the text was either the *Lives of the Saints* or the *Liturgical Year*. Outings with her father were visits to the Blessed Sacrament in various churches, especially the chapel of the Convent of the Carmel. At nine, Thérèse again nearly died, but a vision of Our Lady smiling at the young girl effected an immediate and complete cure. She then wished to enter the convent as a postulant, only to be told she was much too young.

A larger than life marble group in the garden at Les Buissonnets immortalises the day in 1887 when Thérèse, then 13, won her father's backing for what had been a ceaseless but as yet unproductive campaign to enter the Carmel convent before she was 16. He took her on a pilgrimage to Rome, where Pope Leo XIII told her: "You will enter if God wills it." Thérèse accordingly entered the convent as Thérèse de l'Enfant Jesus on 9 April 1888. She was 15. In the normal course of events, the world would have heard no more of Thérèse after the convent gates closed behind her. The happenstance destined to bring millions of pilgrims to Lisieux was an order by the Mother Superior, not a suggestion, that she try her hand at writing. The result was her *Story of a Soul*, subtitled *The Spring-tide Story of a Little White Flower.*

The autobiography clearly strikes a universal chord, although anyone not predisposed towards relentless diminutives — the "little" flower, the "little ball for the Child Jesus to play with", etc – is unlikely to be tempted beyond the first page. Her most famous passage, leaving little scope for indifference, is fusion with Jesus in the form of a wedding invitation.

Racked by consumption, Thérèse died at 25. Normandy led a canonisation campaign which came to fruition in 1925. **Lisieux's famous little ■ saint.**

and there is an exhibition of their work, as well as a flock of black mop-haired Crèvecoeur chickens saved from extinction. Trout fishing is also available.

Pilgrim's rest: Ten miles (17 km) due east of Crèvecoeur is **Lisieux**, a former Roman provincial capital and the main town of the region, with a population of 26,000. Beside the old **Episcopal Palace** is the fine former **cathedral of St-Pierre**, the earliest Gothic church in Normandy. The town was a German base during the war and was subsequently flattened. Signs of its former architectural attractiveness can be seen in the **Musée de Vieux Lisieux**, 30 Boulevard Louis Pasteur, on the opposite bank of the Touques where several timber-framed houses remain.

The main reason many people come here today is to trace the story and see the shrine of St Thérèse (*see facing page*). A tape in various languages guides visitors through the rooms of her middle-class home, **Les Buissonnet**, and a room of memorabilia can be visited beside the **Carmelite convent** where she lived from the age of 15 until her death at 25 in 1897. Above and beyond these, and quite unmissable is her shrine, a vast **basilica** topping 305 ft (93 metres) and reminiscent of Paris's Sacré Coeur. It was begun a year after her canonisation in 1925 and completed in 1954. The neo-Byzantine interior, occasionally embellished with a laser light show, is aesthetically valueless, but it attracts thousands of pilgrims.

Five miles south of Lisieux on the D579, turn left up the D278 to the **Château de St-Germain-de-Livet.** This is a delightful moated manor, settled in the Touques valley beside a church which is popular for weddings. It dates from the 15th century and its chequerboard walls are made not just of limestone and red-brick, but patterned with green glazed bricks as well. Guided tours begin in the guard room, which has 16th-century wall paintings of a tournament, and of John the Baptist. On the first floor are some typical local Pays d'Auge tiles, and some works by the cabinet-making Riesener family,

Below, pilgrims at St Thérèse's basilica. Right, wedding in Lisieux.

former owners who were related to Eugène Delacroix. The 19th-century painter sometimes stayed here and a bedroom contains a yellow canopied bed and other pieces of his furniture.

Two other châteaux lie on the western side of the D579. **Coupesarte** is a beautiful moated manor farm of simple timber infilled with brick. It is privately owned and the grounds are only to the public only on special days. A couple of miles beyond it, near the Aga Khan's stud farm at St Crispin, is the grand 16th-century **Grandchamp-le-Château**, unfortunately not open to the public. Just outside the modern little town of Mézidon-Canon 10 miles (15 km) west on the D47 is the **Château de Canon** approached down an avenue of lime trees. The château's magnificent gardens are laid out with an ornamental pool, statuary and various follies. Outdoor events are put on during the summer, including "nature weekends".

The main town on this western side of the Auge is **St-Pierre-sur-Dives**, just to the south. It is a market town with the largest medieval market hall in all France. Its roof was destroyed in the war but it was subsequently properly rebuilt without nails or screws but with 300,000 chestnut pegs. On Mondays, it is full of farm produce and the squawk of fowl. The market extends over several acres of adjacent dusty wasteland.

The **Halle aux Grains**, some 280 ft (85 metres) long and 70 ft (21 metres) wide, was built in the 13th century by the monks of the **Abbaye de St-Pierre-sur-Dives**, whose church, consecrated under William the Conqueror, survives to dominate the town. Crossing its nave is a sundial rod with zodiac signs embedded in the floor. The best way to see its cloisters and part of the former abbey is to visit the **Musée du Conservatoire des Techniques Fromagères Traditionnelles de Normandie**. Though not the best cheese museum, it gives a picture of the local business in which St-Pierre plays its part, as the prime producer of the boxes the cheeses come in.

On the D911 just northeast of St-Pierre is **Vieux Pont**, where another

Weekly livestock auction in the market town of St-Pierre-sur-Dives.

fine but less well known Normandy cheese comes from. Seek it out at the cheesemaker's Michel Touzé.

Before diving off in search of the cheeses, church connoisseurs might want to take a brief detour 8 miles (12 km) south down the D90 past **Barou-en-Auge** and **Norrey-en-Auge**. The sandstone farms in this part of the Auge take on a golden, Cotswold colour. At Barou-en-Auge the church has lost half its nave, and a side chapel has a primitive black skull-and-crossbone frieze. The church at Norrey-en-Auge is also primitive with wall paintings in need of restoration. The herringbone, or *opus spicatum,* stonework pattern dates the church to around the 10th century.

Just beyond the D90 turning to these churches is **Vendeuvre** where the château has a collection of what initially looks like dolls' furniture. In fact these miniatures are models made by Normandy furniture-makers prior to building the real things.

Cheese greats: The two other cheese towns of the Pays d'Auge are **Livarot**

Below, the Camembert museum, Vimoutiers. Right, mother's milk.

and **Vimoutiers**, the centre for Camembert. Livarot has a cheese museum in a small château on the west side of the town where the traditional way of making this circular, pink-crusted local treat is explained in as much detail as is necessary. The **Route du Fromages** which encircles the town takes in **Ste-Foy-de-Montgomery** where Field-Marshal Rommel was driving in June 1944 when he was caught by aircraft fire, and **Lisores**, a hamlet put on the map by Fernand Léger (1881–1955), the Cubist painter of bright solid shapes, who was born not far away in Argentan. He had an isolated emerald patch of a farm down a lane from Lisores, and in a barn with an outside wall showing one of his pictures in coloured tiles is an exhibition of his works,

Vimoutiers to the south has set itself up as the capital of one of France's most famous cheeses, Camembert, though the village of **Camembert** itself lies just to the west. The town has the best **cheese museum** in the region and a statue to farmer's wife Marie Harell, credited as

having brought this cheese to the attention of a grateful world after getting the recipe from a priest from Brie whom she sheltered during the Revolution.

Marie Harel lived on a farm overlooking Camembert (population: 185) where a modern exhibition hall celebrates her success. Though the Camembert *appellation* is now strictly controlled, the only two farms in Camembert still making this cheese by the traditional method fail to qualify. But they are worth seeking out, just over a mile (3 km) further west on the D246. The Durands' pretty Herronière farm is on the right, and almost opposite is Michel Delorme at Tordouet: produce can be bought at both.

The Risle valley: The solitude of the countryside continues over to the east, in truly rural little towns such as **Orbec**. The exemplary Norman Renaissance **Vieux Manoir** in the main street has 1563 carved on a lintel and its three storeys contain the Municipal Museum devoted to Orbec, once one of Normandy's largest manorial estates. On the right, heading towards the giant 16th-century north tower of the **Notre Dame church**, where unexpected bright dragons grip the nave's hammer beams in their teeth, is the solid stone facade of the 17th-century **Hôtel de Croissy** where Claude Debussy composed *Jardin sous la Pluie* in 1895.

Eleven miles (18 km) northeast of Orbec, is **Bernay**, only a small town of 11,000, but after the countryside it seems full of bustle. Among its lively cafés and bars is the Brasserie de la Commerce on the corner of Rue Thiers and Rue Gaston-Follope, a street of old timbered buildings, antique shops and the small **Norman Museum**. Bernay's abbey church was begun by Guglielmo da Volpiano in 1013, but more lively is Ste-Croix, dating from the 14th century and containing statues and tombstones from Bec-Hellouin, a sign that the great abbey is within reach.

Bernay's singular claim to fame is noted in Rue Alexandre behind the church where there is a plaque to the 12th-century poet Alexandre de Bernay.

Irises in a thatched-roof garden.

He wrote his epic *Romance of Alexander* in lines of 12 syllables, establishing the literary form known as Alexandrine.

Bernay lies on the Charentonne, an attractive tributary of the Risle. The D123 follows it eastwards and crosses the Risle at Beaumont-le-Roger. From the edges of the Forêt de Beaumont, the D123 continues eastwards, rising up on to the fertile plain of **Le Neubourg**. The town of the same name is an airy place with a generously wide main street.

Just outside it is **Champ-de-Bataille**, one of the most curious châteaux in the region. The battle site it commemorates was between Rollo and a rival Norman, who slugged it out for supremacy over these lands. It was not until after World War II that the 17th-century château was given to the Harcourt family, descendants of one of Rollo's stalwart knights, in recompense for their Thury-Harcourt home which had been destroyed in the war. Today it is owned by a rich and successful interior designer who has filled it with antiques and spent a not inconsiderable sum restoring the place. The 250 acres (100 hectares) of Le Nôtre's gardens are next on the list.

In fact, the Harcourts did have another ancestral pile nearby, **Harcourt Château**, a proper castle built by Robert II of Harcourt at the end of the 11th century and in the family hands until it was taken over by the French Agricultural Academy in 1828. With half-hearted displays of flora and fauna, it is a mix of institutional poverty and feudal grandeur which comes from the medieval flavour of its 66ft (20-metre) wide moat and fortified walls. There is also a 15-acre (6-hectare) **arboretum** in the grounds, with 200 species, mainly conifers, from around the world.

From Harcourt it is just 4 miles (6 km) up the D137 to **Brionne** on the Risle. This small town has statuary from **Bec-Hellouin** in its otherwise plain church and a large Sunday market that stretches out in the car-park beside it. Above the town is a fine square 11th-century keep and it was while besieging the duke of Burgundy here in 1047 that William the Conqueror came in contact with Bec-

Vendeuve château's miniatures.

Hellouin and its Italian abbot Lanfranc, who was to become such a help to him in later life.

The abbey is just 4 miles (6 km) north, in the small flat valley of the Bec, a tributary of the Risle. There are regular conducted tours through the day undertaken by urbane and witty white-robed monks. All that remains of the original building destroyed after the Revolution is the solid **belfry of St Nicolas** with a commemorative plaque to the English prelates who came from Bec. The tomb of Herlouin, the knight who founded the abbey in 1034, is in the centre of the new church which has taken over the refectory of the 17th-century building.

The attractive village beside the abbey centres on a small green and a church brimming with statuary the abbey lacks. There is also a small **motor museum** of 50 functioning collectors' pieces. From Bec the D137 crosses the Risle and heads for the wooded hills and **St-Georges-du-Vièvre** 5 miles (9 km) distant. Just before it, on the right-hand side, is the **Château of Lounay**. It is privately owned, but a walk in the grounds is rewarded with the sight of one of the most imaginatively carved dovecotes in Normandy.

Back on the D130, the road follows the Risle through **Montfort-sur-Risle**, squeezed under a cliff beside a ruined 13th-century castle, before crossing to the left bank and the town of **Pont-Audemer**. This is a lively place, a former tannery town with half-timbered houses looking especially attractive beside a bridge over a backwater of the Risle at the southern end of the Rue de la République. This main street also has the unfinished facade of St-Ouen, a saint whose legend is commemorated among the Renaissance stained-glass windows.

The grandest hotel and restaurant in town is the half-timbered Auberge de Vieux Puits, but there are also a number of inexpensive places, which make it a good base for the Pays d'Auge, for the Brotonne Regional Park, and for Honfleur and the pricey Côte Fleurie.

Right, the privately-owned, half-timbered and moated manor farm of Coupesarte.

SOUTHERN HILLS AND PLATEAUX

The landscape of the Eure is not what one expects of Normandy. Instead of small meadows, hedges, orchards, sunken roads, woods and glades, the scene is almost prairie-like, with vast fields of cereal crops stretching in all directions to the horizon, only occasionally interrupted by a copse of trees or farm buildings. Driving along the main roads through the *département* gives a sense of monotony, but anyone prepared to wander away from the beaten track will soon discover there is much to be enjoyed.

Évreux is the capital of the Eure *département*. Although at 50,000 its population is smaller than Rouen's or Caen's, it was chosen by the Normandy Tourist Office as their centre in an attempt to avoid showing a bias towards either Upper or Lower Normandy. Évreux is a lovely city, in spite of having suffered frequent fires and often violent destruction from the 5th century, when the Vandals sacked the old Roman town, up to World War II when German and Allied air raids razed many of the buildings.

Standing high amid its modern buildings, however, the **Notre-Dame cathedral**, which on several occasions has itself suffered the depredations of fire, is the city's pride and joy. Founded in the 6th century, it was rebuilt in the 12th century and again in the 13th and has been restored several times since, giving the building a rich mixture of styles. Especially worth seeing are the stained-glass windows, the carved wooden screens of the side chapels and the intricately sculpted north porch.

Next to the cathedral the former bishopric, built in 15th-century Renaissance style, houses the **municipal museum**, which has a particularly fine archaeological room incorporating part of the town's Gallo-Roman ramparts as one of its walls. Among the exhibits can be found jewellery from the Paleolithic period, Roman bronzes of Jupiter and Apollo found among the Gallo-Roman

remains at nearby Le Vieil-Évreux, medieval tombs, Aubusson tapestries, Nevers and Rouen china, and 17th- and 18th-century paintings.

Often passed unnoticed because of the draw of the cathedral, **St-Taurin** is another church worth seeking out. Just off the Rue Josephine, it is part Romanesque, part Renaissance, and contains the magnificent shrine of Évreux's first bishop, St Taurinus, a 13th-century masterpiece which was crafted from silver-gilt in the form of a miniature chapel decorated with embossed figures and statuettes.

Friendly bells: Contributing to the charm of the city is the River Iton which winds past the cathedral. A riverside walk which follows the old ramparts, and is named after Robert de Flocques, who liberated Évreux from the English in 1441, ends up at a colourful floral square which is further enhanced by an ensemble comprising the Hôtel de Ville, the theatre and the **Tour de l'Horloge**. The latter, an elegant tower built in the 1490s to replace one of the towers of the

main gateway, has a two-ton bell known as La Louyse, which chimes the hours.

Some 8 miles (13 km) east of Évreux, the river that gives the Eure *département* its name flows virtually parallel with the Seine for a while before joining it near **Louviers**. Like the other rivers of the *département*, it has a special beauty with some outstanding stretches.

One of them is found around 5 miles (8 km) northwest of **Pacy-sur-Eure** at **Cocherel**, a straggling village of half-timbered houses beside the tree-shaded river, and the site of a famous battle in 1365, early in the Hundred Years' War when the brilliant, brutal Bertrand du Guesclin defeated the combined forces of England and Navarre.

Aristide Briand, several times premier of France between 1909 and 1929, became attached to this region and he lived in Cocherel for some years before his death in 1932. There is a fine statue of the statesman seated in contemplative mood in an ivy-draped alcove near the river. Close by, a memorial marks the spot where 15 French soldiers were killed in June 1940 as they tried to defend a bridge from the invading German army. Briand himself is buried in the village churchyard.

Pacy, too, has a statue of Briand. He became known as the "apostle of peace" and won the Nobel Peace Prize in 1926 for his efforts on Franco-German reconciliation after World War I. In 1930 he also became known for advocating a federal union of Europe. Otherwise, Pacy has little of interest, though it does produce a cheese not often associated with Normandy: garlic-flavoured Boursin.

Border towns: Further south, the River Eure forms a border between Normandy and the Île-de-France *département* of Eure-et-Loire, continuing nearly as far as Dreux where the River Avre takes over border duties. In the Middle Ages it was an important line of defence and saw many battles.

Ivry-la-Bataille, 10 miles (17 km) south of Pacy on the D836, gets its name from one such engagement, in 1590, when Henry IV defeated the forces of the Catholic League. The battle site is

Inspiring roofs on an imposing half-timbered château in Louviers.

marked by an obelisk, erected in 1804 by Napoleon near the village of **Epieds**.

Ivry itself is a quiet place that has taken to heart its link with the victorious king. In the Rue Henri lV there are the Patisserie Henri lV and the Hostellerie du Roi Henri lV, while in a fine old half-timbered building at 5 Rue de Garennes stands the Boucherie Henri lV. The latter probably has the most legitimate claim to the name, since Henry is supposed to have stayed at the house at the time of the battle.

Though on the wrong side of Normandy's border, the **château** at **Anet**, just south of Ivry, should not be passed by. Built by the beautiful and charming Diane of Poitiers, who bewitched Henry II, it was in its day the most lavish Renaissance palace in all France and enough of it remains to give an idea of those gilded days.

Along the Avre valley west of Dreux, three fortified towns, **Nonancourt**, **Tillières** and **Verneuil-sur-Avre**, built by Henry I of England as a line of defence between Normandy and France,

saw a great deal of bloody action towards the end of the Hundred Years' War. Of the three, Tillières is the least interesting, but Nonancourt has a number of well-restored half-timbered houses around the Place Aristide Briand, including one housing the tourist office that leans so much it seems on the verge of falling over. Around the church, which has an unusual eight-sided belfry with ornate pinnacle turrets, some of the alleyways have a medieval flavour.

Verneuil has the most appeal of the three, and it is a good place to stay, too, with a fine selection of hotels and shops. The Place de la Madeleine is its recognised centre, the giant tiered and multi-styled tower of its Madeleine church casting a long shadow over the square. It is worth looking inside the church to see its numerous statues and works of art, which include a larger-than-life nativity and entombment, as well as the tomb of Count de Frotté, who led the royalist chouans from his base at Flers during the latter days of the Revolution until he met his end in front of a firing

squad at Verneuil. The **Notre-Dame church** is also worth seeing for its remarkable collection of 16th-century statues, more than 20 in all, the work of local sculptors.

Notre-Dame, like several other buildings in the town, is built of *grison*, a distinctive red agglomerate stone found in the area. Part of the town's old fortifications are also made of it, the most notable example being the **Grise Tower**. Alongside stands a short section of the old wall, while behind, a pretty little half-timbered house looks across the River Avre to the delightful leafy gardens of the **Parc André Fourgère**.

Verneuil's ancient houses have been lovingly restored, especially the 15th- and 16th-century buildings distinguished by chequered walls and corner turrets in the Rue de la Madeleine and Rue Notre-Dame and the 18th-century Bournonville Hotel, an *hôtel particulier* or aristocrat's town-house, built of red brick and with wrought-iron balconies.

Breteuil, 8 miles (12 km) north of Verneuil, has some pretty little waterways and an unusual Hôtel de Ville in the Place Lafitte, built in ornate Gothic style but on a strangely small scale. There are a number of half-timbered houses round the square, but more impressive is the church with its 12 massive red *grison* pillars in the nave and decorated panel ceiling.

Conches-en-Ouche, 8 miles (12 km) further north, was founded in the 11th century when it was given its name by Roger de Tosny, who stole some relics of St Foy from Conques, a holy place in Aquitaine on the pilgrim route from Le Puy to Santiago de Compostela in Spain. Hence the reason for the three *coquilles St-Jacques* in the Norman town's coat-of-arms.

Standing on a hill almost enclosed by the Rouloir river, Conches proved a valuable defensive site, especially in the Hundred Years' War when it was occupied on two occasions by the English, the last time for eight years before Robert de Flocques chased them out in 1449. Its castle was finally dismantled in 1591 during the Wars of Religion, but

The native Percheron dray horse.

its ruined keep, overgrown with greenery now, remains an attractive sight.

The church, like the one at Conques, is dedicated to St Foy and, though originating in the 11th century, was almost entirely rebuilt 500 years later. The stained-glass windows, installed in the 16th century and depicting the lives of Christ, the Virgin and St Foy, are among the best in Normandy.

Northwest of Conche-en-Ouche, towards Bernay (*see page 270*), is the château at **Beaumesnil**, built in 1640 with a fine baroque facade. The garden is one of Le Nôtre's which can be walked in even when the building is closed. If the château is open, enjoy the huge library among its treasures. Just to the east is **Le Val Gallerand**, a grand Norman manor farm.

The rugged Perche: To the southwest of Breteuil lies a part of the Orne *département* called the **Perche,** a rugged area of wooded hills and valleys in marked constrast to the gentle scenery of the southern Eure. The town of **L'Aigle**, 15 miles (23 km) west of Verneuil, is the gateway to the region as well as serving as its main market centre.

In fact, L'Aigle has the **largest market** in Normandy (the third largest in France) and every Tuesday morning farmers descend on the town to trade in cattle, horses and other livestock. There's a general market too, which centres on the huge Place Boislandry and spills through several streets linking the Place St-Martin and the Place de la Halle, where the Renaissance café is a reminder of *belle époque* society life.

Overlooking a section of the market, the impressive town hall was formerly a château, built in 1690. Inside, it has an interesting museum of musical instruments, while in an outbuilding which also houses the tourist office, another small museum uses wax figures and recorded voices to illustrate the course of the Battle of Normandy.

The Perche itself is a beautiful part of Normandy, yet feels almost separate from it. Its largest town is **Mortagne-au-Perche**, famous as the home of the Percheron horse and for its **black pud-**

ding fair, held every year in March. Over a weekend, a couple of miles (4–5 km) of sausage are sold.

The Percheron, a strong beast originally bred to carry knights in armour and now finding renewed interest among Japanese horse breeders, is commemorated in statue form in the public gardens. The horse carries Cupid on its back, who in turn carries Neptune's trident and the goddess Ceres, and symbolises Neptune's love for Ceres as a result of which the two become horses.

During the 17th century, many people living in the Perche made the decision to emigrate to Canada, and one of them, Pierre Boucher, the "patriarch" of French Canada, came from Mortagne. A stained-glass window in the Notre-Dame church recalls his exploits. (At **Tourouvre**, 5 miles/8 km to the northeast of the town is the **Musée de l'Émigration Percheronnne au Canada**, which explains how 250 emigrants from the region are responsible for 1½ million descendants today.)

The remaining part of Mortagne's

former fortifications can be seen behind the church, the **St-Denis Gate**, originally built in the 15th century but later topped by a two-storey building now housing the **Perche Museum.** Alongside stands the 17th-century Maison des Comtes du Perche, flanked by turrets and set around an inner courtyard.

Perche capital: Ten miles (16 km) to the south is **Bellême,** regarded as the capital of the Perche, though the casual visitor may wonder why this quiet hilltop town is preferred to Mortagne. Like Mortagne it was once walled, and like Mortagne all that remains is a gateway flanked by towers. The church, dating from the late 17th century, has an ornately decorated interior, especially the baptismal font. More recently, the town has become known for its golf course.

Elsewhere in the Perche, the communities are much smaller, little villages and occasional manor houses hidden among the folds of the hills and between the forests. Few of the manor houses are open to the public, but those at **Les Feugerets**, **Courboyer**, **La Vove** and **L'Angenardière** with their turrets and towers add a touch of the medieval to the general scene.

Among the villages, **Longny-au-Perche**, lying in the Jambée valley, is noted mainly for its pretty Notre-Dame de Pitié chapel on the hill above. West of Bellême, **La Perrière**, a hilltop village with some fine old buildings, has one of the best views in the whole of the Perche. At **La Chapelle-Montligeon**, the village has, since 1911, been dominated by the twin white spires of its neo-Gothic basilica and the château-like proportions of its hermitage.

Another religious centre, the **Abbaye de la Trappe**, is located at the edge of the Perche Forest, a lovely area of lakes, some of which are equipped for boating and family activities. The Trappist order was founded here in 1664 and although the monastery itself can't be visited, the monks have a shop which sells produce from various French abbeys, fruit pastels being the local speciality. And to show this strict, silent order is geared for the modern world, credit cards are accepted.

Left, fountain outside La Trappe monastery.

DOVECOTES

According to an old joke, the fertility of the Norman soil comes from the *fieffe*, the droppings of the pigeons flying over the countryside. Pigeons have had an important part to play in both the diet and the architecture of Normandy, and the attractive, grain silo-sized dovecotes they were kept in, the *colombiers*, are still evident all over the countryside. Some were so grand they caused decrees to be passed and duels to be fought to preserve the special status and privileges they conferred.

Pigeon-rearing started as a quest for a more varied diet in winter, and in the Middle Ages it was fashionable to eat both their flesh and their eggs. But by the early 16th century the economic rewards for selling the droppings became so great that the landed gentry worked to exclude all but themselves from being enriched. In 1583 a royal decree was issued to regulate the number that could be owned (three nests per 1¼ acres/0.5 hectares) and authorising punishment for anyone not returning a ringed pigeon and for anyone caught eating a bird not their own. Pigeons became such a valuable source of income that pairs were used to settle debts and given as wedding presents. Racing pigeons were introduced and fast birds fetched high prices, and dovecotes became increasingly valued works of art.

There were two kinds of dovecotes, the *colombier à pied*, a single-purpose building which the wealthier preferred, and the *colombier bi-fonctionnel* where the ground floor might be used as a stable, while the middle level was used for poultry and pigeons were kept at the top. Their height would depend on the wealth of the owner, and they rose to around 60 ft (18 metres). They could be square, polygonal or round and they were built in all the variety of materials that Normandy has to offer with the roofs originally made of thatch.

Although their materials and exterior shapes differed, they all followed a similar design. The roof was conical or pepperpot shaped, topped with a *lanteron,* a small opening for the birds to enter or leave. One or two *lucarnes* (dormer windows) gave air and additional access. Other small openings were strategically placed in the walls to match the building's design. Families' coats of arms decorated the doors and a stone ledge, known as the "rat bar" encircled the building about a third of the way up the outside wall to keep out rodents.

Interior walls were filled with *boulins*, small niches for nests made of brick or clay. A rotating pole set in a stone base in the centre of the building formed the pivot for the revolving ladders which were used for keeping an eye on the nests. To gather eggs the keeper would climb the ladder, check the *boulins*, climb down again, move the ladder round, and go up once more, and so on all the way round.

Like many fine buildings, a number of Norman dovecotes were destroyed in the Revolution of 1789, as they were viewed as an aristocratic excess. But the Revolution also decreed that pigeon-owning should henceforth be available to everyone. It is still possible to see the old dovecotes. Two Routes de Colombiers are offered by the Seine Maritime and Eure tourist boards, but be warned that the excellent brochures are not followed up with roadsigns to help visitors on the maze of country roads. ∎

Renaissance bird building at the Manoir d'Ango, near Dieppe.

ORNE AND THE NATIONAL STUD

The Orne is the only *département* in Normandy not to have a seaboard, but it makes up for this deficiency by having a greater share of delightful wooded valleys and lush green hills. The fact that it lacks a Mont-St-Michel or a Rouen or a Bayeux Tapestry to draw in the visitors does not appear to worry it overmuch, and in recent years it has been making the most of its wonderful playtime potential to attract those who prefer to expend energy on sports.

The *département* has no great cities, but its largest town and capital, **Alençon**, which today has a population of 32,500, was once capital of all Normandy. The dukes' castle, built in the 14th and 15th centuries and dominated by a crowned tower, still stands and is now a prison. The town survived World War II remarkably well and after its liberation towards the end of the Battle of Normandy, General Leclerc established his headquarters here beside the River Sarthe, in what is now the **Musée de la Dentelle** (Lace Museum). Leclerc's statue stands opposite.

Lace centre: Alençon is famous for its lacework, which became renowned throughout Europe in the mid-17th century, after Louis XIV's chief minister Jean-Baptiste Colbert set up a lace-making centre in the town to specialise in Venetian-style needle-point (*see page 293*). In great demand, it became known as both the "queen of lace" and the "lace of queens". The creation of the Alençon Point National Workshop in 1976, supporting just 12 workers, ensures that the tradition continues. A second lace collection is exhibited at the **Musée des Beaux Arts et de la Dentelle**, alongside paintings by French artists and a display of Cambodian curios collected by Adhemard Leclère from Alençon, governor of the former French protectorate at the beginning of the century.

Lively during the day, Alençon's centre is a delight to wander around. The impressive **Notre-Dame church**, dominating the semi-pedestrianised Grande

Rue, has a particularly fine porch, its delicate tracery a match for any of the lace produced in the town. Among Alençon's many old houses, the most notable are the attractive 15th-century Maison d'Ozé next to the church and the birthplace of St Thérèse of Lisieux, opposite the splendid 17th-century prefecture in the Rue Saint-Blaise.

Hard against Normandy's southern border, Alençon lies amid some fine countryside. A 10-minute drive to the southwest is one of Normandy's prettiest villages, **St-Ceneri-le-Gerei**, built on a granite spur dominating a loop of the Sarthe river in the **Alpes-Mancelles** which, like the Suisse Normande, is an exercise in grandiosity. Inside the Romanesque church are some faded 14th-century frescoes, while in a nearby field close to the river a tiny 14th-century chapel contains a statue of the saint after whom the village is named.

Just north of Alençon the oaks, beeches and conifers spread their branches to form one of the largest forests in Normandy, the magnificent **Forêt**

d'Écouves. The joint highest point in western France is here, too, at the Écouves signal station at 1,370 ft (417 metres), a height it shares with the Mont des Avaloirs a short distance away across the border in the *département* of Maine. During the final days of the Battle of Normandy the forest provided excellent cover for the retreating Germans, and a tank named the Valois at the Croix de Médavy stands in the heart of the forest as a memorial to the French army's success in flushing them out.

At the edge of the forest, **Sées** possesses the Orne's only **cathedral**, a beautiful Gothic building whose twin towers, rising 200 ft (60 metres) above the fields, have been an inspirational landmark for travellers for over 600 years. At night, with superb floodlighting, it is even more outstanding. Spectacular *son-et-lumière* shows telling the cathedral's history are a feature of summer evenings and regular classical concerts are popular. Just across the Orne river, which flows through the town, stands the old **market hall**, built in the form of a rotunda, with an intricate timber-framed roof supported on stone columns.

The N158 from Sées to Argentan passes close to three of the Orne's lovely châteaux. The **château of Médavy** is a stately home built by the Grancey family in the early 17th century, replacing an earlier fortress, two towers of which can still be seen in the grounds. **Sassy** is even grander, a red-brick and white-stone building on a hillside overlooking formal terraced gardens. Although building started in 1760, it was not completed until after the Revolution. Inside there are some fine Aubusson tapestries and a magnificent library installed by Étienne-Denis Pasquier, chancellor of France during the reign of Louis-Philippe. A small chapel in the grounds contains a 15th-century altarpiece carved from oak in the Flemish town of Ghent.

The *pièce de résistance* of all the Orne's châteaux lies between these two, in the shape of the simply named **Château d'O,** near **Mortrée.** Set in an extensive wooded park and surrounded by the still waters of its moat, it has

Alençon, a Normandy capital.

distinctive pepperpot towers and steep, pointed roofs. It was built in Renaissance style in the 15th-century by Jean d'O, chamberlain to Charles VIII. It reached its zenith and was lost under François d'O, finance minister to Henry III, a hedonist and an incompetent, who died bankrupt and the château was sold to pay off his debts. Especially worth seeing inside are 17th-century frescoes in the drawing-rooms. An 800-year-old farm in the grounds has been turned into one of the region's finest restaurants.

Along the road from Sassy, the little village of **St-Christophe-le-Jajolet** is a place of pilgrimage for followers of the patron saint of travellers, St Christopher. On feast days in July and October, pilgrims drive their cars around a large statue of the saint outside the church.

Argentan, like Alençon, is a centre of lace and its *point d'Argentan* is made exclusively by the nuns of the Benedictine abbey on the southern outskirts of the town. Almost everything else of interest centres around the Place St-Germain, where a busy market is held every Tuesday. Towering above the stalls is **St-Germain church**, seriously damaged during the war along with the rest of the town, but some interesting features survived, including its Flamboyant porch, a domed belfry and some excellent 16th-century glass. The chapel of St Thomas inside the church is a reminder that it was from Argentan that the four knights set out after Henry II of England's ill-chosen words, to murder archbishop Thomas Beckett before the altar at Canterbury Cathedral.

Across the square, decorated in part by lawns and floral displays, is the **château**, an imposing building with square towers built in 1372 by Pierre II, count of Alençon, on the site of an earlier fortress. It now serves as the Palace of Justice. The chapel next to it was built around the same time and now houses the library and tourist office.

"A horse's Versailles": As the trotting-horse and carriage symbol for the Orne indicates, this part of Normandy is proud of its equine traditions. The area around Argentan is the heart of the region's

The lavish, steep-roofed château d'O.

horse-breeding country and 9 miles (14 km) east of the town, amid the forests along the N26, is the most famous stud-farm (*haras*) of them all, the Haras du Pin, **the National Stud**.

Created in the late 17th century through another initiative by Louis IV's minister Colbert, the stud's magnificent **château and stables**, at the end of a broad, grassy avenue and grouped round a horse-shoe shaped courtyard, are known as "the horses' Versailles". In the season, it is home to around 80 stallions, a mixture of Arab and English thoroughbreds, French trotters, cobs and giant Percherons. A tour of the stud takes in the stables, and collections of 19th-century carriages, saddles and harnesses. There is always plenty of activity for spectators, with horses being exercised, annual horse-shows and dressage events and, in September and October, racing at the *hippodrome* at the nearby village of **Le Pin au Haras**.

Five miles (9 km) north of the Haras, horse-power of another sort made its mark in the arena of world history half a century ago. Today, the countryside around **Chambois**, a quiet village with the remains of a fortress that guarded the Dives valley in the 12th century, is a peaceful picture of Norman rustic life: dappled cows graze the lush meadows beneath apple trees and country-folk go about their everyday business on small, half-timbered farms.

In August 1944, however, this area, known at the time as the **"Falaise Pocket"**, was where the Nazis' formidable panzer divisions were cornered and smashed as they tried to escape along the Dives Valley, in what General Eisenhower described as one of the biggest slaughterfields of the war. The victory brought the Battle of Normandy to an end after 77 days of conflict. A monument to the American, British, Polish, French and Canadian armoured divisions involved overlooks the site on **Mont-Ormel**, just south of Chambois.

Nature parks: Occupying the southern part of the Orne is one of France's largest regional nature parks, the **Parc Régional de Normandie-Maine**. There

The castle o Lassay.

are several towns within its boundaries, but the honour of "capital" falls on the little village of **Carrouges** on the D2 between Argentan and Alençon, where the Maison du Parc, the park's visitor centre, is housed in a restored chapter-house, an outbuilding of Carrouges's 16th-century château. The centre has information about flora and fauna, walking, cycling and horse-riding.

The château itself is one of the Orne's more outstanding and unusual, being built of red brick. A magnificent gate-house leads to its impressive leafy park, at the centre of which the irregular quadrilateral of the castle stands, square towers at each corner and surrounded by a moat. Not to be missed is a tour of the interior, entered by a drawbridge and inner courtyard and famous for its sumptuous furnishings, decor and paintings. One bedroom is named after Louis XI, who stayed there for a night in 1473.

Carrouges lies between the forests of Écouves and **Andaines** and at the heart of the latter lies the spa town of **Bagnoles-de-l'Orne** and its neighbour **Tessé-la-Madeleine**, for want of a coastline and beach the Orne's main holiday resorts. Bagnoles's heyday was in the Edwardian era and while it still has chic shops, smart hotels and *salons de thé* as well as a lakeside casino, it looks a little faded, despite recent efforts to update its image.

The 25°C (77°F) waters of the **spa**, which is the largest in western France, have been benefitting people since the 6th century, especially those with glandular and circulatory problems, and around 20,000 still come to the Établissement Thermal each year. There are also plenty of activities on hand to ensure the circulation remains in good order, – tennis, golf, swimming, walking, riding, boating and climbing on the rocks of the nearby gorge. Details are available at the Maison de Tourisme.

A detour 10 miles (16 km) south of Bagnoles crosses the Normandy border to **Lassay**, where each summer there is a *son-et-lumière* of the castle built in the reign of Charles VII.

La Ferté-Macé, 4 miles (6 km) north-

east of Bagnoles, is by contrast a market and industrial town. Its church has an unusual patterned facade of coloured bricks and stone and is worth a visit for its **museum** of old and precious ecclesiastical curios. A newly created lakeside leisure centre on the edge of the town has *gîte* accommodation and a full range of activities including swimming, windsurfing, fishing, riding and golf. But La Ferté-Macé's greatest claim to fame is its contribution to Normandy's culinary arts: *tripe-en-brochette*, strips of tripe cooked on skewers.

Lofty pear town: Due west of La Ferté-Macé is one of the Orne's more charming old towns. **Domfront**, dating from the 11th century, stands on a long rocky spur high above the *bocage* countryside of the **Passais**, an area of pear orchards. In spring it becomes a mass of white blossom which from a distance and in hazy sunshine creates the appearance of a frost-covered landscape. *Poiré*, a pear cider, is a popular local drink.

Domfront was built up around a **fortress**, which was dismantled under the

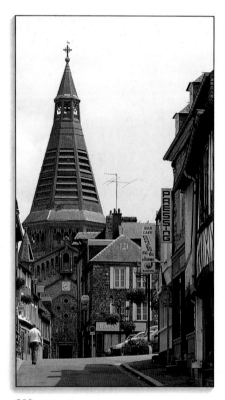

orders of Henri IV in 1608. On a lofty perch are its crumbling towers, ramparts and casemates to be explored and to stir the imagination, though its harsh medieval life is tempered now by beautifully kept gardens. Besieged on numerous occasions, Domfront became an English possession on at least three occasions, the last time, during the Hundred Years' War, for 32 years.

The town was walled too and some sections can still be seen, especially along the Rue des Fosses Plisson where old houses blend into the walls and towers. The best of the towers stands at the foot of the Grande Rue. Within the walls, the medieval character has been preserved, an exploration of the narrow cobbled streets revealing a number of well-restored half-timbered houses, mansions and *hôtel particuliers*. An unexpected sight right in the middle of the town is the **church of St-Julien**, built in 1924 of concrete in a neo-Byzantine style and full of gilt decoration.

A church that is too easily missed lies next to the N176 to Mont-St-Michel in the valley below the fortress. The pretty little Romanesque church of **Notre-Dame sur l'Eau**, built beside the River Varenne in the late 11th century, was the venue for a Christmas Mass celebrated by Thomas Beckett in 1166 during his exile in France. The church has been frequently altered, most savagely during the 19th century when much of the nave was removed to make way for road widening, though fortunately without detriment to the symmetry of the place. Inside are 12th-century frescoes and some interesting tombs.

About 5 miles (8 km) to the northwest is **Lonlay-l'Abbaye**, founded in the 11th century by Guillaume de Bellême. Only the church remains. In a picturesque valley surrounded by hills, it is easy to see why the monks chose this particular point, but they were unable to avoid the ravages of the Wars of Religion and the Revolution and much was destroyed. The village is still worth a visit, as much for its setting as its church, and for the chance to sample the local *sablé de l'Abbaye* biscuits, a type of shortbread made to an old recipe.

Domfront, with St-Julien in the background.

ROYAL LACE

Alençon is the home of Normandy's lacemakers, craftworkers dedicated to textile's most complex and dedicated endeavour. The visitor will find them in the museums and for sale in shops at a high price which reflects the extraordinary amount of work required to produce these intricate examples: it takes 32 hours to make just one square inch (6.5 sq. cm).

The industry grew up here on the back of the textile industry, spurred on by a national economic interest. The court of Louis XIV, the Sun King, was, in its day, the most elaborate in all Europe, and its fashionable and foppish courtiers created a demand for lace. The extravagant lifestyle of the monarchy sailed the state close to bankruptcy and it needed all the guile of Louis's imaginitive chief minister, Jean-Baptiste Colbert, to keep the country solvent.

Lace at the time was manufactured almost exclusively in Venice, and Colbert decided the money would be better spent at home, so he set up a "royal school" of lacemaking at Alençon to provide the king and the court with the trimming they needed. Venetian imports were subsequently banned and the Alençon lace became *de rigueur*. The museum and school in Rue Pont Neuf has a fine veil made for Marie-Antoinette. Napoleon I and the Empress Eugénie also wore the lace.

Point d'Alençon, involving a geometric pattern, was already established when Colbert came along in 1655: he merely added funds and royal approval. In the early 17th-century Alençon was making *vélin,* an antique cutwork made on parchment. After Colbert, *point de France* was introduced. This was had adapted from the Venetian lace which, at its most intricate, involved 6,000 buttonhole stitches to the square inch. Its decorative stitches were characterised by 1mm circles known as "0". Later the designs incorporatesd small bunches of flowers.

Nunneries and convents throughout Normandy produced lace, each providing a prarticular style which could immediately identify their place of origin. In the mid-19th century, women's headdresses, which had grown into the tall and elaborate concoctions now seen as part of the traditional folk costumes, were replaced by small frilled bonnets. But whatever the style of the headwear, identifying their lace was a way of distinguishing which part of Normandy the wearer came from.

Today this industry is still state-run in Alençon and grants go towards a handful of workers who ensure the craft survives. It is arduous, eye-straining work and a single piece may take many years to complete.

It is possible to find lace in other parts of Normandy still made by nuns. In Argentan, for example, *point d'Argentan* is made by the nuns who occupy the Benedictine abbey to the south of the town. Its history is as honourable as Alençon's, and it was also a centre for *point de France*. It was popular at court until the late 18th century, when the lighter Alençon lace came more into vogue, Today the nuns work to a pattern rediscovered and popularised in the 19th century.

In the Augustine convent in Bayeux nuns show visitors examples of the establishment's craft. (The convent's most famous daughter, Marie-Catherine, founded Canada's first hospital, the Hôtel-Dieu in Quebec.) There is also a lace workshop in the town where the Bayeux pattern is being revived. ∎

Point d'Alençon, from the Musée de la Dentelle.

293

SUISSE NORMANDE

The name "Suisse Normande" was invented for a marketing exercise to bring tourists back to a part of France that had just been torn to pieces by the war. And as in many marketing exercises, its creators' imaginations went over the top, for the region's loftiest hill, the 925-ft (282-metre) L'Éminence, is not even the highest point in Normandy.

In this rural backwater south of Caen, there are no mountains, no lakes (except where a dam has been thrown across the River Orne) and only the occasional exposed rocky height among the otherwise heavily wooded hills. Nevertheless, it truly is an area of outstanding natural beauty, much of it barely touched by tourism.

At the core of the Suisse Normande is the **River Orne**, a river of varying moods, sometimes lazy and slow, sometimes flighty, sometimes turbulent, which cuts a winding path from Putanges-Pont-Écrepin in the south through the green hills straddling the border between the Orne and Calvados *départements*, to Thury-Harcourt 25 miles (40 km) to the north. Falaise, William the Conqueror's birthplace, lies to the east and the towns of Vire and Flers to the west.

Much of the area saw a great deal of action during the war and most of the towns and villages have since been rebuilt. As a result they tend to lack inspiration, and must rely on the backcloth of greenery for their attraction. They do, however, all make good tourist centres with comfortable hotels and a good selection of camp-sites.

Thury-Harcourt is a case in point. It is a popular spot for canoeing, but the less sporty may find its chief attraction lies in the grounds of the ruined **Château d'Harcourt**. Built in the reign of Louis XIII for the illustrious Harcourt family, the château was used during World War II by the Germans, who burned it to the ground on their retreat in 1944. The overgrown ruins are evocative, but more appealing still are the grounds where grassy meadows give way to banks of cultivated flowers in the formal gardens. There are also quite lengthy walks along the river bank. A chapel in the grounds contains items salvaged from the château after the war.

Because main roads are few and far between in the Suisse Normande, people travel slowly and can appreciate their surroundings, perhaps stopping now and then for a walk. One of the few main roads is the D562 which runs 12 miles (19 km) south of Thury-Harcourt to **Condé-sur-Noireau** by way of **Clécy**.

Activity centre: Known as the capital of the Suisse Normande, Clécy (population: 1,188) is the liveliest and most attractive of the villages in the valley and it offers a wide range of activities.

Canoeing comes high on the list, but some of the finest climbing faces in Normandy are here, too, and the **Rochers des Parcs**, towering above the Orne, are often swarming with roped-up climbers. It is a good centre for walking, with several *grandes randonnées* (long-distance footpaths) and for horse-riding,

Preceding pages: view over Clécy. **Left**, kayaking on the Orne. **Right**, bikers take to the hills.

fishing and hang-gliding. Hang-gliders launch themselves from the **Rochers de la Houle**, reached by way of the Route des Crêtes, a road running along the ridge of the hills. The panoramas are exceptional, especially from the **Pain de Sucre** and the rocks themselves, which look down on a bend in the Orne and Clécy beyond.

The village is the most tourist orientated in the Suisse Normande. Cafés and restaurants, including the much photographed Moulin de Vey, line the tree-shaded riverside walks near the **Pont du Vey**. Brightly coloured pedalos and water tricycles splash between the banks. Some of Clécy's less sporty attractions include the **Musée du Chemin de Fer Miniature,** which has an extensive miniature railway, and the **Musée Hardy**, which contains 150 works by the Impressionist artist André Hardy, who drew considerable inspiration from the countryside around Clécy.

The Suisse Normande is an area that shouldn't be rushed: in fact the nature of the roads won't allow it. East of the

Orne en route from Clécy to **Pont-d'Ouilly**, 7 miles (11 km) to the south, a maze of narrow winding lanes are an invitation for visitors to lose themselves among the hills, where cattle animate the still life of isolated small farms and their orchards.

Pont-d'Ouilly, both crossroads and border town (between Calvados and the Orne *départements*), lies at the centre of the Suisse Normande and is one of its main resorts. Although rebuilt and modernised after the war, along the valley there is evidence of an earlier age when spinning and tanning were the local industries: granite and red-brick mills stand forlorn and neglected at **St-Christophe** and **Le Bateau**.

From Pont-d'Ouilly the D167 south keeps close to the Orne for a couple of miles (4 km) until it reaches **Pont-des-Vers**, then, by way of the Rouvrou Meander where the river all but loops back on itself, climbs to the **Roche d'Oëtre**, a rocky outcrop that gives a hint of what those marketing men were getting at. It stands beside a café at the

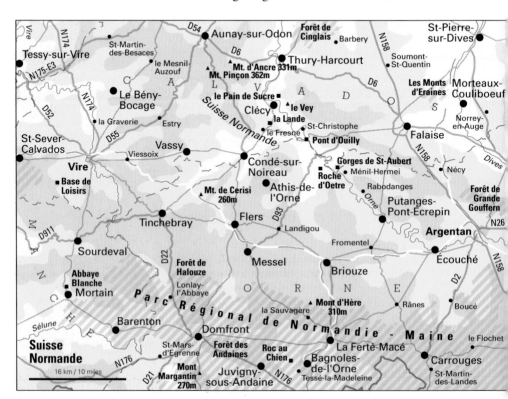

top of a 387-ft (118-metre) precipice, overlooking not the Orne but a tributary called the **Rouvre**, its valley slopes covered in trees and yellow broom. Nearby, a cave called the **Fairies' Room** was a hiding place for brigands and fugitives of the Revolution.

To the south, the Orne passes through the **Gorges de St-Aubert**, a gentle gorge with only the occasional glimpse of a craggy rock face through wooded slopes, before reaching **Rabodanges** where the grey 17th-century **château** appears at the end of an ornamental drive.

The village also gives its name to a dam built across the Orne to the south. Primarily there to create electricity, it forms a long narrow lake which has become a popular leisure centre with water-skiing, jet-skiing, windsurfing and fishing. At the upper end of the dam is **Putanges-Pont-Écrepin**, the Suisse Normande's southern resort town. Quietly attractive, it lies each side of the Orne, which drifts lazily past small boats tied at their moorings and beneath willows leaning from the banks.

The Conqueror's town: While the Suisse Normande may be a fairly confined area, its landscape of rolling, wooded hills, farms, orchards and hidden hamlets extends somewhat farther and brings within its domain much larger centres of interest. **Falaise** is one, just 11 miles (18 km) east of Pont-d'Ouilly, a town that simply shouldn't be missed.

Falaise had more influence on the history of England than any other town in France, for it was here in 1027 that William "the Bastard", son of Robert the Magnificent, duke of Normandy, and Arlette, daughter of a local tanner, was born. Arlette used to wash clothes in the spring beneath the castle keep at Falaise, and Robert, meeting her there one day, fell instantly in love. William was born in the **castle** and at the age of 39 "the Bastard" became "the Conqueror" of England.

Today, the massive walls of the castle and the keep still stand, dominated by the 115-ft (35-metre) **Talbot Tower** built in the 13th century by Philippe-Auguste. Extant, too, is the room where

La Roche d'Oëtre.

William was born. In a chapel is the list of 300 knights who accompanied him on his conquest of Britain.

Beside the spring, near the laundry where Arlette worked, a modern sculpture in relief depicts her fateful meeting with Robert. But the town's most dramatic statue is near the castle's main gate in the cobbled Place Guillaume Le Conquérant. This splendid bronze statue of William on a rearing horse rises above a plinth depicting six of his forebears, from Rollo, first duke of Normandy.

The nearby **Musée Août 1944** traces the story of the Falaise Pocket. There are two sturdy churches in the town, and the small, pretty **St-Laurent**.

Flers, 15 miles (25 km) to the west of Putanges on the D962, is more concerned with commerce and light industry than tourism. However, it makes a good base for excursions into the Suisse Normande. It also has an attractive 16th-century **château**, renovated and enlarged in the 18th century, which during the Revolution became the headquarters of the Chouans, a group of Norman royal-ists led by Count Louis de Frotté who took up arms again against the republicans. The revolt was eventually put down by Napoleon and despite a promise of safe conduct to Paris, the leaders were executed en route at Verneuil.

The château, tower-flanked and partly moated, stands beside its former stables in beautiful grounds, now a public park. As well as housing the town hall, it also contains a **museum** with some 17th- to 19th-century paintings, including works by Daubigny, Boudin and Corot, and a section on local life, going back to the days of cloth-weaving on which the town once relied.

Floral hill: Some 5 miles (8 km) north-west of Flers on the D18, is the village of **Cérisy-Belle-Étoile** which lies at the foot of **Mont de Cérisi**, a modest height of 870 ft (260 metres) with superb views over the surrounding *bocage* towards the Suisse Normande. Access is via a bosky toll road, which winds up the hillside to a ruined **château** at the top. Built by an English aristocrat, Lord Burkinyoung, around 1870, it was a

William the Conqueror and the castle where he was born, Falaise.

victim of bombardment in 1944. Way-marked walks and mountain-bike trails wind through the woods, which rhododendrons turn to a mass of colour in spring. There is a terraced bar and restaurant, and an open-air theatre which is used regularly for traditional music and dancing. At the end of May, the hill is the venue for the Fête des Rhodos.

A short drive from the village are the remains of the 13th-century **Abbaye de Belle-Étoile** at the head of a peaceful valley, its few arches and cloisters now incorporated into an apple orchard. Even though there is little to see, it makes a delightful spot on a sunny day and it is easy to imagine why it attracted monks in the Middle Ages. Nearby buildings are used as a *village des vacances* for children in July and August.

The *bocage* countryside that is such a lovely characteristic of this part of Normandy from time to time throws up some unexpected sights and one of them lies just north of Condé-sur-Noireau. **Château Pontécoulant**, distinguished by its small round towers and row of tall arched windows, dates from the 16th century and comes into view round a bend at the end of a landscaped park hidden in a wooded valley. Now a museum, the château contains some fine pieces of antique furniture.

Another surprise is found in the valleys near **Le Bény-Bocage** on the D577 north of Vire, which is 16 miles (26 km) west of Condé-sur-Noireau. Back in 1889, Gustave Eiffel, the man responsible for Paris's most famous landmark, built a railway viaduct over the Souleuvre valley. After the railway had ceased running, 101 years later, A. J. Hackett came from New Zealand and set up Europe's first **bungee-jumping centre**, using a platform fixed to the top of one of the viaduct's stone pillars. Now thousands of visitors go to watch, even to participate, as dare-devils dive off headfirst, nothing more than a rubber band preventing them from slamming into the ground 200 ft (60 metres) below. For those of a more nervous disposition, it is also a lovely area for picnics and walks.

The best of what remains of **Vire**'s medieval sights is the **Tour de l'Horloge**, a 15th-century belfry on top of a 13th-century gateway, once part of the town's ramparts. Two smaller towers nearby were also part of the fortifications. Beyond the church, the Place du Château looks down on the River Vire which loops round the town. In the Middle Ages this narrow valley, the Vaux de Vire, now quite rural in aspect, was the town's industrial zone, producing textiles. It later became associated with a collection of bawdy workers' songs published under the name *Vaux de Vire*, which is said to have led eventually to the word "vaudeville".

Of the **château**, all that remains is a ruined keep standing amid the trees, the rest having been demolished on the order of Cardinal Richelieu in 1630. Down below, the town **museum**, installed in the medieval Hôtel-Dieu close to the river, is dedicated to local arts and traditions. The town is also famous for its contribution to Norman cuisine, the *andouille*, a type of chitterling and something of an acquired taste.

Europe's first bungee-jumping centre on an old viaduct.

CHERBOURG AND THE COTENTIN

In the north of the Manche *département*, the Cotentin Peninsula juts stubbornly out into the English Channel, a severely eroded remnant of the great mountains of the Armorican Massif that underpin France's northwest corner. In some ways the region is a prelude to Brittany, with its western seaboard similarly blessed with rugged cliffs and magnificent beaches swept clean by strong tides. Maritime traditions come to the fore in this isolated corner of Normandy, where a weatherbeaten coastline of lighthouses, headlands and fortified harbours is tempered by the presence of old-fashioned seaside resorts and stretches of refreshingly undeveloped shore.

At the same time the Cotentin feels thoroughly Norman – as brusque and solid as the belaboured figures painted in the 19th century by Jean-François Millet, born in a small village to the west of Cherbourg. The Norman ego can be held responsible for Mont-St-Michel, a temple to the warrior archangel St Michael, and it was sons of the Cotentin who ventured south to establish lucrative kingdoms in Sicily and southern Italy during the 11th and 12th centuries. They were the descendants of the Vikings who settled on the Peninsula in great numbers, and whose presence is still remembered in its Norse place-names, such as at St-Vaast-la-*Hougue* (hill) and Bricque*bec* (stream).

In the past the Cotentin Peninsula was an island, and a southern band of low-lying land and marshes, known as the **Cotentin Pass**, now stretches between Lessay and Carentan. Watered by the Douve, Seve, Taute and Vire rivers, this area forms the heart of the recently created **Parc Régional des Marais du Cotentin et du Bessin**. Among its extensive patchwork of marshes and water-meadows is the Canal des Espagnols, constructed in 1809 by 400 Spanish prisoners-of-war shipped in as part of an ambitious project of Napoleon's to link the peninsula's east and west coasts.

In the centre of the Parc Régional is the cattle town of **Carentan**, the traditional eastern gateway to the northern Cotentin. This historic function is best acknowledged by passing straight through – a golden rule for enjoying this underappreciated corner of Normandy is to always avoid the N13, where monster-sized lorries pound to and from the port of Cherbourg. Instead take the most minor roads you dare – with sea on three sides you are odds-on to find golden sands at the end.

Branching northeast at **St-Côme-du-Mont** (D913), you can quickly reach the stunning expanses of **Utah Beach**, where the US forces landed on D-Day. Now named the **Route des Alliés**, the D421 runs for 8½ miles (14 km) north from the hamlet of **La Madeleine** to **Quinéville**, following a relentless, haunting stretch of sand that is one of the best coastal drives in Normandy. At La Madeleine a German blockhouse now houses a small **museum** recalling the events of 6 June 1944, including filmed footage of the landings taking

place. By the end of the day 23,000 men and 17,000 vehicles had been brought ashore at Utah, and within three weeks the Cotentin Peninsula was in Allied hands. As at the eastern flank of the D-Day beaches, airborne troops were used to secure inland positions in advance of the seaborne landings. Among the 13,000 men that dropped from the skies that day, one paratrooper gained lasting fame by getting caught on the church steeple of **Ste-Mère-Église**, 6 miles (10 km) inland. For two hours John Steele hung in the air feigning he was dead before being taken prisoner. His ordeal was re-told in a film, *The Longest Day*.

In the town a dummy paratrooper still hangs from the church's spire, and the landings are commemorated in its stained glass. Nearby the **Musée des Troupes Aéroportées** (Airborne Troops Museum) works hard to convey, to a growing audience that has never known war, the reality of D-Day. While some museums are little more than an army surplus store, this one can boast both a C47 dropping plane and a fear-

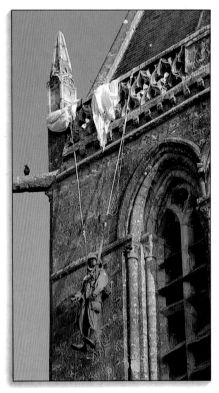

fully-flimsy WACO glider complete with sweet-eyed shop dummies as passengers. Once you have read Jim's poignant "Tonight's the night" letter to his parents, posthumously posted home, their use does not seem so out of place.

On the outskirts of Ste-Mère-Église, the **Musée de la Ferme du Cotentin** offers a useful chance to get inside one of the highly covetable ensembles of stone-and-slate farmhouse buildings that are typical of western Normandy. Built around a courtyard and well, the farm dates back to the end of the 16th century but recreates rural life at the start of this one. Its well-displayed collections of agricultural tools include enough woodcutters' axes to equip a lunatic asylum.

Rural traditions are also on show in the market town of **Valognes** 10 miles (16 km) further north. Here the **Musée Régional du Cidre et Calvados** and its companion **Musée de l'Eau de Vie** pay homage to the Norman zeal for extracting liquid fruits from the apple. Among the expected cider presses, mashing troughs and spiralling copper alembics

is a fantasy-provoking bed carved from a barrel in 1831.

Rural corner: The northeastern corner of the Cotentin Peninsula conceals a scenic surprise: a triangular pocket of rolling countryside adorned with narrow lanes, thick hedges, gorse and wild flowers. Known as the **Val de Saire**, it makes a pleasant rural drive (D25), with a viewpoint at **La Pernelle** offering extensive views along the east coast.

Nearby lies the sprawling oyster port of **St-Vaast-la-Hougue**, guarded by the Fort de la Hougue. This is a survivor of the coastal defences erected by the ubiquitous military architect Sébastien Vauban following the destruction of the French fleet here by Anglo-Dutch ships in 1692. The **fort** is still in use, but a similar one can be visited on the nearby **Île de Tatihou**. This flat island, which has a small **Musée Maritime**, can be reached by a short boat trip from the Quai Vauban and is ideal for a leisurely walk invigorated by sea air.

Further north, the spacious fishing port of **Barfleur** has an easy-going at-

mosphere that belies the strong seas just offshore. It was here in 1120 that the *White Ship* carrying Henry I's son was blown on to the reefs, drowning the English heir and 300 others. Today Normandy's tallest lighthouse stands at the **Pointe de Barfleur**, a short drive north. The climb to the top will particularly appeal to numerologists, as it has 12 storeys, 52 windows and 365 steps.

From here the D116 winds pleasantly along the north coast to **Cherbourg,** passing through an area well-known to seabird-watchers, with attractive wildflowers and *pique-nique* spots.

Visitors to Cherbourg will today find little sign of the illustrious port where Napoleon resolved "to re-create the wonders of Egypt". Although the idea of transforming this exposed fishing village into a naval base was considered as early as 1686, the fortified breakwater now linking its offshore islands was not completed until 1853. Cherbourg subsequently developed a rôle as a transatlantic port, with grand terminals built to receive the prestigious liners that docked here between the two world wars. In 1944 the port was a key objective in the first phase of Operation Overlord, and fell three weeks after D-Day to the US 7th Corps. Hitler had ordered that the harbour be left "a field of ruins", and photographs of its devastation can be seen in Cherbourg's engaging **Musée de la Guerre et de la Libération**. This is housed in the 19th-century hilltop Fort de la Roule, which enjoys a commanding view of the port and was itself the scene of intense fighting.

Plutonium City: Among the museum's many exhibits is a fragment of PLUTO, the Pipe Line Under The Ocean that was laid across the Channel to fuel the war effort. Today, in a rare linguistic twist, Cherbourg is now derisively known as Plutonium City, on account of the spent nuclear fuel shipped here for reprocessing at **La Hague**. It is still a military port where nuclear submarines are based.

Today Cherbourg, which has a population of 90,000, is one of the most likeable and unpretentious of the Channel ports. The historic part of the town is

Left, Notre-Dame church Cherbourg. **Below**, a view of the port.

located in the streets west of the **Bassin du Commerce**, where the Place Général de Gaulle serves as a central square and market venue. For shopping and strolling, head for the pedestrian precincts and narrow streets to its north, such as Rue Tour-Carrée and Rue de la Paix.

Visitors with time to spare before their ferry will find they are well served by bequests to the town from two 19th-century collectors. Just south of the Place Général du Gaulle, in Rue Vastel, the **Musée Thomas-Henry** exhibits a miscellany of fine art including some lively 17th-century Flemish painting, a haunting *Pietà* by Nicolas Poussin, portraits by Millet and homages to *homard* (lobster) and other sea fruits by local artists.

Further west, in the Rue l'Abbaye, the Parc Emmanuel Liais is an oasis of tropical plants camouflaging the **Musée d'Histoire Naturelle**, which has a collection of archaeological finds, ethnographic souvenirs and things stuffed.

West of Cherbourg civilisation peters out as you approach **Cap de la Hague**, Normandy's Land's End. If you have the time, take the D45 which trickles along the coast via the village of **Gréville-Hague**, where a bust of Jean-François Millet celebrates the painter's birth-place. The road then continues to the minimalist harbour of **Port Racine**, which claims with obvious justification to be *le plus petit port de France*, and eventually concludes at **Goury**, where a lighthouse rising from the rocks punctuates the end of the road like an exclamation mark. Satellite photography and excavation have shown that this area north of **Beaumont**, was once defended by a dyke cut by the Celts and consolidated with walls by the Romans. It is not hard to imagine these early settlers appreciating the majestic sweep of the **Baie d'Écalgrain**, to the south of **Auderville**. Today it is skirted by a scenic road (D401) which virtually passes through the living-rooms of **Dannery**, where a right-turn leads out to the cliffs at **Nez de Jobourg**. Here the blustery sea-views are complemented by an agreeable restaurant, the Auberge des Grottes.

After gazing out to sea, it is some-

Cottages at Vauville, which overlooks its own bay.

thing of a shock to look southward and find the landscape blighted by the windowless blocks and chimneys of **La Hague nuclear reprocessing plant**. Opened in 1965, this vast plant employs 8,000 workers and has an Information Centre by its main entrance on the D901. Further south, at the opposite end of the spectacular *plages* along the **Anse de Vauville**, is another nuclear installation, the **Cap de Flamanville**. power station. Guided tours are available.

South of here the coast is characterised by windswept beaches bordered by banks of sand dunes, an area blissfully free of resorts until you reach two seaside towns that sound like a music hall act, **Barneville** and **Carteret**. Both are unashamedly devoted to the traditional summer holiday: here you can take a boat trip to the Channel Islands (the Îles Anglo-Normandes in French), ride on the Train Touristique to **Portbail**, or enjoy their beaches and amusements.

Ten miles (16 km) inland is **Bricquebec**, dominated by a castle with a 75-ft (23-metre) keep and clock tower. The nearby Trappist monastery, Notre-Dame-de-Grâce, can be visited.

Lessay, 17 miles (27 km) south of Barneville, is renowned for its exquisitely Romanesque abbey church, stoically restored after the war. An influential Benedictine abbey was founded here in 1056, which owned estates in Jersey and England. The church has impressive stained glass inspired by Celtic designs, with adjacent conventual buildings dating from the mid-18th century. A somewhat sleepy place, Lessay comes alive in mid-September when it is the venue for the three-day Sainte-Croix Fair. This horse fair has been held here since at least the 12th century and it now attracts up to 400,000 visitors a year.

On the coast 9 miles (14 km) southwest of Lessay is **Château Pirou**, a fine feudal castle which puts on *son-et-lumières* about its Viking past. South of Lessay the D2 crosses the austere **Lande de Lessay** moorland to reach the Cotentin's ancient capital, **Coutances**.

<u>Right</u>, Écalgrain Bay lies on the wilder shores of the Cotentin.

SOUTHERN COTENTIN

The Cotentin gets its name from the diocese of Pagus Constantinus, founded by the 3rd-century Roman emperor Constantius Chlorus. His capital was at Constantia, today the hilltop cathedral town of **Coutances**.

Despite a tragic decision to fill its streets with piped pop music, Coutances is well worth exploring. Approach it from the west (D44), via its companion resort of **Agon-Coutainville**, and you will have a good view of both the cathedral and the remnants of the medieval **aqueduct** that once spanned the Bulsard, one of three rivers that meet to the south of the town. At the top of Rue Tancrède, the Place du Parvis is a market square-cum-car park that squats in front of the cathedral like an irreverent offering.

The **Cathédrale Notre-Dame** is a rocketship in stone, launched in the 1040s by the local De Hauteville family who had recently acquired their kingdoms in southern Italy and Sicily. By 1274 their Romanesque church had been surmounted with Gothic additions scaling new heights – a thundering 135-ft (41-metre) lantern tower and twin spires that soar to 256 ft (78 metres).

As such the cathedral is a fine example of the Norman Gothic style: in the west front the pursuit of slenderness verges on the anorexic, while double flying buttresses dance daringly around the east end. These elegant strains continue inside with a profusion of vertical lines and ambitious vaulting, lightened by the octagonal lantern tower and a delicate stained glass – among which you can see, high up in the north transept, a depiction of Thomas Becket sailing to England.

Herbal gifts: South of the cathedral in Rue Geoffrey de Montbray stands the 15th–16th-century **church of St-Pierre**, with its own rival lantern tower. Having lost its stained glass, the unusually light interior resembles the inside of a sumptuously decorated eggshell. A short walk east of the Place du Parvis is Coutances' **Jardin des Plantes**. Once the grounds

of a splendid 17th-century hotel, the gardens were bequeathed to the town in 1850 on the condition that its herbs be made available to its citizens free of charge. The house is now the **Musée Quesnel-Morinière,** guarded by a giant cider press with a motley collection of fine art and antiques indoors.

Within striking distance of Coutances is **Gratot Château** with an 18th-century pavilion and 15th-century Fairy's Tower, and **Orval church** to the south, the remnants of an important 12th-century priory where St Omer was born.

In 1796 Coutances' position as capital of the Cotentin was usurped by **St-Lô**, 17 miles (27 km) to the east and today the Préfecture of the Manche *département*. The city was all but obliterated in June 1944, then blitzed again by modern architecture. It is worth visiting principally for the uncompromising manner in which its **church of Notre-Dame** was rebuilt: the war left a gaping hole between the two towers of its west front, which was simply filled with a contrasting wall of green stone. On the

north side of the church you can still see an unexploded shell lodged in its walls.

In the town centre a modern **Musée des Beaux Arts** successfully intermingles treasures ranging from an ancient Ethiopian Bible and a Tiepolo drawing to a set of 16th-century Bruges tapestries and works by Corot, Boudin and Millet. On the east side of the town (D972) is the **Haras National**, a national stud farm founded by Napoleon in 1806. Displays featuring its stallions and team-driving are held here during the summer.

South of Coutances and St-Lô, the Cotentin lapses into the relaxing *bocage* countryside of small fields bordered by raised hedges characteristic of Basse Normandie. Through this landscape the River Sienne meanders gently north towards Coutances, while further inland the River Vire aims for St-Lô. Six miles (10 km) north of **Villedieu-les-Poêles,** a strand of the Sienne wanders past the 12th–13th-century ruins of the Benedictine **Abbaye de Hambye**. These provide a worthy excuse to potter through the Sienne valley – take the D198 east of **Gavray** – and are complemented by an idyllic set of farm buildings, orchards and munching cows that make a convincing commercial for the monastic way of life.

Lots of pots: Villedieu-les-Poêles translates as "God's Town of the Frying Pans", a name derived from the pots and pans that coppersmiths have been making here for centuries. It is undoubtedly the shiniest town in Normandy, with a high street bedecked with copper, brass and pewter goods for sale. In the 12th century it was the headquarters of the Knights of St John and a staging post on the pilgrimage route to Mont-St-Michel. The town still has a medieval feel, with narrow alleys branching off from its streets into small *cours* (courtyards), such as along the central Rue Général Huard and the pedestrianised Rue Docteur Havard.

One legacy of its metalworking traditions is the **Fonderie de Cloches** (Bell Foundry), close to the river in Rue du Pont-Chignon. Bells are still made here,

Left, St-Lô's ramparts. **Below**, ruins of the Abbaye de Hambye.

and a guided tour reveals the arcane skills behind this sonorous art. Similar enlightenment is available at the **Atelier du Cuivre** (Copper Workshop), while other museums are devoted to pewter, copperware, clocks, lace and Normandy furniture.

The port of **Granville** stands 17 miles (28 km) due west at the northern end of the vast **Baie du Mont-St-Michel** that bites into the Cotentin's southwestern corner. Its prominence owes a lot to the English, who built fortifications on a rocky spur here in 1439 as part of their assaults on Mont-St-Michel. Within three years the Normans had captured this fortress, and the walled town that grew up on Le Roc is now referred to as the **Haute Ville**. In the 18th century Granville, like St-Malo in Brittany, prospered both from the labours of its cod fishing fleet off Newfoundland and the exploits of its state-sponsored pirates. During the 19th century it developed as a fashionable seaside resort, and Granville is still well-stocked with traditional end-of-the-pier amusements like the **Féerie du Coquillage** (Shell Wonderland), **Palais Minéral** (Mineral Palace) and **Le Roc Marine Aquarium**.

In the main entrance to the Haute Ville, the Grande Porte, the Musée du Vieux Granville recalls the town's seafaring past and makes a useful prelude to a tour of the adjacent ramparts. The upper town's western end is filled by the weatherbeaten **church of Notre-Dame**, its chapel walls decorated with inscribed marble plaques giving thanks to the fishermen's patroness, Notre-Dame du Cap Lihou. At the eastern end, below the panoramic Place de l'Isthme, a walkway crosses the Trenche Anglais cut by the English to separate Le Roc from the mainland. Steps now lead down to Granville's casino and the Promenade du Plat-Gousset.

From the port on the south side of Granville you can take a boat over to the Channel Islands or the nearer **Îles Chausey**, a splash of low-lying granite islands where stone was quarried for the construction of Mont-St-Michel. South of Granville the D911 follows the curve

'an-makers a copper oundry, illedieu-les- oêles.

of the Baie du Mont-St-Michel, along a scenic route signposted "Avranches par la Côte".

At **Bec d'Andaine** there is a good view across the sands to the island of **Tombelaine** and **Mont-St-Michel** beyond (*see page 323*) – as well as signs warning of the danger posed by the tides. If you want to walk across the bay, pay a visit to the **Maison de la Baie** in **Genêts,** where guides can provide safe passage – just as their predecessors did for the pilgrims of the Middle Ages.

The tides around Mont-St-Michel are among the strongest in the world, sometimes reaching 18 miles an hour (30 kph) in spring, with a tidal range of up to 50 feet (15 metres). In March 1993 the highest tidal coefficient since 1918 was recorded, prompting many to scour the sands for a bumper crop of shellfish, and bringing a flood of tourists to Mont-St-Michel to witness *la marée du siècle* engulfing the island.

If the mists permit, there are more good views of Mont-St-Michel to be had from the **Jardin des Plantes** in **Avranches**. Despite damage caused by the war – a memorial on its southern outskirts celebrates General Patton's breakthrough at Avranches on 1 August 1944 – the town has a welcoming atmosphere. If you can't face the claustrophobia of Mont-St-Michel or the tacky band of hotels that line its approaches, consider staying here.

Avranches once had a cathedral, and you can see a model of it in the town's **Musée Municipal**. This hides to the north of Place Littré, the town's central square, and is housed in what was once the Bishop's Palace and later a prison. Its displays provide a good introduction to life in the southern Cotentin, with exhibits that range from decorative tiles rescued from the Abbaye de Hambye to the lovingly-made furniture and costumes of the 19th century. A stupendous collection of **illuminated manuscripts** brought over from Mont-St-Michel in the wake of the French Revolution is now exhibited separately in the nearby Hôtel de Ville.

The position of the old cathedral,

Granville, a port with a swashbucklin‍g history and links to the Channel Islands.

which was pulled down in 1812, can be gauged from a lonely stone in one corner of La Plate-Forme, a grassy terrace that can be reached by walking through an arch north of the Palais de Justice. Here a memorial commemorates the place in front of the cathedral where in 1172 Henry II publicly atoned for the murder of Thomas Beckett.

Valley routes: Inland from Avranches two river valleys run east-west across the southern parts of Manche, both offering leisurely routes for travelling between the Orne and Mont-St-Michel. To the north the D911 follows the River Sée to **Brécey** and **Sourdeval**, passing through a rich countryside of rolling farmland, woods and orchards. Further south the Sélune valley runs via **Ducey** (D78) to **St-Hilaire-du-Harcouët**, with the river's flow stemmed by the **Barrage de Vezins**, south of the N176. The artificial lake created by this hydroelectric dam now lies at the heart of an inland resort where you can walk, fish, cycle, ride and indulge in a variety of water sports.

The southeast corner of the Manche *département* forms part of the **Parc Régional de Normandie-Maine**, where the traditional rural landscape of Normandy is protected and specialist museums pay tribute to local crafts. One worth seeking out is the **Maison de la Pomme et de la Poire** (Apple and Pear House), south of the village of **Barenton** – partly because the surrounding countryside towards **St-Cyr-du-Bailleul** is full of tiny lanes and unrestored half-timbered farm buildings. Here you can pay your respects to La Rouge Vigne, a 200-year-old pear tree that in a good year produces 1.5 tonnes of pears. That's the equivalent of 900 litres of *poiré*, the pear cider described, in all seriousness, as the "champagne of Normandy".

On the edge of the park is **Mortain**, a pleasant town with a small waterfall, called the "Grande Cascade" in the Cance river which tumbles 82 ft (25 metres) through a woodland walk. The nearby 12th-century Cistercian **Abbaye Blanche** beside the Cance is today a retreat, but it can be visited.

Below, a wedding in Avranches. Right, the Grande Cascade in Mortain.

MONT-ST-MICHEL

The story of Mont-St-Michel begins with a hole. Cult-followers, the chronologically-correct and anyone intrigued to know the size of a divine forefinger should pay a prefatory visit to the small treasury of the church of St-Gervais in Avranches, where the time-tanned skull of St Aubert resides in an elaborate gilt reliquary.

According to religious history, one night in 708 the Archangel Michael appeared before Aubert, then bishop of Avranches. He issued instructions for a church to be built on top of Monte-Tombe, a rocky island at the mouth of the River Couesnon. Aubert thought he was dreaming, but the application of an archangelic *doigt de feu* above the right ear got the message through – as well as leaving a sizeable hole in his skull.

Despite this impediment, Aubert managed to construct a small oratory dedicated to St Michael, thus laying the foundations for what has since become the top tourist attraction in France outside Paris. Once part of the Forest of Scissy, this 258-ft (78-metre) high rock is now an island crowned by a fortified abbey nearly as high again.

Perilous place: Mont-St-Michel's phenomenal development can be explained by its strategic position on the frontier between Brittany and Normandy. It stands aloof in the Baie du Mont-St-Michel, where treacherous mists, tides and quicksands serve as natural defences. The threat posed by these sands is borne out by Scene 17 of the Bayeux Tapestry, which shows two trapped Norman soldiers being rescued by the noble Harold.

In AD 966 Duke Richard I installed Benedictine monks from St-Wandrille on the island, with work on an enlarged abbey starting in the early 11th century. By then Mont-St-Michel was already an established place of pilgrimage that attracted Michael-worshippers, known as *miquelots*, from afar. They continued to arrive despite the ducal and Anglo-French wars that raged through the Mid-

dle Ages, with the opposing armies simply demanding a safe conduct payment.

By the end of the 13th century Mont-St-Michel had acquired a three-storey Gothic abbey, with a garrison installed in the lower town. During the Hundred Years' War new defensive walls were constructed that defied repeated English attacks. Two bombards, left behind by the English after their final attempt in 1434, now stand beside the **Porte de l'Avancée**. This gateway was the only break in the medieval ramparts and, as visitors are surprised to discover, is flooded at high tide.

Following the defeat of the English at Formigny in 1450, Mont-St-Michel enjoyed a new popularity. In subsequent centuries it suffered from rule by absentee abbots, a decline partially checked by the arrival of monks from a new Benedictine Order, the Maurists, in 1622. After the French Revolution the abbey became a prison, which only closed in 1863 following a lengthy campaign initiated by Victor Hugo. Eleven years later the abbey was declared a

eceding ges: the ount at low le. **Left,** urch on rock. ght, an th-century all painting St Michael.

national monument. In 1966, 1,000 years after the Benedictines first arrived on Mont-St-Michel, a small community of monks from Bec-Hellouin returned.

Today Mont-St-Michel provides a textbook definition of a tourist-trap. It is at its most impressive when seen from afar, with its famous silhouette rising above the hazy sands and salt marshes like a heavily fortified breast. There is a fair case for just looking and leaving, for as you travel down the **causeway** that has linked the Mount to the mainland since 1880 its aura of enchanted isolation quickly disappears.

Pilgrim hordes: Every year 850,000 people visit Mont-St-Michel, piling on to an island only two-thirds of a mile (1 km) in circumference like angels crowding on to a pin-head. As you join the throng, think of the medieval pilgrims who came before you, sporting cockleshells and lead badges depicting the Archangel. Pilgrims still arrive today, carrying flags and singing hymns as they climb up to the abbey along **La Grande Rue**. This street is the town's principal artery, and at any time of the year it is liable to be blocked with fellow visitors. When faced with such congestion, the only successful means of progress may be to buy an enormous ice cream and carry it before you like a crucifix warding off evil.

Unless you are in urgent need of a fluorescent plastic sword or some Mont-St-Michel dominoes, you can avoid La Grande Rue and its thrusting souvenir shops (wait for the abbey's own shop, which is spacious and well-stocked) by taking the flight of steps opposite the Post Office. These ascend to the town's 13th- to 15th-century **ramparts**, which, turning left, lead via a series of defensive towers to the **abbey entrance**.

On the way you can admire the silvery sands of Mont-St-Michel Bay, with the **Tour du Nord** offering good views of the nearby island of **Tombelaine**. In the 12th century there was a priory here, and English forces erected a castle on the island during the Hundred Years' War. Today the only people to find a use for Tombelaine are the leaders of school

Souvenir shops.

Le Mont St-Michel

100 meters / 109 yards

Chapelle St-Aubert

Fontaine St-Aubert

Tour Gabriel

Jardins de l'Abbaye

Montée aux Poulains

Terrasse de l'Ouest Cloître

La Merveille

Grand Degré

Échauguette du Nord

Réfectoire

Église Abbatiale

Chemin de Ronde Abbatial

Chatelet

Tour du Nord

Port de l'Avancée

Église paroissiale

Bastillion de la Tour Boucle

Port du Roi

Tour du Roi

Post Office

Maison de l'Arcade

Grande

Rue

Musée

Tour Cholet

Courtine

des   Remparts

Tour Basse

Causeway

Tour de la Liberté

parties, who like to point to it as an illustration of what Mont-St-Michel looked like before the monastic skyscrapers arrived.

With more than 80 chapels, cells, towers and public chambers, a guided tour of the **abbey complex** is a necessarily complicated progress through the succession of buildings and social hierarchies that have been stacked up on the island over the past 1,000 years. Visits normally begin on a wide terrace to the west of the abbey, near to a point called **Gautier's Leap** after a prisoner who jumped to his death from its heights. This is reached by climbing a grand inner staircase – the adjacent buildings are where the eight members of today's religious community live.

Work on the **abbey church** began in 1017, with the transept built over what was once the island's highest point. The architects made use of an earlier 10th-century church to form its crypts and supports – a remnant of this original, pre-Benedictine building lies directly below the terrace, now known as the

chapel of **Notre-Dame Sous Terre** (not always included in tours). The terrace itself was once covered by the three westernmost bays of the abbey's nave, which were removed in 1776 after falling into disrepair.

Inside the church four bays of the Romanesque nave survive to face the chancel, rebuilt in 1446–1521 in the Flamboyant Gothic style. The transept crossing and lantern date from the restorations of the 1890s, when the famous skyline of neo-Romanesque belfry, neo-Gothic spire and golden statue of St Michael was created.

Visitors are then taken into **"La Merveille"**, the name commonly given to the early 13th-century Gothic masterpiece added to the north side of the church. Constructed in only 16 years, this marvel of the medieval world stands in ghostly tribute to the island's monks and the society that once revolved around them. Built on three levels, each divided into two rectangular rooms, it reflects the social strata of its day. On the top floor is the enclosed world of the mo-

3th-century loister.

nastic order. Here you find the **cloister**, open to the skies, where the monks could meet and meditate. Next to this is the **refectory**, where rows of narrow windows filter the sunlight and a pulpit reminds us of the holy words that would have been read aloud in Latin during meal times.

Beneath the cloister is the **calefactory** and **scriptorium** (misleadingly named the Salle des Chevaliers in the 18th century), where huge fireplaces enabled the monks to get some warmth, and large windows allowed them to work on the abbey's illuminated manuscripts. Adjacent to this is the **Salle des Hôtes**, formerly reception rooms for the rich and powerful guests visiting the abbot. On the lowest floor were storage cellars and the **almonry**, where pilgrims were received and alms dispensed to the poor. This is now, appropriately, a bookshop and souvenir hall.

Gothic horror: If the great granite carcass of the abbey now seems more like a horror film set than a place of devotion, it is partly because it has been denuded of the stained glass, religious statuary, tapestries and hangings that would have once adorned its walls. Furthermore, the years the abbey served as a political prison have left a grim stain. During that time, the delicate columns and arches of the cloister were made into cell walls, and you can still see the hoist, powered by prisoners walking like hamsters in a tread-wheel, which was used to haul up supplies.

Today visitors can escape to the fresh air of the **Abbey Gardens**, reached through a door at the western end of the almonry. This allows access to the steep and wooded north side of the island, with interesting views back up to La Merveille. Below the western corner of the gardens is the small 15th-century Chapelle St-Aubert.

After leaving the abbey, you can explore the higher reaches of the town by walking south past the **Musée Grévin**, part of a trio of museums that suck tourists in from the Mount's crowded streets. All three offer inessential "experiences" about the abbey and its past: the Grévin favours waxworks, while the **Musée Historique et Maritime** and the **Archéoscope**, both in La Grande Rue, prefer dusty model ships and fatuous audiovisuals respectively.

West of the Musée Grévin, the Chemin de Ronde Abbatial curls round the island to a series of terraces and paths that descend to the **Tour Gabriel**, constructed in 1524 and later crowned with a windmill. An alternative descent to the mundane is to take the steps leading below the Musée Grévin, a route that passes the cemetery of the island's parish church, **St-Pierre**.

The entrance to this predominantly 15th-century church is in La Grande Rue. Inside, the walls are covered with plaques, banners and *ex-votos* brought here by pilgrims – many of them the result of a patriotic upsurge in the 1870s. In a chapel a large silver statue of the Archangel Michael stands with sword raised high. The silent worshippers at his feet, surrounded by flickering candles and devotional pamphlets in foreign languages, are proof that the cult of St-Michel is alive and well.

Left, fortified round tower. **Right**, view from above. **Following page**: deckchairs at Trouville.

326

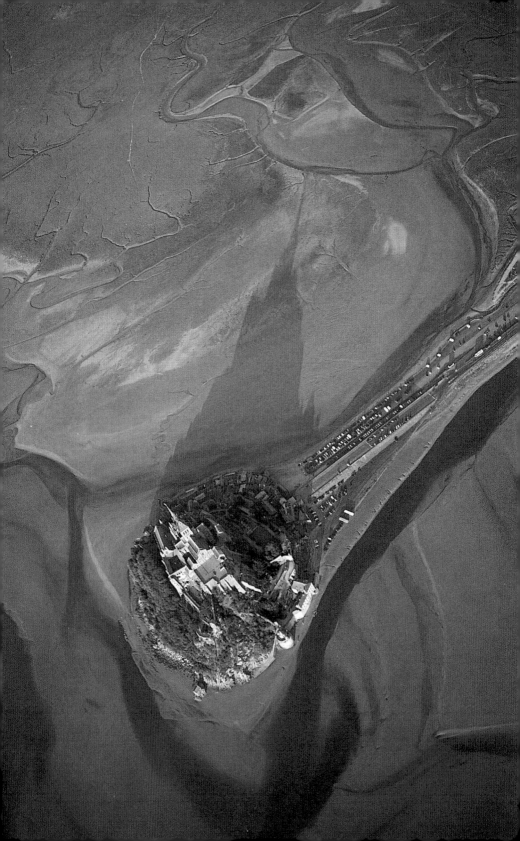

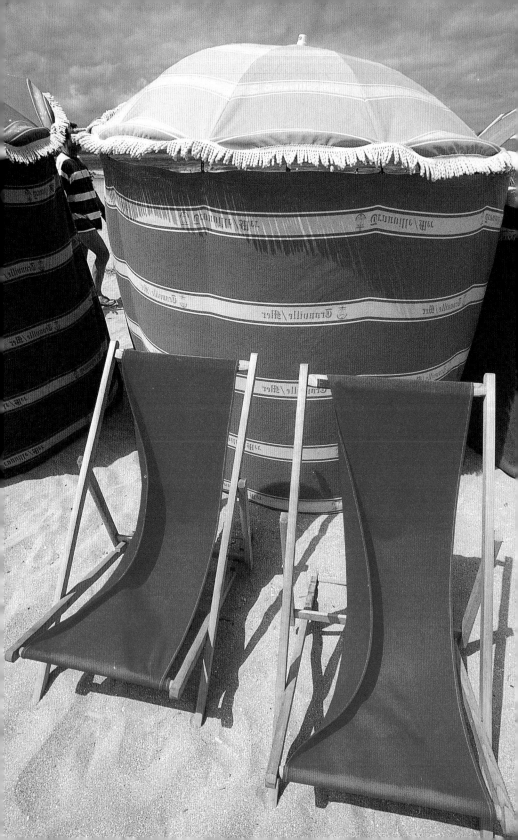

Driving flat-out direct to Holiday France.
(Or Spain)

Lights glitter in the distance.
Is it a cruise-liner, is it a ferry?
Nothing so ordinary. It's Brittany Ferries,
one of a new generation of cruise-ferries that
thinks it's a luxury hotel.
It glides by. It's vast.
And behind countless cabin doors,
discerning travellers are sped direct to the
most convenient port for their holiday,
bypassing busy ports miles out of their way.
And all for the price of an ordinary ferry.
Brittany Ferries are the most modern fleet on
the Channel. We have perfect sailings, great
value fares and a range of marvellous holidays.
For a brochure see your travel agent or ring

(0752) 269926 or (0705) 751708.

So, you're getting away from it all.

Just make sure you can get back.

AT&T Access Numbers
Dial the number of the country you're in to reach AT&T.

*ANDORRA	19◇-0011	GERMANY**	0130-0010	*NETHERLANDS	06-022-9111
*AUSTRIA	022-903-011	*GREECE	00-800-1311	*NORWAY	050-12011
*BELGIUM	078-11-0010	*HUNGARY	00◇-800-01111	POLAND†◆²	0◇010-480-0111
BULGARIA	00-1800-0010	*ICELAND	999-001	PORTUGAL†	05017-1-288
CROATIA†◆	99-38-0011	IRELAND	1-800-550-000	ROMANIA	01-800-4288
*CYPRUS	080-90010	ISRAEL	177-100-2727	*RUSSIA† (MOSCOW)	155-5042
CZECH REPUBLIC	00-420-00101	*ITALY	172-1011	SLOVAKIA	00-420-00101
*DENMARK	8001-0010	KENYA†	0800-10	SPAIN	900-99-00-11
*EGYPT† (CAIRO)	510-0200	*LIECHTENSTEIN	155-00-11	*SWEDEN	020-795-611
*FINLAND	9800-100-10	LITHUANIA◆	8◇196	*SWITZERLAND	155-00-11
FRANCE	19◇-0011	LUXEMBOURG	0-800-0111	*TURKEY	9◇9-8001-2277
*GAMBIA	00111	*MALTA	0800-890-110	UK	0800-89-0011

Countries in bold face permit country-to-country calling in addition to calls to the U.S. *Public phones require deposit of coin or phone card. **Western portion. Includes Berlin and Leipzig. ◇Await second dial tone. †May not be available from every phone. ◆ Not available from public phones. ¹Dial "02" first, outside Cairo. ²Dial 010-480-0111 from major Warsaw hotels. ©1993 AT&T.

Here's a travel tip that will make it easy to call back to the States. Dial the access number for the country you're visiting and connect right to AT&T **USADirect**® Service. It's the quick way to get English-speaking operators and can minimize hotel surcharges.

If all the countries you're visiting aren't listed above, call **1 800 241-5555** before you leave for a free wallet card with all AT&T access numbers. International calling made easy—it's all part of **The *i* Plan.**℠

THE *i* PLAN™

AT&T

TRAVEL TIPS

GETTING THERE

BY AIR

Air France is the main agent for all flights to France (*see Useful Addresses*); as well as their own services they also handle bookings for smaller operators such as Brit Air and Régional Airlines (formerly Air Vendée). Travellers from America and other countries can get direct flights to Paris although for long-haul passengers a charter flight to London, then onward from there may work out cheaper. Nouvelles Frontières offer some of the most competitive fares on both scheduled and charter flights to Paris and London from the US and Canada.

Availability of charter flights is variable; details from their offices at:

London: 11 Blenheim Street, London W1Y 9LE. Tel: 071-629 7772.

New York: 125 West 55th Street, New York, NY 10019 Tel. 212-247 0100.

Montreal: 800 Boulevard de Maisonneuve Est, Montreal, Quebec H2L 4M7. Tel: 514-288 4800.

Air France flies direct to Paris from London, and operates a rail package with flights available from 16 airports around the UK and Ireland (not Heathrow) to Paris, then onward by train to the region. These inclusive tickets can also be combined with a rail pass (*see By Train*). For schedules and booking, contact Air France at 177 Piccadilly, London W1, tel: 081-750 4306, (reservations: 081 742 6200). Brit Air offer services from Gatwick to Caen and Le Havre, bookable through Air France, as above.

Rouen's Vallé de Seine airport has flights to Amsterdam, Barcelona, Brussels, Frankfurt, Geneva and London-Gatwick. Operators are Régional Airlines, Rouen Boos 76520, tel: 35 76 41 20, fax: 35 80 52 36. Air France are agents abroad.

Le Havre has flights to Dusseldorf and Frankfurt (Régional Airlines, Aéroport du Havre, tel: 35 46 09 81, fax: 35 44 88 74); and London (Brit-Air, Aéroport du Havre Octeville, tel: 35 46 09 81, fax: 35 44 88 74). Book abroad through Air France.

Aurigny Air Services fly to Cherbourg from the Channel Isles of Jersey, Guernsey and Alderney. Contact the company at Victoria Street, St Anne's, Alderney. Tel: 0481-822886.

Other low-price charter flights can be obtained through "bucket shops", although France is not as well served by these as other European destinations;

check the national press, or *The European* newspaper for offers.

Students and young people can normally obtain discounted charter fares through specialist travel agencies in their own countries.

In the UK try Campus Travel, 52 Grosvenor Gardens, London SW1W 0AG, tel: 071-730 3402, for your nearest branch. Campus is part of the international group USIT, whose main US address is New York Student Centre, 895 Amsterdam Avenue, New York, NY 10025. Tel: 212-663 5435.

Also in the US is CIEE Council Travel, 205 East 42nd Street, New York, NY 10017.

Discounts on internal flights in France are available from Air Inter under their Grands Bleus tariff which gives young people under 25, and students under 27 up to 65 percent reduction on off-peak flights. For information and booking, contact Air France as above.

BY SEA

Several ferry services operate across the English Channel from the UK, Ireland and the Channel Islands to Normandy. All carry cars as well as foot passengers.

Brittany Ferries offer sailings from Portsmouth to Caen, and a slightly cheaper "Les Routiers" service from Poole to Cherbourg (summer only). They also sail to St Malo, just west of the region from Portsmouth and Cork (Ireland). For details contact: The Brittany Centre, Wharf Road, Portsmouth PO2 8RU, tel: 0705-827701; or from Millbay Docks, Plymouth PL1 3EW. Tel: 0752-221321.

P & O European Ferries sail from Portsmouth to Cherbourg and Le Havre, and also operate the short sea route from Dover to Calais. Fares and schedules: P & O, Channel House, Channel View Road, Dover CT17 9TJ. Tel: 0304-203388.

Stena Sealink Line operate between Southampton and Cherbourg and also offer the northern routes from Newhaven to Dieppe (which offers speedy access to Rouen) and Dover to Calais. Information and bookings: Charter House, Park Street, Ashford, Kent TN24 8EX. Tel: 0233-643381.

Irish Ferries run daily sailings June–August from Rosslare or Cork to Le Havre and Cherbourg. Contact them at 2-4 Merrion Row, Dublin 2. Tel: 01-661 0511.

Companies plying the waters between Normandy and the Channel Islands are:

Emeraude Lines, 1-3 Rue Lecampion, 50400 Granville. Tel: 33 50 16 36. Jersey and Guernsey to Granville.

HAG Marine Services, BP 1, 50340 Flamanville. Tel: 33 04 46 50. Guernsey to Auderville and Flamanville.

Iltour, BP 15, 50270 Barneville-Carteret. Tel: 33 53 87 21. Guernsey and Jersey to Cherbourg and Carteret.

THE NOBLE TIME

JUVENIA

—— 1860 ——

Golden Age ®

COLLECTION

STEEL - STEEL/GOLD - 18KT GOLD AND WITH PRECIOUS STONES

Worldwide list of JUVENIA Agents available on request

JUVENIA MONTRES SA - 2304 LA CHAUX-DE-FONDS - SWITZERLAND
Tel. 41/39 26 04 65 Fax 41/39 26 68 00

Vedettes Amoricaines, 12 Rue Georges Clemenceau, 50400 Granville. Tel: 33 50 77 45. Jersey and Guernsey to Granville.

Alternative routes to the northern ports of France are operated by:

Hoverspeed offer hovercraft or Seacat catamaran service from Dover to Calais and Boulogne (crossing time approx. 30 minutes). Hoverspeed Ltd, Marine Parade, Dover CT17 9TG. Tel: 0304-240241.

North Sea Ferries connect travellers from the north of England and Scotland to France, from Hull to Zeebrugge in Belgium, 35 miles (56 km) from the French border. The overnight services include a five-course dinner and breakfast in the fare. Contact the company at King George Dock, Hedon Road, Hull HU9 5QA. Tel: 0482-795141.

Sally Line ferries use the smaller ports of Ramsgate and Dunkerque in the north of France. For details: 81 Piccadilly, London W1V 9HF, tel: 071-409 2240; or the Argyle Centre, York Street, Ramsgate, Kent CT11 9DS. Tel: 0843-595522.

BY RAIL

France has a fast and efficient rail network operated by the SNCF (Société Nationale des Chemins de Fer de France). There are direct connections to the main cities of the region from Paris Saint-Lazare and Montparnasse stations. Paris to Rouen takes 1 hour 20 minutes, Paris-Caen 3 hours, Paris-Cherbourg 4 hours, Paris-Deauville 2 hours (for Deauville you may have to change at Lisieux where there is a 10-minute wait).

From Saint-Lazare there are through trains to Bayeux, Caen, Carenten Evreux, Gisors, Le Havre, Liseux, Rouen, Vernon, Yvetot. And, in season, to Houlgate and Dives-Cabourg.

From Montparnasse there are through trains to L'Aigle, Argenton, Briouze, Flers, Vire and Granville.

Trains from Gar du Nord go to Eu and Le Tréport.

For other destinations, change at Caen, Lisieux or Rouen.

The fastest route to Mont-St-Michel is by TGV to Rennes in Brittany, and then a local connection.

Tickets may be booked for through journeys from outside France. In the UK tickets can be booked from any British Rail station, including ferry travel. BR travel centres can supply details of continental services, or contact British Rail International Enquiries, International Rail Centre, Victoria Station, London SWl, tel: 071-834 2345. Students and young people under 26 can obtain a discount. Eurotrain, tel: 071-730 3402, offers 30 percent off standard two-month return tickets for those under 26.

French Railways has opened a new telephone service in London to provide an instant booking service. The lines, however, are usually very busy and a little patience is required. The service includes ferry bookings, discounted tickets for young people, a

"Carte Vermeil" for senior citizens, which a gives generous discount on tickets and Eurodomino rail passes (*see below*). Lines are open Monday–Friday and Saturday morning. Tel: 0891-515477 (information only) or 071-495 4433 (reservations only).

Any rail ticket bought in France must be validated by using the orange automatic date-stamping machine at the entrance to the platform. Failure to do so incurs a surcharge.

RAIL PASSES

There are several rail-only and rail combination passes available to foreign visitors. These must always be bought before departing for France. In the UK a Eurodomino Pass offers unlimited rail travel on any 3, 5 or 10 days within a month. This can also be purchased in conjunction with an Air France-Rail ticket (*see By Air*).

Visitors from North America have a wider choice of passes, starting with the basic France Railpass which offers four or nine days' unlimited travel within a month. Then there are various types of Eurail Pass which offer varying periods of first-class travel throughout Europe; the Eurail Youthpass offers a similar deal for young people under 26. The France Rail 'n' Drive pass offers a flexible rail and car rental package, while the Fly Rail and Drive Pass combines internal flights on Air Inter with train travel and car hire.

Similar passes are available to travellers from other countries, although the names of the tickets and conditions may vary slightly.

In the UK, information and reservations for all the above services can be obtained from French Railways Ltd, 179 Piccadilly, London W1 0BA, tel: 071-493 9731; or via the Rail Shop (*see above*).

In the US from Raileurope Inc. at the following locations: 226-230 Westchester Ave, White Plains, NY 10604; 360 Post Street, San Francisco, CA 94102, tel: 415-982 1993; 100 Wilshire Boulevard, Santa Monica, CA 90401, tel: 213-451 5150; II E Adams Street, Chicago, IL 60603, tel: 312-427 8691; 800 Corporate Drive, Suite 108, Fort Lauderdale, FL 33334, tel: 305-776 2729; 6060 N Central Expressway, Suite 220, Dallas, TX 75206, tel: 214-691 5573.

In Canada from Raileurope Inc: 2087 Dundas East, Suite 100, Mississauga, Ontario L4X IM2, tel: 416-602 4195; 643 Notre Dame Ouest, Suite 200, Montréal, Quebec H3C 1HB, tel: 514-392 1311; 409 Granville St, Suite 452, Vancouver, BC V6C IT2.

In Australia and **New Zealand** details are available from Thomas Cook offices.

SCNF has a central reservation office in Paris, tel: (1) 45 65 60 60, and an information service in English tel: (1) 45 82 08 41, in French tel: (1) 45 82 50 50. The SNCF office in Paris is at 10 place de Budapest, 75436 Paris Cedex 09. Tel: (1) 42 85 60 00.

Most French railway stations accept payment by Visa and Amex.

For the fastest weekend refunds anywhere in the world.

Ensure your holiday is worry free even if
your travellers cheques are lost or stolen by buying
American Express Travellers Cheques from;

Lloyds Bank	Leeds Permanent Building Society[*]
Royal Bank of Scotland	Woolwich Building Society[*]
Abbey National[*]	National & Provincial Building Society
Bank of Ireland	Britannia Building Society[*]
Halifax Building Society[*]	American Express Travel Offices.

As well as many regional building societies and travel agents.

[*]Investors only.

Not all travellers cheques are the same.

CHANNEL TUNNEL

The long-awaited Channel Tunnel will offer fast, frequent rail services between London (Waterloo) and Paris (Gare du Nord) – expected journey time is three hours – for connection to other destinations. Subject to the usual delays which are encountered with any major project, the Chunnel will be fully operational by the end of 1994.

Rail passenger services will be operated by a consortium of the French, British and Belgian railway companies and tickets will be bookable through French Railways or British Rail (*see above*).

Le Shuttle is the name for the service to take cars and their passengers from Folkestone to Calais on a simple drive-on-drive-off system, expected journey time 35 minutes. Payment will be at toll booths (which will accept cash, cheques or credit cards). Prepaid tickets will be available, but no booking will be necessary as you will just turn up and take the next available service. Le Shuttle will run 24 hours a day, all year round, with a service at least once an hour through the night. The toll-free motorway link between Rouen and Neufchâtel will be extended to Abbéville by the end of 1994 to make this a reasonable alternative for motorists to the longer ferry crossings.

For information, contact the Eurotunnel Exhibition Centre, St Martin's Plain, Cheriton High Street, Folkestone, Kent CT19 4QD. Tel: 0303-270111.

BY BUS

Eurolines is a consortium of almost 30 coach companies, operating in France and throughout Europe. They operate a service from Bristol to Le Havre and Rouen, via Portsmouth, with connections available from London (Victoria). It operates daily in summer; Friday and Sunday in winter. One of the cheapest ways of reaching France, discounts are available for young people and senior citizens. The ticket includes the ferry crossing (via Dover) and National Express coaches have connections with the London departures from most major towns in the UK. For details contact: Eurolines UK, 52 Grosvenor Gardens, Victoria, London SW1W 0AU. Tel: 071-730 0202.

BY ROAD

Normandy is an ideal destination for car travellers, with good motorways from Paris (N13 to Evreux and Caen, N14 to Rouen) and the Belgium border (N28). The roads are good in the region, and reasonably uncrowded, except on the main routes to and from Paris at peak holiday times (e.g. public holidays, and the first and last weekends in August). Almost all the motorways in France are privately owned and subject to tolls (credit cards are usually acceptable). A toll is also payable on the Brotonne bridge and the Tancarville bridge over the Seine. The

new bridge, opening in 1994, connecting Le Havre to Honfleur, will improve access from the port to the coastal resorts of Deauville, Trouville etc., and the south of the region.

Caen centre is less than 30 minutes from the port of Ouistreham and Rouen is only about an hour away from the channel ports of Le Havre or Dieppe.

TRAVEL ESSENTIALS

VISAS & PASSPORTS

All visitors to France need a valid passport. No visa is currently required by visitors from any EC country or from the US, Canada or Japan. Nationals of other countries do require a visa. If in any doubt check with the French consulate in your country, as the situation may change from time to time. If you intend to stay in France for more than 90 days at any one time, then a *carte de séjour* must be obtained (again from the French consulate) – this also applies to EC members until restrictions are relaxed.

MONEY MATTERS

The Franc is divided into 100 centimes – a 5-centime piece being the smallest coin and the FF500 note the highest denomination bill. Banks displaying the "*Change*" sign will change foreign currency and in general, at the best rates (you will need to produce your passport in any transaction). If possible avoid hotels or other independent bureaux which may charge a high commission. Credit cards are widely accepted, but Visa is by far the most common and can now be used in petrol stations, hypermarkets and many supermarkets. Access (Mastercard/Eurocard) and American Express are also accepted in many establishments. Credit cards can also be used to obtain cash from cashpoints outside banks, using a PIN number. Eurocheques, used in conjunction with a cheque card, drawn directly on your own bank account, can be used just like a cheque in the UK and are commonly accepted. Apply for these, or if you prefer, travellers' cheques, from your own bank, allowing a couple of weeks before your departure.

CUSTOMS

All personal effects may be imported into France without formality (including bicycles and sports equipment). It is forbidden to bring into the country any narcotics, pirated books, weapons and alcoholic liquors which do not conform to French legislation. Certain items (e.g. alcoholic drinks, tobacco, perfume) are limited as to the amount you may take in or out, and these amounts vary for those coming from the EC, other European countries or outside Europe. From 1 January 1993 customs barriers within Europe for alcoholic drinks and tobacco (bought and duty paid in France) practically ceased to exist, but for goods bought at duty-free shops on the ferry or aeroplane the old restrictions still apply. The current allowances are shown below (with on-board duty-free shop allowances in brackets), although these can be exceeded, provided proof is shown that the goods bought are for personal consumption (e.g. a family wedding, and not for resale). If in doubt, check with yopur local customs office (In the UK HM Customs and Excise, Dorset House, Stamford Street, London SE1 9NG. Tel: 071-928 3344 or any Excise enquiry office.)

Customs allowances, for each person over 18 years of age:

10 litres (1 litre) of spirits or strong liqueurs, over 22 percent vol.

20 litres (2 litres) fortified wine.

90 litres (2 litres) wine (of which no more than 60 litres may be sparkling wine).

200 cigars (50 cigars); *or* 400 cigarillos (100 cigarillos); *or* 800 cigarettes (200 cigarettes).

ANIMAL QUARANTINE

No animal under three months of age may be taken into the country. It is not advisable to take animals to France from the UK because of the six months' quarantine required by the British authorities on your return. However, if you do wish to take a pet you need to have either a vaccination certificate for rabies, or a certificate to show that your country has been free of the disease for three years. For further information, contact the French consulate in your country.

GETTING ACQUAINTED

GEOGRAPHY

Normandy in northern France is an ancient province of 11,825 sq. miles (30,627 sq. km), which is about the size of Belgium, and it has some 375 miles (600 km) of coastline. It can be divided into an upper and a lower region. Upper Normandy lies to the east around the basin of the River Seine, which leads on to Paris. The younger geology of its chalk, clay and limestone tends to a flat landscape. This rises to a plateau of around 400 ft (122 metres) in the Perche region towards the south where the Neubourg Plain is particularly featureless. To the north is the Normandy Vexin, a chalk plain which continues into the Caux region and the Alabaster Coast where dramatic white cliffs can be seen in such resorts as Etretat. The northeast Bray region is a depression between the two. The Seine Valley, which towards its estuary meanders through reclaimed marshland, is also marked by chalk cliffs. In the west of the region bordering Lower Normandy is the Auge, an undulating land of small hills and valleys where orchards flourish.

Geologically, Lower Normandy is much older than Upper Normandy. Its main feature, rising to the west of the Caen Plain, is the Amorican Massif made of shale and granite rocks which form the Cotentin peninsula and produce the highest hills in western France in Mount Alavoirs and the Ecouves Forest Beacon which both rise to 1,368 ft (417 metres). This is a typical *bocage* region, a wooded landscape of small fields enclosed by ancient hedgerows. Woodlands were once a great feature of the whole of Normandy and two large tracts of land come under the protection of the Parcs Naturels de France; the Normandie-Maine Regional Park extends to 580,000 acres (234,000 hectares) in the centre and south of the region, while the Brotonne Regional Park covers a more modest 100,000 acres (40,000 hectares) northwest of Rouen.

Heavy clay soil has resulted in the local architectural feature of *colombage,* the half-timbering style infilled with clay. The other memorable building material is the cream-coloured Caen stone and in the Perche region there is a red sandstone used for building called *grison.*

GOVERNMENT & ECONOMY

The name Normandy derives from the Northmen, or Vikings who from AD 820 invaded and settled in the region, and from whom William the Conqueror, 6th Duke of Normandy, was directly descended. However, the Norsemen were not the first to succumb to the subtle charms of this pleasant land. Around AD 280 the Romans established a peaceful rule in the region which lasted many years, during which time they founded many of the towns still in existence, such as Rouen, Bayeux and Avranches. There are signs that Normandy was first settled around the time of the Stone Age, but it is for its connections with England, conquered by William in 1066 and the scene of the great Allied beach landing of World War II, that a large number of British people are acquainted with the region.

Haute (Upper) Normandie, comprises the *départements* of Seine-Maritime and Eure, and Basse (Lower) Normandie covers the *départements* of Orne, Manche and Calvados.

Each *département* (roughly comparable to an English county) is divided into a number of disparately-sized communes whose district councils control a town, village or group of villages under the direction of the local mayor. Until recently, France was ruled largely by central government, but the Paris-appointed *préfets* lost much of their power under the socialists (1981–86) when the individual *départements* gained their own directly elected assemblies, giving them far more financial and administrative autonomy. Each *département* still has a *préfet*, but the role is now more advisory than executive; the *préfecture* is based in the principal town of each *département*. Communes are now responsible for most local planning and environmental matters; decisions relating to tourism and culture are mostly dealt with at regional level, while the state controls education, the health service and security.

French *départements* are identified by an individual number which is used as a convenient reference for administrative purposes, for example it forms the first two digits of the postcode in any address and the last two figures on vehicle licence plates. The *département* numbers follow a simple alphabetical order, i.e. Calvados–14, Eure–27, Manche–50, Orne–61, Seine-Maritime–76.

Normandy's economy is still largely based on agriculture; primarily dairy farming, but also the production of apples, giving rise to the three "Cs" of Normandy: cream, cider and Calvados. Although some small traditional farms still survive – the French seem to have hung on to their small parcels with more tenacity than elsewhere in Europe – economics have demanded that much of the farming is now more commercial. A sizeable proportion of the population works in agricultural-related industries, such as food processing. Heavy industry is mostly confined to the Seine Valley, with the river being accessible to ocean-going vessels as far as Rouen; and also the ports, particularly Le Havre, which is second only to Marseille in the importation of petrol products, and Dieppe and Cherbourg, which still have active shipyards.

Another important industry is vehicle production, with Citroën, and Renault's truck division around Caen accounting for 19 percent of the region's employees, while Renault's car plant in the north has around 24,000 employees. The electronics industry and production of electrical domestic equipment is also a healthy sector of the economy; Moulinex have eight plants around the region and recently opened a research centre near Caen. The textile industry in the *départements* of Orne and Manche has remained fairly stable over the past 10 years. Tourism too, accounts for a growing portion of the region's wealth.

POPULATION

Normandy hasd a population of 3.1 million. The main centres of population are in three principal cities, which form an industrial triangle based along the River Seine. The biggest is Rouen and former capital of Normandy, which has a population of 380,000. Le Havre, the second largest port in France after Marseilles, has a population of 198,000. Caen, capital of Lower Normandy and seat of the Normandy regional council, has a population of 117,000. Evreux, chosen as the base for the Normandy Tourist Office, has a population of just 49,000.

TIME ZONE

For most of the year, France is one hour ahead of Greenwich Mean Time (GMT), so if it is noon in London, the time is 1pm in France, 7am in Washington DC, and 7pm in Singapore.

CLIMATE

The Cotentin peninsula benefits from the warming effect of the Atlantic Gulf Stream. The countryside inland is verdant – there is plenty of rain here, mostly in the autumn. Much of the countryside is given over to pasture and orchards – a visit during blossom time (roughly mid-April to mid-May) is well rewarded. It is often said that the climate of Normandy is similar to that of England. It is true that it is quite variable, but it is generally a few degrees warmer, whatever the season. Winters are fairly mild (average temperature in January is 46°F/7.6°C) and it rarely gets stifling hot in summer (average temperature in August is 72°F/22°C).

CULTURE & CUSTOMS

Normans are in general conservative, Catholic, courteous, country people. They like their traditions and have a pride in the countryside and in their

PART OF
THE ART

swatch+
automatic

swatch+
SCUBA 200

POP
swatch

swatch+
C·H·R·O·N·O

swatch+

SWISS
made

homes. Their history is celebrated on such occasions as the William the Conqueror festival in Cabourg and the Joan of Arc festival in Rouen. *Pardons* and pilgrimages tend to be more popular in the Cotentin, where they have more in common with neighbouring Brittany.

Like all French people, Normans believe their food to be the best, and family meals are something of an occasion. Many of the annual festivals celebrate the harvests of cider, flowers and fish; and there are seasonal markets for cherries, apples and plums.

The region has some of France's most famous artistic sons, particularly in the realms of literature and art (see *Literature* and *Impressionism* chapters). The playwright Pierre Corneille (1606–84) was born at Rouen, as was the writer Gustave Flaubert (1821–80); Guy de Maupassant (1850–93) was born in Seine-Maritime. In the art world, the region is particularly noted for the development of the Impressionists, who were inspired by the coastal region around Dieppe, Le Havre, Deauville and Trouville. Nicolas Poussin (1594–1665), Jean François Millet (1814–75), Eugène Boudin (1824–98) and Raoul Dufy (1877–1953) were all born in the region. Claude Monet (1840–1926) had a house at Giverny, now open to the public, and much visited. In music, Erik Satie (1886–1925) was born in Honfleur, and Maurice Ravel (1875–1937) and Claude Debussy (1862–1918) were inspired by the region.

LANGUAGE

Standard French, which has its roots in the Vulgar Latin of its Roman conquerors, is spoken throughout the region. Local accents should not cause any particular problems. The Viking legacy can be encountered in some place names; places with *bec* in the title for instance imply proximity with a stream.

ELECTRICITY

Electric current is generally 220/230 volts, but still 110 in a few areas. It alternates at 50 cycles, not 60 as in the US, so Americans need a transformer for shavers, travel irons, hairdryers etc., which also takes care of the fact that outlet prongs are different.

WEIGHTS & MEASURES

The metric system is used in France for all weights and measures, although you may encounter old-fashioned terms such as *livre* (about 1 pound weight – 500 grammes) still used by small shop-keepers.

For quick and easy conversion remember that 1 inch is roughly 2.5 centimetres, 1 metre roughly equivalent to a yard, 4 ounces is just over 100 grammes and a kilogram is just over 2 lbs. As a kilometre is five-eights of a mile, a handy reckoning whilst travelling is to remember that 80 kilometres = 50 miles, thus 40 kilometres = 25 miles.

Accurate conversions are given below:

Weight:

3.5 ounces (oz)	=	100 grammes (g)
1.1 pound (lb)	=	500 g
2.2 lb	=	1 kilogram (kg)

Length:

0.39 inch	=	1 centimetre (cm)
1.094 yard	=	1 metre (m)
0.62 mile	=	1 kilometre (km)

Liquid:

2.113 pints		= 1 litre (l)
0.22 Imp gallon; 0.26 US gallon		= 1 litre
2.2 Imp gallons; 2.6 US gallons		= 10 litres

Temperature:

Temperatures are always given in celsius (centigrade). Here are some fahrenheit equivalents:

$0°C = 32°F$; $10°C = 50°F$; $15°C = 59°F$; $20°C = 68°F$; $25°C = 77°F$; $30°C = 86°F$; $35°C = 95°F$

BUSINESS HOURS & PUBLIC HOLIDAYS

Office workers normally start early – 8.30am is not uncommon, and often stay at their desks until 6pm or later. This is partly to make up for the long lunch hours (from noon or 12.30pm for two hours) which are still traditional in banks, shops and other public offices. Many companies are beginning to change to shorter lunchbreaks as employees appreciate the advantages of getting home earlier to families in the evening.

A list of major public holidays is given below. It is common practice, if a public holiday falls on a Thursday or Tuesday, for French business to *faire le pont* (literally "bridge the gap") and have the Friday or Monday as a holiday too. Details of closures should be posted outside banks etc. a few days before the event but it is easy to be caught out, especially on Assumption Day in August, which is not a holiday in the UK.

New Year's Day	1 January
Easter Monday (but not Good Friday)	
Labour Day	Monday closest to 1 May
VE Day	8 May
Ascension Day	
Whit Monday Pentecost	
Bastille Day	14 July
Assumption Day	15 August
All Saints Day-Toussaint	1 November
Armistice Day	11 November
Christmas Day	25 December
(but not Boxing Day, 26 December).	

Banks are normally open Monday–Friday 9am–noon and 2pm–4 or 5pm, but these hours may vary slightly.

*B*REAK THE LANGUAGE BARRIER!

...ou travel internationally, for business or pleasure - or ...you are learning a foreign language - TI's electronic ...guage -products can make communication a lot easier.

...e **PS-5800** is a versatile 3-language dictionary with ...,000 entry words in each language. Available in ...glish/German/French or English/Italian/French, it ...ludes, travel sentences, business words, memory space ...build and store your own vocabulary, currency and ...tric conversions, and more.

...e **PS-5400** is a powerful 5-language translator fea-

turing up to 5,000 words and 1,000 structured sentences in English, German, French, Italian, and Spanish. Travel-related sentences, conveniently grouped by category, facilitate conversation in the language of your choice. To keep you on time and on top, there's also world time, alarm reminders, calculator, and metric conversions.

The **PS-5800** and **PS-5400**. Two pocket-sized ways to break the language barrier!

For more information, fax your request to:
Texas Instruments France, (33) 39 22 21 01

TEXAS INSTRUMENTS

COMMUNICATIONS

POSTAL SERVICES

Provincial post offices – *Postes* or PTTS (pronounced *Pay-Tay-Tay*) are generally open Monday–Friday 9am–noon; 2–5pm and Saturday 9am–noon (opening hours are posted outside); in cities and main towns, such as Caen and Rouen they are generally open continuously from 8am–7pm. Inside major post offices, individual counters are marked for different requirements – if you just need stamps, go to the window marked *Timbres*. If you need to send an urgent letter overseas, ask for it to be sent *par exprès*, or through the Chronopost system which is faster but very expensive.

To cut down queues, many post offices have now installed coin-operated franking machines which produce franked stickers. These machines, marked *Libre service affranchissement*, are easy to operate and have instructions (similar to bank cash machines) in English.

Stamps are often available at tobacconists (*tabacs*) and other shops selling postcards and greetings cards.

Telegrams (*cables*) can be sent during post office hours or by telephone (24-hours); to send a telegram in English dial 16-1 42 33 21 11. Expect to pay around FF75 for a minimum of 15 words to the US, Canada or the UK.

For a small fee, you can arrange for mail to be kept *poste restante* at any post office, addressed to Poste Restante, Poste Centrale (for main post office), then the town's post code and name, e.g. 14000 Caen. A passport, or identity card is required when collecting mail.

Many post offices have coin-in-slot photocopying machines and fax facilities.

TELEPHONE

The French telephone system is now one of the most efficient in the world. That is not to say that you can be guaranteed to find telephone boxes (*cabine publiques*) that are always operational, but most are. Telephone numbers have been rationalised to 8 figures, given in sets of two, e.g. 99 44 63 21, the only codes necessary are for dialling into or out of Paris or overseas. To dial Paris from Normandy, dial 16-1, then the subscriber's number; to dial out of Paris, just dial 16 then the number. International calls can be made from most public booths, but it is often easier to use a booth in a post office – ask at the counter to use the phone, then go back to settle the bill – but you have no record of the cost of the call until the end.

Coin-operated phones take most coins, but the majority are being replaced by card phones. A phone card – *une télécarte* – in different denominations can be purchased from post offices, stationers, railway stations, some cafés and tobacconists. You can even buy one before you go from Voyages Vacances Int., 34 Savile Row, London W1X 1AG, tel: 071-287 3171. Several main post offices now also have telephones that can be used with credit cards.

If you use a phone (not a public call box) in a café, shop or restaurant you are likely to be surcharged. Some hotels and cafés now have computerised public telephones whereby the caller receives a printed statement of the details of his call on payment of the bill at the bar – a useful asset for people travelling on business.

To make an international call, lift the receiver, insert the money (if necessary), dial 19, wait for the tone to change, then dial the country code (*see below*), followed by the area code (omitting any initial 0) and the number.

Some international dialling codes:

Australia	61
Canada	1
Ireland	353
UK	44
US	1

Useful numbers: operator services 13
                directory enquiries 12

Note that numbers will be given in pairs of figures, unless you ask for them to be given *chiffre par chiffre* (singly).

Some main post offices in France have now replaced their traditional telephone directories with the computerised Minitel system. Members of the public can use this free of charge to look up any number in the country. The instructions (in French) are fairly simple to understand, and you simply tap in the name of the town, *département* and person (or company) whose number you seek for it to be displayed on the small screen, connected to the telephone. It can also be used in the same way as *Yellow Pages* to find, for example, all the dry cleaners listed in a particular town.

If you need to make a phone call in rural areas, or small villages with no public phone, look out for the blue plaque saying "*téléphone publique*" on private houses. This means the owner is officially required to allow you to use the phone and charge the normal amount for the call.

You cannot reverse charges (call collect) within France but you can to countries which will accept such calls. Go through the operator and ask to make a PSV (*Pay-Say-Vay*) call. Telephone calls can only be received at call boxes displaying the blue bell sign.

To take advantage of cheap rates, use the

THE WORLD IS FLAT

A.R. SMITH

Its configuration may not be to Columbus' liking but to every other traveller the MCI Card is an easier, more convenient, more cost-efficient route to circle the globe.

The MCI Card offers two international services—MCI World Reach and MCI CALL USA—which let you call from country-to-country as well as back to the States, all via an English-speaking operator.

There are no delays. No hassles with foreign languages and foreign currencies. No foreign exchange rates to figure out. And no outrageous hotel surcharges.

If you don't possess the MCI Card, please call **1-800-842-9144.**

The MCI Card. It makes a world of difference.

MCI

telephone weekdays between 10.30pm and 8am and at weekends after 2pm on Saturday when you will have 50 percent more time for your money.

MEDIA

Regional newspapers, as in the US, contain national and international as well as local news, and have a far higher standing in France than their counterparts in the UK and are often read in preference to the national press. The principal regional paper in Normandy is *Ouest France*. The main national dailies are *Le Monde* (good for a liberal overview of political and economic news), the more conservative *Le Figaro* and the communist papers, *Libération* and *L'Humanité*. *Le Point* and *L'Express* are the major weekly news publications. British and American dailies, notably *The Times*, *The European* and the *International Herald Tribune* are widely available in major towns and cities.

France News is a a bi-lingual newspaper published in Falaise 10 times a year and aimed principally at the business community. *Normandy Today*, a glossy bi-lingual monthly magazine on the life and culture of the region, is widely available.

Television viewers can receive the two main national channels: TF1 (commercial) and Antenne 2 (state-owned but largely financed by advertising; as well as FR3 which offers regional programmes). French houses are beginning to be defaced by satellite dishes at about the same rate as their British counterparts. Cable TV provides access to BBC channels, but as the French TV system is different from the British one; portable black and white sets are the only ones which can pick up French programmes.

France Inter is the main national radio station (1892m long wave) and it broadcasts English-language news twice a day in summer (generally 9am and 4pm). BBC Radio 4 can be received fairly well in parts of the region on long wave (198 kHZ) as can the World Service.

EMERGENCIES

SECURITY & CRIME

Sensible precautions regarding personal possessions is all that should really be necessary when visiting France. Theft and other crime exists here as elsewhere but it is not a serious problem as far as tourists are concerned. Drivers should follow the rules of the road and always drive sensibly. Heavy on-the-spot fines are given for traffic offences, such as speeding, and drivers can be stopped and breathalysed during spot checks. The minimum fine for speeding is FF1,300 and immediate fines of up to FF30,000 can be levied for drink-driving offences (if you do not have enough cash you will be required to pay a deposit). Police are fairly visible on the main roads of France during the summer months.

LOST PROPERTY

If you lose something on a bus or a train, first try the terminus to see if it has been handed in.

To report a crime or loss of belongings, visit the local *gendarmerie* or *commisariat de police*. Telephone numbers are given at the front of local directories, or in an emergency, dial 17. If you lose a passport, report first to the police, then to the nearest consulate (*see Useful Addresses*). If you have the misfortune to be detained by the police for any reason, ask to telephone the nearest consulate for a member of the staff to come to your assistance.

HEALTH CARE

The International Association for Medical Assistance to Travelers (IAMAT) is a non profit-making organisation which anyone can join, free of charge (although a donation is requested). Benefits include a membership card, entitling the bearer to services at fixed IAMAT rates by participating physicians, and a Traveller Clinical Record, a passport-sized record completed by the member's own doctor prior to travel. A directory of English-speaking doctors belonging to IAMAT and on call 24 hours a day, is published for members' use.

EC nationals should check before leaving for France that they qualify for subsidised treatment under the EC (most British nationals do: check with the Department of Health and acquire from them the form E111). The E111 does not cover the full cost of any treatment so you may find it worthwhile to take out private insurance too.

IAMAT offices:

US: 417 Center Street, Lewiston NY 14092. Tel: 716-754 4883.

Canada: 1287 St Claire Ave, W Toronto, M6E 1B9, Tel: 416-652 0137; or 40 Regal Road, Guelph. Ontario N1K 1B5, Tel: 519-836 0102.

New Zealand: PO Box 5049, Christchurch 5.

Switzerland: 57 Voirets, 1212 Grand-Lancy, Geneva.

For minor ailments it may be worth consulting a pharmacy (recognisable by its green cross sign), who have wider "prescribing" powers than chemists in the UK or US. They are also helpful in cases of snake or insect bites and identifying fungi!

If you need to see a doctor, expect to pay around FF100 for a simple consultation, plus a pharmacist's fee for whatever prescription is issued. The doctor will provide a *feuille des soins* which you need to keep to claim back the majority of the cost (around 75 percent) under the EC agreement. You have to attach to the *feuille* the little sticker (*vignette*) from any medicine prescribed to enable you to claim for that too. Refunds have to be obtained from the local *Caisse Primaire* (ask the doctor or pharmacist for the address).

In cases of medical emergency, either dial 15 for an ambulance or call the Service d'Aide Médicale d'Urgence (SAMU) which exists in most large towns and cities – numbers are given at the front of telephone directories.

The standard of treatment in French hospitals is generally high, and you should be able to find someone who speaks English to help you. You may prefer to try to get to either the American Hospital at 63 boulevard Victor-Hugo, 92292 Neuilly. Tel: (1) 47 47 53 00; or the British Hospital Hortford, 3 rue Barbes, 92300 Levallois. Tel: (1) 47 58 13 12, both just outside Paris. Show the hospital doctor or authorities your E111 and you will be billed (once you are back home usually), for approximately 25 percent of the cost of treatment.

GETTING AROUND

MAPS

A first essential in touring any part of France is a good map. The Institute Géographique National is the French equivalent of the British Ordnance Survey and their maps are excellent; those covering the region are listed below:

Red Series (1:250,000, 1 cm to 2.5 km) sheet No. 102 covers the region at a good scale for touring.

Green Series (1:100,000, 1 inch to 4 miles or 1 cm to 1 km), are more detailed, local maps. Sheet Nos. 6 and 7 cover the north and much of the centre of the region, Nos. 16 and 17 the south, Nos. 18 and 8 the east. The Green Series are quite good for walking too, although serious walkers will need IGN's highly detailed 1:50,000 and 1:25,000 scales (**Blue Series**).

Another particularly good series for touring are the Telegraph (**Recta Foldex**) maps which cover France on four maps; the northwest sheet being the appropriate one for Normandy.

Michelin Regional maps are published at a scale of 1;200,000 (1 cm to 2 km); sheet No. 231 covers the whole of Normandy. Local maps are published at the same scale; sheet No. 52 covers the northeast, Nos. 55 and 60 the centre, No. 54 the Cherbourg peninsula and sheet No. 59 covers the southwest.

Michelin also publish a special historical map, sheet No. 102: Battle of Normany map, also at 1:200,000 scale.

Town plans are often given away free at local tourist offices, but if you wish to purchase them in advance, they are available from Michelin or Blay.

Stockists in London are Stanfords International Map Centre, 12–14 Long Acre, Covent Garden WC2, tel. 071-836 1321; The Travel Bookshop, 13 Blenheim Crescent, London W11 2EE, tel: 071-229 5260; Travellers' Bookshop, 25 Cecil Court, London WC2N 4EZ, tel: 071-836 9132; and The European Bookshop, 5 Warwick Street, London W1, tel: 071-734 5259.

World Leisure Marketing, 117 The Hollow, Littleover, Derby, tel: 0332-272020, are the UK agents for IGN and McCarta and offer a mail order service.

Compass Books, Freepost, Dereham, Norfolk NR19 1TE, tel: 0362-691623, offers a mail order service (7-day money-back guarantee) and carries a wide range of maps and guides for whole of France.

In France, most good bookshops should have a range of maps, but they may cost less in hypermarkets or service stations. Motorway maps can often be picked up free of charge at rest areas.

DOMESTIC TRAVEL

Car hire is expensive if rentals are organised locally (*see Driving*), but bikes (*vélos*) are fairly readily available for hire, often from cycle shops. Local tourist offices keep information on hire facilities. French Railways have them for hire at several stations in the region; they do not necessarily have to be returned to the same station. Bikes can be carried free of charge on buses and some trains (Autotrains), on other, faster services you will have to pay. Travelling by a combination of bike and bus or train can be an excellent way of touring, and relieves you of some of the legwork. For further information *see Sports*.

TAXIS

Taxis are normally readily available at railway stations and at official taxi ranks in city centres.

BY BUS

Details of routes and timetables are generally available free of charge either from bus stations (*gare routière*) which are often situated close to rail stations, or from tourist offices. They will also give details of coach tours and sightseeing excursions which are widely available.

BY TRAIN

Information on services is available from stations (*gare* SCNF). If you intend to travel extensively by train it may be worth obtaining a rail pass before leaving home (*see Getting There*). Before buying any tickets in France check on any discounts available, e.g. the *Carte Couple* for married couples travelling together on off-peak services. Children under 4 travel free, from 4 to 12 for half-fare. People travelling in groups of six or more can also obtain discounts (20–40 percent depending on numbers). All tickets purchased at French stations have to be put through the orange machines at the stations to validate them before boarding the train. These are marked "*compostez votre billet*".

DRIVING

British, US, Canadian and Australian licences are all valid in France and you should always carry your vehicle's registration document and valid insurance (third party is the absolute minimum, and a green card – available from your insurance company – is strongly recommended).

Additional insurance cover, which can include a get-you-home service, is offered by a number of organisations including the British and American Automobile Associations and Europ-Assistance, 252 High Street, Croydon CRO 1NF. Tel: 081-680 1234 or 0444-442211; in the US Europ Assistance Worldwide Services Inc., 1133 15th Street, Suite 400, Washington DC 20005. Tel: 202-347 7113. The Automobile Club National is the umbrella organisation of France's 40-odd motoring clubs. They will assist any motorist whose own club has an agreement with it. Contact them at 9 rue Anatole-de-la-Forge, 75017 Paris. Tel: (1) 42 27 82 00, fax: (1) 40 53 90 52.

RULES OF THE ROAD

Britons must remember to drive on the right: it doesn't take long to get used to, but extra care should be taken when crossing the carriageway, for instance, to use a service station. It is very easy to come out and automatically drive on the left – especially if there's no other traffic around.

The minimum age for driving in France is 18; foreigners are not permitted to drive on a provisional licence.

Full or dipped headlights must be used in poor visibility and at night; sidelights are not sufficient unless the car is stationary. Beams must be adjusted for right-hand drive vehicles, but yellow tints are not compulsory.

The use of seat belts (front and rear if fitted) and crash helmets for motorcyclists is compulsory. Children under 10 are not permitted to ride in the front seat unless fitted with a rear-facing safety seat, or if the car has no rear seat.

Priorité à la Droite: An important rule to remember is that priority on French roads is always given to vehicles approaching from the right, except where otherwise indicated. In practice, on main roads the major road will normally have priority, with traffic being halted on minor approach roads with one of the following signs:
Stop
Cedez le passage – give way
Vous n'avez pas la priorité – you do not have right of way
Passage protégé – no right of way

Particular care should be taken in towns, where you may wrongly assume you are on the major road, and in rural areas where there may not be any road markings (watch out for farm vehicles). Note that if a driver flashes the headlights it is to indicate that *he* has priority, not the other way round. Priority is always given to emergency services and also public utility vehicles e.g. gas, electricity and water companies.

The French recently changed the rules concerning roundabouts – in theory drivers already on the roundabout now have priority over those entering it, but beware; some drivers still insist that priority belongs to the drivers entering a roundabout.

SPEED LIMITS

Speed limits are as follows, unless otherwise indicated: 80 mph (130 kph) on toll motorways; 68 mph (110 kph) on other motorways and dual carriageways; 56 mph (90 kph) on other roads except in towns where the limit is 30 mph (50 kph). There is also a *minimum* speed limit of 50 mph (80 kph) on the outside lane of motorways during daylight with good visibility and on level ground. Speed limits are reduced in wet weather as follows: toll motorways: 68 mph (110 kph), dual carriageways: 62 mph 100 kph, other roads: 50 mph (80 kph).

On-the-spot fines can be levied for speeding; on toll roads, the time is printed on the ticket you take at your entry point and can thus be checked and a fine imposed on exit. Nearly all *autoroutes* (motorways) are toll roads.

Autoroutes are designated "A" roads and national highways "N" roads. "D" roads are usually well maintained, while "C" or local roads, may not always be so.

Carry a red warning triangle to place 55 yards (50 metres) behind the car in case of a breakdown or accident (strongly advised, and compulsory if towing a caravan). In an accident or emergency, call the police (dial 17) or use the free emergency telephones (every 1 mile/2 km) on motorways. If another driver is involved, lock your car and go together to call the police. It is useful to carry an European Accident Statement Form (obtainable from your insurance company) which will simplify matters in the case of an accident.

Unleaded petrol (*essence sans plomb*) is now widely available in France. If in doubt, a map showing the location of filling stations is available from main tourist offices.

For information about current road conditions, telephone the Inter Service Route line on (1) 48 94 33 33 (this is a recorded anouncement in French and not always terribly clear).

MOTORCYCLES & MOPEDS

Rules of the road are largely the same as for car drivers. The minimum age for driving machines over 80cc is 18. GB plates must be shown and crash helmets are compulsory. Dipped headlights must be used at all times. Children under 14 years are not permitted to be carried as passengers.

CAR HIRE

As previously mentioned, hiring a car is an expensive business in France, partly because of the high VAT (TVA) rate – 33 percent on luxury items. Some fly/drive deals work out reasonably well if you're only going for a short visit. French Railways offer a good deal on their combined train/car rental bookings. Weekly rates often work out better than a daily hire and it can be cheaper to arrange hire in the UK or US before leaving for France. The minimum age to hire a car is 18, but most companies will not hire to anyone under 23, or 21 if paying by credit card and the hirer must have held a full licence for at least a year. Apart from Avis, most companies have an upper age limit of 60–65. The central reservation offices of the major car hire companies and local offices in some of the main towns of the region are listed below.

Avis:
Central Reservation: Tour Franklin, 92042 Paris-La-Défense Cedex 11. Tel: (1) 49 06 68 68, fax: (1) 47 78 98 98.
Alençon: Garage Kosellek, 45 Rue Paris, 61000. Tel: 33 29 40 67.
Caen: 44 Place de la Gare, 14000. Tel: 31 84 73 80.
Cherbourg: 5 Avenue Carnot, 50100.
Tel: 33 43 16 00.
Deauville: Gare SNCF (main station), 14800.
Tel: 31 88 16 73.
Dieppe: Gare de Dieppe, Boulevard Georges Clemenceau, 76200. Tel: 35 84 40 84.
Evreux: Rue Pierre Sémard, 27000. Tel: 32 39 38 07.
Lisieux: Hall de la Gare SNCF (main station), 14100. Tel: 31 31 71 54.
Rouen: 36 Rue Verte, 76000. Tel: 35 89 87 05.
Budget/Milleville:
Central Reservation: Rue des Hauts-Flouviers, 94517 Thiais. Tel: (1) 46 86 65 65, fax: (1) 46 86 14 13.
Alençon: 28 Rue Mans, 61000. Tel: 33 32 89 00.
Caen: 54 Place de la Gare, 14000. Tel: 31 83 70 47.
Cherbourg: 16 Boulevard Pierre Mendès, 50100.
Tel: 33 94 32 77.
Deauville: 29 Avenue de la République, 14800.
Tel: 31 98 43 37.
Le Havre: 161 Boulevard Strasbourg, 76600.
Tel: 35 22 53 52.
Saint-Lô: 29 Rue Valvire, 50000. Tel: 33 57 77 69.
Citer:
Central Reservation: 125 bis Rue de Vaugirard, 75015 Paris. Tel: (1) 44 38 60 00, fax: (1) 40 56 08 08.
Alençon: Roques SA, RN 138, 61000.
Tel: 33 28 10 20.
Bayeux: Route de Cherbourg, 14400.
Tel: 31 92 18 35.
Caen: Place du 36ème R.I., 14000. Tel: 31 86 58 25.
Deauville: Garage Citroën, 14800. Tel: 31 88 85 44.
Evreux: 81 Route Orléans, 27000. Tel: 32 82 38 39.
Le Havre: 50 Rue Docteur Piasuki, 76600. Tel: 35 25 60 60.
Lisieux: 41 Rue de Paris, 14100. Tel: 31 62 20 73.
Rouen: 180 Avenue Mont Riboudet, 76000. Tel: 35 07 39 78.
Eurodollar/Mattei:
Central Reservation: Place des Reflets, Z.I. Parc Nord II, 165 Avenue du Bois-de-la-Pie, BP 40002, 959111 Roissy-Charles-de-Gaulle Cedex. Tel: (1) 49 38 77 00, fax (1) 49 38 77 02.
Rouen: 134 Avenue Mont Riboudet, 76000. Tel: 35 71 62 42.

Europcar/National/Interrent:
Central Reservation: 65 Rue Edouard-Vaillant, 92100 Boulogne. Tel: (1) 49 10 55 55, fax: (1) 46 20 47 81.
Alençon: 99 Avenue Rhin et Danube, 61000. Tel: 33 28 91 11.
Caen: 36 Place de la Gare, 14000. Tel: 31 84 61 61.
Cherbourg: 4 Rue Tanneries, 50100.
Tel: 3344 53 85.
Deauville: CID, 14800. Tel: 31 98 38 83.
Dieppe: 33 Rue Thiers, 76200. Tel: 35 04 97 10.
Lisieux: 18 Rue de la Gare, 14100. Tel: 31 62 88 80.
Saint-Lô: 41 Boulevard Alsace-Lorraine, 50000. Tel: 33 05 56 57.

Hertz:
Central Reservation: 4 Avenue du Vieil-Etang, 78180 Montigny-le-Bretonneux. Tel: (1) 30 45 65 65, fax: (1) 30 58 46 21.
Bayeux: Boulevard du 6 juin, 14400.
Tel: 31 21 80 40.
Alençon: 26 Avenue Quakenbrück, 61000. Tel: 33 31 08 00.
Caen: AA Calvados Auto, 34 Place de la Gare, 14000. Tel: 31 84 64 50.
Cherbourg: 43 Rue Val de Saire, 50100.
Tel: 33 20 48 11.
Deauville: Garage Hoche, 32 Rue Hoche, 14800. Tel: 31 88 21 79.
Dieppe: 8 Boulevard Général de Gaulle, 76200. Tel: 35 84 01 10.
Evreux: Route Paris, 27000. Tel: 32 33 41 96.
Rouen: 35 Quai G. Boulet, 76000. Tel: 35 98 16 57.

ROUTES

Following a tourist circuit, or route is a sure way of getting to see the major sites of a region. Some are designed to help appreciate the countryside, such as the apple route (Route de la Pomme), but many have an historical significance, such as those connected to World War II. Here are a few suggestions; local tourist offices will provide more complete itineraries, and usually maps.

The **Historical Route of the Norman Master Builders**, is contained in a leaflet published, in English, by the Caisse Nationale des Monuments, 62 Rue Sainte-Antoine, 75004 Paris. Tel: (1) 42 74 22 22. This route largely follows the west coast from Cherbourg down to Mont-St-Michel, dipping inland to Valognes, a town of many noble houses, Coutances, with its splendid cathedral, and Hambye for its ruined abbey in classic Norman gothic style.

The same organisation will also provide details of the **Route Historique des Ducs de Normandie** covering much of Calvados and including many reminders of William the Conqueror, such as his birthplace at Falaise and the Abbaye-aux-Hommes and Abbaye-aux-Dames built for William and his wife in Caen. **Liberty Road** follows the itinerary of the battles during the liberation of France in 1944, all the way to Bastogne in Belgium. Special kilometre markers show the route. Kilometre "0" stands in front of the town hall in Sainte-Mère-Eglise which was liberated on the night of 5 June 1944, but there is also a "00" km marker at Utah Beach. Further information is available from the Manche Tourist office (*see Useful Addresses*).

La Route Normandie-Vexin offers a 124 miles (200 km) cultural tour from Rouen towards Paris ending at Monet's house and garden at Giverny, and taking in some spectacular sights en route, such as the Cistercian abbey at Fontaine-Guérard, the majestic ruins at Les Andelys and the 18th-century Château de Bizy.

Normandy is famed for its riding stables and in the Orne you can follow the **Route Historique des Haras et des Châteaux de l'Orne**, which includes the important national stud farm (*haras*) at Le Pin-au-Haras. Other important sites on the route are Sées cathedral, Sassy Manor with its formal gardens, and the Château d'O at Mortrée. Also in the Orne the **Suisse Normande Route** is signposted through the lovely Orne valley, passing through Thury-Harcourt (where you can forsake the car for a little tourist train), Condé-sur-Noireau and Clécy with its narrow streets and museums.

The **Cider Route** is signposted, "Route du Cidre" in the Pays d'Auge, linking charming country towns such as Cambremer, Beuvron-en-Auge and Beaufour-Druval. Along the way many small farms will offer tastings of their wares, not just cider, but also the apple brandy, Calvados, and *pommeau*, the aperitif made from cider apples.

The Seine-Maritime tourist board have come up with no less than eight routes around their *département* and beyond, including the **Route du Fromage de Neufchâtel** for cheese-lovers and the **Route du Val de Seine et des Abbayes**. The Eure tourist board have also poduced their own guide to marked routes: *Circuits en Vallée de Risle et Alentours*. For details of all these write to main tourist offices in the *départements* concerned (*see Useful Addresses*).

A further source of information about historic routes and monuments is Demeure Historique, 57 Quai de la Tournelle, 75005 Paris. Tel: (1) 43 29 02 86.

RAMBLERS

France has a network of waymarked footpaths, called Grandes Randonnées, which are well signposted and in the main offer good facilities for walkers en route. The paths are classified with a GR number and there are countless opportunities for exploring Normandy by foot, either following a long route, or on one of the shorter circular tours. Suggested tours might be the GR2: Cliffs on the Seine; GR223 Cotentin tour from Avranches to Barfleur; GR261: Normandy Landing Beaches; GR36 Ouistreham to Ecouché via the Orne Valley or a 155 miles (250 km) tour of the Pays d'Auge. Other GR paths in the region include the Pays de Caux (GR21, 211 and 212);

Suisse Normande (GR221); Eure valley and forests (GR222); the Normandy-Maine Regional Park (GR22 and 36) and the GR26 which runs from Feucherolles via Evreux and Bernay to the coast at Deauville.

These GR routes come under the protection of the French Ramblers' Association, Fédération Française de la Randonnée Pédestre (FFRP) based at 8 Avenue Marceau, 75018 Paris. Tel. (1) 47 23 62 32, fax: (1) 47 20 00 74. The FFRP publishes *Topoguides* (guide books incorporating IGN 1:50,000 scale maps) to all France's footpaths but they are only available in French. These guides are available in good book-shops in France, or in the UK try Stanfords in London.

McCarta's Footpaths of Europe series are regional walking guides based on the *Topoguides*, in English, with IGN mapping. There are two titles for the region: *Normandy and the Seine* covering the 435 miles (700 km) of footpaths along the Seine from Paris to the coast; and *Coastal Walks in Normandy and Brittany*, a guide to the 560 miles (900 km) of footpaths bordering the fascinating coastline across the two regions. A good basic guide book for serious walkers is Rob Hunter's book *Walking in France*, published by Oxford University Press. The IGN Blue series maps at a scale of 1:25,000 are ideal for walkers. For a grid, contact the stockists mentioned in the Maps section above.

Each *département* has its own ramblers' organisation (operating under the FFRP umbrella) which arranges a variety of activities throughout the year: guided walks taking a day, a weekend or more, as well as walks with a particular theme, flora, or wildlife for example.

For more information, contact the Centre d'Information Sentiers et Randonnée, 64 Rue Gergovie, 75014 Paris. Tel: (1) 45 45 31 02, or the regional offices of the FFRP as follows:
Seine-Maritime: Comité Départemental de la Randonnée Pédestre, BP 680, 76008 Rouen Cedex.
Calvados: Comité Départemental de Tourisme Pédestre, 6 Promenade de Mme de Sévigné, 14050 Caen Cedex. Tel: 31 88 33 02.
Eure: Coderando 27, BP 187, 27001 Evreux Cedex. Tel: 32 32 07 88 (after 8.30pm).
Orne: Délégation du Comité National des Sentiers de Grande Randonnée, Centre Social et Culturel, Rue E Branly, 61000 Alençon. Tel: 33 29 22 56.
Manche: Coderando 50, Maison du Département, 50008 Saint-Lô. Tel: 33 05 98 70.

Tourist offices will also give information about local clubs and events.

Various walking holidays with accommodation either in hotels or under canvas are available; try the following:
Office National des Forêts, 36 Rue St-Blaise, 61000 Alençon. Tel: 33 26 28 12. Tour the forests of Orne.
Clés de France, 13 Rue Saint-Louis, 78100 Saint-Germain-en-Laye. Tel: (1) 30 61 23 23. The national

organisation for holidays in France's regional parks offers a weekend exploring the Brotonne Park.

Independent travellers can take advantage of low-priced accommodation offered in *gîtes d'Étapes*, hostels offering basic facilities which are to be found on many of the GR routes and in mountain regions. For more information contact the Gîtes de France organisation (*see Where to Stay*).

HITCHHIKING

With sensible precautions, hitchhiking can be an interesting and inexpensive way to get around France. Would-be hitchhikers may be discouraged by the difficulty of getting a lift out of the channel ports, so it may be worth taking a bus or train for the first leg of your journey. Hitching is forbidden on motorways, but you can wait on slip roads or at toll booths. Allostop is a nationwide organisation which aims to connect hikers with drivers (you pay a registration fee and a contribution towards the petrol). Tel: (1) 42 46 00 66.

WHERE TO STAY

Advice to visitors to the celebrations for the 50th Anniversary of the Normandy Landings: much of the accommodation in the proximity of the landing beaches has been booked up well in advance of the celebrations in the summer of 1994.

Stopover suggestions for the travelling motorist are given later in the *Restaurant* section.

HOTELS

Hotels are plentiful in the main towns of the region and along the main highways, but those tucked away in the smaller country villages can be the best. All hotels in France conform to national standards and carry star-ratings, set down by the Ministry of Tourism, according to their degree of comfort and amenities. Prices (which are charged per room, rather than per person) range from as little as FF90 for a double room in an unclassified hotel (i.e. its standards are not sufficient to warrant a single star, but is likely to be clean, cheap and cheerful), to around FF400 for the cheapest double room in a 4-star luxury hotel.

Hotels are required to display their menus outside, and details of room prices should be visible either outside or in reception, as well as on the back of bedroom doors. It is possible for a hotel to have a 1-star rating, with a 2-star restaurant. This is ideal if you are on a budget and more interested in food than wallpaper or plumbing.

When booking a room you should normally be shown it before agreeing to take it; if it doesn't suit you, ask to be shown another (this may sound odd advice, but rooms can vary enormously within the same building). Prices are charged per room; supplements may be charged for an additional bed or a cot (*lit bébé*). You may be asked when booking if you wish to dine, particularly if the hotel is busy – though you are not obliged to take a meal along with the room, preference may in fact be given to hungry customers as there is not a lot of profit in letting rooms alone. Also the simple request, "*On peut dîner ici ce soir?*" will confirm that the hotel's restaurant is open (many are closed out of season on Sunday or Monday evenings).

Lists of hotels can be obtained from the French Government Tourist office in your country or from regional or local tourist offices in France. It is also worth buying from the Tourist Office in London the *Logis et Auberges de France* guide. This is an invaluable guide to an excellent and reasonably priced network of family-run hotels who aim to offer a friendly welcome and good local cuisine. The guide can be bought in bookshops in France but it is more expensive. It can be used to book hotels before travelling (for the central reservation office in Paris, tel: (1) 45 84 83 84); they also offer a "*Logis en Liberté*" or "Go as you please" service, whereby you can book several different hotels, participating in the scheme, for a flat rate. Some tourist offices will make hotel bookings for you, for a small fee.

Several other hotel chains and associations offer central booking facilities. These range from the very cheap and simple groups such as the Balladins chain of modest but very modern 1-star hotels, to the Concorde group of 4-star and de-luxe hotels.

A list of central booking offices follows, with UK and US contacts mentioned where available.

Altéa/Mercure, 7 Allée du Brévent, 91021 Evry Cedex Résinter. Tel: (1) 60 77 27 27, fax: (1) 60 77 21 08. UK office: Tel: 081-741 4655, fax: 081-748 3542. The Altéa group are also linked with Hotels Pullman, and between them they have several smart hotels in Normandy, including the Grand Hotel in Cabourg.

Balladins, 20 Rue du Pont-des-Halles, 94656 Rungis Cedex. Tel: (1) 49 78 24 61, fax: (1) 46 86 41 44. Budget-priced hotels.

Campanile, 31 Avenue Jean-Moulin, 77200 Torcy. Tel: (1) 64.62.46.46, fax: (1) 64 62 46 61. UK office: Tel: 081-569 6969, fax: 081-569 4888. Chain of mostly modern purpose built hotels.

Climat de France, 5 Avenue du Cap-Horn, ZAC de Courtaboeuf, BP 93, 91943 Les Ulis. Tel: (1) 64 46 01 23 or 05 11 22 11 (toll-free in France), fax: (1) 69 28 24 02. UK office: Tel: 071-287 3181. Moderate to 4-star hotels.

Formule 1, Immeuble le Descartes, 29 Promenade Michel-Simon, 93163 Noisy-le-Grand. Tel: (1) 43 04 01 00, fax: (1) 43 05 31 51. Budget-priced hotels, offering a booking service from one hotel to another in the chain.

Ibis/Urbis, 6-8 Rue du Bois-Briard, 91021 Evry Cedex. Tel: (1) 60 77 27 27, fax: (1) 60 77 22 83. UK office: Tel: 071-724 1000, fax: 081-748 9116.

Minotels France Accueil, 85 Rue du Dessous-des-Berges, 75013 Paris. Tel: (1) 45 83 04 22, fax: (1) 45 86 49 82. UK office: France Accueil, 10 Salisbury Hollow, Edington, Westbury, Wilts BA13 4PF. Tel: 0380-830125; or Minotels Great Britain, 5 Kings Road, Cleveleys, Lancs FY5 1BY. Tel: 0253-66266, fax: 0253-866251. US office: Minotels Europe, 683 South Collier Boulevard, Marco Island, Florida 33037. Tel: 813-394 3384 (toll free 1-800-336 4668), fax: 813-394 3384. Canadian office: Tours Chanteclerc, 65 Rue de Brésoles, Montréal, Québec H2Y 1V7. Tel: 514-845 1236, fax: 514-845 5794.

The following are hotel groups which do not have central booking facilities. Most of these groups offer something other than the average hotel. Each group produces its own brochure or list of hotels, available from the addresses below, but bookings have to be made with the individual establishments.

Châteaux-Demeures de Tradition et Grandes Etapes de Vignobles, BP 40, 13360 Roquevaire. Tel: 42 04 41 97, fax: 42 72 83 81. Elegant hotels.

Relais et Châteaux, 9 Avenue Marceau, 75116 Paris. Tel: 47 23 41 42, fax: (1) 47 23 38 99. Independently-owned hotels and restaurants in former castles and other historic buildings (guide available from French Government Tourist Offices abroad). UK information office: 28 Basil Street, London SW3 1AT.

Les Relais du Silence, 2 Passage Duguesclin, 75015 Paris. Tel: (1) 45 66 77 77, fax: (1) 40 65 90 09. Two to 4-star hotels in particularly tranquil settings.

It is not possible to offer a comprehensive list of hotels for the whole region, for which we recommend the Michelin Red Guide. The following is just a small selection to suit all budgets. Star ratings are given thus ✩; CC means credit cards. Double room prices are given but should be taken as a rough guide only.

SEINE MARITIME

CAUDEBEC-EN-CAUX

Le Cheval Blanc, 4 Place René Coty, 76490. Tel: 35 96 21 66. Small hotel; reasonably-priced restaurant. CC: Amex, Diners, Eurocard, Visa. FF160–280.

DIEPPE

La Présidence ✩✩✩, Boulevard de Verdun, BP 32, 76200. Tel: 35 84 31 31. Spacious and central. FF340–530.

L'Univers ✩✩✩, 10 Boulevard de Verdun, 76200. Tel: 35 84 12 55. Fading elegance, right by the sea. CC: most. Around FF200.

ETRETAT
Le Donjon, Chemin de St Clair, 76790. Tel: 35 27 08 23. A small château in its own quiet grounds overlooking the sea. CC: Amex, Visa.

EU
Pavillon de Joinville ☆☆☆, Route du Tréport, 76260. A former hunting lodge, set in delightful grounds. CC: most. FF255–335.

FORGES-LES-EAUX
Le Havre Foch ☆☆, 4 Rue de Caligny, 76600. Tel: 35 42 50 69. Quiet surroundings near the marina. CC: Amex, Diners, Visa. FF175–280.

La Paix, 17 Rue de Neufchâtel, 76440. Tel: 35 90 51 22. A small, simple hotel and restaurant. CC: Amex, Diners, Eurocard, Visa. FF107–165.

MARTIN EGLISE
Auberge du Clos Normand ☆, 22 Rue Henri IV, 76370. Tel: 35 04 40 34. Attractive hotel and restaurant, not far from Dieppe. Closed: Monday evening, and Tuesday; 22 November–22 December. CC: Amex, Diners, Eurocard, Visa. FF260–360.

NEUFCHÂTEL-EN-BRAY
Le Grand Cerf, 9 Grande Rue Fosse Porte, 76270. Tel: 35 93 00 02. Hotel and restaurant set in its own grounds. CC: Eurocard, Visa. FF200–250.

ROUEN
De Dieppe ☆☆☆, Place Bernard-Tissot, 76000. Tel: 35 71 96 00. Convenient for the station, but quiet rooms. CC: Amex, Diners, Visa. FF350–520.

Du Gros Horloge ☆☆, 91 Rue du Gros Horloge. Tel: 35 70 41 41. Near the famous clock in the old part of town. From FF150.

SAINT VALÉRY EN CAUX
Les Terrasses ☆☆, 22 Rue le Perrey sur Front de Mer, 76460. Tel: 35 97 11 22. Hotel and restaurant of the Logis de France association. Closed: Wednesday, and 20 December–31 January. CC: Diners, Eurocard, Visa. FF300–350.

VARENGEVILLE SUR MER
De la Terrasse ☆☆, 76119. Tel: 35 85 12 54. Seaside hotel in own grounds. Tennis court and children's play area. CC: Eurocard, Visa. Menus from FF80 (children FF45). Rooms: FF240–280.

CALVADOS

ARROMANCHES
De la Marine ☆☆, Quai du Canada, 14117. Tel: 31 22 34 19. An ideal base for visiting the landing beaches. Good restaurant. CC: Amex, Eurocard, Visa. FF200–340.

AUDRIEU
Château d'Audrieu, 14250. Tel: 31 80 21 52. Very convenient for Bayeux and Caen, set in its own grounds in verdant countryside. Excellent restaurant. CC: most. FF560–1,800.

BAYEUX
Grand Hôtel du Luxembourg, 25 Rue des Bouchers, 14403. Tel: 31 92 00 04. It *is* quite grand. FF320–520.

CABOURG
Du Golf ☆☆☆, Avenue Michel d'Ornano, 14390. Tel: 31 24 12 34. Resort hotel of medium size to suit medium budgets. CC: most. FF275–440.

CAEN
Le Relais des Gourmets ☆☆☆☆, 15 Rue de Geôle, 14000. Tel: 31 86 06 01. In a central location, with a traditional restaurant. FF240–430.

Le Dauphin ☆☆☆, 29 Rue Gemare, 14000. Tel: 31 86 22 26. Hotel in the *Logis* de France association. Restaurant closed Wednesday lunchtime; and mid–July to 10 August. CC: Amex, Diners, Eurocard, Visa. FF310–460.

Le Jasmine ☆, 37 Rue Pierre Girard, 14000. Tel: 31 52 08 16. Small, modest hotel for those on a budget. FF95–115.

DEAUVILLE
Le Royal ☆☆☆☆, Boulevard Cornuché, 14800. Tel: 31 98 66 33. Majestic hotel – one of the top places to stay in this elegant resort; some rooms have good sea views. CC: most. Rooms: FF860–2,000.

Les Sports ☆☆, 27 Rue Gambetta, 14800. Tel: 31 88 22 67. Small hotel for those with a somewhat lower budget. FF190–395.

FALAISE
De la Poste ☆☆, 38 Rue Georges Clémenceau, 14700. Tel: 31 90 13 14. Stay in the town where William the Conqueror was born. CC: Amex, Eurocard, Visa. FF190–360.

HONFLEUR
La Ferme-St-Siméon ☆☆☆☆, Route A Marais, 14600. Tel: 31 89 23 61. Unashamed luxury in a hotel of the Relais et Châteaux chain. Facilities include an indoor swimming-pool and health club. CC: most. FF990–3,250.

Le Cheval Blanc ☆☆☆, 2 Quai des Passagers, 14600. Tel: 31 89 13 49. Near the quaint harbour; good restaurant. FF365–580.

LISIEUX
La Bretagne ☆☆, 30 Place de la République, 14100. Tel: 31 62 09 19. Has rooms suitable for the disabled. CC: Amex, Diners, Eurocard, Visa. FF170–356.

PONT L'EVÊQUE
Climat de France ☆☆, 14130. Tel: 31 64 64 00. Modern hotel set in a lakeside leisure complex. CC: most. FF245–350.

TROUVILLE
Carmen ☆☆, 24 Rue Carnot, 14360. Tel: 31 88 35 43. Reasonably priced hotel in this popular resort. Closed: Monday evening, Tuesday low season, and 6 January–9 February. CC: Amex, Diners, Eurocard, Visa. FF180–380.

VIRE
Des Voyageurs ☆, 47 Avenue de la Gare, 14500. Tel: 31 68 01 16. Moderately priced *Logis* de France hotel near the station. CC: Amex, Diners, Eurocard, Visa. FF132–220.

EURE

LE BEC HELLOUIN
L'Auberge de l'Abbaye ☆☆☆, 27800. Tel: 32 44 86 02. Charming inn on the village square with rooms overlooking the rolling Risle valley. CC: most. FF320–350.

EVREUX
De France ☆☆, 29 Rue Saint-Thomas, 27000. Tel: 32 39 09 25. Has a good restaurant overlooking a garden. The restaurant is closed Sunday evening and Monday. CC: Diners, Eurocard, Visa. FF260–330.

PONT-AUDEMER
Auberge du Vieux Puits ☆☆, 6 Rue Notre-Dame-du-Pré, 27500. Tel: 32 41 01 48. Tudor-style mansion near the centre of this charming old town. Lovely courtyard. CC: most. FF180–360.

PONT-SAINT-PIERRE
La Bonne Marmite ☆☆☆, 10 Rue René Raban, 27360. Tel: 32 49 70 24. Pleasant hotel in the Andelle valley, convenient for visiting Les Andelys, Château Gaillard, etc. CC: Amex, Diners, Eurocard, Visa. FF350–420.

SAINT-PIERRE-DU-VOUVRAY
Hostellerie Saint-Pierre ☆☆☆, 1 Chemin des Amoureux. Tel: 32 59 93 29. Traditional, half-timbered residence on the bank of the Seine. Closed: 10 January–28 February. CC: Eurocard, Visa. FF450–790.

VERNEUIL-SUR-AVRE
Hostellerie du Clos ☆☆☆☆, 98 Rue de la Ferté-Vidame, 27130. Tel: 32 32 21 81. Delightful hotel in Relais et Châteaux chain set in parkland, with a tennis court and sauna. Closed: December–February, and Monday low season. CC: most. FF600–780.

VERNON
Le Normandy ☆☆☆P, 1 Avenue Pierre Mendès France, 27200. Tel: 32 51 97 97. Convenient for visitors to Monet's house and the garden at Giverny. CC: most.

ORNE

L'AIGLE
Le Dauphin ☆☆☆, 4-6 Place de la Halle, 61300. Tel: 33 24 43 12. Centrally situated, upmarket hotel with a 4-star restaurant. CC: most. FF337–432.

ALENÇON
Du Grand Cerf ☆☆☆, 21 Rue St-Blaise, 61000. Tel: 33 26 00 51. Has a garden and reasonably-priced restaurant. CC: most. FF270–380.

Le Grand Saint Michel, 7 Rue du Temple, 61000. Tel: 33 26 04 77. Small *Logis* de France hotel participating in the "Go as you please" scheme. Closed: Sunday evening in low season, and February school holiday. CC: Visa. FF160–280.

ARGENTAN
La Renaissance, 20 Avenue de la 2eme DB, 61200. Tel: 33 36 14 20. This hotel (in the course of being reclassified) boasts a 4-star restaurant. CC: Amex, Diners, Eurocard, Visa. FF220–300.

BAGNOLES DE L'ORNE
Le Celtic ☆☆, 14 Boulevard Albert Christophe, 61140. Tel: 33 37 92 11. Family-run Logis de France. Closed: January, Sunday evening, and Monday in low season. CC: Visa. FF200–260.

Savoy-Hotel P, 3 Boulevard Lemeunier-de-la-Raillère, 61140. Tel: 33 37 84 02. Reasonably-priced hotel with its own garden. Menus from FF68. CC: most. Rooms: FF190–200.

BELLÊME
Relais Saint Louis, 1 Boulevard Bansard-des-Bois, 61130. Tel: 33 73 12 21. Small, moderately priced *Logis* de France hotel and restaurant. Closed: Sunday in low season. CC: Eurocard, Visa. FF200–250.

LA FERTÉ-MACÉ
Auberge d'Andaine, La Barbère, Route de Bagnoles, 61600. Tel: 33 37 20 28. Hotel and restaurant in its own grounds in this country resort. Closed: Sunday in low season. CC: Eurocard, Visa. FF180–280.

FLERS
De l'Ouest ☆☆, 14 Rue de la Boule, 61100. Tel: 33 64 32 43. Hotel and restaurant with a garden. CC: Eurocard, Visa. FF174–240.

GACÉ
Hostellerie Les Champs ☆☆, Route d'Alençon, 61230. Tel: 33 39 09 05. Has its own swimming-pool and tennis court. CC: most. FF190–365.

SÉES
Le Cheval Blanc ☆☆, 1 Place Saint-Pierre, 61500. Tel: 33 27 80 48. Small hotel in a town with a notable cathedral. Closed: Friday evening, and Saturday low season; Thursday evening, and Friday high season. CC: Eurocard, Visa. FF165–260.

TESSÉ-LA-MADELEINE
Chanteclerc ☆☆, 2 Boulevard du Dr. R-Louvel, 61140. Tel: 33 37 82 20. Modest hotel in this spa town. Closed: November–March. CC: most. FF133–190.

MORTAGNE AU PERCHE
Du Tribunal, 4 Place du Palais, 61400. Tel: 33 25 04 77. Stands in its own grounds in this country resort. Menus from FF59. A *Logis* participating in the "Go as you please scheme". CC: Amex, Eurocard, Visa. Rooms: FF125–350.

MANCHE

AVRANCHES
Du Jardin des Plantes, 10 Place Carnot, 50300. Tel: 33 58 03 68. Good family hotel with children's play area and menu. CC: Eurocard, Visa. FF160–290.

BRÉVILLE SUR MER
La Mougine des Moulins à Vent ☆☆, 50290. Tel: 33 50 22 41. A small hotel three minutes from the seaside resort of Granville. CC: Diners, Visa. FF325–395.

CHERBOURG
Le Louvre ☆☆, 2 Rue H Dunant, 50100. Tel: 33 53 02 28. No restaurant. CC: Visa. FF160–220.

COUTANCES

Cositel ☆☆, Route de Coutainville, 50200. Tel: 33 07 51 64. Well equipped to welcome the disabled and good facilities for children, including mini-golf. CC: Amex, Diners, Eurocard, Visa. FF320–340.

GRANVILLE

Marmotte ☆, 57 Avenue des Matignons, 50400. Tel: 33 50 05 05. Moderately priced with rooms from around FF100.

MONTPINCHON

Hostellerie Château de la Salle ☆☆, 50210. Tel: 33 46 95 19. An old manor house in a quiet spot near Coutances. Closed: January–Easter. CC: Amex, Diners, Visa. FF500–680.

MONT-ST-MICHEL

Les Terrasses Poulard ☆☆☆, Intra Muros, 50116. Tel: 33 60 14 09. Modern and offering all the comforts, but beware the tourist hordes. CC: Amex, Diners, Visa. FF320–770.

SAINT-LÔ

Les Voyageurs ☆☆, 5-7 Avenue de Briovère, 50000. Tel: 33 05 08 63. Near the station. Closed: 20 December–10 January; Sunday evening, and Monday. CC: Amex, Diners, Eurocard, Visa. FF260.

SAINT-VAAST-LA-HOUGUE

De France et des Fuschias ☆☆, 18 Rue Maréchal Foch, 50550. Tel: 33 54 42 26. Delightful old hotel, offering a good fish menu. CC: Amex, Diners, Eurocard, Visa. FF130–450.

SAINTE-CÉCILE

Manoir de l'Acherie ☆☆, 50800. Tel: 33 51 13 87. A lovely 17th-century manor house in a peaceful setting near Villedieu-les-Poëles. Good restaurant. Closed: Monday (except hotel in July–August), and 22 June–7 July. CC: Eurocard, Visa. FF220–320.

BED & BREAKFAST

Bed and breakfast accommodation is fairly widely available in private houses, often on working farms, whose owners are members of the Fédération Nationale des Gîtes Ruraux de France. All such accommodation is inspected by a local representative of the Fédération to ensure that standards are maintained in accordance with its "star" rating (which in fact is shown by ears of corn on a scale of one to four). Bookings can be made for an overnight stop or a longer stay. Breakfast is included in the price (from around FF140 for one person, FF180 for a couple) and evening meals – usually made with local produce and extremely good value – are often available.

Staying with a family in this way provides an ideal opportunity really to get to know the local area and its people. Brochures of all recognised Gîtes-Chambres d'hôtes are available from Gîtes de France organisation in each *département* some are bookable through the Gîtes de France office in London (*see Self-Catering*).

B&B Abroad offer a straightforward bed and breakfast service which can include ferry bookings if desired. They will book accommodation at either a single destination or various stops around the region. Contact: 5 Worlds End Lane, Green St Green, Orpington, Kent BR6 6AA. Tel. 0689-855538.

Café-Couette is a Paris-based organisation offering B&B, or as they call it, *Hébergement chez l'habitant*. Contact them at 8 Rue de l'Isly, 75008 Paris, tel: (1) 42 94 92 00, fax: (1) 4294 93 12. The Café-Couette brochure is also available from the French Government Tourist Office in London, price £6 (£7 by post).

For B&B on a slightly grander scale, try Château Welcome, PO Box 66, 94 Bell Street, Henley-on-Thames RG9 1XS, tel: 0491-578803. They organise stays in privately-owned châteaux where an evening meal is often also available. In Canada: book through Tours Chanteclerc, 65 Rue de Brésoles, Montréal, Québec H2Y 1V7, tel: 514-845 1236; and at 100 Adelaide Street West, Toronto, Ontario M11 1S3, tel: 416-867 1595.

If you do not wish to book anything in advance, just look out for signs along the road (usually in the country) offering *chambres d'hôtes*. You will be taking pot luck, but you may be delighted by the simple farm food and accommodation on offer.

SELF-CATERING

France has what is probably the best network of self-catering holiday cottages anywhere in Europe. The Fédération des Gîtes Ruraux de France was set up around 40 years ago with the aim of restoring rural properties (by means of offering grants to owners) on the condition that these properties would then be let as cheap holiday homes for the less well-heeled town and city dwellers. These *gîtes* (literally: a place to lay one's head) have now become extremely popular with the British in particular, as an inexpensive way of enjoying a rural holiday in France. The properties range from very simple farm cottages to grand manor houses and even the odd château.

The properties are all inspected by the Relais Départemental des Gîtes Ruraux de France (the county office of the national federation) and given an *épi* (ear of corn) classification. The *gîtes* are completely self-catering (in many cases expect to supply your own bed-linen), but most have owners living nearby who will tell you where to buy local produce (and if on a farm, often provide it). One salutary note – many of these cottages are on farms, and as such, are surrounded by wildlife so if you are squeamish about the odd mouse in the kitchen, stay in a hotel. Having said that, the properties should be, and generally are, kept clean and in good order.

Many *gîtes* are rather off the beaten track and a car, or at least a bicycle, is usually essential. Bicycles can often be hired locally or sometimes from *gîte* owners. Car hire is expensive, but some fly/drive packages still make this a relatively inexpensive way to visit the region, as gîtes can cost as little as FF1,000 per week for the whole house.

Gîtes can get heavily booked in high season, so start the process in the New Year. If you wish to deal directly with France, write to the addresses below from whom you can obtain a list of all the Gîtes de France in each individual *département*. Alternatively, you can book through the London booking office: Gîtes de France, 178 Piccadilly, London W1V 9DB. Tel. 071-493 3480. For just a few pounds' membership you have the choice of a selection of *gîtes* in the region.

FÉDÉRATION DES GÎTES RURAUX FRANCE

Seine-Maritime: ADETER, Chambre d'Agriculture, Chemin de la Brétèque, BP 59, 76232 Bois Guillaume Cedex. Tel: 35 60 73 34.
Calvados: Chambre d'Agriculture, 6 Promenade Madame-de-Sévigné, 14039 Caen Cedex. Tel: 31 82 71 65.
Eure: 9 Rue de la Petite-Cité, BP882, 27008 Evreux Cedex. Tel: 32 39 53 38.
Orne: Comité Départemental du Tourisme, 88 Rue Saint-Blaise, BP 50, 61002 Alençon Cedex. Tel: 33 32 09 00.
Manche: Maison du Département, BP 419, 50000 Saint-Lô. Tel: 33 56 28 80.

Seine-Maritime is one of the first *départements* to participate in a new national organisation of reasonably priced holiday lets, called *Cléconfort*. Members of the association abide by a charter and the houses, flats or other accommodation are inspected regularly by the tourist authorities and awarded a "key" symbol on a rating of one to four. All the accommodation in Seine-Maritime is by the sea, at Etretat, Fécamp, Saint-Valéry-en-Caux and Le Tréport. Prices for a week's rental range from FF1,200 for a 2-"key" house for four people in May, June or September, to FF3,500 for a 3-key fisherman's cottage of character for up to six people in July or August. Bookings are made direct with the owners. For a brochure, write to Cléconfort Seine-Maritime, BP 680, 76008 Rouen Cedex. Tel: 35 88 61 32.

The main ferry companies also offer *gîte* holidays in association with the Gîtes de France office in London – apply to the ferry companies for their brochures (*see Getting There for addresses*). Many other tour operators and private individuals also offer self-catering accommodation, ranging from a simple farm cottage to an apartment in a luxurious château. Sometimes these properties are official gîtes and so have to conform to the Féderation's standards, but others are not subject to any form of inspection at all. Try the private advertisements in the national press. A selection of UK-based companies, who will usually handle your travel arrangements as part of the package, are listed:

AA Motoring Holidays, PO Box 128, Fanum House, Basingstoke RG21 2EA. Tel: 0256-493878.
Air France Holidays, Gable House, 18-24 Turnham Green Terrace, London W4 1RF. Tel: 081-742 3377.
Allez France, 27-29 West Street, Storrington RH20 4DZ. Tel: 0903-742345.
Blakes Holidays, Wroxham, Norwich NR12 8DH. Tel: 0603-784141, fax: 0603-782871.
Hoseasons Holidays Abroad, Sunway House, Lowestoft NR32 3LT. Tel: 0502-500555, fax: 0502-500532.
Kingsland Holidays, Brunswick House, Exeter Street, Plymouth PL4 0AR. Tel: 0752-251688.
Vacances en Campagne, Bignor, Pulborough, West Sussex RH20 1QD. Tel: 07987-433, fax: 07987-343. The company has overseas agents in the US, and Canada (contact Sussex office for addresses).
VFB Holidays, Normandy House, High Street, Cheltenham GL50 3HW. Tel: 0242-526338.

CAMPING

There is a good choice of campsites in Normandy, many of them situated near the coast. The Regional tourist offices produces a list of all recognised sites, with details of star-rating and facilities (also available from the French Government Tourist Office in London – send an address label and £1 of stamps). As with other types of holiday accommodation, the sites can get booked up in high season, so do consider advance booking. Members of the Camping Club or Camping and Caravanning Club of Great Britain may make use of their booking services. The Michelin Camping/Caravanning Guide lists sites which accept (or insist on) pre-booking. The Camping Service at 69 Westbourne Grove, London W2 4UJ, tel: 071-792 1944, can book sites either from their own brochure of 3 and 4-star sites or any other site and will also book ferries.

A camping carnet is useful (some sites will not accept a booking without one). It is available in the UK to members of the AA, RAC or the Camping Clubs mentioned above; or for a small fee from the GB Car Club, PO Box 11, Romsey, Hants SO5 8XX.

Campsites, like hotels have official classifications from 1-star (minimal comfort, water points, showers and sinks) to 4-star luxury sites with more space to each pitch, and offer above-average facilities, often including a restaurant or takeway food, games areas and swimming-pools. The majority of sites nationwide are 2-star. Average prices are around FF20 per person per night at a 1-star site, to around FF45 at a 4-star site.

If you really like to get back to nature, and are unimpressed by the modern trappings of hot water and electric power, look out for camp-sites designated "Aire naturelle de camping" where facilities will be absolutely minimal and prices to match. They have a maximum of 25 pitches so offer the opportunity to stay away from some of the more commercial sites (which can be huge). These sites are listed in the FFCC Guide (*see Useful Addresses next column*).

Some farms offer "official" sites too under the auspices of the Fédération Nationale des Gîtes Ruraux (*see Self-Catering*) – these are designated "Camping à la ferme". Again facilities are usually limited but farmers are only allowed to have six pitches and if you are lucky you will get to know and enjoy the farm life and some of its produce. A national guide to these sites is *Camping à la Ferme*, published by the Gîtes de France organisation, available from their London office (*see Self-Catering*). Another option, currently becoming popular on some sites, are wooden huts which are rather more attractive than caravans, but offer the same sort of facilities. There are several such sites in Seine-Maritime; write to the tourist office in Rouen for details (*see Useful Addresses*).

Packaged camping holidays are now very popular with British holidaymakers and ideal for other overseas visitors too, as all the camping paraphernalia is provided on the site – you only have to take your personal luggage. Many companies now offer this type of holiday, mostly with ferry travel included in the all-in price. Like other package tours, the companies have couriers on the sites to help with any problems. It is interesting to note that where such companies have taken over sections of existing sites, that facilities have improved to meet the demands of their customers and so benefit all campers. Many companies offer good opportunities for sports and leisure, such as wind-surfing or surfing; often the equipment, and sometimes instruction too is covered by the cost of the package. Be warned though that some of the sites are very large, so might not suit those who wish to get away from it all.

Here is a selection of the package operators, for others check the Sunday press.

Canvas Holidays, 12 Abbey Park Place, Dunfermline KY12 7PD. Tel: 0383-621000. Pioneers in the field; offer a nanny service.

Eurocamp Travel, Canute Court, Toft Road, Knutsford, Cheshire WA16 0NL. Tel: 0565-626262.

French Country Camping, 126 Hempstead Road, Kings Langley, Herts WD4 8AL. Tel: 0923-261316.

French Life Holidays, 26 Church Road, Horsforth, Leeds LS18 5LG. Tel: 0532-390077, fax: 0532-584211. Offer a "multicentre" deal.

Keycamp Holidays, Ellerman House, 92-96 Lind Road, Sutton SM1 4PL. Tel: 081-395 4000.

Solaire International Holidays, 1158 Stratford Road, Hall Green, Birmingham B28 8AF. Tel: 021-778 5061.

Sunsites, Canute Court, Toft Road, Knutsford, Cheshire WA16 0NL. Tel: 0565-652222.

USEFUL ADDRESSES & PUBLICATIONS

The *French Federation of Camping and Caravanning Guide* (FFCC), lists 11,300 sites nationwide, and also shows which have facilities for disabled campers. Available in the UK from Springdene, Shepherd's Way, Fairlight, East Sussex TN35 4BB.

Michelin *Green Guide – Camping/Caravanning France*. Very informative and also lists sites with facilities for the disabled. Published annually in March. Camping and Caravanning Club, 11 Lower Grosvenor Place, London SW1.

Caravan Club, East Grinstead House, East Grinstead, Sussex RH19 1UA.

YOUTH HOSTELS

Holders of accredited Youth Hostel Association cards may stay in any French hostels which are in fact run by two separate organisations; Fédération Unie des Auberges de Jeunesse (FUAJ), 27 Rue Pajol, 75018 Paris, tel: (1) 46 07 00 01, fax: (1) 46 07 93 10, which is affiliated to the International Youth Hostel Federation, and the Ligue Francaise pour les Auberges de Jeunesse (LFAJ), 38 Boulevard Raspail, 75007 Paris, tel: (1) 45 48 69 84. Expect to pay around FF60 per night. The British YHA publishes the International Youth Hostel Handbook, Vol. I (revised each March), which includes all the hostels in the region, by post from Youth Hostel Association, 14 Southampton Street, London WC2E 7H7, tel: 071-836 8541. They also handle membership queries, tel: 071-836 1036.

In the US apply to the American Youth Hostels Inc, PO Box 37613, Dept USA, Washington DC 20013/7613. Tel: 202-783 6161.

Gîtes d'Étapes offer hostel accommodation and are popular with ramblers, climbers and horse riders (some offer stabling). All official gîtes d'Étapes come under the auspices of the Relais Départementaux des Gîtes Ruraux (for addresses *see Self-Catering*). These are a popular form of cheap accommodation particularly in the national parks. Prices are similar to youth hostels – around FF50 per night for basic accommodation, but up to FF110 or more in the slightly luxurious establishments which may be on farms offering riding facilities and/or stabling. You do not have to be a member of any organisation to use them.

Other holiday centres for groups of young people are also available in the region. Some the region's hostels (Auberge de Jeunesse) are listed below. Advance booking is advisable in high season.

SEINE-MARITIME
Auberge de Jeunesse, BP 15, 76460 Saint-Valéry-en-Caux. Tel: 35 97 03 98. Open: 1 June–30 September.

CALVADOS
Centre International de Séjour, 1 Place de l'Europe, 14200 Hérouville (Caen). Tel: 31 95 41 00. Open: all year.

Auberge de Jeunesse, 61250 Damigny (near Alençon). Tel: 44 29 00 48. Open: all year.

Auberge de Jeunesse, Avenue Louis-Lumière, 50100 Cherbourg. Tel: 3344 26 31.

Centre Régional de Nautisme, BP 140, Blvd des Amiraux, 50401 Granville Cedex. Tel: 33 50 18 95.

FOOD DIGEST

WHAT TO EAT

France enjoys a reputation throughout the world for its fine cuisine and good wine. Indeed, the French pay very serious attention to their food and it is only in the past few years that fast foods have started to creep into French supermarkets, and on to the high streets. It may be argued, however, that the French have always enjoyed convenience foods provided by their splendid *traiteurs* and *charcutiers*. Visit a delicatessen (*charcuterie*) and pick a selection of their prepared dishes for a delicious picnic.

Normandy is noted in particular for its dairy products, cheese and cream, especially *crème fraîche* which is now becoming increasingly available abroad; and anything to do with apples, notably cider and Calvados, the brandy distilled from it. Of course, seafood is also in much evidence on restaurant tables around the coast. As in neighbouring Brittany, another notable speciality of the region is *crêpes* (pancakes), and there are many *crêperies* which offer an alternative to a traditional restaurant meal – ideal for a light lunch.

RESTAURANTS & OVERNIGHT STOPS

When travelling around Normandy, you will often find that eating and sleeping go hand-in-hand, as many hotels have good kitchens. In small towns and villages, the only place to eat may be a hotel. There are, however, places to search out just for eating or just for sleeping. The following list is a mix of both, specially chosen by the *Insight Guide* writing team. They will give those touring the region a flavour of its intimate atmosphere. Both rooms and restaurants are divided into three categories: Expensive, moderate and inexpensive.

SEINE MARITIME

AUMALE

Le Mouton Gras, 2 Rue de Verdun. Tel: 35 93 41 32. Small half-timbered *Logis* on Normandy's eastern border and an agreeable stopover for motorists using Boulogne or Calais. Rooms (Moderate) are in a separate building from the restaurant which serves copious Normandy fare marred by an overpriced wine list. (Moderate)

AUTIGNY

Heluin Chambre d'Hote is signposted on the D142 3 miles (5 km) south of Fontaine-le-Dun, 35 minutes from Dieppe. Tel: 35 60 48 60. A barn has been converted into five accommodation units. Breakfast is taken on the ground floor which is large enough to accommodate children on a rainy day. (Moderate)

LE BOUILLE

Le St-Pierre, Place de Bateau. Tel: 35 18 01 01. This pretty spot on the Seine just outside Rouen has a number af restaurants and hotels vying for trade. The seven-room St-Pierre has the best views (Expensive). But the restaurant is the main event, with a sophisticated gastronomic menu. (Expensive)

DIEPPE

Au Grand Duquesne, 15 Place Saint Jacques. Tel: 35 84 21 51. A small hotel of character situated near St-Jacques itself. (Moderate). The restaurant succeeds in bringing originality to its menus: on their cheapest – *saumon fumé crêpes*. (Moderate)

Hôtel du Rocher de Cancale, 47 Rue de l'Épée. Tel: 35 84 17 91. Located in the heart of the old quarter between the Plage and the Grand Rue. Modest 18th-century house of character. Rooms with *petit dejeuner* only; no restaurant. (Inexpensive)

Hôtel Windsor, 18 Boulevard de Verdun. Tel: 35 84 15 23. Edwardian-modern hotel on sea front with a magnificent panoramic dining troom overlooking lawns and the Plage. Food so good they even taught cooking. Prices more than justified. (Expensive)

La Musadière, 61 Quai Henry IV. Tel: 35 82 94 14. Restaurant with covered pavement terrace opposite car ferry. Friendly, welcoming service and a good choice of set menus in traditional Norman cuisine. Wine expensive, but entertainment from passing crowds free. (Moderate)

Les Tourelles, 43 Rue du Cammandant Fayolle. Facing the medieval town gate of that name and behind the casino, a restaurant with an imaginitive menu, strong on seafood that extends to *couscous* and *paella* at weekends. (Inexpensive)

HARFLEUR

L'Auberge du Priuré, 52 Rue de la République. Tel: 35 45 02 20. A charming restaurant in a 17th-century pharmacy, with a courtyard where meat is barbecued in summer. (Inexpensive)

LE HAVRE

Monaco, 16 Rue Paris. Tel: 35 42 21 01. Near the ferry terminal, this 2-star hotel has 11 rooms (Moderate). The food is well above average, particularly the fish dishes. (Moderate)

Our history could fill this book, but we prefer to fill glasses.

When you make a great beer, you don't have to make a great fuss.

JUMIÈGES

Auberges des Ruines, Place de la Mairie. Tel: 35 37 24 05. Restaurant with rooms just a stone's throw from the abbey ruins. The rooms are simple. (Inexpensive). The food is excellent. (Moderate)

LYONS-LE-FORÊT

La Licorne, Place Bensérade. Tel: 32 49 62 02. Picturesque 3-star hotel in the centre of an extremely pretty town. Comfortable rooms (Moderate) are complemented by a busy restaurant serving traditional dishes. (Moderate)

MARTIN EGLISE

Auberge du Clos Normand. Tel: 35 82 71 01. Once a farmhouse, this handsome red-brick building, now a first-class restaurant, still retains that character. Food is prepared at one end of the large dining room and eaten here or at tables under the trees in the orchard beside the trout stream at its borders. A la carte and worth every franc: closed Monday evening, and Tuesday. (Expensive). A small number of beds available in the half-timbered annexe: a truly rural idyll. (Moderate)

OFFRANVILLE

Parc des Loisirs du Colombier. Tel: 35 85 19 58. Your choice of Indian, Ceylon or Earl Grey tea in the stylish *Salon de Thé* in a beautifully renovated carriage shed set in the delightful park of the *Manoir*. There is a restaurant in another converted farm building. (Moderate)

ROUEN

Couronne, 31 Place Vieux Marché. Tel: 35 71 40 90. The building witnessed the immolation of Joan of Arc. The elegant interior matches the quality of the food, and is right for a special occasion. (Expensive)

Hotel de Québec, 18-24 Rue de Québec. Tel: 35 70 09 38. Compact 2-star hotel on the right bank of the Seine. Close to the river and a short walk from the city's sites. Parking. (Inexpensive)

Ibis Centre, 56 Quai Gaston Boulet. Tel: 35 70 48 18, fax: 35 71 68 95. Perfect for those who want a central location, all modern facilities and value for money, but checking into an Ibis is like going to McDonalds: no matter where you are it looks and tastes the same. (Rooms and restaurant both moderate)

Les Nymphéas, 7-9 Rue de la Pie. Tel: 35 89 26 69. This is the place to take yourself for a treat. In an old house off the market square, it is elegantly furnished and has a small patio at the back. Try the Rouen duck. (Expensive)

La Pêcherie, 29 Place de la Basse-Vieille-Tour. Tel: 35 88 71 00. Unpretentious restaurant specialising in fish and seafood. (Moderate)

Le Queen Mary, 1 Rue du Cercle. Tel: 35 71 52 09. Just west of the Place du Vieux Marché, a friendly, no-nonsense restaurant to suit all needs. Majors in *moules* and chips, with a good range of *menu fixe* and prompt service. (Inexpensive)

45 Rue aux Ours. Tel: 35 70 99 68. The Aunay family has lived at this wonderful 17th-century townhouse for more than a century. Only 100 yards from the cathedral, and ideal for exploring. A

drawback, the nearest car park is 10 minutes away, and loading and unloading must be quickly accomplished. (Moderate)

ST-LEONARD

Auberge de la Rouge, on the D940 a few miles south of Fécamp. Tel: Tel: 35 28 07 59. Six purpose-built ground-floor rooms surround a small garden (Moderate). Superb kitchen. (Moderate). Booking essential for both rooms and restaurant.

VALMONT

Hotel de l'Agriculture, Place du Docteur Dupont. Tel: 35 29 03 63. On the main square with views of the château from the front windows, which can be a little noisy at night. Rooms and bathrooms newly decorate. (Moderate). The restaurant is in a charming half-timbered building 114 ft (50 metres) away and serves excellent regional dishes. (Moderate)

VEULES LES ROSES

Les Galets, 3 Rue Victor Hugo. Tel: 35 97 61 33. Described as "one of the best restaurants in Normandy" and merits it, though the price of menus reflects its reputation. Situated where France's shortest river reaches the mini *plage* in this most charming of resorts on the Alabaster coast. Victor Hugo thought so, too. (Expensive)

CALVADOS

ARROMANCHES-LES-BAINS

Marine, Quai du Canada. Tel: 31 22 34 19. Well-established three-chimneys *Logis* on the seafront with a restaurant that quickly fills up at lunchtime. (Moderate)

BAYEUX

Luxembourg, 25 Rue des Bouchers. Tel: 31 92 00 04. Quality 3-star hotel in the centre of town with a smartly furnished restaurant that brings home the riches of Normandy cuisine. (Expensive)

Mogador, 20 Rue Alain Chartier. Tel: 31 92 24 58. Courteous and adequate 2-star hotel in the northwest of the town. Some rooms overlook the market square of Place St-Patrice. (Inexpensive)

BEUVRON-EN-AUGE

Le Pavé d'Auge, Place du Village, Tel: 31 79 26 71. Dubbed with a Micehlin star, this is the smartest of the restaurants in this picturesque Auge village, which offers several attractive places to eat out, at differing prices. This at the top of the range. (Expensive)

BONNEBOSQ

Le Manoir du Champ Versant. Tel: 31 65 11 07. There were are only two bedrooms in this impeccable small manor house and on special days the ground floor is open to visitors. (Moderate)

CAEN

Le Boeuf Ferré, 10 Rue Froide. Tel: 31 85 36 40. Tucked away in Caen's old quarter, this has long been a favourite local eating place and people are often prepared to queue at weekends. (Inexpensive-Moderate)

La Bourride, 15-15 Rue du Vaugueux. Tel: 31 93 50 76. Small, top-class restaurant in the city's old quarter serving *"cuisine de coaur et de passion"*. (Expensive)

Ibis Centre, 6 Place Cortoinne. Tel: 31 95 88 88, fax: 31 43 80 80. Part of a chain of motels for the business traveller on a budget. Wonderful location on the Port de Plaisance and near the centre of town for sightseeing and restaurants. Excellent value for money. (Moderate)

St Etienne. 2 Rue de l'Academie. Tel: 31 86 35 82. Delightful period town house dating from the Revolution. Tiny dining room for breakfast, which they are happy to bring to your bedroom. (Inexpensive)

DOUVILLE-EN-AUGE

Ferme de l'Oraille. Tel: 31 79 25 49. Mme Houlet has three guest rooms in her 17th-century farmhouse 11 miles (7 km) from Deauville and a good place for exploring the coastal area. A herd of dairy cattle are part of the farm scene. (Inexpensive)

COURSEULLES-SUR-MER

La Crémaillère, Boulevard de la Plage. Tel: 31 37 46 73. Large three-chimney *Logis* on the seafront with a seaview restaurant serving locally caught seafood. (Moderate)

FALAISE

De La Poste, 38 Rue George Clemenceau. Tel: 31 90 13 14, fax: 31 90 01 81. *Logis* in the centre of town with comfortable rooms, though some can be noisy. (Moderate). Good Kitchen. (Moderate)

HONFLEUR

Les Bagues d'Argent, 30-32 Rue de l'Homme de Bois. Tel: 31 89 27 97. Friendly plant-filled restaurant with a limited but satisfactory menu. Usefully distant from the crowds circulating in the Vieux Bassin below. (Moderate)

MONTREUIL-EN-AUGE

Auberge la Route du Cidre. Tel: 31 63 12 27. Tucked right in the middle of rolling cider country near Cambremer, the auberge consists of a *chambre d'hote* in the grand old farmhouse, plus two *gîtes*. (Moderate). There is also an excellent restaurant in a huge barn with picture windows giving views over the valleys. Everything seems to be cooked with apples and cider. (Moderate)

ST-LOUP-DE-FRIBOIS

Le Pirieuré, on the outskirts of Crèvecouer-en-Auge is a *gîtes* in one of the most authentic old farms in the Auge. The tipsy half-timbered buildings and flatstone-floored kitchen date from the 14th century. Taste home-made cider and see Calvados being distilled.

TROUVILLE

Les Vapeurs, 160 Boulevard F. Moreau. Tel: 31 88 15 24. This is *the* place is eat in Deauville-Trouville. It is not much different from some of the neighbouring restaurants, such as the Central, but it has been decided that where one should be seen eating seafood, or *moules frites*. Open late. (Moderate–Expensive)

VIMOUTIERS

L'Escale du Vitou, Route d'Argenton. Tel: 33 39 12 04. Basic *Logis* in the grounds of an outdoor leisure centre with lake, riding, swiming and small restaurant. (Inexpensive)

EURE

ANET

Auberge de la Rose, 6 Rue Charkls Cacherel. Tel: 37 41 90 64. An eight-room hotel in this charming chateau town. (Moderate) The restaurant is the main reason for staying here. (Expensive)

BEAUMESNIL

L'Etape Louis XIII. Route de la Barre. Tel: 32 44 44 72. The restaurant is housed in a former presbetry and dates from 1612. Good traditional Norman cooking. (Moderate)

BONCOURT

Beghini Tel: 32 36 92 44. An 18th-century barn in a farming village between Evreux and Pacy-sur-Eure. The Benghinis have turned the barn into breakfast-room/lounge and six rooms are in a row with a patio at the front. Each room is charmingly decorated. (Moderate)

BEC HELLOUIN

L'Auberge de l'Abbaye. Tel: 32 44 86 02. Located on the village green and a short walk from the monastery, this 18th-century inn has 10 rooms. (Expensive). Its local cuisine makes good use of apples and cider. (Moderate–Expensive)

Évreux Hospital, Angle Rue Buzot/Rue G. Bernard. Tel: 32 29 45 00. Modern hotel and restaurant a short walk from the Hôtel de Ville. Stylish furniture and colourful decor hide behind a dull exterior. (Moderate)

LES ANDELYS

La Chaine d'Or, 27 Rue Grande. Tel: 32 54 00 31. This riverside, charmingly decorated, 12-room hotel is a perfect place for a special weekend. (Moderate). Dining in the restaurant is definitely a high spot and its regional dishes rate three Michelin forks.

PACY-SUR-EURE

L'Etape. 1 Rue Isambard. Tel: 32 36 12 77. This old 2-star hotel is in a fine situation right on the river and you may have to book one of its 17 rooms (Moderate). The food is good solid country fare. (Moderate)

PONT-AUDEMER

Auberge du Vieux Puits, 6 Rue Notre-Dame-du-Pré. Tel: 32 41 01 48, fax: 32 42 37 28. Anyone who likes to be at the centre of life in an old market town should stay at this famous 17th-century coaching inn. Rooms are smallish but well decorated. (Moderate). The excellent restaurannt is well patronised and the menu of traditional favourites pleases its regular clientele. (Expensive)

VERNON

Restaurant de la Poste, 26 Avenue de Gambetta. Tel: 32 51 10 63. Somewhere to go after visiting Monet's Giverny nearby. Excellent value local dishes appreciated by shoppers and stallholders on Market day. (Inexpensive)

ORNE

ALENÇON
Au Peti Vatel, 72 Place du Cdt Desmeulles. Tel: 33 26 23 78. A small restaurant on the outskirts of town, this is something of an institution, thanks largely to its genial proprieter. Good Normady cooking. (Medium–Expensive)

BAGNOLES DE L'ORNE
Lutétia Boulevard Paul Chalvet. Tel: 33 37 94 66. This 3-star hotel, open Easter to November, has rooms in an old house and a new annexe and it retains an intimate atmosphere. (Moderate–Expensive). The restaurant is good. (Moderate)

CARROUGES
Du Nord, Place Gen de Gaulle. Tel: 33 27 20 14. A small *Logis* on the main square with comfortable rooms. (Moderate). Local business people crowd the dining room at lunchtime.

MORTAGNE-AU-PERCHE
Du Tribunal 4 Place du Palais, near St-Denis Gate and Notre-Dame cathedral. Tel: 33 25 04 77, fax: 33 83 60 83. The rooms in this 18th-century half-timbered building are charming if somewhat small. (Moderate). The kitchen is excellent. (Moderate)

MORTRÉE
Restaurant de la Ferme d'O, in the grounds of the Chateau d'O. Tel: 33 35 35 27. Visitors will probably go to see one of Normandy's finest châteaux, but many go just for the excellent restaurant – a stable wing with flag-stoned floor. Open for tea and coffee, too. (Moderate)

OCCAGNES
Les Mesnil. Tel: 33 67 11 12. A farm 3 miles (5 km) from Argenton has bedrooms with separate entrances from the main house. Limited cooking facilities. (Moderate)

PUTANGES-PONT-ÉCREPIN
Lion Verd, Place de l'Hotel de Ville. Tel: 33 35 01 86. At the southern end of the Suisse Normande, a large, confident *Logis* with a spacious restaurant overlooking the river. (Moderate)

TOUROUVRE
De la France, 19 Rue de 13 Aôut. Tel: 33 25 73 55, fax: 33 25 73 55. On the main road opposite the town hall square. Don't be put off by the building's ugly facade and entrance. The service is excellent, the staff friendly and the rooms simple but comfortable. (Moderate). There is a limited menu and the food is very good. (Moderate)

SÉES
Normandy Garden Hotel, 12 Rue des Ardillers. Tel: 33 27 98 27. One of three good hotels in this town that make a good stopping place. It was revamped by an Australian who started the Boomerang restaurant opposite the Cathedral. Spacious rooms (Moderate)

MANCHE

AVRANCHE
Jardin des Plantes, 10 Place Carnot. Tel: 33 58 03 68. Next to the town's public gardens and ample parking. The restaurant is popular with locals, so service can be slow. (Inexpensive). Simple but cosy rooms above. (Moderate)

BARNEVILLE-CARTARET
Les Isles, 9 Boulevard Maritime. Tel: 33 04 90 76. Peaceful and comfortable beachside hotel with small rooms. (Moderate). The restaurant has a limited menu catering mainly for its *demi-pension* guests. (Moderate)

CHERBOURG
Napoléon, 14 Place de la République. Tel: 33 93 32 32. 2-star hotel with a splended facade close to the Port de Plaisance and ferry terminal. (Inexpensive)

DOMFRONT
De La France, 7 Rue du Mont-St-Michel. Tel: 33 38 51 44, fax: 33 30 49 54. Comfortable *Logis* in the centre of town near the station and within walking distance of the old town. Good for those travelling without a car.

FRESVILLE
Manoir de Grainville, Tel 33 41 10 49, fax: 33 21 07 57. An 18th-century stone farmhouse *chambre d'hôte*, centrally located is 5 miles (8 km) from St-Mère-Eglise and less than an hour from Cherbourg. Evening meals sometimes served. English and German spoken. (Moderate)

GRANVILLE
Le Hérel, Port de Hérel. Tel: 33 90 48 08. Modern box hotel next to the port with a bar well used by nautical types. (Moderate)

HAMBYE
Auberge de l'Abbaye. Tel: 33 61 42 19. Country hotel and restaurant with only seven rooms, close to the entrance of the Abbaye d'Hambye. (Inexpensive)

LE NEZ DE JOBOURG
Auberge des Grottes. Tel: 33 52 71 44. Small restaurant close to the cliffs, deservedly popular as a lunch stop for motorists touring the Hague peninsula. (Moderate)

MONT-ST-MICHEL
St-Pierre, Grand Rue. Tel: 33 60 14 03. Comfortable, welcoming 3-star hotel with some rooms (as common with many hotels on the island) in separate buildings. Book well ahead and be prepared to carry your luggage up from the causeway car park. (Expensive)

ST-VAAST-LA-HOUGE
France et des Fuchsias, 18 Rue Maréchal Foch. Tel: 33 54 42 26. Pleasant, simple hotel with simple rooms, good food – and masses of fuchsias. (Moderate)
La Granitière, 64 Rue de Maréchal Foch. Tel: 33 54 58 99. Smart but friendly hotel with a small restaurant and thoughtfully furnished rooms. Good for a treat (Expensive)

Le Louvre, 28 Rue des Religieuses. Thoroughly old-fashioned market-town hotel that gets packed out with locals for Sunday lunch. (Moderate). Comfortable rooms (Inexpensive)

St-Pierre et St-Michel, 12 Place de la République. Tel: 33 61 00 11, fax: 33 61 06 52. Comfortable *Logis* in the centre of town with parking. (Moderate). Weekend evenings and Sunday lunch finds the dining rooms full of locals. (Moderate)

Hotel Manoir de L'Archerie, L'Archerie, Sta-Cécile. Tel: 33 51 13 87. Near Villedieu-les-Poelles and within striking distance of Mont-St-Michel, this 16th-century manor house is very peaceful in lovely surroundings. There are 14 comfortable rooms. (Moderate). The restaurant serves good local food. (Moderate)

DRINKING NOTES

Wine drinkers are familiar with the term *appellation d'origine contrôlée*, but now other producers are adopting the same label, as a proof of quality, in particular for cheeses. Some of the best known cheeses of the region are Camembert, Neufchâtel (the oldest known cheese of Normandy), Livarot and Pont l'Evêque, but one of the delights of shopping in France, particularly in local markets, is to find all the individual cheeses that come from small producers. You will usually be invited to try before you buy.

So confident are the Normans in the quality of their produce that they hold a fair, le Salon Horial, every other year at Saint-Lô. Intended to show off their produce to professional buyers, the fair is also open to the public where they are invited to sample the gastronomic delights of the region. The next fair will be in the spring of 1995.

CIDER

This traditional alcoholic drink is often drunk as an accompaniment to meals in preference to wine. It is made from the juice of apples and is produced all over Normandy, but predominantly in the Auge region. To discover more about the drink, follow the "cider route" and visit the producers and museums devoted to this golden, sparkling liquid. Particular varieties of apples are used, harvested in October. The juice is squeezed out and left to mature so the sugar can turn to alcohol (around 5 percent by volume). It is left to ferment for just a short while before being bottled. It is drunk fairly young, preferably the following summer, and it is either *sec* (dry) or *doux* (sweet).

CALVADOS

Calvados is produced by evaporating the alcohol from cider and condensing it in a still. When removed from the still the alcoholic content of Calvados is around 70°, but this is reduced to around 40°–45° after being aged in oak casks. The Calvados is then blended with brandies of different ages to create a full flavour. There are two recognised *appellation contrôlée* labels for Calvados: Appellation contrôlée Calvados and Appellation contrôlée Calvados du Pays d'Auge, the later undergoing a double distillation in a traditional pot still. There is a custom in Normandy (borne out by the many postcards depicting it) of taking a small glass of Calvados halfway through a copious meal, as an aid to digestion. Known as a "Trou Normand", this can sometimes be served as an apple sherbert soaked in Calvados.

POMMEAU

This sherry-strength *apéritif* is made by blending the "must" of cider and Calvados in the ratio of 2:1. It is matured in oak casks and makes an ideal companion to oysters, *foie gras* and melon.

WINE

Vines have been cultivated in France since the ancient Romans first planted them. To exclude cider or wine from the dinner table is almost like forgetting the salt and pepper. It is not regarded as a luxury; everyday wine (*vin de table*) is produced for everyday consumption. On the other hand France produces some of the finest vintages in the world, and the pomp, ceremony and snobbery that accompany their production show just how important it is to the culture and economy of France. Normandy is one of the few regions which does not have a wine industry as such.

READING THE LABEL

Wines are graded according to their quality and this must be shown on the label. The grades are as follows:

Vin de Table, usually inexpensive everyday table wine. Quality can be variable.

Vin de Pays, local wine.

VDQS **or Vin délimité de qualité supérieure**, wine from a specific area, and of higher quality than a vin de table.

AOC or Appellation d'origine contrôlée, good quality wine from a specific area or château where strict controls are imposed on the amount of wine produced each year.

If the label bears the words "*mis en bouteille au château*" it has been bottled at the vineyard. This is also indicated by the words, *récoltant* or *producteur* around the cap; the term *négociant* means that it has been bought by a dealer and usually bottled away from the estate. However, this is not necessarily to the detriment of the wine; there are many excellent *négociants* in business today.

Several UK companies offer holidays in the region which include gastronomic tours or cookery courses. A selection is given below:

Allez France, 27-29 West Street, Storrington RH20 4DZ. Tel: 0903-742345.

Discover France Holidays, c/o Wessex Continental Travel, PO Box 43, Plymouth PL1 1SY. Tel: 0752-846880.

La France des Activités, Model Farm, Rattlesden, Bury St Edmunds IP30 0SY. Tel: 0449-737678. Five-day courses in a château.

InnTravel, The Old Station, Helmsley, York YO6 5BZ. Tel: 0439-71111. Three-day cookery holidays in Normandy.

P & O European Ferries Holidays, Channel View Road, Dover, Kent CT13 0RA. Tel: 0304-214422. Gastronomic breaks in Caen and Deauville.

THINGS TO DO

PLACES OF INTEREST

The listing below covers a variety of different activities: parks and gardens, miniature railways, craft workshops, technical visits and so forth. Some of the suggested venues are specific to the region and are well worth seeking out.

All the places listed are open daily, morning and afternoon (not including public holidays) except where otherwise specified. Most close for a long lunch break – noon or 12.30 until 2 or 2.30pm – although many of the major sites stay open throughout the day at high season. Opening times are subject to change, so if making a special journey it is wise to check. Expect to pay an entrance fee at most venues. A list of museums and art galleries, historic buildings (including churches) and archaeological sites are given under the heading of *Culture Plus*.

Most major towns offer guided tours – enquire at the Office de Tourisme or Syndicat d'Initiative, just the main sights are listed here.

SEINE MARITIME

ANEVILLE-SUR-SCIE

Duchy de Longueville orchards. Visit the orchards and see the cider makers at work. Open: Monday–Friday morning. Tel: 35 83 32 76.

AUZOUVILLE-SUR-SAÂNE

Le Gloopi, leisure park with 70 amusements. Open: 1 April–30 October. Tel: 35 83 23 47.

CLERÈS

Parc du Bocasse, leisure park with many attractions including pedalo, an enchanted river, etc. Open: daily 10 April–10 September; 1 March–31 October Wednesday and weekends. Tel: 35 33 22 25.

Parc zoologique, animals and birds roaming free. Closed: December, and the beginning of March. Tel: 35 33 23 08.

DIEPPE

Cité de la Mer, L'Estran, BP 1031, this new attraction only opened in 1993; five themed areas to discover, including an aquarium and exhibits about the history of the sea, the fishing industry, naval construction and new technology. Tel: 35 84 24 42.

EPRETOT

Le Canyon, St-Romain-de-Colbosc, leisure park with 50 different amusements, including carousels. Open: daily 1 June–31 August; 1 March–15 November Wednesday and weekends. Tel: 35 20 42 69.

ETRETAT

Parc de loisirs des Roches, 76790, featuring over 100 species in a marine aquarium. Tel: 35 27 01 23.

LE HAVRE

Parc forestier de Montgeon, 667 acres (270 hectares) of wooded parkland where amenities include a lake with pedalos, a zoo and sports facilities.

ISNEAUVILLE

Le Jardin de Papillons, 76230, huge tropical glasshouse where butterflies from Asia, Africa and the Americas can be observed flying free. Open: May–October. Tel: 35 61 31 22.

OISSEL

The town's public park extends over 16 acres (6 hectares), bordering the Seine, with a good selection of trees.

ROUEN

Jardin des Plantes, 25 acres (10 hectares) of botanical gardens with some rare species, including the spectacular giant Amazonian water-lily, "Victoria Regia". Open: daily until dusk; glasshouses open 9–11.30am and 2–5pm.

VARENGEVILLE-SUR-MER

Moutiers floral park, botanical gardens which have won international acclaim. Open: Easter–November. Tel: 35 85 10 02.

CALVADOS

BAYEUX

Jardin des Plantes, Route de Port-en-Bessin, botanical gardens.

BRÉCY

Jardins du Château, Saint Gabriel de Brécy, formal French gardens open Tuesday, Thursday and Sunday afternoons from 1 April–30 September. The château can be viewed by written appointment only. Tel: 31 80 11 48.

BRETTEVILLE-SUR-ODON
Festyland, Carpiquet, near Caen, leisure park with many attractions including mini-golf, tourist train, electric cars, adventure playground and a *crêperie*. Open: April–September 11am–7pm. Tel: 31 75 04 04.

LE BREUIL-EN-AUGE
Château de Breuil, Pont l'Evêque, visit to the distillery and cellars of this Calvados producer. Closed: weekends out of season. Tel: 31 65 07 76.

CAEN
Jardins des Plantes et Jardin Botanique, 5 Place Blot. Open: daily (glasshouses 2–5pm only except by appointment). Tel: 31 86 28 80.

CLÉCY
La Suisse Normande Miniature, park with miniature railway and museum. Open: daily Easter–30 September; low season Sunday afternoon only. Tel: 31 69 07 13.

COQUAINVILLIERS
Calvados Boulard, Distillerie du Moulin de la Foulonnerie, Calvados producer open daily (closed weekends 16 September–15 April). Tel: 31 62 29 26.

COURSEULLES-SUR-MER
La Maison de la Mer, Place du 6 Juin, shell museum, aquarium tunnel and oyster exhibition. Open: daily, continuously from 9am–7pm in July and August . Tel: 31 37 92 58.

DAMPIERRE
Le Pressoir Dajon, producers of cider and Calvados. Open: every afternoon from Easter–September. Tel: 31 68 72 30.

DEAUVILLE
Parc Calouste Gulbenkian, Domaine des Enclos. Open: 2–7pm weekends and public holidays from 1 July–15 September. Tel: 31 87 90 06.

HOTOT-EN-AUGE
Atelier de Brocottes, pottery and ceramics studio. Open: daily except Monday.

JURQUES
Parc Zoologique de la Cabosse, over 24 acres (10 hectares) of wild animals. Closed: 15 December–15 January. Tel: 31 77 80 58.

LISIEUX
Cerzä Parc-Lisieux, Hermival-les-Vaux, wild animals roaming free in a 123 acre (50 hectare) park. Restaurant. Open 9.30am–7.30pm (10.30am–5pm in low season). Tel: 31 62 17 22.

MERVILLE-FRANCEVILLE
Réserve Ornithologique du Gros Banc, 330 hectare reserve for the protection of sea birds in the Baie de l'Orne. Waymarked circuits and guided tours available. Information from the Maison de la Nature de Sallenelles. Tel: 31 78 71 06.

NORON-LA-POTERIE
An important centre for the local pottery industry; several workshops are open to the public, including Poter Dubost, tel: 31 92 56 15 and Poterie Turgis, tel: 31 92 56 49.

PONT-L'EVÊQUE
Chais du Père Magloire, Route de Deauville, visit the cellars and Calvados museum. Tel: 31 64 12 87.

SAINT-PIERRE-DU-MONT
Reserve for seabirds, including albatross. Park at la Pointe du Hoc; the reserve is half a mile (1 km) from there.

SANNERVILLE
Zone Artisanale, Rue de Liroze, copper and pewter workers open their studios to the public; gift shop. Tel: 31 23 30 51.

THURY-HARCOURT
Parc et jardins du Château d'Harcourt, 173 acres of parkland bordering the River Orne and the ruined former residence of the Governors of Normandy. Well designed gardens. Open: Sunday and public holiday afternoons in April and October; every afternoon 1 May–30 September. Tel: 31 79 65 41.

TROUVILLE
Aquarium Ecologique, 17 Rue de Paris, diverse collections in fairly natural surroundings. Open: daily, continuously from 10am–8pm in July–August; afternoons only November–Easter. Tel: 31 88 46 04.

EURE

AMFREVILLE-SUR-ITON
La Mare Hermier, visit a producer of *foie gras*; tasting possible and sale of produce.

BEAUMESNIL
Classical gardens attributed to La Quintine, a pupil of Le Nôtre, set around the early 16th-century château. Open: every afternoon 1 May–30 September.

BOURNEVILLE
La Maison des Métiers, a showcase for local crafts and trades; also includes the regional Musée des Métiers; demonstrations, gift shop. Open: every afternoon from February–October (closed: Tuesday except in July and August); weekends only in November and December. Tel: 32 57 40 41.

GISORS
Parc de Loisirs du Bois d'Hérouval, leisure park, 2½ miles (4 km) from the town on the road to Cergy-Pontoise. Many different activities and a miniature train; picnic site. Open: daily 15 May–September; Wednesday and weekends Palm Sunday–15 May. Tel: 32 55 33 76.

GIVERNY
The house and gardens (easily recognisable from his famous paintings) of Claude Monet. Visit too, the Museum of American Impressionists. Both open: April–31 October. Closed: Monday. Tel: 32 51 28 21. (For the museum, tel: 32 51 94 65.)

HARCOURT
Le Neubourg Arboretum, the second oldest arboretum in France with many rare trees. Open: June–September daily 10am–7pm; October–May 2–7pm (closed: Tuesday).

HAUVILLE
Moulin de Hauville, one of the few stone windmills left in Normandy. Built in the 12th century, it has been restored and is open to the public on Sunday afternoons March–November; also Saturday May, June and September; every afternoon in July and

August. The thatched cottage next door serves hot pancakes.

LA BONNEVILLE-SUR-ITON
Domaine de la Noé, leisure park with golf, tennis, canoeing, pony riding and many other attractions. Coaching available. Open May–September. Tel: 32 30 20 41 (town hall).

LA HAYE DE ROUTOT
Two buildings have been restored in this village as living history exhibitions: one is a bakery where bread is baked in traditional manner every Sunday from April–October plus exhibition; the other is a clog-maker's workshop. Open: every afternoon July–August; Saturday and Sunday May, June and September; Sunday only March, April, October and November.

LOUVIERS
Jardin Aristide Briand, well-kept public gardens.

PLASNES
Bird sanctuary, on the RN 138, 2 miles (4 km) from Bernay, 100 cages with birds from all over the world; models and prehistoric animals and a collection of dogs and cats. Children's play area. Open: daily 15 March–31 October. Tel: 32 43 21 22.

ROUTOT
La Maison du Lin, Upper Normandy is one of the world's largest flax producers, and this House of Flax is dedicated to the industry. Open: every afternoon, except Tuesday April–October (open daily July–August); weekends in November–December. Tel: 32 56 21 76.

SAINTE-OPPORTUNE
La Maison de la Pomme, this House of Apples is situated in a former presbytery, and displays apples in all its forms: cider, Calvados and pommeau. Open: weekends and public holidays in the afternoon March–October (daily July–August); also the first Sunday in the month in winter to coincide with the apple markets in the town.

THEVRAY
Paradise Valley Parc, leisure park in the Risle valley with miniature golf, tourist train, etc. Open: every afternoon June–15 September; Wednesday, Sun. and public holidays 15 April–31 May. Tel: 32 30 71 80.

TOSNY
Tolysland, leisure park near Les Andelys, with tourist train, miniature golf, fun tunnel and water games etc. Open every afternoon in July–August; Wednesday, Sunday and public holidays in May, June and September. Tel: 32 54 00 19.

ORNE

L'AIGLE
Les Caves de Normandie, 64 Rue Louis Pasteur, producer of cider, Calvados and pommeau. Open to the public: weekdays in May, June and July. Tel: 33 24 14 54.

ECOUCHÉ
La Marionnetterie, Le Moulin, puppetmakers open to the public, with possibly the largest permanent exhibition of puppets in Europe. Phone for an appointment, open all year. Tel: 33 35 17 97.

LE HARAS DU PIN
Le Haras National, national stud farm, known as the "Versailles of the horse-world" in a *département* dedicated to everything equine. Established in 1665, its grounds were laid out by France's most famous landscape artist, Le Nôtre. Open: daily (afternoons only from 10 October–11 July); there is a special display every Thursday at 3pm from 14 May–17 September.

JUVIGNY-SOUS-ANDAINES
La Ferme du Cheval de Trait, la Michaudière, 61140, 3½ miles (6 km) from Bagnoles-de-l'Orne, a working farm where you can relive the time when horses still did all the heavy work; 19th-century tools. At 4.30pm daily April–October, there is a display of horses, carriages and races, topped off by a country meal. For details, tel: 33 38 27 78.

TESSÉ-LA-MADELEINE
Arboretum du Château, over 120 species of trees in the 44 acres (18 hectare) park of the château (19th century) in this spa town. Tel: 33 37 93 03.

VIMOUTIERS
Escale du Vitou, leisure park with a lake and other attractions, including grass skiing. Tel: 33 39 12 04.
Cidrerie Sopalgy Réunies, 27 Rue du Perré, producer of cider, Calvados and pommeau. Open: daily with free tastings. Tel: 33 39 00 40.
Ferme de la Héronnière, Camembert, 61120 Vimoutiers, see the cheese being made at this farm; sale of produce. Open: daily except Sunday. Tel: 33 39 08 08.
La Maison du Camembert, discover how the famous local cheese is made; sale of produce. Open: Easter–November. Tel: 33 39 43 35.

MANCHE

AUVERS
Cidrerie Héroult Filts, Cantepie, farm producing cider, pear perry and Calvados. Open to the public: Monday–Friday and Saturday morning May–September. Tel: 33 42 04 24.

BARENTON
Maison de la Pomme et de la Poire, La Logerai, learn all about the production of cider, Calvados and other products made from apples and pears; tastings, shop. Open: daily March–September. Tel: 33 59 56 22.

BELLEFONTAINE
Le Village Enchanté, the Enchanted Village, a fairytale land with various attractions, including a theatre of automata, miniature train and craft exhibitions. Open: Easter–30 September. Tel: 35 59 01 93.

BLAINVILLE-SUR-MER
Coopérative d'Aqua-Culture, an oyster farm, also producing mussels and other shellfish. Open: daily except weekend. Tel: 33 47 13 47.

BRÉVILLE-SUR-MER

Parc d'attractions de la Baleine Blanche, amusement park with many facilities: go-karts, miniature golf, pony rides, etc. Open: every afternoon in summer; weekends in low season May–October. Tel: 33 90 83 00.

CHAMPEAUX

Permanent exhibition of local fauna on the clifftops, on the D 911 road. Displays over 600 species of birds and 60 mammals. Open: daily July–15 September; Sunday only in May and June. Tel: 33 48 05 56.

CHAMPREPUS

Modern zoo where the comfort and environment of the animals is paramount. Ninety species of animals and birds; amuseuments, bar and snack bar. Open: daily 10am–6pm. Tel: 33 61 30 74.

COUTANCES

Parc l'Evêque, unusual medieval park, founded in the 11th-century, in the process of restoration; home to much wildlife. Open: 2–7pm, weekends 15 May–1 November (daily in July–August).

See too the public gardens around the **Coutances Museum**, noted for its maze, rare trees and mosaic arrangements. *Son et lumière* show every evening except Tuesday in summer.

FLAMANVILLE

Centrale Nucléaire de Flamanville, guided tour (English spoken) and exhibition at the nuclear station. Take some form of identity with you. Open: daily (afternoons only Sunday and school holidays). Tel: 33 08 95 95 ext: 4100.

GRANVILLE

L'Aquarium du Roc, Le Palais du Coquillages (shell palace) and Le Palais Minéral et le Jardin des Papillons et des Insectes (butterfly house) are all open daily from Palm Sunday to November. Tel: 33 50 03 13.

See too, the **public gardens** created by Christian Dior in 1920 around his family home.

GRATOT

Les Chevaliers d'Argouges, Le Pavement, 50200. Chocolate makers. Open to the public: every afternoon June–15 September. Tel: 33 45 89 50.

ILE DE TATIHOU

Opened in 1992, a natural environment of sandy moors and dunes, with an observatory for bird-watching, plus a scientific cultural centre and maritime museum. Access by amphibious craft from Saint-Vaast-la-Hougue; departures every 35 minutes daily June–October. Information from Acceuil Tahitou, Quai Vauban, 50550 Saint-Vaast-la-Hougue. Tel: 33 23 19 92.

ISIGNY-LE-BUAT

Coopérative Fermière des Calvados du Bocage (FERMICALVA), BP 5, Le Grand Chemin, 50540. Calvados distillery. Open to the public; free tastings; shop. Open: 10am–5pm weekdays. Tel: 33 48 00 16.

LE POMMIER

Chèvrerie de la Huberdière, Le Pommier, Liesville-sur-Douve. Cheesemaker, offering visits and tastings. Tel: 33 71 01 60.

MONTAIGU-LA-BRISETTE

Parc animalier Saint-Martin, animals roaming free in the Barnavast wood. Opens at: 11am daily 15 May–31 August, but 2pm on weekends and public holidays, also weekends 15 March–14 May; Sunday in September–15 November. Tel: 33 40 40 38.

SAINT-MARTIN-DE-LANDELLE

Ange Michel leisure park, with amusements for adults and children as well as a craft and agricultural museum. Open: weekends Easter–September; daily except Monday 20 June to mid-September. Tel: 33 49 04 74.

SAINT-SYMPHORIEN-DES-MONTS

L'Eden Parc, on the RN 176, 4 miles (7 km) from Saint-Hilaire-du-Harcouët; rare and endangered species in an 18th-century park; also floral gardens, amusements, crêperie and picnic site. Open: daily at 9am 15 May–11 November. Tel: 33 49 02 41.

SAINT-VAAST-LA-HOUGUE

Huîtres et Moules de Saint-Vaast, 31 bis Rue d'Isamberville. Oyster farm. Open: weekdays according to the tides. Tel: 33 54 42 70.

TOURLAVILLE

Parc du château, romantic park with beautiful glasshouses erected in 1877. Free entry to the gardens daily.

VILLEDIEU-LES-POÊLES

La Fonderie de Cloches, Atelier Cornille-Havard, Rue du Pong-Chignon, famous bell foundry. Open to the public: daily (closed: Sunday and Monday in low season, and from 23 December–18 January). Tel: 33 61 00 56. The town is full of souvenirs of copper and pewter work.

See too the **Atelier du Cuivre**, a copper workshop and the Maison de l'Etain, pewter workshop, both in Rue Général Huard. Open: daily (closed: Sunday and Monday in low season). Tel: 33 51 31 85.

VILLIERS-FOSSARD

La Vallée aux Oiseaux, 5 miles (8 km) from Saint-Lô, a zoo specialising in birds (over 160 species), plus amusements, café and picnic site. Open: daily 10am–7pm in summer; Wednesday and weekends 2pm–dusk in winter.

NATIONAL PARKS

Normandy's Regional Parks (Parcs Naturels) come under the protection of the Fédération des Parcs Naturels de France. Covering some of the most outstanding areas of natural beauty, these parks offer a sanctuary for wildlife and a host of leisure opportunities.

The main agency concerned with promoting the parks nationally is Clés de France, who provide information regarding facilities in individual parks, as well as details about excursions and activity holidays. Contact Clés de France at 13 Rue St-Louis, 78100 St-Germain-en-Laye. Tel: (1) 30 61 23 23.

Local offices for the parks, where you can find out about guided tours and local events are as follows over page:

Parc Naturel Régional de Brotonne, 76940 Notre-Dame-de-Bliquetuit. Tel: 35 37 23 16.

Parc Naturel Régional des Marais du Cotentin et du Bessin, Le Trivial, Le Butel, 50190 Marchesieux. Tel: 33 47 32 32.

Parc Naturel Régional de Normandie-Maine, Le Chapitre, 61320 Carrouges. Tel: 33 27 25 15.

EXCURSIONS

All kinds of excursions are possible to make your stay in France a little different. From rides on tourist trains, trips in hot air balloons or by horse-drawn carriage. Tourist offices will have details of all kinds of local facilities. Some possibilities are listed below.

BOAT TRIPS

There many opportunities for boat trips around the coast, or inland on the Seine and smaller rivers. At seaside resorts, just stroll along the quay to find notices offering tourist or fishing trips, or book through the companies listed below. In the Manche *département* there are regular trips to the Channel Isles, the Isles of Chausey and Tatihou. Information is available from the Granville tourist office, tel: 33 50 02 67.

SEINE CRUISES

Aqua Viva, 30 Avenue Franklin Roosevelt, 75008 Paris. Tel: (1) 45 61 16 41. Upmarket cruises of one week between Paris and Honfleur, aboard *Le Normandie*, a floating hotel.

Fleuves et Loisirs, 29 Avenue Claude Monet, BP 5 95510 Vetheuil. Tel: (1) 34 78 16 15. Operates *River's King* a cruise vessel with restaurant from Les Andelys or Vernon. Booking essential.

M. Fortin, Quai de la Marine, BP 1086, 76062 Le Havre Cedex. Tel: 35 42 01 31. Visit the port of Le Havre, or cruise on the Seine (departures from Le Havre, Honfleur, Caudebec-en-Caux, etc.).

Port of Rouen. Trips are available around the port on board the *Cavelier de la Salle*. Book through the Rouen tourist office, 25 Place de la Cathédrale, BP 666, 76008 Rouen. Tel: 35 71 41 77.

Rives de Seine Cruises offers cruises from Rouen to Vernon on the *Guillaume le Conquérant*, which has a restaurant. Information from the Les Andelys tourist office. Tel: 32 21 61 94.

Société Maritime de la Rance, Quai Boisguilbert, Hangar 5, 76000 Rouen. Tel: 35 15 21 31. Gastronomic cruises between Rouen and the Seine estuary, October–April.

CALVADOS

"Barbey d'Aurevilly", Port Jourdan, RN 13. Trips with commentary for a full day or half-day, on the *Douves*, through the Marais Cotentin. Tel: 33 71 55 81 or 33 42 74 01 (Carentan tourist office).

MANCHE

Cherbourg Harbour. One-hour guided excursions depart from the Pont Tournant, daily from April–

September. Information from the tourist office. Tel: 33 52 59 40.

M. Guerin, Le Petit Port, 50270 Barneville-Carteret. Tel: 33 04 71 51. Cruises aboard the *Long John Silver* to the Channel Isles and Brittany.

Manche Fluvial, La Ville, 50540 Les Biards. Tel: 33 60 50 50. Day and night-time cruises on the Vezins lake (between Mont-Saint-Michel and Saint-Hilaire-du-Harcouët), aboard the *Sélune* which has a restaurant. Board at La Mazure leisure centre in Les Biards (booking necessary).

Trans Canal, 96 Quai Vendeuvre, 14000 Caen. Tel: 31 34 00 00. Cruises on the Caen canal; cruises with a meal also possible, April–October.

Vedettes "Jolie France", Gare Maritime, 50400 Granville. Tel: 33 50 31 81; a year-round service to the Isles of Chausey.

M. Vicquelin at Grandcamp-Maisy offers mini cruises to the landing beaches and the Point du Hoc. Information from Quai Nord, or Boutique Tentations, 11 Rue Aristide Briand, 14450 Grandcamp-Maisy. Tel: 31 21 42 93.

TOURIST TRAINS

The **Chemin de Fer Touristique du Mont des Avaloirs**, installed in 1992, a 1950s-style American railroad, the longest in world, takes you through Suisse Normande (two hours one-way), between Alençon and Pré-en-Pail. Weekends and public holidays 4 July–13 September. Information from: Association Chemins de fer touristiques de l'ouest, 203 Rue Lucien-Lelièvre, 50600 Saint-Hilaire-du-Harcouët. Tel: 33 49 27 68, or 43 03 89 38.

Le Train Touristique du Cotentin and **le Train du Marais** are operated by l'Association Tourisme et Chemin de Fer de la Manche, Place Patton, 50250 La Haye-du-Puits. Information from the Carentan tourist office. Tel: 33 42 74 01.

L'Autorail le "Picasso" runs through the La Londe forest from Elbeuf station to Petit-Couronne, with departures every two hours in either direction. No booking required, it operates Sunday and public holidays.

Le Train Touristique de la Suisse Normande runs on Sunday (and by prior booking during the week) in summer from Caen to Clécy. Departures from Caen-La Prairie, Route de Louvigny (near the Cavée viaduct). Information from TTSN, BP 20, 14220 Thury-Harcourt. Tel: 31 79 02 02.

IN THE AIR

Balloon trips are available at Tessé-la-Madeleine 61140, near Bagnoles-de-l'Orne. Information from the local tourist office. Tel: 33 38 87 76. Ultramagic, 13 Rue de la Coursoupe, 95510 Cherence. Tel: 16-1 34 78 18 72 also offers balloon trips with champagne and certificate for first-timers on landing. Book a minimum of one week in advance. The British School of Ballooning offers weekend ballooning breaks at the Lutetia Hotel, tel: 33 37 94 77; and the Manoir du Lys Hotel, tel: 33 37 80 69.

The Museum of Ballooning at Balleroy in Calvados stages a spectacular ballooning festival annually in June (*see Diary of Events* and *Museums*).

Light aircraft trips are available from Aéroclub de l'Eure, at Evreux-Fauville, tel: 32 33 13 86; and the Aéroclub de Granville, Aérodrome de Granville, tel: 33 50 24 24.

Helicopter flights are available from Heli-Ouest, 28340 Boissy-les-Perche, tel: 37 37 63 42; and Heli-Time, BP2, 27500 Corneville-sur-Risle, tel: 32 57 00 38.

COACH TRIPS

Let someone else do the driving and you can take in all the scenery and sights. Day or half-day trips are widely available to major tourist sights, usually with a guide. Well Income Tours, offers a range of trips, with departures from Rouen or Dieppe. Contact the company at 36 Place St Marc, 76000 Rouen. Tel: 35 07 79 79. Illuminated tours of the Bessin region by night are offered by Tourisme Verney, Place de Gaulle, 14150 Ouistreham. Tel: 31 96 30 10. For further information contact local bus stations or tourist offices. If being shepherded in groups is not your style, then try taking a guided taxi tour, available from many taxi companies.

WAR & PEACE

Normandy was devastated by World War II, and attracts many visitors to its memorials and cemeteries. In 1994, the 50th anniversary of the D-Day Landings, there are many special events and tours planned. Hotel accommodation for the summer of 1994 is scarce and around 5 and 6 June, there will be problems with blocked roads and parking restrictions. Only those invited will be able to take part in the ceremonies. The following tour operators are offering specialist trips during 1994. This list is by no means comprehensive, for other operators contact the regional or departmental tourist offices (*see Useful Addresses*).

UK TOUR OPERATORS

Miss Burton's Historical Tours, PO Box 161 Shotley, Ipswich, Suffolk IP9 1PF. Tel: 0473-787308.
Major & Mrs Holt's Battlefield Tours Ltd, Golden Key Building, 15 Market Street, Sandwich, Kent CT13 9DA. Tel: 0304-612248. A well-established company which has a special programme in France for June and July 1994.
STS Travel, 24 Culloden Road, Enfield, Middlesex EN2 8QD. Tel: 081-367 1767.

US TOUR OPERATORS

Battlefield Tours Inc., 118 Village Street, Suite C, Slidell, Louisana 70458. Tel: 1-800-428 1097.
Mr Burton's Historical Tours, c/o Britannia Roads, 880 Del Rio Avenue, San Luis Obispo, California 93405. Tel: 1-800-457 0464.

Convention & Group Travel, 7 West 11th Street, Lawrence, Kansas 66044. Tel: 913-841 8687.
STS Travel, 795 Franklin Avenue, Franklin Lakes, New Jersey 07417. Tel: 1-800-752 6787.
Tours of Historic and Important Places, 134 Gold Club Drive, Longwood, Florida 32779-4693. Tel: 1-800-869 9576.

For independent travellers, two books may prove useful: *Holt's Battlefield Guides: Normandy-Overlord* and *Holt's Visitor's Guide to the Normandy Landing Beaches*. Both are packed with factual and historical information, and include a fairly comprehensive list of military cemeteries. Available from Major and Mrs Holt's Battlefield Tours, address as above.

WAR MUSEUMS & MEMORIALS

The following are the principal museums in the region. (*See Museums listing for general entry conditions*.) For a complete list of military cemeteries, apply to the departmental tourist offices, or refer to the Holt's guides above.

CALVADOS

ARROMANCHES
Musée du Débarquement. Tel: 31 22 34 31. By the landing beach, includes a cinema and models of the Mulberry Harbour. Open: daily 9am–6.30pm 15 May–31 August.

BAYEUX
Musée de la Bataille de Normandie, Boulevard Fabian Ware. Tel: 31 92 93 41. It stands opposite the largest British military cemetery in Normandy. Open: daily 9am–7pm June–August.
Musée Mémorial du Général de Gaulle, 10 Rue Bourbesneur. Tel: 31 92 45 55. With written texts, photographs and other souvenirs, recording his five visits to the town between 1944 and 1946. Open: daily 15 March–15 November.

BÉNOUVILLE
Musée des Troupes Aéroportées, Pegasus Bridge. Tel: 31 44 62 54. The history of the air assault led by Major Howard. Open: daily 1 April–15 October (continuously 9am–7pm in July–August).

CAEN
Le Mémorial, a Museum for Peace. Tel: 31 06 06 44. Impressive, spacious, opened in 1991. It gives an overview of the war in the context of the history of the 20th century, using the latest computer and audiovisual techniques. The Nobel Peace Prize Gallery lists all the winners of the prize since 1901. Allow at least two or three hours for your visit. Open: daily 9am–7pm (9pm 11 July–31 August).

COLLEVILLE
Omaha Beach, 14710 Trévières. Tel: 31.22.40.62. The beach is dominated by the most important American military cemetery in Normandy; over 9,000 servicemen lay buried here and over 1,500 more are commemorated as missing, on the memorial. Open: all year.

FALAISE

Musée "Août 1944". Tel: 31 90 37 19. Tells the story of the closing stages of the battle for Normandy in August 1944, when the German army lost 10,000 men and 50,000 were captured. Also a room dedicated to the French Resistance. Open: daily March–November. Closed: Monday and Tuesday except June-August.

GRANDCAMP-MAISY

Musée des Rangers, Quai Crampon. Tel: 31 22 64 34. Dedicated to the élite American force, specially trained for D-Day. Open: daily except Monday April–October; daily 10am–7pm June–August.

MERVILLE-FRANCEVILLE

Musée. Tel: 31 24 23 57. Four concrete shelters, captured by the British 9th Parachute Battalion on 5/6 June, with a museum.

OUISTREHAM

Musée du Débarquement No. 4 Commando. Tel: 31 96 63 10. Commemorating the D-Day landings. Open: daily Palm Sunday–October; 9am–6.30pm June–September except weekends.

PORT-EN-BESSIN

Musée des Epaves sous-marines du Débarquement. Tel: 31 21 17 06. Remains of boats and aeroplanes and personal effects retrieved from the sea bed. Visit by appointment.

ST-MARTIN-DES-BESASCS

Musée. Tel: 31 68 75 00. Museum of the British breakthrough in the *bocage*.

SURRAIN

Musée de la Libération. Tel: 31 22 57 56. Commemorating the liberation of Surrain.

TILLY-SUR-SEULLES

Musée. Tel: 31 80 80 26. The museum commemorates the Battle of Tilly, liberated on 8 June.

VIERVILLE-SUR-MER

"Omaha". Tel: 31 22 43 08. Exhibition of the 6 June US landings on Omaha Beach.

MANCHE

AVRANCHES

Musée de la Seconde Guerre Mondiale, Le Moulinet, le Val-Saint-Père. Tel: 33 68 35 83. Varied collections on two floors. Open: daily in summer; weekends and bank holidays only, out of season.

CHERBOURG

Musée de la Guerre et de la Libération, Fort du Roule. Tel: 33 20 14 12. Open: daily except Tuesday in low season.

QUINEVILLE

Musée de la Libertée. Tel: 33 21 40 44. An evocation of the war in photographs and video. Open: daily April–October, continuously 9.30am–6.30pm June–September.

SAINTE-MARIE DU-MONT

Musée du Débarquement à Utah Beach, 50790. Tel: 33 71 53 35. The closest town to the first landings, commemorated by the 0 km marker on the "Liberty Road" (*see Tourist Routes* in *Getting Around* sec-

tion). Apart from the museum of the landings, there are several other monuments. Open: daily Easter–1 November; 9.30am–6.30pm July–September; Sunday and public holidays in winter. Closed: January.

SAINTE-MÈRE-EGLISE

Musée des Troupes Aéroportées. Tel: 33 41 41 35. Commemorates troups which were dropped by air into the battlefield, exhibits of a Douglas C 47 transport plane and other equipment and souvenirs. Open: daily 1 February–15 November; weekends 16 November–15 December.

Ecausseville. Aviation museum with World War II fighter planes.

ORNE

L'AIGLE

Musée "Juin 44", Place Fulbert-de-Beina. Tel: 33 24 19 44. Waxworks. Open: daily except Monday Palm Sunday–11 November.

MONT-ORMEL

Mémorial de Coudehard-Montormel. Tel: 33 28 88 71. Northeast of Chambois, this commemorates the climax of the Battle of Normandy on Mont-Ormel, after 77 days fightling with a monument to British, Canadian, French, Polish and US combatants.

MILITARY CEMETERIES

AMERICAN

Colleville-Saint-Laurent, on the coast between Arromanches and Grandcamp: 9,386 graves.

Saint-James (Montjoie St Martin), between Avranches and Fougères: 4,410 graves.

BRITISH

Banneville-Sannerville, between Caen and Troarn: 2,175 graves.

Bayeux: 4,868 graves.

Brouay, between Caen and Bayeux: 377 graves.

Cambes-en-Plaine, between Caen and Courseulles: 224 graves.

Chouain (Jerusalem), between Bayeux and Tilly-sur-Seulles: 40 graves.

Douvres-la-Délivrande, between Caen and Luc-sur-Mer: 927 graves.

Fontenay-le-Pesnel, between Caen and Caumont-l'Eventé: 520 graves.

Hermanville-sur-Mer, on the coast: 986 graves.

Hottot-Longraye, between Caen and Caumont-l'Eventé: 965 graves.

Ranville, near Pegasus Bridge: 2,151 graves.

Ryes, between Bayeux and Arromanches: 987 graves.

St-Charles-de-Percy, near Bény-Bocage: 792 graves.

St-Désir-de-Lisieux, near Lisieux: 589 graves.

St-Manvieu, between Caen and Caumont-l'Eventé: 2,186 graves.

Secqueville-en-Bessin, between Caen and Bayeux: 117 graves.

Tilly-sur-Seulles, between Caen and Balleroy: 1,224 graves.

CANADIAN

Bény-sur-Mer – Reviers, near Courseulles: 2,048 graves.

Bretteville-sur-Laize-Cintheaux, between Caen and Falaise: 2,959 graves.

GERMAN

La Cambe, between Bayeux and Isigny: 21,160 graves.

La Chapelle-en-Juger, Marigny between Saint-Lô and Coutances: 11,169 graves.

Huisnes-sur-Mer, near the Mont-St-Michel: 11,956 graves.

Orglandes, south of Valognes: 10,152 graves.

St-Désir-de-Lisieux, near Lisieux: 3,735 graves.

FRENCH

Memorial to the 2nd Armoured Division, Alençon.

POLISH

Grainville-Langannerie, between Caen and Falaise: 650 graves.

CULTURE PLUS

MUSEUMS & ART GALLERIES

There is a great variety of museums and galleries to visit in Normandy, ranging from sparkling new prestigious museums to simple local collections in town halls around the region. Here we list some of the best and some of the more unusual. For War Museums, see separate listing.

Most museums charge an entrance fee; for those that are state owned expect to pay between FF10 and FF25 (half price on Sunday). Reductions are usually given for children, senior citizens and students – on production of a valid card. Some major towns and cities offer a multi-site ticket; enquire at tourist offices. The museums listed here, are open every day, mornings and afternoons (opening is variable on public holidays), except where specified otherwise. As a general rule national museums are closed on Tuesday and municipal museums on Monday. Remember, most close for a long lunch from noon–12.30pm to around 2.30pm, although major sites are often open continuously, especially during the summer months.

SEINE MARITIME

CAUDEBEC-EN-CAUX

Musée de la Marine de Seine. Tel: 35 96 27 30. Dedicated to the life and times of the great river, including the last sailing barge that operated on it. Open: daily 15 March–31 October; closed Tuesday except July–August; open weekends in November–December.

CLÈRES

Musée d'Automobiles de Normandie. Tel: 35 33 23 02. Motor museum including 50 vehicles from World War II. Open: daily 9am–7pm.

CROISSET

Musée Flaubert. Tel: 35 36 43 91. The only remaining building in the grounds of the writer's former home. Closed: Tuesday and Wednesday mornings and public holidays.

FÉCAMP

Musée de la Bénédictine, 110 Rue Alexandre-le-Grand. Tel: 35 28 00 06. Find out all about the production of this famous liqueur and the abbey where its production started.

Musée Centre des Arts, ceramics from Rouen, religious art, and local furniture. Tel: 35 28 31 99. Closed: Tuesday.

LE HAVRE

Musée des Beaux-Arts André Malraux, Place Guynemer. Tel: 35 42 33 97. Fine collection of paintings from the pre-Impressionists and Impressionists to the present day. Closed: Tuesday and public holidays.

Other museums in the town are the museum of **Old Le Havre**, The **Maritime** and **Port Museum** and the **Natural History Museum**.

MOULINEAUX

Musée des Vikings, Château Robert le Diable. Tel: 35 18 02 36. Waxworks telling the story of the Viking invasions and the first dukes of Normandy in the impressive remains of the château. Open: daily 2am–7pm March–15 November, Sunday only in winter. Closed: January.

ROUEN

Galerie Bovary (Musée d'Automates). Tel: 35 23 61 44. 500 working automata, of which 300 represent the principal scene's from Flaubert's *Madame Bovary*. Open: daily July–August; Saturday, Sunday, Monday and public holidays Easter–31 October.

Musée des Beaux-Arts. Tel: 35 71 20 40. Good collections from the 16th–18th centuries, including works by Monet, David, Rubens and Fragonard. Closed: Tuesday, and Wednesday morning and public holidays.

Musée de la Céramique. Tel: 35 07 31 74. Rouen *faïence* from the 17th and 18th centuries. Closed: Tuesday, Wednesday morning and public holidays.

Musée Corneille, 4 Rue de la Pie, the dramatist and poet's birthplace.

Musée Flaubert et d'Histoire de la Médicine, Hôtel-Dieu, 41 Rue de Lecat. Tel: 35 08 81 81 ext: 52467. The birthplace of Gustav Flaubert whose father was chief surgeon at the hospital.

Musée Jeanne d'Arc, Place du Vieux Marché. Tel: 35 88 02 70. Closed: Monday in winter.

Musée Le Secq des Tournelles, Eglise Saint-Laurent, Rue Jacques-Villon. Tel: 35 71 28 40.

Named after the donator of the most important collection of antique wrought-ironwork in the world. Exhibits date from the Roman period to the present day. Closed: Tuesday, Wednesday morning and public holidays.

National Museum of Education. Of particular interest is the School of the Jews an 11th-century site excavated in the 1970s under the courtyard of the Palace of Justice, which bears witness to the strong Jewish culture and community in medieval Rouen. For visits, enquire at the tourist office.

VILLEQUIER

Musée Victor Hugo. Tel: 35 56 91 86. Souvenirs of the writer, in particular of *Contemplations* written after the death by drowing of his daughter and her husband in the Seine nearby. Closed: Tuesday.

CALVADOS

BALLEROY

Musée des Ballons, in the grounds of the château. Tel: 31 21 60 61. The world of hot-air balloons from the Montgolfier brothers onwards, the collections of Forbes, the American millionaire enthusaist. A spectacular balloon festival is held annually in June. Open: daily except Wednesday 15 April–31 October.

BAYEUX

Musée de la Tapisserie, Centre Guillaume le Conquérant, Rue de Nesmond. Tel: 31 92 05 48. Excellent museum, displaying the whole of the historic Bayeux Tapestry depicting the story of the conquest of England by William the Conqueror. To see it "in the flesh" is quite breathtaking. Also background exhibition and cinema. Open: daily 9am–7pm 16 May–15 September.

Musée Baron Gérard, Place de la Liberté. Tel: 31 92 14 21. Displays of porcelain, faïence, lace and paintings. Open daily 9am–7pm June–August. There is also a museum of religious art, a war museum (see *War and Peace* three pages back) and a clock museum (latter open by appointment only. Tel: 31 92 70 76).

CAEN

Musée des Beaux Arts, in the château, the former home of William the Conqueror. Tel: 31 85 28 63. Collections include faïence and important Italian and French works of the 17th and 18th centuries. Closed: Tuesday.

Musée de Normandie, Château de Caen. Tel: 31 86 06 24. Arts, crafts and traditions of the region. Closed: Tuesday.

Musée de la Poste et des Techniques de Communication. Tel: 31 50 12 20. Fascinating history of the postal service. Open: every afternoon except Sunday and Monday, also mornings 15 June–15 September.

Le Mémorial museum. For details *see War Museums*.

CLÉCY

Musée du Chemin de Fer Miniature. Tel: 31 69 07 13. Dedicated to miniature railways; 14 layouts. Open: Easter–30 September.

HONFLEUR

Musée Eugène-Boudin, Place Erik Satie. Tel: 31 89 54 00. 19th and 20th-century paintings, particularly the Saint-Siméon school; also costumes and temporary exhibitions. Open: afternoons only. Closed: Tuesday 1 October–15 March.

See too the **Museum of Old Honfleur** and the **Maritime Museum** in the Vieuix Bassin (joint ticket).

LE MOLAY-LITTRY

Musée de la Mine. Tel: 31 22 89 10. Reconstruction of a coal mine. Also the **Musée de la Meunerie**, Moulin de Marcy. Tel: 31 21 42 13. A 19th-century working mill. Both open: 1 April–30 September. Closed: Wednesday, Thursday, Saturday and Sunday afternoons 1 November–31 March.

PONT-L'EVÊQUE

Musée du Calvados et des Métiers anciens. Tel: 31 64 12 87. Dedicated to the production of Calvados and old trades of the region.

Musée "La Belle Epoque de l'Automobile", Château de Betteville. Tel: 31 65 05 02. Displays 100 vehicles produced between 1898 and 1950. Open: 9.30am–6.30pm Easter–11 November.

TROUVILLE

Villa Montebello, 64 Rue de Gen Leclerc. Tel: 31 88 16 26. An 1886 mansion housing works of the first artists to come to the coast, plus the history of sea bathing. Open: daily except Tuesday, Easter–September.

VENDEUVRE

Musée du mobilier miniature in the orangerie of the château, Saint-Pierre-sur-Dives. Tel: 31 40 93 83. Fine collection of miniature furniture and other works. Open: afternoons daily June–15 September; weekends and public holidays 15 March–2 November.

EURE

BERNAY

Musée Muinicipal, Place Guillaume de Volpiano. Tel: 32 46 63 23. Rich art collection, including Rouen faïence. Closed: Tuesday.

BOURNEVILLE

Ecomusée de la Basse Seine, La Maison des Métiers, one of a group of museums comprising the Ecomuseum, devoted to the life and crafts of the lower Seine. Other sites include Caudebec-en-Caux, Ytetot, Hauville and others.

GIVERNY

Maison et jardins de Claude Monet, Gasny. Tel: 32 51 28 21. The charming house where Monet lived and worked has been restored to the condition it was in during Monet's time. The famous gardens are recognisable from greetings cards worldwide. Open: 10am–6pm daily except Monday April–October.

Musée des impressionistes américains. Tel: 32 51 94 65. New museum of paintings executed by American artists either at Giverny or back home in the States. Open: 10am–6pm daily except Monday April–October.

LA COUTURE-BOUSSEY

Musée des Instruments de Musique à Vent. Tel: 32 36 28 80. Discover how wind instruments are made. Open: every afternoon except Tuesday and public holidays.

LE NEUBOURG

Musée du Charron-forgeron, 82 Rue O. Bonnel. Tel: 32 35 00 10. A new museum dedicated to the work of the blacksmith and cartwright. Open: May–November.

LES ANDELYS

Musée Nicolas Poussin, Rue Sainte-Clotilde. Tel: 32 54 04 16. Works of art from prehistoric to modern times of the region. Open: every afternoon except Tuesday.

LOUVIERS

Musée des Décors. Tel: 32 40 22 80. Collection devoted to design in the theatre, opera and cinema. Closed: Tuesday except July–September.

VASCOEUIL

Le Château de Vascoeuil, Rue Jules Michelet. Tel: 35 23 62 35. An important regional cultural centre. The Michelet Museum in the grounds is dedicated to the famous 19th-century French historian, who lived in the castle, while the château itself stages an annual exhibition of modern art in summer, as well as a programme of other events. Pleasant restaurant. Open: April–November.

VERNON

Musée Alphonse-Georges Poulain. Tel: 32 21. 28 09. Local history and fine art, particularly Monet, Bonnard, Vuillard and the American impressionists; also good collection of animals in art. Open: every afternoon except Monday.

ORNE

ALENÇON

Musée des Beaux-Arts et de la Dentelle, near Place Foch. Tel: 33 32 40 07. Important collections of graphic art and ethnic art from Cambodia; also the lacemaking for which the area is famous. Closed: Monday.

Musée de la Dentelle au Point d'Alençon, 33 Rue du Pont-Neuf. Tel: 33 26 27 26. The national gallery for this particular craft. Closed: Sunday .

BAGNOLES-DE-L'ORNE

Musée des Sapeurs Pompiers, 16 Boulevard Albert-Christophe. Tel: 33 38 10 34. Houses France's biggest collection of horse-drawn fire appliances. Open: daily except Wednesday 1 April–30 October.

FLERS

Musée du Bocage Normand, in the château. Tel: 33 64 01 02. Arts, crafts and local customs of the *bocage* – rural Lower Normandy. Open: every afternoon except Tuesday Easter–30 September.

Musée de la Blanchardière, 16 Rue Durmeyer. Tel: 33 65 42 22. Representing 40 local trades, tools, agricrutural machinery and vehicles. Open: daily except Friday and Sunday morning 30 April–1 November.

GACÉ

Musée de la Dame aux Camélias. Tel: 33 35 50 24. Dedicated to the Lady of the Camelias, who was born in the Orne, celebrated in films, TV, theatre and literature. Open: 2–6pm daily except Monday 15 June–1 September.

LIGNEROLLES

Musée de l'Epicerie. Tel: 33 25 91 07. Unusual museum displaying 4000 objects connected with the grocery trade from the turn of the century to the 1950s. Open: Sunday afternoon June–15 September.

VIMOUTIERS

Musée du Camembert. Tel: 33 39 30 29. Reconstruction of a farm producing the famous local cheese. Open: daily 1 March–31 December. Closed: Monday morning 1 May–31 October, Saturday afternoon and Sunday morning in March, April, November and December.

MANCHE

AVRANCHES

Musée Municipal, Palais Episcopal. Tel: 33 58 25 15. Local history, arts and crafts in the former Bishop's palace. Open: daily except Tuesday, Easter–15 October.

See too the exhibition of manuscripts from Mont-St-Michel in the Bibliothèque du Fonds Anciens at the Mairie (town hall). Tel: 33 68 33 18. Open: daily June–August.

BARENTON

Maison de la Pomme et de la Poire, La Logeraie. Tel: 33 59 56 22. Learn all about making cider, Calvados and related products in an old farm. Open: 1 March–15 November.

MARCHÉSIEUX

La Maison des Marais. Tel: 33 07 15 20. Traditional crafts and way of life on the Marais (marshland). Open: daily afternoons July–August; Sunday only from Easter–1 November.

MONT-ST-MICHEL

l'Archéoscope. Tel: 33 60 14 09. A new multi-media spectacle showing the history and legends surrounding the Mount. Open: daily 9am–6pm from the February school holiday until 11 November.

Musée Grévin. Tel: 33 60 14 09. Waxworks showing the life and work of the monks and the story of the building of the abbey. Open: daily 9am–6pm from the February school holiday until 11 November.

SAINT-MICHEL-DU-MONTJOIE

Musée du Granit. Tel: 33 59 84 94. Exhibition of the uses of stone, in building, agriculture, etc. in a vast wooded park. Open: daily 15 June–15 September; weekends Easter–30 October.

VALOGNES

Musée Regional du Cidre. Tel: 33 40 22 73. In a 15th-century house, discover the history of the production of cider in the region over the last 500 years, plus old Norman costumes and furniture. Open: daily. Closed: Sunday and Wednesday morning 1 June–30 September.

Musée des Vieux Métiers, Hôtel de Thieuville, Rue Pelouze. Tel: 33 40 26 25. Old tools and machines for traditional trades and crafts in the region. Open: daily. Closed: Sunday and Wednesday morning 1 June–30 September.

VILLEDIEU-LES-POÊLES

Maison de la Dentellière et Musée du Cuivre Ancien. Tel: 33 90 20 92. Lacemaking and copperworking in a working museum. Open: daily except Tuesday morning Easter–1 November.

Musée du Meuble Normand, Rue du Reculé. Norman furniture. Open daily except Tuesday morning Easter–1 November.

See too the Atelier du Cuivre and the Maison de l'Etain, (see Things to Do).

Bicycle Museum on the road to Avranches (RN 175). Tel: 33 61 13 00. Open: daily 10am–7pm 1 April–31 October.

LIVE ARTS

There is a variety of live entertainment performed in Normandy. In the summer, many major cities (and even small towns) present a programme of events, including music and drama festivals (often including street theatre and other outdoor performances). Of particular note is the contemporary music festival in Caen in March, the Jazz festival at Coutances in May, the chamber music festival in Mortagne in June, the summer music festival in Bayeux and the September music festival which has events all over the *département* of Orne. The Château de Vascoeuil in Eure is a regional arts centre with a full programme of cultural events during the summer season (*see Museums*). An annual programme listing all the major festivals and fêtes is available from the departmental tourist offices, or in Calvados from the Office Départemental d'Action Culturelle du Calvados, 28 Rue Jean Eudes, 14000 Caen. Tel: 31 85 25 93. (See also *Diary of Events*.)

Son-et-lumière displays are now a popular way of presenting historical events, these started at the châteaux in the Loire valley and have spread to historic monuments all around the country. Performances normally at around 9 or 10pm, with often several shows a night in July–August. For information and reservation contact the local tourist offices; a national guide of historical shows is published annually and is available from the Fédération Nationale des Fêtes et Spectacles Historiques, Hôtel de Ville, 60000 Beauvais. Tel: 44 79 40 09.

Spectacles particularly worth noting are "Les Imaginaires du Mont-Saint-Michel", a night-time tour of the abbey with full illuminations, mid-June to mid-September; also the *son-et-lumière* display at the Château de Martainville-Epreville (Seine-Maritime) with "actors" in full costume, every Friday and Saturday from the end of June to the beginning of August (for bookings, tel: 35 33 51 31). The Sées Musilumières in June combines three days of art events with the sound and light shows

around the cathedral (which continue weekly until September). Bagnoles-de-l'Orne is the setting for the annual Lancelot of the Lake festival, culminating in a huge firework display at the lakeside on 15 August.

DIARY OF EVENTS

Listed here are brief details of the main annual events. For more specific information, contact the local tourist offices.

FEBRUARY

Granville: Manche, Carnival.

MARCH

Caen: Calvados, Aspects de la Musique Contemporaine (contemporary music festival).
Lisieux: Calvados, Foire aux Arbres (tree fair).
Mortagne: Orne, Foire au boudin (black pudding fair); Livestock fair.
Le Tourneur: Calvados, Daffodil festival.

APRIL

Alençcon: Orne, Children's film festival.
Argentan: Orne, Quasimodo fair.
Caen: Calvados, Easter fair. Deauville: Calvados, Classical music festival.
Domfront: Orne, Foire des Rameauux (Palm Sunday fair).
Lisieux: Calvados, Easter celebrations at the Basilica.
Vimoutiers: Orne, Easter fair.

MAY

Bernay: Eure, Flower festival.
Beuvron: Calvados, Geranium festival.
Coutances: Manche, Jazz sous les Pommiers (jazz festival).
Deauville: Calvados, Postcard collectors' fair.
Evreux: Eure, May festival and carnival at the end of the month.
Falaise: Calvados, Maupassant fortnight.
Le Havre: Seine Maritime, Poetry festival.
Honfleur: Calvados, Bénédiction de la mer (sailor's festival).
Mont-St-Michel: Manche, Spring festival (religious celebrations and folk festival).
Pont-l'Evêque: Calvados, Cheese fair.
Saint-Sever: Calvados, Music festival.
Rouen: Seine-Maritime, International fair; Jeanne d'Arc festival.

JUNE

L'Aigle: Orne, arts festival.
Les Andelys: Eure, June festival.
Balleroy: Calvados, International hot-air balloon festival.
Cabourg: Calvados, International romantic film festival.
Caen: Calvados: "A Caen la Paix" festival.
Falaise: Calvados, les Polyfolies de Falaise (choral festival).
Fécamp: Seine-Maritime, Music weeks (until September).
Forges-les-Eaux: Seine-Maritime, Poetry festival.
Sainte-Mère-Eglise: Calvados, annual D-Day landings celebrations.

Mortagne: Orne, Chambre music festival.

JULY

Bastille Day: celebrated throughout France on the 14th.

Bagnoles-de-l'Orne: Orne, Lancelot of the Lake festival.

Bayeux: Calvados, Marché médiéval (market in medieval style); Eté Musical de Bayeux, continues into August.

Carrouges: Orne, Festival tradition et terroir (local festival with market of regional produce).

Creully: Calvados, baroque music festival.

Crouttes: Calvados, Musique au Prieuré; series of concerts and master classes.

Deauville: Calvados, world Bridge championships; jazz festival; international dog show.

Dieppe: Seine-Maritime, international dog show.

Fécamp: Seine-Maritime, Fêtes de la Mer (sea festival).

Forges-les-Eaux: Seine-Maritime, Horse fair.

Le Havre: Seine-Maritime, festival of wind instruments.

Honfleur: Calvados, Music festival, continues in August.

Gavray: Manche, Marché Normand (colourful market).

Mantilly: Orne, Perry festival.

Mont-St-Michel: Manche, Festival des heures musicales (music festival), continues in August.

Trouville: Calvados, Jazz festival.

AUGUST

Berville-sur-Mer: Eure, Sailor's festival.

La Colombe: Manche, Harvest festival.

Le Havre: Seine Maritime, Corso fleuri (flower festival parade).

Saint-Vaast-la-Hougue/Ile de Tatihou: Manche, Festival of the sea.

Savigny: Manche, Harvest festival.

SEPTEMBER

Alençon: Orne, Normandie-Maine Agricultural Show; September Musical de l'Orne: concerts all around the *département*.

Bellême: Orne, Mycologiades de Bellême (mushroom festival).

Deauville: Calvados, American film festival.

Lisieux: Calvados, Grandes fêtes de Sainte Thérèse.

Mont-St-Michel: Manche, Fête de la Saint-Michel (autumn pilgrimage).

OCTOBER

La Chapelle d'Andaines: Orne, Journées mycologiques (mushroom fair).

Crèvecoeur: Calvados, Apple fair.

Gavray: Manche, Saint Luc fair.

Soumont Saint-Quentin: Calvados, Cider festival.

Vimoutiers: Orne, Apple fair.

NOVEMBER

Liery: Eure and Dieppe; Seine-Maritime, Herring fair.

Sommery: Seine-Maritime, Apple fair.

DECEMBER

La Chapelle-d'Andaines and Sées: Orne, Turkey fair.

Evreux: Eure, Saint Nicolas fair.

ARCHAEOLOGY & ARCHITECTURE

A listing is given below of some of the major architectural sites of the the region – ecclesiastical, secular, historic, or just interesting. Opening hours are given where necessary, for general information about visits, see the *Museums* listing.

SEINE MARITIME

ETELAN

This flamboyant Gothic castle has a notable Renaissance staircase and a restored chapel. Open: every afternoon except Tuesday 15 July–31 August. Tel: 35 39 91 27.

ETRETAT

Château des Aygues, Rue Offenbach, 76790, in a romantic setting, this 19th-century castle was the former home of two queens of Spain. Open: every afternoon, Easter–31 October. Tel: 35 28 92 77.

EU

The Château d'Eu was the former residence of Louis-Philippe (he received Queen Victoria here once). Houses a Glass Museum. Open: daily except Tuesday 15 March–7 November. Tel: 35 86 44 00.

See too the Collegiate Church and the Jesuit College Chapel.

FÉCAMP

The Holy Trinity church, a masterpiece of Gothic architecture was the former abbey church for the Benedictine monastery built in the 12th century. The only other remaining monastic building now houses the Town Hall next door.

The Palais Bénédictine, built in the 19th century to compete with the excesses of Renaissance and Gothic styles, now housing the distillery for Benedictine liqueur, a museum and contemporary art gallery. Open: 20 March–14 November; 9.30am–6pm June–12 September; in winter visits possible at 10.30am and 3.30pm. Tel: 35 10 26 10.

FILIÈRES

Built from Caen stone in the 16th–18th centuries, this castle stands in extensive grounds which include the remains of an older fort. Gardens also open. Open: daily Easter–November. Tel: 35 20 53 30.

JUMIÈGES

The ruins of the Jumièges Abbey are in a delightful parkland setting, and should not be missed. The Museum of Sculpture. Open: daily 9am–6.30pm 15 June–15 September. Tel: 35 37 24 02.

LES ANDÉLYS

Château Gaillard is a ruin standing in a splendid setting overlooking the Seine. It was built by Richard Lionheart in 1196 and was the last bastion of the Dukes of Normandy which fell to the King of France in 1204. Open: 15 March–15 September except Tuesday and Wednesday morning. Tel: 32 54 04 16 (town hall).

MESNIÈRES-EN-BRAY

The beautiful Château de Mesnières, now an Ecclesiastical College. Would not look out of place among the splendours of the Loire Valley. Open: weekend and public holidays in the afternoons Easter–November. Tel: 35 93 10 04.

MIROMESNIL
Château de Miromesnil, 76550 Tourville-sur-Arques, 6 miles (10 km) from Dieppe, this 18th-century château was the birthplace of the writer, Maupassant. It boasts two contrasting facades and lovely gardens. Open: every afternoon except Tuesday 1 May–15 October. Tel: 35 04 40 30.

ORCHER
Overlooking the sea, this 18th-century castle stands on the site of an ancient fort. It is set in wooded park. The grounds are open all year except on Thursday; the house every afternoon July–15 August. Tel: 35 45 45 91.

ROUEN
The Gothic splendour of the Cathedral of Notre Dame announces it as one of the finest in the country. The Lady Chapel is notable for its fine stained glass (not many windows survived two world wars), and there are several interesting tombs, including Richard the Lionheart's. The elaborate west front is famous for its Tree of Jesse in the tympanum. Also of particular note is the famous clock, le Gros Horloge in the road of the same name. The seat of the former Normandy Parliament, the Palais de Justice is another fine building, all the more notable for the archaeological site which was excavated there in 1976 – the Monument Juif d'Epoque Romane (*see Museums*). Much of the old quarter of half-timbered houses has been carefully restored in recent years, in particular Rue Damiette and Eau-de-Robec. The old market square (Place du Vieux Marché) in the heart of the shopping centre is notable as the spot where Joan of Arc was burnt at the stake.

SAINT-PIERRE-DE-MANNEVILLE
Manoir de Villers, 30 Route de Sahurs, 76113, in this family home you can trace the history of Norman architecture from the 16th century to the present day. Tel: 35 32 07 02.

SAINT-ROMAIN-DE-COLBOSC
The remains of Tancarville Castle dominate the Seine, and offer sweeping views. Also an art gallery and restaurant. Open: in season. Tel: 35 96 00 21.

SAINT-WANDRILLE
Saint-Wandrille abbey is a fine site, a combination of 14th-century ruins and the present buildings dating from the 17th century. It was used for theatrical productions during the early part of this century, but the monks moved back in in 1931 and it is now a thriving Benedictine community. Tel: 35 96 23 11.

VALMONT
Renaissance-style castle and leisure park. Open: afternoons Saturday and Sunday April–October (daily July–August). Tel: 35 29 84 36.

The Abbaye de Valmont. Much of it is in ruins, but the Lady Chapel remains intact and is quite charming. Tel: 35 29 83 02.

CALVADOS

BALLEROY
This château built by Mansart in the 17th-century, this château's rather plain exterior hides a wealth of riches inside, including some superb paintings by Mignard. See the Balloon Museum in grounds (see Museum's listing). Open: daily except Wednesday 15 April–31 October. Tel: 31 21 60 61.

BAYEUX
Cathédrale de Notre Dame, built in the 11th century on the site of a former Roman temple, restored in the 12th and 19th centuries. Closed: at lunchtime September–July.

BÉNOUVILLE
The castle was built in the 18th century by Nicolas Ledoux in neoclassical style. Open: afternoon at weekends, public holidays and Easter–30 September, also Wednesday July–30 September. Tel: 31 95 53 23.

CAEN
Much of the city was destroyed during World War II and has been rebuilt in local stone. The Abbaye-aux-Hommes survived unscathed, and indeed was used as a shelter by local people during the bombings. Now used as the Town Hall, the abbey was built on the orders of William the Conqueror; his tomb is marked here, but the grave was ransacked and his bones scattered. Around the same time the Abbaye-aux-Dames was founded by his wife, Matilda of Flanders.

CANAPVILLE
The traditional half-timbered Manor House dates back to the 15th century and is one of the most picturesque in the Auge region. Entry by appointment only. Tel: 31 65 22 23.

CREULLY
Fortified castle originally built in the 11th century when the Barons of Creully were the most powerful lords in the region. Rebuilt in the 14th–6th centuries. The first BBC transmitter was sited in Creully during the Allied Landings. Open: daily July–August. Tel: 31 80 18 65.

FALAISE
The castle where William the Conqueror was born in 1027 was probably one of the first stone castles to be built in Normandy. It has been closed for extensive restoration work; check at the local tourist office for future opening times. Tel: 31 40 05 24.

FONTAINE-HENRY
Built in stages the château is a fine record of architectural styles from the 15th and 16th centuries. It is notable for its ornamental sculptures on the facade. Visits by appointment. Tel: 31 80 00 42.

JUAYE-MONDAYE
The classical church and monastery of Mondaye are still in use today as a thriving cultural centre. Open: every afternoon July–30 September; Sunday and public holidays out of season. Tel: 31 92 58 11.

LISIEUX
Much of the town, including some fine Gothic buildings were destroyed in the war; the Musée du

Vieux Lisieux gives a picture of what it was like. Saint Peter's Cathedral survived, as did the Basilica, built in 1929 and consecrated in 1954, to commemorate Saint Thérèse who spent her childhood in the town, and is now a place of pilgrimage.

LA LUCERNE-D'OUTREMER
This 12th-century abbey is particularly notable for its Gregorian chant sung every Sunday at 10am and 6pm; also a collection of liturgical clothing. Open: daily 15 March–14 November; weekends only in winter. Tel: 33 48 83 56.

PONTECOULANT
Two towers and the southern pavillion are all that remain of the 16th-century fortified manor house, but the 18th-century extension is also beautiful. Now houses a regional museum. Open: daily except Tuesday; afternoons only from 16 November–4 April when also closed on Monday. Closed: October. Tel: 31 69 62 54.

SAINT-GERMAIN-DE-LIVET
This half-timbered moated manor house, with beautiful checkered stonework, is a fine example of the architecture of the Auge region. Closed: 1–15 October and 15 December–1 February. Tel: 31 31 00 03.

SAINT-PIERRE-SUR-DIVES
The abbey church (12th–13th century) is one of the finest examples of Gothic architecture in the region. While in the area visit the covered market (market day Monday).

SAINT-SAUVEUR-LE-VICOMTE
This 11th-century abbey is a centre of pilgrimage and has exhibitions of historic documents and important Roman remains. Tel: 33 41 60 37.

The ancient fortress in the town was built by the English Captain Chandos and played an important role in the Hundred Years' War. Tel: 33 41 60 26 (town hall).

VENDEUVRE
The château, built for the chief engineer of the city and castle of Caen, is a fine country residence. Visit the museum of miniature furniture in the orangery. Open 15 March–1 November, by appointment. Tel: 31 40 93 83.

EURE

BEAUMESNIL
The château is one of the finest examples of Louis XIII in France. Also houses a bookbinding museum. Open: 1 May–30 September by appointment. Tel: 32 44 40 09.

BERNAY
The abbey is a fine example of a Romanesque abbey church dating from the 11th century. The churches of Sainte-Croix and Notre-Dame de la Couture are worth a visit to see the stained glass windows. Closed: Tuesday.

EVREUX
The Cathedral of Notre Dame is a mixture of architectural styles due to having suffered attack many times over the centuries. It boasts some good stained glass and wrought ironwork. The adjacent Bishop's Palace houses a museum.

FLEURY-LA-FORÊT
The château was rebuilt in the 18th century after a fire. It boasts a remarkable roof and classical French park with rose gardens; rides available on a miniature tourist train. Also houses an exhibition of antique dolls. Visits all year by appointment. Tel: 32 49 63 91.

GAILLON
This splendid Renaissance castle, a former residence of the Archbishops of Rouen, has been undergoing restoration. Open: July, August. Tel: 32 29 60 35.

GUICHAINVILLE
Château du Buisson Garembourg, elegant 17th-century castle with 18th-century furnishings and a chapel in the grounds where there is also a picnic site. Open: daily except Sunday morning 1 May–31 September. Tel: 32 23 12 48.

HEUDICOURT
This elegant 17th-century château was a gift from Napoleon I to his Treasurer, Count Estève, to whose family it still belongs. See the collection of tapestries. Open: by appointment Easter–1 November. Tel: 32 55 86 06.

LE BEC-HELLOUIN
Abbaye Notre-Dame, substantial ruins of a formerly important ecumenical centre which served as a school for diplomats and royal officials as well as theologians. Has connections with Canterbury cathedral. Also a car museum. Closed: Tuesday. Tel: 32 44 86 09.

LE NEUBOURG
Château du Champ de Bataille, recently re-opened, this late 17th-century mansion is one of the most sumptuous in Normandy. The park includes an 18-hole golf course. Open: every afternoon. Tel: 32 31 84 34.

MONTAURE
This 18th-century manor house stands in a vast park with a cider museum in the grounds. Open: afternoons in summer except Wednesday, out of season on Sunday and public holidays. Tel: 32 50 64 99.

VASCOEUIL
This fine old house includes a museum dedicated to the historian Michelet, also contemporary art exhibitions. The grounds include a classical French garden and sculptures. Open: every afternoon April–November. Tel: 35 23 62 35.

VERNON
Château de Bizy, a former royal castle built in the 18th century. It is noted for its tapestries and souvenirs of the Bonaparte family. In the grounds admire the fountains and the stables copied from Versailles. Open: daily, closed Friday April–November. Tel: 32 51 00 82.

ORNE

CARROUGES
A vast castle, surrounded by a moat and gardens, it

remained in the same family from the time it was built in the 14th century until it was presented to the Monuments Historiques (French National Trust) in 1936. Closed: public holidays. Tel: 33 27 20 32.

CROUTTES
Prieuré Saint-Michel, a group of monastic buildings (13th–18th century) often used for exhibitions and conferences. Its attractive gardens contain medicinal plants and old roses. Open: afternoon 4 July–29 August. Tel: 33 39 15 15.

LE BOURG-SAINT-LÉONARD
Beautiful late 18th-century castle, with fine furnishings, including a Chinese boudoir, and Aubusson tapestries. See too the orangerie and stables. Open: daily except Wednesday 15 June–10 October. Tel: 33 67 15 36.

MÉDAVY
Notable moated mansion dating back to the 16th century on the bank of the River Orne, classical French gardens. Open: 14 July–14 September. Tel: 33 35 34 54.

MORTRÉE
Château d'O, a combination of flamboyant Gothic and Renaissance styles, this château is still inhabited. The lovely 12th-century commandery now houses a restaurant. Open: daily except Tuesday; afternoons only 1 October–31 March. Tel: 33 35 34 69.

SAINT-CÉNERI-LE-GÉREI
At the heart of the Alpes Mancelles, this delightful village has been classified as one of the 100 most beautiful in France.

SAINT-CHRISTOPHE-LE-JAJOLET
Château de Sassy, this 18th-century castle is still inhabited and is notable for its gardens and terraces. Gardens open all year; the château every afternoon from Palm Sunday–1 November. Tel: 33 35 32 66.

SÉES
The cathedral of Notre-Dame is dwarfed by its big sister in Rouen, but this magnificent work of Gothic Norman art should not be missed.

VILLERS-EN-OUCHE
Castle and gardens dating from the 17th century. Open: daily except Tuesday Easter–1 November. Tel: 33 34 90 30.

MANCHE

BRIQUEBEC
The château houses the regional museum of ethnography. Open: daily July–August. Tel: 33 52 21 13 (town hall).

CÉRISY-LA-FORÊT
Abbaye Bénédictine Saint-Vigor, all that remains of this 6th-century monastic foundation are the 11th-century church and some other ruins. A permanent exhibition on the Romans in Lower Normandy is on view. Open: daily 9am–6.30pm Easter–15 November. Tel: 33 57 34 63.

COUTANCES
Splendid Gothic cathedral, built to replace an earlier one which was destroyed by fire. Note the scenes from Thomas à Becket's life in the chapel window. Tel: 33 45 17 79.

CROSVILLE-SUR-DOUVE
This castle (15th–17th century) is remarkable for its ceiling painted with mythological scenes and a monumental fireplace. Still inhabited, it is open to the public afternoons Easter–1 October. Exhibitions and concerts are often stage. Tel: 33 41 67 25.

GRATOT
Flanked by four towers, this old castle dates back to the 14th-century. It has been restored by a group of dedicated volunteers and now houses an exhibition "Eight centuries of life" about the local area. Tel: 31 85 25 93.

HAMBYE
Abbey church and ruined convent; see the collections of furniture, liturgical ornaments and tapestries. Closed: Tuesday; Wednesday morning in winter and from 20 December–1 February. Tel: 33 61 76 92.

LESSAY
The former abbey, now the parish church was damaged in 1944, but well restored in Romanesque style. On the surrounding moorland, the colourful Millenial Holy Cross Fair takes place every September. Open: daily; guided tours in July and August. Tel: 33 46 46 18 (town hall).

MARTINVAST
Domaine de Beaurepaire, English-style gardens surround the remains of this Norman fortress; the 11th-century keep is the only part intact, which is linked to the 16th-century castle by an extension built in the 19th century. Open: afternoons Saturday, Sunday and public holidays. Tel: 33 52 02 23.

MONT-SAINT-MICHEL
One of the most important sites of Normandy, indeed of France. This fantastic abbey rises on a rock in the St-Michel Bay, well fortified against the sea and invaders. Its religious community thrived until the Revolution, then the monastery became a prison, but it has been well preserved since 1874 when it was declared a national monument and it remains remarkably intact. The foot of the mount is crowded with souvenir shops, but those with the fortitude to climb to the top and enter the abbey itself will be rewarded as the tourist hordes thin out somewhat and the views are splendid. Open: 15 May–14 September from 9.30am–6pm, closed on public holidays. Tel: 33 60 14 14.

MORTAIN
On a hill at the entrance to the Normandy-Maine Regional Park, Mortain is worth visiting for its Abbaye Blanche (White Abbey), a former Cistercian abbey of the 12th century. Closed: Tuesday. Tel: 33 59 00 21.

PIROU
Pirou is said to be the oldest castle in Normandy. Dating back to the 12th century, it houses an exhibition of tapestries depicting the Norman conquest of Sicily. Open: every afternoon except Tuesday; every day including mornings July–August. Tel: 33 48 83 56.

SAINT-VAAST-LA-HOUGUE

This picturesque fishing port is protected by the defensive tours of Hougue and Tahitou, remains of the Vauban's 17th-century fortifications.

TORIGNI-SUR-VIRE

Building on the castle started in the 16th century, but was not completed until the reign of Louis XIV. Now houses 17th-century furniture and tapestries and stages exhibitions. Open: afternoons during the Easter holidays; 12–30 June and 1–15 September; other periods by appointment. Tel: 33 56 71 44.

VAINS

Le Manoir de Vains stands in an attractive setting which includes a 16th-century chapel. Exhibitions of old manuscripts. Open: weekday afternoons 1 July–15 September. Tel: 33 58 24 46.

VALOGNES

The Hôtel de Beaumont is a fine town house, known as the Little Versailles of Normandy. It has richly decorated rooms and classical French gardens. Guided visits every afternoon 1 July–15 September and Easter weekend. Tel: 33 40 12 30.

NIGHTLIFE

The most lively nightlife in the region is to be found in the more sophisticated seaside resorts, such as Deauville and Trouville, and the major cities, such as Rouen and Caen. Here you will find a variety of nightclubs, discothèques and, particularly around the coast, casinos – some of which also offer other entertainment away from the gaming tables. Many towns around the region organise cultural festivals during the summer for the local people and tourists; also popular are *son-et-lumière* displays (*see Live Arts* and *Diary of Events*).

If you are staying on a farm or in a country area, you may be invited to join in local festivities. Almost every town and village has its own fête during the summer; these can range from a simple *boules* competition finished off with a dance, hosted by an enthusiastic (and sometimes excruciating) band, playing traditional music (or if you're unlucky, ancient pop songs), to a full-blown carnival with street theatre, fireworks and sophisticated entertainment.

Information about all kinds of entertainment is available from the tourist offices, or at your hotel. The lists below are by no means comprehensive.

CASINOS

The following casinos are open all year; there are plenty of others which are only open in the high season. You may be required to show your passport to gain admittance.

SEINE MARITIME

DIEPPE

Casino: Roulette, baccarat, chemin de fer, blackjack, gaming machines. Tel: 35 82 33 60.

FORGES-LES-EAUX

Casino: Gaming machines, baccarat, roulette, blackjack; regular entertainment in summer including magicians and dinner dances; restaurant. Tel: 35 09 80 12.

CALVADOS

DEAUVILLE

Casino: Roulette, blackjack, chemin de fer, over 200 gaming machines. Le Régine's night club is downstairs. Tel: 31 98 66 66.

LUC-SUR-MER

Casino, Rue Guynemer: Roulette, blackjack, gaming machines; piano bar. Tel: 31 97 32 19.

OUISTREHAM

Queen Normandy Casino, Place Alfred Thomas: Gaming machines, billiards; nightclub, bars and a restaurant. Tel: 31 36 30 00.

TROUVILLE-SUR-MER

Casino: Blackjack, roulette, craps, 200 gaming machines. Tel: 31 87 75 00.
L'Embellie night club. Tel: 31 88 76 09

ORNE

BAGNOLES-DE-L'ORNE

Casino du Lac: Blackjack, roulette, chemin de fer, gaming machines; old-time dancing; Sunday afternoon tea dances. Tel: 33 37 84 00.

MANCHE

CHERBOURG

Casino de l'Amirauté: Gaming machines; nightclub, American bar and shows. Tel: 33 43 00 56.

GRANVILLE

Casino: Blackjack. Tel: 33 50 00 79.

NIGHTCLUBS & DISCOTHEQUES

CALVADOS

BAYEUX

Le Royal, 9 Rue Genas Duhomme. Tel: 31 21 18 00.

CABOURG

Le Privé and Le Palace, two nightspots at the casino; also a piano bar, "Du côté de chez Swann". Tel: 31 91 11 75.

CAEN

Le Chic, Place Courtonne. Tel: 31 94 48 72.
Le Diam's, 10 Place du 36ème R.I. Tel: 31 84 71 23.
Le Paradis, 10 Rue de Strasbourg. Tel: 31 85 40 40.

CLÉCY

La Potinière, café, jazz and theatre every Friday July–August. Tel: 31 69 76 75.

DEAUVILLE

Le Glamour, Rue Désiré-le-Hoc. Tel: 31 88 30 91.
Melody, 13 Rue Albert-Fracasse. Tel: 31 88 34 83.
Le Régine's, below the casino. Tel: 31 98 66 66.

HOULGATE

Allison's Bar, 2 Rue Beaumier. Tel: 31 24 13 92.
Manhattan, at the Casino which also has a cinema. Tel: 31 91 60 94.

OUISTREHAM

Les 2 Flo, Avenue Pasteur. Tel: 31 97 19 22.

EURE

EVREUX

Le Blue Note, 8 Rue Georges-Bernard. Piano bar. Tel: 32 31 26 49.
Le Night-Bird, 43 Rue St-Louis. Piano bar. Tel: 32 33 06 77.
Le Privé, 33 Avenue Winston Churchill. Tel: 32 31 17 00.
Top-Gun, 47 Rue St-Sauveur. Tel: 32 38 01 68.

LE NEUBORG

Le Jingles, Quitteboeuf (out of town). Tel: 32 34 08 83.
Les Pleiades, Hectomare (out of town). Tel: 32 35 30 83.

MANCHE

CHERBOURG

L'Ascot, cabaret and piano bar. Tel: 33 22 10 32.
Le Teppaz, Port Chantereyne. Tel: 33 94 44 48.

HAMBYE

L'Appocalypse discothèque.

HAUTEVILLE-SUR-MER

Les Dunes discothèque and billiard club.

SAINT-LÔ

Cotton-Club, 2 Rue des Fossés. Tel: 33 05 13 60.

SAINT-PAIR-SUR-MER

Discothèque at the casino. Tel: 33 50 06 51.

SAINT-VAAST-LA-HOUGUE

L'Ascage. Tel: 33 20 12 23.

ORNE

L'AIGLE

Le Moulin d'Antan, 35 Rue des Jetées. Tel: 33 24 55 24.

ALENÇON

L'Arc en Ciel, 11 Rue de la Halle aux Toiles. Tel: 33 26 32 15.
Le Saint-Germain, Rue Elan, St-Germain du Corbeis. Tel: 33 26 25 19.

BAGNOLES-DE-L'ORNE

Club Discothèque "Le Privé", Avenue Robert Cousin. Tel: 33 37 86 15.

FLERS

Le Calypso, 3 Rue de la Chaussée. Tel: 33 64 83 07.

SHOPPING

Over the last couple of decades most major towns in France have made the sensible decision to keep town centres for small boutiques and individual shops. Many of these areas are pedestrianised and very attractive (although beware – some cars ignore the *voie piétonnée* signs). The large supermarkets, hypermarkets, furniture stores and do-it-yourself outlets are grouped on the outskirts of the town, mostly designated as a Centre Commercial. The biggest centres are vast and are to be found on the edge of the major conglomerations of Rouen, Caen, etc.

These centres, although aesthetically quite unappealing, are fine for bulk shopping, for self-catering or for finding a selection of wine to take home at reasonable prices. But for gifts and general window-shopping the town centres are far more interesting. It is here that you will find the individual souvenirs with a particularly local flavour, alongside the beautifully dressed windows of delicatessens and patisseries. Caen is said to have the best shopping centre outside Paris, and is well served by department stores and individual boutiques.

MARKETS

The heart of every French town is its market; they mostly start early and close at midday, although some bigger ones are open in the afternoon too. The French themselves usually visit early to get the best of the produce. Markets are full of colour and bustle; the best have all kinds of stalls from flowers to domestic animals (do not be deceived – these are for the pot). Local cheeses, honey, cider, sausage, pâté and other specialities are often offered for tasting to tempt browsers to buy. Fish markets are often held by the harbour early in the morning in many coastal towns. Some of the best weekly markets are:

MONDAY

Calvados: Pont-l'Evêque, Saint-Pierre-des-Dives.
Eure: Bourg-Achard, Gisors, Pont-Audemer.
Orne: L'Aigle and Briouze (livestock), Soligny-la-Trappe, Vimoutiers (afternoon).
Manche: Briquebec, Carentan.

Seine-Maritime: Goderville.
Calvados: Deauville, Dives-sur-Mer (summer only), Grandcamp-Maisy.
Eure: Evreux (St-Michel).
Orne: L'Aigle, Argentan, Soligny-la-Trappe.
Manche: Hambye, Lessay, Villedieu-les-Poêles.

WEDNESDAY
Seine-Maritime: Yvetot.
Calvados: Bayeux, Villers-Bocage, Luc-sur-Mer (summer only).
Eure: Evreux (centre), Le Neuborg, Vernon.
Orne: Flers, Longny-au-Perche, Le Mêle-sur-Sarthe.
Manche: Cérisy-la-Forêt, Granville.

THURSDAY
Seine-Maritime: Etretat, Forges-les-Eaux.
Calvados: Condé-sur-Noireau, Houlgate, Le Molay-Littry.
Eure: Brionne, Lyons-la-Forêt.
Orne: Alençon, Bellême, La Ferté-Macé.
Manche: Carentan, Coutances.

FRIDAY
Seine-Maritime: Auffay, Eu.
Calvados: Caen (Place St-Sauveur), Cambremer, Deauville, Vire.
Eure: Broglie, Tillières-sur-Avre.
Orne: Argentan, Courtomer, Ecouché.
Manche: Agon, Valognes.

SATURDAY
Seine-Maritime: Dieppe.
Calvados: Bayeux, Honfleur, Lisieux.
Eure: Les Andelys, Bernay, Louviers.
Orne: Carrouges (afternoon), Flers, Gacé and Mortagne-au-Perche (afternoon), Sées.
Manche: Avranches, Saint-Lô.

SUNDAY
Calvados: Caen (Place Courtonne), Cabourg, Trouville.
Eure: Brionne, Evreux (La Madeleine).
Orne: Alençon, Mortrée.
Manche: Barenton, Hauteville-sur-Mer.

There are more and more antique or second-hand (*brocante*) markets springing up around the provinces, as well as flea markets (*marché aux puces*), which are also fun to look around – you may find a genuine bargain antique amongst all the old junk. Try Saint-Pierre-sur-Dives, in Calvados, held on the first Sunday in every month. Antique and bric-a-brac fairs are usually held annually as below:
February: Lisieux and Honfleur (Calvados).
April: L'Aigle (Orne), Neufchâtel-en-Bray and Rouen (Seine-Maritime), Bernay (Eure).
May: Argentan (Orne).
June: Beaumont-le-Roger (Eure), Le Tréport (Seine-Maritime).
August: Mortagne-au-Perche (Orne).

Look out for special fairs held all over the country at various times throughout the year, such as harvest times, Jumièges in Seine-Maritime, for example has a cherry market in July, a plum market in August and an apple market in October. Some of the most important are listed in the Diary of Events section (*see Culture Plus*), for others check with the local tourist office for details.

BUYING DIRECT

Around the country, you may be tempted by all the signs you see along the road for *dégustations* (tastings). Many cider producers and farmers will invite you to try their cider, Calvados, and other produce. This is a good way to try before you buy and can sometimes include a look around the farm. Sometimes farm produce is more expensive to buy this way than in the supermarkets, but do not forget that it is home produced and not factory processed.

PRACTICAL INFORMATION

Food shops, especially bakers, tend to open early; boutiques and department stores open about 9am, but sometimes not until 10am. In most town centres, almost everything closes from noon until 2.30 or 3pm but in seaside resorts and other tourist areas, it is becoming more common for shops to remain open. Most shops close in the evening at 7pm. Out of town, the hypermarkets are usually open all day until 8 or even 9pm. Most shops are closed Monday mornings and many all day. If you want to buy a picnic lunch, remember to buy everything you need before midday. Good delicatessens (*charcuterie*) have a selection of delicious ready-prepared dishes, which make picnicking a delight.

On most purchases, the price includes TVA (VAT or Valued Added Tax). The base rate is currently 18.6 percent, but can be as high as 33 percent on luxury items. Foreign visitors can claim back TVA; worth doing if you spend more than FF2,400 (FF1,200 for non-EC residents) in one place. Some large stores and hypermarkets have information bureaux or welcome desks where you can obtain a refund form. This must be completed to show (with the goods purchased) to customs officers on leaving the country (pack the items separately for ease of access). Then mail the form back to the retailer who will refund the TVA in a month or two. Certain items purchased (e.g. antiques) may need special customs clearance.

If you have a complaint about any purchase, return it in the first place to the shop as soon as possible. In the case of any serious dispute, contact the local Direction Départementale de la Concurrence et de la Consommation et de la Répression des Fraudes (see telephone directory for number).

CLOTHING

Most shops will let you try on clothes (*essayer*) before buying. Children's sizes, in particular, tend to be small compared with UK and US age ranges. Hypermarkets have good-value children's clothes.

SPORTS

PARTICIPANT

Normandy offers opportunities for all kinds of sporting activities. Most medium-sized towns have swimming-pools and even small villages often have a tennis court, but you may have to become a temporary member to use it – enquire at the local tourist office or *mairie* (town hall) which will also provide details of all other local sporting activities. It seems to be a quirk of the French tourist industry that they do not always take full advantage of their facilities. Even though there may be good weather in early summer and autumn, open-air swimming-pools and other venues often limit their seasons to the period of the summer school holidays (July and August).

Wind-surfing is popular along the coast and inland; many of the sailing schools also offer courses. Sand yachting is mostly practised on the sandy stretches of beach in Calvados and Manche.

Most of the resorts have beach clubs for children where youngsters can be entrusted to the care of supervisors for all kinds of fun and games. A fee is normally payable, but no prior booking is usually required.

Many companies offer sporting and activity holidays in France; a selection is given under each sports heading below.

WATERSPORTS

With its miles of coastline, there are many opportunities for sailing, wind-surfing and all kinds of water sports. It is impossible to list all the facilities here, but a selection is given under each heading.

SAILING

The national organisation for leisure sailing is the Fédération Française de Voile, 55 Avenue Kléber, 75784 Paris Cedex 16. Tel: (1) 45 53 68 00. Another useful address is the Yacht Club de France, 4 Rue Chalgrin, 75116 Paris. Tel: (1) 45 01 28 46. The regional tourist office (*see Useful Addresses*) publishes a leaflet detailing all the yachting harbours in the region and their facilities. It is possible to hire a self-skippered yacht, or one with a crew for a week or a weekend; try the companies listed below:
Accastillage Diffusion, Bassin de Plaisance, 14150

Ouistreham-Riva-Bella. Tel: 31 97 17 41.
Aries Location, Port-Chantereyne, 50100 Cherbourg. Tel: 33 03 46 94.
Centre Nautique, Krischarter, Port-Deauville, 14800 Deauville. Tel: 31 88 67 32.
Granville Plaisance, Port de Hérel, 50400 Granville. Tel: 33 50 23 82.
Lespesqueux Sail, 3 Rue Clément-Desmaisons, BP 422, 50404 Granville Cedex. Tel: 33 50 18 97.
Serra Marine, Port de Plaisance, 14150 Ouistreham-Riva-Bella. Tel: 31 97 17 41.

There are almost 100 sailing clubs and sailing schools in the region, offering courses at all levels; information is available from departmental tourist offices; a selection is listed below:
Cabourg Yacht Club, Cap Cabourg, 14390 Cabourg. May–November. Tel: 31 91 23 55.
Centre de Formation à la Croisière de Carentan, Port de Plaisance BP 401, 50500 Carentan. Tel: 33 71 19 65.
Club Nautique de Trouville-Hennequeville, Ecole de Voile, Digue des Roches Noires, 14360 Trouville. Tel: 31 88 13 59.
Deauville Yacht Club, Quai de la Marine, 14800 Deauville. Tel: 31 88 38 19.
Jeune Ariane Sailing School, 13 Rue du Nord, 50400 Granville. Tel: 33 50 12 23.
Luc Yachting Club, Ecole de Voile, Rue Guynemer, 14530 Luc-sur-Mer. Tel: 31 96 74 39.
Noroit Marime, 1 Rue Destrais, 50110 Tourlaville. Tel: 33 20 30 64.

CANOEING

The national organisation for the sport is Canoë-Kayak de France, 47 Quai Ferber, 94360 Bry-sur-Marne. Tel: (1) 48 81 54 26. Other offices in the individual *départements* will also give details of courses, possibilities of hire and suitable stretches of water:

SEINE-MARITIME
Canoë-Nature, 12 Rue des Tanneurs, 76680 Saint-Saëns. Tel: 35 34 87 40. Details of activities and hire possibilites on the Varenne, Béthune, Eaulne and Yères.

CALVADOS
Comité Départemental de Canoë-Kayak, Stade Nautique, Avenue A. Sorel, 14000 Caen.

EURE
Departmental Tourist Office (*see Useful Addresses*). Recreation centres for canoeing exist in Pose, Dangu, Brionne and La Bonneville; navigable rivers are the Risle, Epte, Eure, Andelle and Charentonne.

ORNE
Comité Départemental de Canoë-Kayak, Auberge de Jeunesse, 61250 Damigny. Tel: 33 29 00 48. There ae good facilities in Damigny and the Normandie-Maine Reginal park.

MANCHE
Try the following clubs who hire canoes and offer tuition:

Canoë-Kayak de Saint-Sauveur-le-Vicomte, Chemin du Moulin, 50390 Saint-Sauveur-le-Vicomte. Tel: 33 21 10 56.

Centre Régional de Nautisme de Granville. Tel: 33 50 18 95. Sea kayak club, open all year, courses in July and August.

Club de Canoë-Kayak d'Avranches, 81 Rue de la Liberté, 50300 Avranches. Tel: 33 68 33 22.

SWIMMING & DIVING

The national organisation for the sport is the Fédération Française de Natation, 148 Avenue Gambetta, 75020 Paris. Tel: (1) 40 31 17 70. There are hundreds of swimming-pools throughout the region. Sea bathing is usually controlled by means of flags on supervised beaches.

The following clubs offer facilities and courses for deep-sea diving; the clubs are usually based at the local swimming-pool.

ASAM Cherbourg, BP 10, 50115 Cherbour Naval. Tel: 33 92 64 59.

Club de Plongée de Trouville, 14360 Trouville, information at the swimming-pool. Tel: 31 88 89 81.

Club Subaquatique du Calvados, Stade Nautique, Avenue A. Sorel, 14000 Caen. Tel: 31 86 04 12.

Club Subaquatique "l'Hippocampe" 21 Avenue Maréchal Leclerc, 50400 Granville. Tel: 33 61 75 09.

Ecole de plongée de Port-en-Bessin, Quai Letourneur, 14520 Port-en-Bessin. Tel: 3151 74 01.

WATER SKIING

The national organisation for the sport is the Fédération Française de Ski Nautique, 16 Rue Clément-Marot, 75008 Paris. Tel: (1) 47 20 05 00. The Léry-Poses leisure in Eure offers the best inland facilities in the region (*see the Base de Loisirs*).

BASES DE LOISIRS

Inland, there are many "Base de Loisirs" (leisure centres) where water sports can be practised. On lakes and quiet river stretches, they offer various activities, maybe tennis, riding, or miniature golf – not just water sports. They usually have a café or bar, maybe even a restaurant, as well as picnic areas, and often a campsite.

Many such centres offer tuition in the various sports available – canoeing, wind-surfing etc; fees are usually charged at an hourly or half hourly rate. Where boating and windsurfing is permitted, equipment is often available for hire, or you may take your own.

SEINE-MARITIME

Cany-Barville – Lac de Caniel: sailing, water skiing, pedalos, etc. Tel: 35 97 40 55.

Jumiège-le-Mesnil – Base de Loisirs UCPA: sailing, windsurfing, catamarans, canoes, plus tennis, archery, golf and climbing. Tel: 35 37 93 84.

Longroy-Gamaches – Etang Ste-Marguerite: canoe/ kayak, windsurfing, mountain biking, etc. Open: 15 March–15 November. Tel: 22 30 91 65.

Saint-Aubin-le-Cauf – Etang de la Varenne: sailing, windsurfing, canoe/kayak. Open: all year. Tel: 35 85 69 05.

CALVADOS

Pont-l'Evêque – Leisure centre based around a lake of almost 140 acres (56 hectares).

EURE

Brionne – Leisure centre with sailing, fishing, pedalos and supervised bathing. Tel: 32 43 66 11.

Conches – Domaine de la Noé leisure centre offers canoeing, windsurfing, pedalo and other amenities such as pony rides, golf and tennis. Open: May–end September. Tel: 32 30 20 41 (town hall).

Dangu – Water sports centre on Gisors Lake: canoeing, wind-surfing, fishing, miniature golf and a play area. Open all year; good campsite. Tel: 32 55 43 42.

Grosley-sur-Risle – Lake for water sports (no equipment available), plus pony rides, miniature golf, micro-light aircraft and campsite. Tel: 32 46 25 28.

Poses – Les Etangs des Deux Amants: The Lery-Poses leisure centre offers the best inland water-skiing facilities in the region on its two lakes. Also a campsite. Tel: 32 59 13 13.

Toutainville – Centre Nautique de Toutainville: sailing, windsurfing and water skiing. Tel: 32 41 52 16.

Venables – Aubevoye water sports centre on 300 acres (86 hectares) of water running into the Seine: power boats, sailing, windsurfing, water skiing and fishing. Open 15 April–21 November. Tel: 32 53 41 45.

ORNE

La Ferté-Macé – A lake of almost 70 acres (28 hectares) in a large park, with sandy beach, bathing, pedalos, windsurfing and other amusements. Tel: 33 37 10 97.

Le Mele-sur-Sarthe – Leisure centre based around a lake: sailing, windsurfing, bathing, tennis. Tel: 33 27 61 02.

Soligny-la-Trappe – A small lake with supervised bathing, punts, pedalos and miniature golf. Tel: 33 34 50 29.

Vimoutiers – Escale du Vitou leisure centre in a pleasant setting with a small lake, swimming-pool, riding centre, tennis and children's games; accommodation available. Tel: 33 39 12 04.

ANGLING

Sea fishing trips are widely available on the coast – look out for sign boards advertising trips on the quayside. A permit (*permis*) is usually required for coarse fishing: enquire at local tourist offices or the national organisations listed below:

Angling: Fédération Française de Pêche au Coup, 20 Rue Emile-Zola, 93120 La Courneuve. Tel: (1) 48 34 45 01.

Sea Fishing: Fédération Française des Pêcheurs en Mer, 8 Rue de la Constellation, 40520 Biscarosse Plage. Tel: 58 78 20 96.

Sport Fishing: Fédération Française des Groupements de Pecheurs Sportifs, 5 Rue Jules-Verne, 69740 Genas. Tel: 72 36 30 33.

Fishing is such a popular sport in Normandy that the regional tourist board has set up a special service "Club Pêche Normandie" which gives information about trips, accommodation and the best places to fish. For information, contact the regional tourist office in Evreux (*see Useful Addresses*).

CYCLING

To take your own *vélo* to France is easy – they are carried free on most ferries and trains – or you can rent cycles for a reasonable cost; main railway stations usually have them for hire and you can often arrange to pick up at one station and leave the bike at a distant one. Alternatively try bicycle retailers/repairers or ask at the local tourist office. Some hirers have signed a charter to enable them to become a "Point-Vélo Accueil", offering a high standard of service and information for cyclists.

Some youth hostels rent cycles and also arrange tours with accommodation in hostels or under canvas. For more information, contact the YHA (*see Where to Stay*). French Routes, 1 Mill Green Cottages, Newbridge, Yarmouth, Isle of Wight, PO41 0TZ, tel: 0983-78392, offers a route planning service for individual tourists and will also arrange bicycle hire and accommodation.

Cycling holidays are offered by various organisations; with campsite or hotel accommodation with the advantage that your luggage is often transported for you to your next destination. Some operators are listed below:

Bicyclub S.A., 8 Place de la Porte-Champerret, 75017 Paris. Tel: (1) 47 66 55 92.

Fédération Française de Cyclotourisme, 8 Rue Jean-Marie-Jégo, 75013 Paris. Tel: (1) 45 80 30 21. Organises tours of 40–60 miles per day (60–100 km). Bring your own bike.

Fédération Française de Cyclisme, Bâtiment Jean-Monnet, 5 Rue de Rome, 95561 Rosny-Sous-Bois. Tel: (1) 49 35 69 00.

Rando Bike, 16 Passage des Ursulines, 76000 Rouen. Tel: 35 89 63 50.

Vélo-Relais/Hexaclub, 38 Rue du Mesnil, 78730 St-Arnoult-en-Yvelines. Tel: (1) 30 59 34 09.

Cyclists Touring Club, Cotterell House, 69 Meadrow, Godalming, Surrey GU7 3HS. Tel: 0483-417217.

It is advisable to take out insurance before you go. Obviously the normal rules of the road apply to cyclists (*see Getting Around*). Advice and information can be obtained from The Touring Department of the Cyclists Touring Club. Their service to members includes competitive cycle and travel insurance, free detailed touring itineraries and general information sheets about France. The club's French counterpart,

Fédération Française de Cyclotourisme offers a similar service. Rob Hunter's book *Cycle Touring in France* is also useful as a handbook.

Such is the French passion for cycling that local clubs organise many trips lasting a day or more and visitors are often more than welcome to join in. Weekend or longer tours are organised by the national Bicyclub. Lists of clubs and events are also organised by local members of the Fédération Française de Cyclotourisme, who also produce leaflets giving suggested cycle tours for independent travellers, ranging from easy terrain, to very hard going for the more experienced cyclist, with details of accommodation en route, cycle repairers and other facilities. The following offices in each *département* offer a similar service:

Seine-Maritime: Comité Départemental de Cyclotourisme-VTT, Appt 135, 27 Place du Mont-Gaillard, 76620 Le Havre. Tel: 35 44 37 07.

Calvados: Comité Départemental de Cyclotourisme, 11 Avenue de la Duchesse Gonnor, 14760 Bretteville-sur-Audon.

Eure: Comité Départemental de Cyclotourisme, 9 Rue du Docteur Roux, 27200 Evreux. Tel: 32 24 01 41.

Orne: Comité Départemental de Cyclotourisme, Les Fieffes, 61700 Domfront. Tel: 33 38 57 83.

Manche: Comité Départemental de Cyclotourisme, La Blinière, 50290 Brehal. Tel: 33 90 82 45.

MOUNTAIN BIKING

This sport has really taken off in recent years, particularly among the French, many of whom are already dedicated cyclists. Many of the organisations listed under Cycling above offer mountain bike holidays, or contact the Association Française de Mountain Bike, 3 Villa des Sablons, 92200 Neuilly-sur-Seine. Tel: (1) 46 24 48 53.

Mountain bikes (in French, VTT – Vélo Tout Terrain) and protective gear can be hired locally, try the local tourist office, or cycle shops/repairers.

There several special terrains suitable for mountain biking, in particular, the Centre de Loisirs VTT at Domfront offers 590 miles (950 km) of marked routes at four levels of difficulty. For information, contact Cycles Sachet. Tel: 33 38 53 97. Other marked trails are to be found in the Valcongrain forest in Calvados (information from the Aunay-sur-Odon tourist office, tel: 31 77 60 32); at Ferrière-Harang, 125-mile (200-km) circuit, tel: 31 67 95 63); and at Amayé-sur-Orne where accompanied tours depart from the Auberge du Pont du Coudray each Sunday at 9.30am. Tel: 31 80 53 55.

HORSE-RIDING

Normandy, particularly the *département* of Orne, is real horse country and there are countless opportunities for those who wish to ride or watch equestrian events. All riding holidays in France come under the umbrella of the Délégation Nationale au Tourimse

Equestre de la Fédération Française d'Equitation (ANTE) based at Ile Saint-Germain, 170 Quai de Stalingrad, 92130 Issy-les-Moulineaux. Tel: (1) 40 93 52 88. The regional office is the Association Régionale de Tourisme Equestre, Rue de la Fontaine Bulant, 27380 Charleval. Tel: 32 49 20 48. Information about marked bridleways, maps, riding centres and insurance is available from them or via the departmental offices as follows:

Seine-Maritime: Comité Départemental de Tourisme Equestre, Rue Villate, 76200 Dieppe. Tel: 35 84 29 48.

Calvados: Comité Départemental de Tourisme Equestre du Calvados, Chambre d'Agriculture, 6 Promenade de Mme de Sévigné, 14050 Caen Cedex.

Eure: Comité Départemental de Tourisme Equestre, Club hippique du Bec-Hellouin, 27800 Brionne. Tel: 32 44 86 31.

Orne: Comité Départemental d'Equitation, Le Châtelet, 61210 Les Aspres. Tel. 33 34 21 12.

Treks lasting a day or more and also longer holidays on horseback can be organised locally, try the following riding centres; otherwise information can be obtained from the organisations mentioned above, and from tourist offices.

ADTER, BP 59, 76232 Bois-Guillaume. Tel: 35 60 73 34. Organises riding holidays based at gîtes or fermes équestres (farms).

Centre Hippique de Bellengreville, 76630 Envermeu. Tel: 35 85 76 21. Weekend stays near the Arques forest.

Centre Equestre du Parc, Le Fief du Wuy, 76940 La Mailleraye-sur-Seine. Tel: 35 37 34 46. Weekend stays in the Brotonne Regional Park.

Ferme de la Boisette, 76950 Les Grandes Ventes. Tel: 35 83 47 13. Riding weekends with a guide in the Eawy forest.

Poney-Club de Bois Guilbert, 76750 Buch. Tel: 35 34 42 51. Riding holidays with accommodation in tents or gîtes in the Bray region.

Le Village du Cheval, 61600 St Michel-des-Andaines. Tel: 33 37 12 79. Offers all kinds of equestrain activities, including courses for children and senior citizens, trips to nearby Bagnoles-de-l'Orne in a horse-drawn carriage, etc. Open all year.

If you fancy being a cowboy for the day, go to the only American Riding school in France, the American Equitation Centre, 61120 Vimoutiers. Tel: 33 39 12 05.

Horse-drawn caravans can be hired from the following organisations:

Attelages du Pays d'Ouche, 27300 Saint-Aubin-le-Vertueux. Tel: 32 43 50 85. Trips from half a day to a week in the Risle valley, or Charentonne or Ouche region (book at least one month ahead).

La Ferme du Clairet, 27240 Manthelon. Tel: 32 34 41 09. Let the huge Percheron horses take the strain while you meander through the Iton Vallet, the Villalet or Breteuil forests.

It is also possible to have a holiday trekking with a pack mule, with or without a guide, exploring the Risle, Roumois and Lieuvin valleys or the Brotonne forest. Information from La Frangousane, Le Grand Hardouin, 27350 Rougemontier. Tel: 32 57 00 20.

Local tourist offices will provide details of stables if you simply wish to hire a horse by the hour or day. Expect to pay around FF75 per hour/FF350 per day.

For details of some of the many events around the region, (*see Spectator Sports*). For details of the national stud le Haras du Pin, see *Things to Do*.

GOLF

In recent years, golf has caught on in a big way in France and the Regional Tourist Boards have joined forces with the French Golf Federation in an effort to promote it better and set standards. The resulting organisation, France Golf International, embraces over 100 golf courses around the country which must provide a certain standard of facilities available to all. They require courses to have weekend reservation systems, and have multilingual staff on hand. Information can be obtained from the Comité Régional au Tourisme (see *Useful Addresses*). Expect to pay around FF180 for green fees for a day's play.

Many tour operators offer golfing holidays in Normandy, here is a selection:

Cresta Holidays, 32 Victoria Street, Altrnicham WA14 1ET. Tel: 061-926 9999.

French Expressions, 4 Belsize Crescent, London NW3 5QU. Tel: 071-794 1480.

French Life Holidays, 26 Church Road, Horsforth, Leeds LS18 5LG. Tel: 0532-390077.

Golf en France, Model Farm, Rattlesden, Bury St Edmunds IP30 0SY. Tel: 0449-737678.

Golf Weekend, 25 Hambidge Lane, Lechland GL7 3BJ. Tel: 0367-241636.

Below are the principal courses in each *département*:

SEINE-MARITIME

Golf de Dieppe, Route de Pourville, 76200 Dieppe. Tel: 35 84 25 05. 18 holes. Driving range, equipment rental.

Golf d'Etrétat, Route du Havre, 76790 Etrétat. Tel: 35 27 04 89. 18 holes.

Golf de la Forêt Verte, 76710 Bosc-Guérard. Tel: 35 33 92 94. 18 holes. Driving range, equipment rental.

Golf du Havre, Hameaux Saint-Supplix, BP 10, 76930 Octeville-sur-Mer. Tel: 35 46 36 50. 18 holes. Driving range.

Golf de Rouen Mont-Saint-Aignan, Rue Francis Poulenc, 76130 Mont-Saint-Aignan. Tel: 35 76 38 65. 18 holes. Driving range.

Golf public du Parc Régional de Brotonne, 76480 Jumièges. Tel: 76480. Tel: 35 05 32 97. 18 holes. Driving range.

Golf de Saint-Saëns, Hameau du Vaudichon, BP 20, 76680 Saint-Saëns. Tel: 35 34 25 24. 18 holes. Driving range, equipment rental.

CALVADOS

The Calvados tourist offices offers a "Golf Pass", covering five green fees to be used on nine consecutive days on five out of a possible six participating courses in the Calvados area, with an option for a sixth day at the new Deauville golf course on payment of a supplement. The pass is available all year round. Simply buy one at the first course you book (participating courses are marked PG below). Further information from the Calvados tourist office (see *Useful Addresses*).

Golf de Bayeux Omaha Beach (PG), La Ferme Saint-Sauveur, 14520 Port-en-Bessin. Tel: 31 21 72 94. 18 holes. Lessons available July and August; equipment rental.

Golf de Cabourg Le Home (PG), 38 Avenue du Président René Coty, Le Home Varaville, 14390 Cabourg. Tel: 31 91 25 56. 18 holes. Driving range, equipment rental.

Golf Public de Cabourg, Avenue de l'Hippodrome, 14390 Cabourg. Tel: 31 91 70 53. 12 holes. Driving range, equipment rental.

Golf de Caen (PG), Le Vallon, 14112 Biéville-Beuville. Tel: 3194 72 09. 18 holes. Driving range, lessons in school holidays.

Golf de Clécy (PG), Manoir de Cantelou, 14570 Clécy. Tel: 31 69 72 72. 18 holes. Driving range, lessons available, equipment rental, accommodation.

Golf de Deauville (PG), 14800 Saint-Arnoult. Tel: 31 88 20 53. 27 holes. Driving range, equipment rental; accommodation.

Golf Club de l'Amirauté, Tourgeville, 14800 Deauville. Tel: 31 88 38 00. 27 holes. Driving range, equipment rental; lessons available.

Golf de Garcelles, Route de Lorguichon, 14540 Garcelles-Secqueville. Tel: 31 39 08 58. 18 holes. Driving range, putting, lessons; 4 covered tennis courts.

Golf de St-Gatien (PG), La Ferme du Mont St-Jean, 14130 Saint-Gatien-des-Bois. Tel: 31 65 19 99. 24 holes. Driving range, lessons in school holidays.

Golf de Saint Julien (PG), Saint-Julien-sur-Calonne, 14130 Pont-l'Evêque. Tel: 31 64 30 30. 27 holes. Driving range, equipment rental.

EURE

Golf du Champ de Bataille, 27110 Le Neubourg. Tel: 32 35 03 72. Private club, 18 holes.

Golf du Center Parcs, Domaine des Bois-Francs, 27130 Verneuil-sur-Avre. Tel:32 23 50 02. 9 holes. Driving range and equipment rental.

Golf de Léry-Poses, Base de Loisirs de Léry-Poses, BP 7, 27740 Poses. Tel: 32 59 47 42. 18 holes. Driving range, equipment rental.

Golf du Vaudreil, 27100 Le Vaudreuil. Tel: 32 59 02 60. 18 holes. Course designed by the English golf architect Hawtree in 1961.

ORNE

Golf de Bagnoles-de-l'Orne, Route de Domfront, 61140 Bagnoles-de-l'Orne. Tel: 33 37 81 42. 9 holes. Driving range and equipment rental.

Golf de Bellême Saint-Martin, Les Sablons, 61130 Bellême. Tel: 33 73 00 07. 18 holes. Driving range, equipment rental.

MANCHE

Golf Club de Coutainville, Avenue du Golf 50230 Agon-Coutainville. Tel: 33 47 03 31. 9 holes. Driving range.

Golf de Granville-Bréville, Chalet du Golf, 50290 Bréville. Tel: 33 50 23 06.

Swin Golf, Route de Surtainville, Le Vretot, 50260 Bricquebec. Tel: 33 04 38 59. 12 holes. Free beginners' lessons at the weekend.

OTHER SPORTS

There are opportunities for all kinds of less common sports in the region. The Suisse Normande area and the Seine valley are good for rock climbing, there is even a permanent site for Bungee jumping (*saut à l'élastique*) at the Souleuvre viaduct in Calvados (information from A.J. Hackett, 14350 La Ferrière-Harang. Tel: 31 67 37 38). If your particular kind of excercise is not featured here, try contacting Insolite, 7 Rue des Basnages, 76000 Rouen. Tel: 35 71 20 20. *Insolite* means unusual and they offer many different activities from go-karting to pot-holing.

SPECTATOR

There are many **equestrian events** in the region, particularly in Orne. There are races almost all year round at Argentan race course and there is an important horse show in September in the grounds of the Château de Carrouges in the Normandie-Maine Regional Park, which also stages other events. A three-day event is held in Caen in October and the Harcourt four-in-hand competition is held annually in June. There are international jumping events at Flers in August, and at Val-de-Reuil and Beaumont-le-Roger. Many competitions are held at the Haras du Pin national stud.

There is a **24-hour speed boat race** at Rouen at the end of April, and the **Cowes-Deauville yacht race** takes place at the end of May.

The **Paris-Camembert cycle race** takes place in June; the **Paris-Deauville vintage car race** is staged in October.

Details of sporting events can be obtained from the nearest tourist office, or from national organisers of events.

SPECIAL INFORMATION

DOING BUSINESS

Business travel now accounts for roughly a third of French tourism revenue. This important market has lead to the creation of a special Conference and Incentive Department in the French Government Tourist Office in both London and New York (*see Useful Addresses*) to deal solely with business travel enquiries. They will help organise hotels, conference centres and incentive deals for any group, large or small.

For general information about business travel and facilities contact the regional or *départemental* tourist offices (*see Useful Addresses*), who will provide lists of hotels with conference facilities, etc. Another good source of business information and local assistance, are the Chambres de Commerce et d'Industrie (CCI) in the region. Here you can obtain details about local companies, assistance with the technicalities of export and import, interpretation/translation agencies and conference centres.

Chambre Régional de Commerce et d'Industrie de Haute-Normandie, 9 Rue Robert Schuman BP 124, 76002 Rouen Cedex. Tel: 35 88 44 42, fax: 35 88 06 52.

Chambre Régional de Commerce et d'Industrie de Basse-Normandie, 21 Place de la République, 14052 Caen Cedex. Tel: 31 38 31 38, fax: 31 85 76 41.

Seine-Maritime: CCI de Rouen, Palais des Consuls, Quai de la Bourse, BP 641, 76007 Rouen Cedex. Tel: 35 14 37 37, fax: 35 70 80 92.

CCI de Dieppe, 4 Boulevard du Général de Gaulle, BP 62, 76202 Dieppe Cedex. Tel: 35 06 50 50, fax: 35 06 50 51.

Calvados: CCI de Caen, 41 Boulevard du Maréchal Leclerc, BP 511, 14035 Caen Cedex. Tel: 31 85 85 85, fax: 31 86 45 76.

Eure: CCI de l'Eure, 35 Rue du Dr. Oursel, BP 187, 27001 Evreux Cedex. Tel: 32 38 81 00, fax: 32 38 81 07

Orne: CCI d'Alençon, 12 Place du Palais, BP 42, 61002 Alençon Cedex. Tel: 33 82 82 82, fax: 33 32 10 16.

Manche: CCI de Granville-Saint-Lô, Place Albert Godal, BP 232, 50402 Granville Cedex. Tel: 33 50 05 35, fax: 33 50 63 11.

CCI de Cherbourg, Hôtel Atlantique, Boulevard Félix Amiot, BP 839, 50108 Cherbourg Cedex. Tel:

33 23 32 00, fax: 33 23 32 28.

There is also a French Chamber of Commerce in London (Tel: 071-225 5250) which exists to promote business between the two countries, and at the same address is French Trade Exhibitions: 2nd floor, Knightsbridge House, 197 Knightsbridge, London SW7 1RB. Tel: 071-225 5566.

A calendar of trade fairs all over France is published every year and this is available in August, for the following year, from the Chambre de Commerce et d'Industrie de Paris, 16 Rue Chateaubriand, 75008 Paris.

CONFERENCE HALLS

The region has plenty of venues suitable for conferences, some purpose-built, some in the gracious surroundings of châteaux or other old buildings. A complete list is available from the regional tourist board; here is a selection:

Alençon: Parc des Expositions, 61100 Alençon. Tel: 33 26 23 98.

Bagnoles-de-l'Orne: Manoir du Lys, 611240 Bagnoles-de-l'Orne. Tel: 33 37 80 69, fax: 33 30 05 80.

Caen: Centre de Congrès, 13 Avenue A. Sorel, 14000 Caen. Tel: 31 85 10 20, fax: 31 50 15 12.

Deauville: Centre International de Deauville, 14800 Deauville. Tel: 31 14 14 14, fax: 31 14 15 16.

Evreux: Château de Trangis, La Madeleine. Tel: 32.31.52.52 (town hall) or Le Cadran, Palais de Congrès, 27000 Evreux. Tel: 32 29 63 00, fax: 32 29 63 33.

Granville: Centre Régional de Nautisme, BP 140, 50400 Granville. Tel: 33 50 18 95.

Le Havre: Service Congrès, Place de l'Hôtel de Ville, BP 649, 76600 Le Havre. Tel: 35 21 22 88 – three possible venues.

Rouen: Palais des Congrès, 6 Place de la Cathédrale, 76000 Rouen. Tel: 35 98 29 66, fax: 35 89 68 25.

The following selection of tour operators specialise in organising conferences, congresses and other similar events:

Centre International Deauville Congrès, Place de la Mairie, BP 79, 14800 Deauville. Tel: 31 98 06 71, fax: 31 98 10 33.

Deauville Organisation, 31 Avenue Florian de Kergorlay, 14800 Deauville. Tel: 31 81 81 18, fax: 31 81 81 01.

Formule Magique, 14 Rue de la Grâce de Dieu, 14610 Epron. Tel: 31 94 80 90, fax: 31 44 87 00.

Frêne Conseil, 20 Rue des Eglantiers, 14000 Caen. Tel: 31 75 31 00, fax: 31 73 43 43.

Optimum, 1 Rue des Mathurins, 14100 Lisieux. Tel: 31 61 08 45, fax: 31 32 23 40.

Other useful addresses are:

French Trade Exhibitions, The Colonnades, 82 Bishopsbridge Road, London W2 6RB. Tel: 071-589 6211.

DATAR (French Industrial Development Board), 21-24 Grosvenor Place, London SW1X 7HQ. Tel: 071-823 1895.

CHILDREN

In France generally, children are treated as people, not just nuisances. It is pleasant to be able to take them into restaurants (even in the evening) without heads being turned in horror at the invasion. It has to be said, however, that French children, being accustomed to eating out from an early age, are on the whole well behaved in restaurants so it helps if one's own offspring are able to understand that they can't run wild.

Many restaurants offer a children's menu; if not, they will often split a *prix-fixe* menu between two children. If travelling with very young children, you may find it practical to order nothing specific at all for them but just to request an extra plate and give them tasty morsels to try from your own dish. It is a good introduction to foreign food for them, without too much waste. French meals are generally generous enough to allow you to do this without going hungry yourself, and you are unlikely to encounter any hostility from *le patron* (or *la patronne*). Another option is to order a single simple, inexpensive dish from the à la carte menu, such as an omelette or fresh soup of the day and plenty of bread (which comes automatically to a French restaurant table) which is often enough to satisfy a small child's appetite with ice-cream or fruit to follow.

If you prefer not to eat in a formal restaurant with young children, many brasseries and cafés also offer light snacks such as *croque monsieur* (toasted cheese and ham) or salads; while at coastal resorts there are plenty of take-away options.

Most hotels have family rooms so children do not have to be separated from parents and a cot (*lit bébé*) can often be provided for a small supplement, although it is a good idea to check availability if booking in advance.

Many of the activities listed in the *Things to Do* section are suitable for, or aimed specifically at children. Many of the seaside resorts have children's clubs on the beach, where for a fee children can be left for a few hours to take part in organised sports and fun events.

It is also possible to organise holidays for unaccompanied children, including stays in *gîtes d'enfants* or on farms, or activity holidays. Naturally, children would only be happy to be left if they have a reasonable command of French, but it is quite common in France, as in the United States, for children to spend at least a part of their summer vacation at a holiday centre. For more information, contact Gîtes de France in individual *départements* (*see Where to Stay*). Loisirs de France Jeunes is a national organisation which offers good value activity holidays for young people. Contact them at

30 Rue Godot de Mauroy, 75009 Paris. Tel: (1) 47 42 51 81.

TRAVELLERS WITH SPECIAL NEEDS

Most less able travellers will be keen to book accommodation in advance rather than arriving "on spec". Most of the official list of hotels (available from the FGTO or the regional tourist office – *see Useful Addresses*) include a symbol to denote wheelchair access, but it is always advisable to check directly with the chosen hotel as to exactly what facilities are available. Balladins is a chain of newly-built, budget-priced hotels throughout France which all have at least one room designed for disabled guests and restaurants and all other public areas are accessible. For a complete list, contact Hotels Balladins, 20 rue du Pont des Halles, 94656 Rungis Cedex. Tel: 49 78 24 00, fax: 46 86 41 44.

An information sheet aimed at disabled travellers is published by the French Government Tourist Office; for a copy, send an SAE. There is a guide, *Où Ferons Nous Etape?* (published in French only) which lists accommodation, throughout France, suitable for the disabled, including wheelchair users, but again if you have specific needs you would need to double check when booking. It is available (for FF40 by post) from the Association des Paralysés de France, Service Information, 17 Boulevard August Blanqui, 75013 Paris. Tel: (1) 40 78 69 00. This organisation may also be able to deal direct with specific enquiries and can provide addresses of their branches throughout France. The *Rousseau H Comme Handicapé* guide may also prove useful. It is available from Hachette bookshops or at SCOP, 4 Rue Gustave-Rouanet, 75018 Paris. Tel: (1) 42 52 97 00.

The Michelin Red Guide *France*, for hotels and their *Camping-Caravanning – France* both include symbols for disabled welcome.

The Royal Association for Disability and Rehabilitation (RADAR), 25 Mortimer Street, London WIN 8AB. Tel. 071-637 5400, has some useful information for tourists, including a guide book, *Holidays and Travel Abroad*. This is a general country by country guide and provides information about France as a whole, including hotel chains offering suitable accommodation, and tour operators offering specialist holidays.

France's sister organisation to RADAR, the Comité National Français de Liaison pour la Réadaption des Handicapés (CNFLRH), is based at 38 Boulevard Raspail, 75007 Paris. Tel: (1) 45 48 90 13. It offers a good information service for visitors with special needs to France, although they do not have an specific information about the region itself.

For young people, the Centre d'Information et de Documentation Jeunesse, 101 Quai Branly, 75740 Paris Cedex 15 provides information on services for young less able travellers. It publishes *Vacances pour Personnes Handicapées* and annual leaflets on acitivity and sports holidays for young disabled people. Parents may also find the following organisation helpful: Union Nationale des Associations de Parents d'enfants Inadaptés (UNAPEI), 15 Rue Coysevox, 75018 Paris. Tel: (1) 42 63 84 33.

The Comité de Liaison pour le transport des personnes handicapées, Conseil National des Transports, 34 avenue Marceau, 75009 Paris publishes a booklet called *Guide des Transport à l'usage des Personnes à Mobilité Réduite*. This gives brief information on the accessibility and arrangements for less able passengers on all forms of public transport and contacts for special transport schemes throughout France.

Brittany Ferries offers free passage for cars of registered disabled travellers on all their routes (except Plymouth-Santander). More information about air and sea travel is also available in a guide entitled Door-to-Door. For a free copy write to Department of Transport, Door-to-Door Guide, Freepost, Victoria Road, South Ruislip, Middlesex HA4 0NZ who can also provide copies on cassette for the vision-impaired.

In the US, the following organisations offer services to disabled travellers:

Travel Information Service, Moss Rehabilitation Hospital, 1200 West Tabor Road., Philadelphia, PA 19141-3099. Tel: 215-456 9600 – has general information for would-be travellers.

Society for the Advancement of Travel for the Handicapped (SATH), 26 Court Street, Brooklyn, New York 11242. Tel: 718-858 5483 – offers advice and assistance in travel matters.

Accessible Journeys, 35 W Sellers Avenue, Ridley Park, Philadelphia, 19078-2113 – offers tours using wheelchair accessible transport in Europe.

In Canada the following organisation may be of help:

Canadian Rehabilitation Council for the Disabled, 45 Sheppard Avenue E, Toronto, Ontario, M2N 5W9. Tel: 416-250 7490 – national organisation producing some material relating to travel.

STUDENTS & YOUNG PEOPLE

Students and young people under the age of 26 can benefit from cut-price travel to France and rail cards for getting around the country – for details *see Getting There*.

If you wish to have a prolonged stay in the region, it may be worth finding out about an exchange visit or study holiday. Several organisations exist to provide information or arrange such visits. In the UK, the Central Bureau for Educational Visits and Exchanges, Seymour Mews House, Seymour Mews, London W1H 9PE. Tel: 071-486 5101 produces three books; *Working Holidays* (opportunities in France are limited, there may be some work on farms in hotels or at seaside resorts), *Home from Home* (a wealth of useful information about staying with a French family) and *Study Holidays* (details of

language courses). Another option, for those with decent French is to approach one of the UK-based camping holiday operators who often employ students as site courriers during the vacation (for companies, see *Where to Stay* section).

Organisations in the US include:

American Council for International Studies Inc., 19 Bay State Road, Bost, Mass. 02215. Tel: 617-236 2051.

The Council on International Educational Exchange (CIEE), 205 E 42nd Street, New York, NY 10017. Tel: 212-661 1414. A wide range of services, including travel.

Youth for Understanding International Exchange, 3501 Newark Street, NW, Washington DC 20016. Tel: 202-966 6800.

There are many several French tour operators which organise study tours and language courses. The Union National des Organisations de Séjours Linguistiques, 293 Rue de Vaugirard, 75015 Paris. Tel: (1) 42 50 44 99 is a national association of organisations offering language courses and carries out quality checks on the 18 members of the organisation. Write to them for a list of schools, or try the following:

Accueil des Jeunes en France, 12 rue des Barres, 75004 Paris. Tel: (1) 42 72 72 09. Offers French study programmes, inexpensive accommodation (or with a family), and tours for individuals or groups.

Acceuil France Famille, 5 Rue François Coppée, 75015 Paris. Tel: (1) 45 54 22 39.

Centre des Echanges Internationaux, 104 rue de Vaugirard, 75006 Paris. Tel. (1) 45 49 26 25. Sporting and cultural holidays and educational tours for 15–30 year olds. Non-profit making organisation.

Students will find a valid student identity card is useful in obtaining discounts on all sorts of activities. including admission to museums and galleries, cinema, theatre, etc. If you do not happen to have your ID card with you reductions may sometimes be allowed by proving your status with a passport.

The Centre d'Information et Documentation de Jeunesse (CIDJ), based at 101 Quai Branly, 75740 Paris. Tel. (1) 45 67 35 85 is a national organisation which disseminates information pertaining to youth and student activities. There is also a Centre d'Informantion Jeunesse at 16 Rue Neuve Saint-Jean, 1400 Caen. Like the Paris office, it has information on all kinds of facilities in the region, including sports, accommodation and activity holidays, as well as riding and holiday centres for disabled youngsters. Young people can call in to the office in Caen where a noticeboard gives all sorts of additional information, including casual jobs.

For individual holidays, the cheapest way to stay is generally under canvas, or in a hostel (expect to pay around FF55 per night without meals). *See Where to Stay* for details of the French youth hostels organisations.

USEFUL ADDRESSES

IN FRANCE

Air France, 119 Champs Elysées, 75384 Paris Cedex 08. Tel: (l) 42 99 21 24. Central reservation. Tel. (1) 45 35 61 61.

Maison de la France, 8 Avenue de l'Opéra, 75001 Paris. Tel: (1) 42 96 10 23.

Comité Régional de Tourisme de Normandie, Le Doyenné, 14 Rue Charles Corbeau, 27000 Evreux. Tel: 32 33 79 00, fax: 32 31 19 04.

Departmental tourist offices (CDTS):

CDTS **de Seine-Maritime**, 2bis Rue du Petit-Salut, BP 680, 76008 Rouen Cedex. Tel: 35 88 61 32, fax: 35 71 00 37.

CDTS **du Calvados**, Place du Canada, 14000 Caen. Tel: 31 86 53 30, fax: 31 79 39 41.

CDTS **de l'Eure**, Hôtel du Département, Boulevard Georges Chauvin, 27003 Evreux Cedex. Tel: 32 31 51 51, fax: 32 31 05 98.

CDTS **de l'Orne**, 88 Rue Saint-Blaise BP 50, 61002 Alençon Cedex. Tel: 33 28 88 71, fax: 33 29 81 60.

CDTS **de la Manche**, Maison du Départment, 50008 Saint-Lô Cedex. Tel: 33 05 98 70, fax: 33 56 07 03.

Clés de France (tour operator for the French Regional Parks), 13-15 Rue Saint-Louis, 78100 Saint-Germain-en-Laye. Tel: (1) 30 61 23 23.

Ligue Française pour la protection des Oiseaux (bird protection league), La Corderie Royale, BP 263, 17305 Rochefort.

Office National des Forêts (Forestry Commission), 217 Rue Grande, 77300 Fontainebleau. Tel: (1) 64 22 18 07.

UK & IRELAND

Maison de la France/French Government Tourist Office, 178 Piccadilly, London W1V 0AL. Tel: 071-491 7622, fax: 071-493 6594.

Comité Régional de Tourisme de Normandie, British Representative, 6 Transom House, Victoria Street, Bristol BS1 6AH. Tel: 0272-253853, fax: 0272-253009.

Air France, 177 Piccadilly, London W1. Tel: 071-750 4306.

Air France, 29-30 Dawson Street, Dublin 2. Tel. 01-77 8272 (reservations: 01-77 8899).

Consulat Général de France, 21 Cromwell Road, London SW7 2DQ. Tel: 071-581 5292. Visa section: 6a Cromwell Place, London SW7. Tel: 071-823 9555.

Consulat Général de France, 11 Randolph Crescent, Edinburgh EH3 7TT. Tel: 031-225 7954.

French Embassy, 58 Knightsbridge, London SW1X 7JT, tel: 071-201 1000. Commercial department: 21-24 Grosvenor Place, London SW1X 7HU, tel: 071-235 7080. Cultural department: 23 Cromwell Road, London SW7, tel: 071-581 5292.

French Consulate General Edinburgh, 11 Randolph Crescent, Edinburgh EH3 7TT. Tel: 031-225 7954.

US & CANADA

Air France, 666 Fifth Avenue, New York NY 10019, tel: 212-315 1122 (toll-free reservations: 1-800-237 2747); 850l Wilshire Boulevard, Beverly Hills, Los Angeles, CA 90211, tel: 213-688 9220.

Air France, 979 Ouest Boulevard de Maisonneuve, Montreal, Quebec H3A 1M4, tel: 514-284 2825; 15l Bloor Street West, Suite 600, Toronto, Ontario M5S 1S4, tel: 416-922 3344.

Maison de la France/French Government Tourist Office, 610 Fifth Avenue, Suite 222, New York, NY 10020-2452, tel: 212-757 1125, fax: 212-247 6468; 9454 Wilshire Boulevard, Beverley Hills, Los Angeles CA 90212-2967, tel: 310-271 7838; 645 North Michigan Avenue, Suite 630, Chicago, Illinois 606ll-2836, tel: 312-337 6301; Cedar Maple Plaza, 2305 Cedar Springs Road, Suite 205, Dallas, Texas 75201, tel: 214-720 4010, fax: 214-702 0250.

Business Travel Division, 610 Fifth Avenue, Suite 222, New York, NY 10020-2452, tel: 212-757 1125, fax: 212-247 6464.

Maison de la France/French Government Tourist Office, 1981 Avenue McGill Collège, Tour Esso, Suite 490, Montreal H3A 2W9, Quebec, tel: 514-288 4264, fax: 514-845 4868; 30 St Patrick Street, Suite 700, Toronto M5T 3A3 Ontario, tel: 416-593 4723.

CONSULATES

In most cases, the nearest consular services are in Paris.

American Consulate: 2 Rue St-Florentin, 75001 Paris. Tel: (1) 42 96 14 88.

Australian Embassy: 4 Rue Jean-Rey, 75015 Paris. Tel: (1) 45 75 62 00.

British Consulate: 9 Avenue Hoche, 75008 Paris. Tel: (1) 42 66 91 42.

Canadian Consulate: 35 Avenue Montaigne, 75008 Paris. Tel: (1) 47 23 32 00.

Irish Embassy: 12 Avenue Foch, 75116 Paris. Tel: (1) 45 00 20 87.

German Consulate: 34 Avenue d'Ilena, 75016 Paris. Tel: (1) 42 99 78 00.

FURTHER READING

For details of the authors from the area, see the *Writers* chapter on pages 115–119.

A Holiday History of France, by Ronald Hamilton. London: The Hogarth Press. Illustrated guide to history and architecture.

A Traveller's History of France, by Robert Cole. London: The Windrush Press. Slim volume for background reading.

France Today, by John Ardagh. London: Secker and Warburg. Up-to-date, hefty tome on modern France.

Holt's Battlefield Guides: Normandy-Overlord and *Holt's Visitor's Guide to the Normandy Landing Beaches*, by Holt, Tonie & Valmai. Both available from Major and Mrs Holt's Battlefield Tours, 15 Market Street, Sandwich, Kent CT13 9DA.

Madame Bovary, by Gustav Flaubert. Translated by Gerard Hopkins. OUP. This book is the best place to start with this essential Norman writer.

Normandy Gastronomique, by Jane Sigal. Conran Octopus.

Odo's Hanging, by Peter Benson. London: Hodder & Stoughton. A fascinating fiction about the making of the Bayeux Tapestry.

Pierre Deux's Normandy, by Dannenberg, Moulin and LeVec. London: Phaidon. Photographic record of Normandy today.

Six Armies in Normandy, by John Keegan. Jonathan Cape (hardback), Pimlico (paperback). The story of the Battle for Normandy.

The Bayeux Tapestry, by David M. Wilson. London: Thames and Hudson. A full colour representation of the complete tapestry, its history and commentary by the Director of the British Museum.

The Food Lover's Guide to France, by Patricia Wells. London: Methuen. The best restaurants, food shops and markets in France, plus regional recipes.

The French, by Theodore Zeldin. New York: Random House. How the French live today.

The Identity of France, by Fernand Braudel. London: Fontana Press.

Writers' France, by John Ardagh. London: Hamish Hamilton. A region-by-region guide to the literature and great writers of France.

OTHER INSIGHT GUIDES

Companion *Insight Guides* which highlight destinations in this region include: *Brittany*, *Burgundy*, *Loire Valley* and *Paris*.

Other volumes cover *Alsace*, *Provence* and the *Côte d'Azur*.

Two *Insight Pocket Guides*, to *Brittany* and to *Paris*, provide visitors who have limited time with detailed itineraries to these destinations, compiled by an expert "host".

ART/PHOTO CREDITS

INDEX

A
B
C
E
F
G
H
I
J
a
b
c
d
e
f
g
h
i
j
l